Philosophy, Dissent
and Nonconformity

Philosophy, Dissent and Nonconformity

Alan P.F. Sell

James Clarke & Co

To my friends in theological education
at home and abroad

James Clarke & Co
P.O. Box 60
Cambridge
CB1 2NT

www.jamesclarke.co.uk
publishing@jamesclarke.co.uk

ISBN 0 227 67977 6

British Library Cataloguing in Publication Data
A catalogue record is available from the British Library

Copyright © Alan P.F. Sell, 2004

First Published in 2004

All rights reserved. No part of this edition may be reproduced,
stored in a retrieval system, or transmitted in any form or by any means,
electronic mechanical, photocopying, recording or otherwise, without the
prior permission in writing from the Publisher.

Printed in the United Kingdom by

Contents

Abbreviations		6
Preface		7
1.	Introduction	9
2.	Philosophy and Philosophers: The Eighteenth Century	17
3.	The Eighteenth-Century Dissenters' Contribution to Moral Philosophy	55
4.	Philosophy and Philosophers: 1800-1920	105
5	Nonconformist Contributions to Ethics and Apologetics: 1800-1920	149
6.	Epilogue	205
Notes		207
Bibliography		257
Index of Academies, Colleges and Universities		281
Index of Persons		285
Select Index of Subjects		295

Abbreviations

BDEB	*The Blackwell Dictionary of Evangelical Biography*, 1995
BH	*The Baptist Handbook*
BQ	*The Baptist Quarterly*
CHST	*Transactions of the Congregational Historical Society*
CR	A.G. Matthews, *Calamy Revised*, 1934
CYB	*The Congregational Year Book*
DECBP	*Dictionary of Eighteenth-Century British Philosophers*, 1999
DMBI	*A Dictionary of Methodism in Britain and Ireland*, 2000
DNB	*Dictionary of National Biography*
DNCBP	*Dictionary of Nineteenth-Century British Philosophers*, 2002
DSCHT	*Dictionary of Scottish Church History and Theology*, 1993
DSCBP	*Dictionary of Seventeenth-Century British Philosophers*, 2000
DTLC	Alan P.F. Sell, *Dissenting Thought and the Life of the Churches*, 1990
DWB	*Dictionary of Welsh Biography*
EEUTA	Herbert McLachlan, *English Education under the Test Acts*, 1931
FAE	Alexander Gordon, *Freedom After Ejection*, 1917
JURCHS	*Journal of the United Reformed Church Historical Society*
PWHS	*Proceedings of the Wesley Historical Society*
UHST	*Transactions of the Unitarian Historical Society*

Preface

In this volume I bring together two of my long-standing interests: philosophy and Dissenting and Nonconformist history. As far as I am aware this is the first attempt to examine the place of philosophy in the Dissenting academies and Nonconformist colleges of England and Wales from the Toleration Act of 1689 to 1920, and to survey the philosophical writings of their professors and alumni.

The work has been germinating in my mind for some years, and from time to time colleagues have prompted me to attend to aspects of it. Thus, at the invitation of Professor Paul B. Wood I gave a paper to the British Society for the History of Philosophy, a version of which was published in *History of Universities*, XI, 1992. I gave a hitherto unpublished paper to the same Society in 2000, at the kind invitation of Professor G.A.J. Rogers; and Professor Joachim Hruschka invited me to participate in a consultation in Erlangen which yielded a contribution to the *Jahrbuch für Recht und Ethik*, VII, 2000. I have valued these opportunities and I have drawn upon the resulting articles in two chapters in the present work; I have not, however, simply reproduced them. Over the years I have resorted to my collection of research materials and lecture notes in order to respond to invitations to write short dictionary articles on some of the philosophers here discussed. I have not consulted these articles in writing the present work, but I have noted the dictionaries in which they appear as appropriate.

In the course of writing this book it has been a pleasure to mine the resources of the following libraries: The Bodleian Library, Oxford; The British Library, London; The Congregational Library and Dr. Williams's Library, London; Harris Manchester College Library, Oxford; The National Library of Wales; The Angus Library, Regent's Park College, Oxford; and The United Theological College Library, Aberystwyth.

I am grateful to Adrian Brink for his willingness to publish my book, and for his kindness throughout the process. It appeals very much to my sense of history to appear on the list of so venerable an institution as

James Clarke, publishers of theological works since 1859. I should like also to express my thanks to Clare Pibworth for her patient and precise editorial work.

For a number of years past I have had the pleasure of giving lectures and conducting courses in theological institutions in many places, and the flow of such work shows no sign of abating. I dedicate this book to my friends in theological education around the world in much appreciation of their friendship and hospitality.

Alan P.F. Sell
Milton Keynes

1

Introduction

In this book an attempt is made to tell the story of the teaching and writing of philosophy by those who pursued their vocation in pastorates, or in Dissenting academies and Nonconformist theological colleges (of which there were well over one hundred in the period under review) because their religious convictions excluded them from the Anglican-Oxbridge establishment. A bald summary of highly intricate matters will set the scene.

The continuing influence of the medieval idea of the unity of the realm was thrown into relief by Henry VIII's disengagement of the English Church from that of Rome. The conviction was fostered that an important constituent of the cement of national unity was religious uniformity. Hence the attempts to secure such uniformity by legislation – attempts stoutly resisted by the Separatist harbingers of English Dissent. In the wake of the Civil War, and under Cromwellian rule, the lot of Dissenters was easier, but reaction against them set in with the Restoration of the monarchy in 1660. The times were politically and religiously turbulent, and once again the authorities sought religious uniformity as the mainstay of national unity. To this end a series of five measures, known to Dissenters of the period as 'the five-thonged whip', found their way to the statute books. The Corporation Act of 1661 barred Nonconformists (Roman and Dissenting) from holding civil office. Between 1660, when the Convention Parliament's Act restored sequestered clergy to their livings, and 1662, and speeded by the Act of Uniformity of the latter year, some two thousand clergymen left, or were ejected from, their livings because they could not in conscience give their 'unfeigned assent and consent' to the Book of Common Prayer of the Church of England. The Act applied also to schoolmasters and university teachers, and among the ejected in the latter category was John Owen, Dean of Christ Church, and formerly Vice-Chancellor of Oxford University. There followed the Conventicle Act (1664), which prohibited religious meetings of five or more persons over the age of sixteen (other than members of the same household); and the Five Mile Act (1665), which was designed to separate ejected ministers from their former pastorates by imposing penalties upon any of them who resided within five miles of any corporate town, or of the place in which they had formerly ministered. The provisions of the First Conventicle Act were reinforced by those of the Second, in 1670.[1]

If the Act of Uniformity excluded Dissenting teachers from the ancient universities, the university statutes effectively excluded Dissenting students; for at Oxford all entering students were required to subscribe to the doctrines of the Thirty-Nine Articles of the Church of England, and all members of that University were prohibited from having relations with any Dissenting societies. Some degrees at Cambridge were open only to those who were members of the Church of England, while other degrees were awarded only upon the candidate's subscription to the articles of the Thirty-sixth Canon of the Church of England.[2]

Under the circumstances described, the earliest Dissenting academy tutors lived dangerously. Richard Frankland, for example, threatened by the penalties of the Five Mile Act, migrated with his academy (1669-1698) on no fewer than five occasions between 1683 and 1689.[3] The arrival of William of Orange in 1688 was, however, soon followed by the enactment of what has come to be known as the Toleration Act of 1689 – despite the fact that the term 'toleration' appears neither in the title of the Act nor anywhere in the text. Without repealing earlier adverse legislation, the Act provided that the penalties attaching to the earlier laws would no longer be imposed upon orthodox Protestant Dissenters (the concession was denied to Roman Catholics, Socinians and Jews). Hence, although they continued to be barred from civic office, and were subject to numerous other restrictions, orthodox Protestant Dissenters were now in a position to worship freely, to organize their religious life, to open meeting-houses, and to do all of this legally and under the protection of the law. In particular, Protestants who assented to the doctrines of the Thirty-Nine Articles (with a concession to Baptists on their doctrinal *raison d'être*) could now provide openly for the higher education of their young. They thus began to establish more permanent academies for this purpose, and philosophy was among the disciplines for which they made provision.

It is well at this point to utter a cautionary word. Those who were trained in philosophy when the conviction widely prevailed that the discipline comprised nothing more than 'talk about talk', and who have not been able to modify this opinion, will simply have to swallow hard when turning to the eighteenth and nineteenth centuries. For here almost anything goes. Philosophers, many of them divines, will discuss all

Introduction

manner of questions, sometimes out of deep interest, frequently because they are spurred on by controversy, and – not least in the Dissenting academies and Nonconformist colleges – because of a shortage of teachers and/or of funds. The more philosophically talented eighteenth-century tutors would glide elegantly from logic to metaphysics to ethics to theology and back again, and even the less gifted were expected to familiarize students with all of these fields. Their efforts were generally worthy, their results sometimes unfortunate. Nor was the need of polymaths soon over. When in 1804 John Pye Smith delivered his inaugural lecture at Homerton Academy (1730-1820), he listed the subjects he intended to cover: natural philosophy, astronomy, chemistry, natural history, logic, ontology, philosophy of the human mind, composition and rhetoric, history, mathematics, Hebrew, Greek, Latin and English.[4] Two years later he assumed the duties of the theological chair. All of which seems awesome, especially when one recalls reports (no doubt malicious and ill-founded) of some in our own time who experience difficulty in keeping one chapter between themselves and their students in one discipline. Our awe must be tempered, however, by the realization that the post-Renaissance explosion of knowledge was in its adolescence, our modern disciplines had yet to receive their now-familiar shapes,[5] and the progressive eighteenth-century person was expected to have a nodding acquaintance with many things. But deeper than the matter of personal interest, or the requirements of controversy, or the shortage of teachers, many Dissenters would have endorsed the words of Thomas Barnes at the opening of the Manchester academy in 1786:

> Of all subjects, DIVINITY seems most to demand the aid of kindred, and even of apparently remoter sciences. Its objects are GOD and MAN: and nothing, which can either illustrate the perfections of the one, or the nature, capacities, and history of the other, can be entirely unimportant.
>
> But how extensive a field do these subjects open? Natural Philosophy, in its widest sense, comprehending whatever relates to the history or properties of the works of Nature, in the Earth, the Air, the Ocean, and including Natural History, Chemistry, &c. has an immediate reference to the one – and to the other belong, all that Anatomy and Physiology can discover relating to the body, and all that Metaphysics, Moral Philosophy, History, or Revelation declare concerning the mind. But here again the field still opens upon us. For History, as well as Revelation, demands the knowledge of Languages; and these again, of Customs and of Arts, of Chronology and

> Manners – the stream of science still branching out into more and wider channels. And to the highest furnishing of the mind are necessary, those subjects which belong to cultivated Taste, which regulate the Imagination and refine the Feelings, and which give correctness to vigour, and elegance to strength.[6]

In a word, those who were seriously concerned with the ways and works of God and humanity, and who wished to provide a university-level education to those otherwise excluded from it, could not consistently balk at a curriculum which ran over the entire field of available knowledge.

Less loftily, there was a widespread conviction in educated circles that philosophy was an important part of a person's intellectual equipment, though some evangelicals, among them the Anglican John Newton, who proffered advice to William Bull on the setting up of Newport Pagnell academy, were wary of the subject on the ground that too much free enquiry could unsettle the faithful. On the other hand, in *A Lecture Introductory to the Study of Philosophy, delivered in Cheshunt College, Herts, November 14, 1838* (1839) the evangelical Independent, Joseph Sortain, contended that philosophy would not only cultivate the minds of intending ministers but would assist them in demonstrating their points in preaching. Lest it be thought that conservative evangelicals alone were suspicious of philosophy we may cite the case of Gilbert Wakefield (1756-1801). In 1790 he was appointed classical tutor at the liberal Hackney College (1786-1796), having previously held a similar post at Warrington academy (1779-83). where he proved to be a 'troubler of Israel'. In 1791 he published a tract in repudiation of public worship;[7] he taught Greek without accents, 'against which he was as violent as he was against the Trinity';[8] he declared that systematic doctrinal teaching produced 'a harvest of *theological coxcombs*,'[9] and he lamented that 'in these institutions young men are dosed with such infusions [of metaphysics, morals, history and politics] to a degree that makes even the strongest stomach regurgitate under the operation.'[10] Wakefield resigned before he had completed his first year at Hackney, and he was, to put it mildly, atypical.

If the position of philosophy in the academies and theological colleges was sometimes precarious either on principle or because of a dearth of teachers, there is more than enough evidence to show that the subject was taught more often than not (though there may be a gap, unperceived by subsequent generations, between what a syllabus specifies and what is actually taught). It is also clear that some at least of the tutors were philosophically active, and a handful of them distinguished, in publishing terms.

Introduction

So to the plan of this book: in the next chapter we shall consider the place of philosophy in the eighteenth-century academies. Those tutors and alumni who published philosophical works will be introduced as we proceed, except that we shall reserve to chapter three our treatment of moral philosophy – a prominent concern of a number of Dissenting philosophers. Chapter four will comprise an account of the place of philosophy in the Nonconformist colleges from 1800 to 1920. As with their eighteenth-century predecessors, we shall note the varied philosophical writings tutors and alumni, but on this occasion holding over our consideration of both moral philosophy and apologetics to chapter five. In chapter six some brief concluding remarks will be offered.

It would be quite unrealistic to attempt a detailed discussion of every published item; indeed, to be frank, some contributions do not merit more than a passing reference. Rather, the objectives here are first, to indicate the place of philosophy in the academies and colleges (a difficult enough task given the paucity of information at a number of points); and secondly, to indicate the variety and range of philosophical interests espoused by Dissenters and Nonconformists. In other words, this survey represents an attempt to answer the question: What was done in the name of philosophy teaching and writing by the tutors and alumni of the Dissenting academies and Nonconformist colleges of the period 1689 to 1920? It will be noted that throughout this book we are concerned with Dissent/Dissenters and Nonconformity/Nonconformists *and philosophy*. That is to say, we are not here concerned with *The Philosophy of Dissent* (to borrow the title of a book of 1900 by the Methodist T. Courtenay James) in the sense of specific Dissenting principles *vis à vis* the Church-state question. This, it seems to me, is fundamentally a theological question, and as such I have sought to discuss it elsewhere.[11]

It must be confessed that in narrative terms this study is far from being a seamless robe. By this is meant first, that quantities of material regarding academies, colleges and the place of philosophy in the curriculum range from the ample through the adequate to the non-existent, and this not simply because some institutions enjoyed a longer life than others. Secondly, with respect to the philosophical works by tutors and alumni, these vary greatly in scale, value and theme; and some philosophy tutors published little or nothing in that field. Accordingly, our account of the course of philosophy in Dissenting and Nonconformist circles in chapters two and four below, though broadly chronological, will be somewhat jerky, for we shall speak of the place of philosophy on the curriculum, introducing the tutors and (where they exist) their works (other than their ethical and apologetic contributions) as we come to them. Thus narrative will from time to time be interrupted by exposition. In chapters three and five there will be a greater unity of theme, and more of a sense that there is an ongoing conversation in which Dissenting and Nonconformist philosophers are participants. Thirdly, there is an almost complete hiatus in the story at the end of the eighteenth century, when a number of Dissenting tutors died and, for that and other reasons, a number of academies closed. Old Dissent required new institutions and new tutors as the nineteenth-century opened, and, after a certain amount of sanctified reluctance, the Methodists decided that they needed such establishments and personnel for the first time.

As to the influence of the tutors on the discipline and on their students: here again the picture is mixed. Whereas Isaac Watts's *Logic* was used until well into the nineteenth century; whereas Richard Price initiated a discussion of freedom and necessity among Dissenters and others; whereas in the nineteenth century George Payne's *Elements of Mental and Moral Science* passed through a number of editions and was referred to by his peers, frequently the philosophers worked independently on themes in ways quite unrelated to the thought of their immediate contemporaries within or without Dissent and Nonconformity. As for the tutors' influence upon their students: while we shall read some fulsome tributes as we proceed, we may not unjustifiably surmise that if Thomas Amory was greatly indebted to his uncle Henry Grove, and if A.M. Fairbairn's vision inspired many, not all tutors (Richard Price among them) excelled in the classroom, and the majority of students (the eighteenth-century non-vocational academies apart) were more likely to regard themselves as budding pastors than as aspiring philosophers. It is not unkind to suppose that of these a proportion, then as now, displayed a remarkable facility for excising Hume, Kant and the rest from their memories between the final examinations and the award of the leaving certificate. Insofar as influence can be negative, we may, for example, note that among the idealist philosopher Edward Caird's most searching critics were his former students, the Congregationalists Robert Mackintosh and A.E. Garvie.[12]

As we go forward we shall do well to remember that much of the education provided was done on a shoe string; that tutors were frequently required to cover enormous amounts of territory in both arts and divinity and even – more especially in the eighteenth century – in classics, science and mathematics; that some of the tutors held pastorates concurrently with their teaching duties, and even those who did not were normally expected to preach far and wide in the churches; that prior to the spread of popular education their entering students frequently had only the slightest grounding in basic disciplines; and that proposed amalgamations

Introduction 15

of colleges seldom met with ready approval.[13] In a word, given the circumstances, the wonder is that philosophy received as much attention as it did, and that those teachers who produced books and articles in the field managed to put pen to paper at all.[14]

A final introductory question remains: Why this study's terminal date of 1920? In the first place, with the opening of Oxford and Cambridge universities to Nonconformists and the increasing use by Nonconformists of the facilities of the then new universities – especially London and Manchester and, later, Bristol, Leeds, Birmingham and Nottingham, the Nonconformist denominations no longer had to supply ministerial personnel and funds for all of the teaching required by their students. Secondly, with the general laicizing of the theological disciplines it was no longer necessary that philosophy be taught by Nonconformist ministers, or even by Christians; though, as it happens, a leaven of ordained philosophers has been found in the secular universities since 1920.[15] In view of these developments, it is not altogether surprising that the amount of philosophical writing undertaken by Nonconformist theological college teachers has declined. Nor, in view of the overall reduction in Nonconformist church membership during the twentieth century, the higher average age of ordinands in recent years, and the determination in some quarters to 'professionalize' the ministry (philosophy sometimes being an early casualty – as if the attempt to wrestle with the problem of evil, for example, were not a clamant *pastoral* necessity), is it surprising that few of today's ministers (unlike a number of Nonconformist lay persons)[16] regard philosophical writing as part of their calling.

2

Philosophy and Philosophers: The Eighteenth Century

The Toleration Act did not meet with universal approval. To some it did not go far enough; but what disturbed the orthodox Dissenters were the attempts to repeal it, which flared up intermittently until 1734, when George II ordered that charges against Philip Doddridge, the Northampton pastor and academy tutor, be dropped. The narrowest squeak was in 1714. The Schism Bill requiring the closure of Dissenting academies was passed in June 1714, and was to have reached the statute book on 1 August. But on that very day Queen Anne, whose signature was needed, died. To many Dissenters this was unparalleled evidence of a favourable Providence; indeed, the Congregationalist Thomas Bradbury, known to Queen Anne herself as 'bold Bradbury', is said to have preached a memorial sermon on II Kings 19 : 34, 'Go, see now this accursed woman, and bury her, for she is a king's daughter.' The textual reference is, of course, to Jezebel. Implacable opposition to Dissenters continued, notably on the part of the Tory Anglican, Henry Sacheverell, a Jacobite incensed at the prospect of the accession of George I. He preached a virulent sermon in Sutton Coldfield Parish Church on 20 October 1714, the day of George's coronation, and riots followed in which a number of Dissenting meeting-houses were destroyed.[1]

In these somewhat precarious circumstances the eighteenth-century Dissenters set about their higher education. As we shall see, although all Dissenters were alike in operating outside of the establishment, their academies were by no means identical in type, longevity or ethos. Some, like Henry Grove's at Taunton (1670?-1758), Philip Doddridge's at Northampton (1729-1751), and that at Warrington (1757-1783), whose tutors included John Taylor, John Aikin and Joseph Priestley, offered a general higher education to students with a variety of vocational aspirations. Others, such as that at Bridgewater (1688-1747) were for theological students only. With the Evangelical Revival the number of specifically theological academies multiplied, and one of them, founded in 1752 by Congregationalists at Ottery-St-Mary, Devonshire, is the oldest of a constellation of colleges to which the present-day Northern College, Manchester, traces its origins.[2] While some academies, notably Doddridge's, were open to a variety of theological views, and others, notably Warrington, were decidedly on the liberal side, those at Trevecca (1768) and Newport Pagnell (1772) were distinctly evangelical.

To pursue the hint dropped in the preceding sentence: if the political context was volatile, the theological air which the eighteenth-century Dissenters breathed was in its own way invigorating. While only the briefest indication of the theological excitements can here be given, we should note that there were issues surrounding the doctrine of the Trinity and confessional subscription which transcended the Church-chapel divide. Indeed, the Anglican Samuel Clarke's book, *The Scripture Doctrine of the Trinity* (1712) was a catalyst in the debate over eighteenth-century Arianism.[3] For Dissenters, matters came to a head at the Salters' Hall conference of 1719. It there became clear that the requirement to subscribe to 'man-made' formulae was what exercised the non-subscribers, who were on the whole younger than their subscribing colleagues, but, with the exception of the decided Arians Benjamin Avery and Nathaniel Lardner,[4] were no less insistent than the subscribers in professing belief in the Trinity.[5] Nevertheless the eighteenth century witnessed a movement in most Presbyterian and General Baptist circles towards 'Arianism' and thence, in some cases – notably that of Priestley, to Unitarianism.[6] On this occasion only the Arianism of the eighteenth century is placed in inverted commas by way of signalling that it was varied in kind and differently motivated from the Arianism of Arius (d. 336), who, against Athanasius, proposed a subordinationist view of the person of Christ in the Christological debates of his day. The eighteenth-century Arians, who could be 'high' like Micaijah Towgood (1700-92) in approving of the worship of Christ, or 'low' like Richard Price (1723-91)[7] in not so doing, took their stand on the Bible, and could find neither the doctrine of the Trinity nor its associated terminology in Scripture, the sole sufficiency of which (over against accumulated Church tradition) they were determined to uphold. Thus John Taylor, whom we shall later meet as a Warrington tutor, thundered against

> high swelling Words of Vanity; such as *Entity, Tri-unity, Quoddity, Quiddity, Formalities, Essentialities, Primalities, Consubstantiality, necessary Emanation, hypostatical Union, mutual Circumplexion, a Trinity of Modes, Communication of Properties, Oeconomical, Co-essential, Co-equal, Co-eternal.* These, Christians, are barbarous sounds, unknown to the pure and divine Mouth of thy Saviour, and the inspired Voice of his

Apostles, whereby the Principles of thy Religion, in themselves noble and heavenly, simple and plain to every Capacity, have been worked into pompous Nonsense and profound Darkness.[8]

Again, there were disputes over baptism and church order. The former are exemplified in the inner-Dissenting pamphleteering of John Taylor the Presbyterian and the Baptist Grantham Killingworth. Killingworth had first taken Taylor to task on the issue in 1740, but when in 1757 Taylor published *The Covenant of Grace and Baptism the Token of it, Explained upon Scripture Principles*, Killingworth returned to the fray with *A Forerunner to a Farther Answer, if need be, To the Rev. Dr. John Taylor of Norwich, His Covenant of Grace and Baptism the Token of it* (1758). At the heart of the dispute was Taylor's assertion, and Killingworth's denial, of the analogy between circumcision as prescribed in the Old Testament and paedobaptism, both being regarded by Taylor as entrances to God's covenant family.[9] As to church order, here the disputes frequently concerned Dissent *vis à vis* the Church of England. With varying degrees of civility, especially having regard to the fragility of toleration throughout the century, Dissenters managed from time to time to make the point that the Church of England was not a true Church since it owed allegiance both to Christ and to the monarch, and not to Christ alone. Perhaps the most important phase of the debate was that between the Anglican John White and the Presbyterian Micaijah Towgood. White published three letters *To a Gentleman Dissenting from the Church of England*, the first in 1743, the second and third in 1745. Towgood gave *The Dissenting Gentleman's Answer* in three letters (1746, 1747, 1748), and recourse was had to his arguments by Nonconformists until well into the nineteenth century. But if Towgood, who disliked controversy, is the model of propriety, the palm for the most swashbuckling attack on the Church of England must go to an altogether rougher diamond, the Unitarian John Gisburne, who deliverd a sermon at Soham, Norfolk, the burden of which was that 'no natural, well-formed body could have more than one head, but the Church of England had two heads, King JESUS and King *George*, and therefore the Church of England was a monster.'[10] The prominent Baptist Andrew Fuller and the Unitarian leader Robert Aspland became embroiled in the dispute, the latter observing that while he regretted the use of coarse and irritating language in the pulpit, Gisburne had 'uttered no more in his blunt, uncourteous manner, than the vital principle of nonconformity.'[11]

If we may say that disputes over the Trinity occurred broadly between those who may be designated rationalistic Arminians and Calvinists,[12] we should also note that there were arguments, notably over the doctrine of double predestination, in which both rationalistic and evangelical

Arminians stood over against Calvinists. Thus, for example, John Taylor and John Wesley, representing the major varieties of Arminianism stood opposed to the high Calvinist Baptists John Brine and John Gill.[13] Not the least important aspect of this dispute was the accusation of antinomianism which was levelled against high Calvinists by Arminians. Indeed, to give an example which shows how doctrinal differences can have ecclesiological consequences, the Happy Union of the 1690s engineered by the Independents and Presbyterians foundered in part because some of the latter, Richard Baxter among them, suspected some of the former of having espoused antinomianism. The dispute was occasioned by the publication in 1690 of the posthumous *Works* of Tobias Crisp (1600-43). The Presbyterian Daniel Williams found antinomianism in Crisp's writings, only to be charged with Socinianism himself: a slur which both bishop Edward Stillingfleet and Jonathan Edwards sought to remove.[14] That there could also be inner-evangelical doctrinal strife is exemplified by the difference of opinion between the evangelical Calvinist George Whitefield and the equally evangelical Arminian John Wesley. When the latter published a sermon of *Free Grace* in 1739 relations between the two men temporarily broke down. The nub of the problem was God's sovereign grace in election in relation to the sinful human being's ability or otherwise to respond to the Gospel offer.[15]

When divines were not busy manning the doctrinal barricades they frequently found themselves in hot pursuit of the deists.[16] On this issue the rationalistic Arminians sided with the Calvinists, for they did not wish their devotion to reason to be mistaken, as it sometimes was in those nick-naming days, for deism with its denial of supernatural revelation. At the turn of the seventeenth century John Locke was repudiating the labels 'deist' and 'Socinian' which some applied to him,[17] while to the end of the eighteenth century Priestley was making it clear that between deism and Socinianism there was a great gulf, notably in connection with belief in a future state.[18] Too disparate to be designated a school or even a movement, the deists were for the most part sincere individuals intent upon reasoning to what they regarded as tenable conclusions concerning God and the natural order. It is quite wrong to say, as is frequently reiterated, that they were *en bloc* opposed to revelation. By far the majority of them insisted on God's having revealed himself in the natural order, and they did not wish to be mistaken for atheists; but, apart from a few early deists who gave a limited place to supernatural revelation provided that its deliverances were sanctioned by reason, they saw no need for a further revelation over and above the one God had given in the book of nature. By the same token, they did not, as is popularly supposed, think that God, having created the universe, had then retreated from it, leaving it to its own devices. Any later thinkers who have espoused this view do not owe it to the early-to-mid eighteenth-century deists.[19]

I

In the context of the lively theological situation as just briefly and selectively described, the eighteenth-century Dissenting philosophers did their teaching and writing. As well as acquainting students with the classical sources, a number of them strove to introduce current concerns.[20] But what inheritance of philosophical equipment did they bring to the task? To hazard a one-sentence answer: the eighteenth-century Dissenters learned and practised their philosophy under the influence of experimentally-modified scholastic method flowing down from the Middle Ages, with recourse to the contributions of Dutch thinkers and Descartes, and with reference to Locke – especially to his quest of reasonableness in religion. Before attempting to unpack this sentence which, as it stands, may obscure more than it reveals, I should like to underline the importance of the last clause in it. It would be quite wrong to suppose that rational Arminians alone were concerned with the application of reason to questions of belief, while the evangelical were mindless enthusiasts. Such was the impact of scholastic method, and so widespread was the recourse to natural theology – the eighteenth century has been branded the age of the cosmological argument as well as the age of Revival – that evangelical Calvinists would frequently set out from the deliverances of natural theology (understood as appealing to, and comprehensible by, all persons of reason) and subsequently come to the deliverances of revealed theology; and this whether they were writing theological treatises or addressing congregations. Thus, for example, the Congregationalist Thomas Ridgley (1667?-1731), tutor at Hoxton academy, published *A Body of Divinity* in 1731. This is an exposition of the *Larger Catechism* (1648) of the Westminster Assembly. Question II of the *Catechism* reads as follows: 'How doth it appear that there is a God?' The answer given is that 'The very light of nature in man, and the works of God, declare that there is a God; but his word and Spirit only do sufficiently and effectually reveal him unto men for their salvation.' Ridgley declares that we ought to be able 'to prove by arguments, or give a reason of our belief, that there is a God,' and he proceeds to give his own proof at some length. Fundamental to it is the cosmological argument; in a nutshell: creatures cannot make themselves, they are made by one who is not a creature, namely, God.[21] The identical line is taken in many evangelical or moderate Calvinist sermons of the period, and it occurs not least in a number of confessions of faith delivered at ordination services. For example, on the occasion of his ordination on 22 July 1735 the Independent John Notcutt began his confession of faith as follows:

> When I take a Survey of this visible Creation, and seriously reflect on the several Objects which therein do continually offer themselves to our View, I cannot suppose this World, and the Things therein contained, to be independent; since nothing can cause itself to exist. I must therefore conclude, that there is one supreme Being, who is independent, and upon whom all Things do depend for their Existence: And this great Being is God.[22]

The quest for a reasonable faith was thus not the concern of one party only among the eighteenth-century Dissenters: many were indebted to the theistic arguments flowing down especially from Aquinas, the mention of whose name returns us to the vast and complicated issue of scholasticism as an aspect of the Dissenters' philosophical inheritance.

From the method of Ridgley's system and Notcutt's ordination statement we can see how prevalent the view was that by reasoning we may establish the existence of God, and that the knowledge thus gained is supplemented by revelation: natural theology paves the way for revealed theology. How far this understanding truly represents Aquinas's position has been questioned by Arvin Vos, who points out that Aquinas 'consistently holds that the light of faith is higher and more certain than the natural light of reason,' and quotes him thus: 'If . . . an opponent believes nothing of what has been divinely revealed, then no way lies open for making the articles of faith reasonably credible.'[23] Thus, for Aquinas, while faith and reason are complementary, faith, the assent of which is prompted by God's gracious working within us, perfects reason. Vos proceeds to speculate why, in subsequent Protestant thought, Aquinas's emphasis upon faith receives less attention than his view that the theistic proofs are preambles to faith. He surmises, following de Broglie,[24] that with Descartes the function of reason is circumscribed. It is now an analytical or deductive tool. Moreover, Descartes' psychological criterion of clear and distinct ideas as being knowledge-producing gave a subjective twist to reason's function. Such knowledge was then employed to judge the credibility of faith's claims. By this time we are at a considerable remove from Aquinas's position. We may observe in passing that in repudiating the Aristotelian syllogism as the pathway to knowledge on the ground that it was too abstract and formal, Descartes' substitution of the criterion of clear and distinct ideas was no less abstract and formal.

Few did more to modify the received Aristotelianism than Peter Ramus (1515-72). He set out to disencumber the syllogism from the qualifications and additions which had become attached to it over the centuries, and to apply a reinvigorated logic to all the disciplines in the humanities. Whereas Aristotle himself had used logic in an informal, discursive way, his followers had codified it. Ramus advocated discourse understood as the adumbration of self-evidently true axioms, rather than as a matter of advancing a series of correctly argued and related syllogisms. His criticisms of Aristotelianism, *Animadversiones Dialecticae*, and his constuctive work, *Institutiones Dialecticae*, were published in 1543. In the Epistle to the Reader of *The Logike* (1574), prospective readers are urged not to fear that they will waste their time in studying the book, for it is not like 'many books going abroad under glorious names, having in deed little or no utility, but wrapped all together with innumerable difficulties. . . .'[25] The book offers unadulterated classical logic in brief, easily assimilable, compass. If it be asked how it can be so brief, when others have written at such length, the answer given is that the author has strictly confined his attention to logic and has not introduces extraneous matter from other disciplines; that he makes only statements which are necessarily true, and does not clutter his text with 'tricks of poisonable sophistry';[26] and that general and special rules are treated at the appropriate time, and once only: there are no 'vain repetitions'.[27]

The method of Ramus was adopted in England by the Puritans William Perkins and his pupil William Ames, and applied for experimental purposes. Thus in a brief but helpful article on Ames, J.D. Eusden has pointed out that whereas in an Aristotelian syllogism such as:

If you believe in the Lord Jesus Christ you shall be saved;
I believe in the Christ;
Therefore I am saved,

Aristotle would emphasise the major premiss as directing the argument to its conclusion, to Ames the minor premiss would be of critical importance, for it implicitly raises the experimental questions, Do I believe in Christ? What is it to believe in Christ?[28]

Reference was earlier made to the Dutch aspect of the Dissenting philosophical inheritance. Over and above Ames's sojourn and Locke's period of exile in the Netherlands, the philosophical works of two Dutchmen were used in a number of Dissenting academies: the logical text book of the Leiden Protestant scholastic, Franco Burgersdyck (1590-1635), and the logical and ethical writings of the Cartesian Adrian Heerebroord (1614-61), also of Leiden.

As if all of this were not enough there was the new science flowing down from Bacon and Newton, to which the contributions of Hartley and others were soon to be added. As explorers were discovering new worlds so scientists were applying themselves to empirical enquiry as never before. Experience and observation came to the fore and, especially in the case of Locke, they stimulated psycho-epistemological enquiries into what, and how, we can know.

Since the earliest Dissenting academy tutors were educated at Oxford or Cambridge we shall do well to note that whereas the method of Ramus was popularized by Perkins and Ames, both Cambridge men, at Oxford received Aristotelianism in general held sway. It is true that Edward Tatham, while he deferred to Aristotle on ethics, was keener than most of his colleagues to exchange Aristotelian logic for the methods of Bacon and Locke, but he was in a minority. As for Ramus, the first book published by Oxford University Press, John Case's *Speculum Moralium Quaestionum* (1585) comprised an attack upon him, and by and large the forces of conservatism prevailed against him at Oxford University. By contrast John Woodhouse, tutor at Sheriffhales academy (1663-97), Francis Tallents of Shrewsbury (1680?-1715?) and Richard Frankland of Rathmell all used Ramus's work in their teaching, and all of them were Cambridge graduates.[29] In this connection the observation of Irene Parker is interesting: when Henry Fleming went up to The Queen's College, Oxford, in 1678, he read the same logic text books as those prescribed at Sheriffhales and Shrewsbury academies – except that the latter recommended Ramus, who was apparently unknown to Fleming.[30] Frankland's pupil, James Clegg, informs us that where logic was concerned, 'One Tutor was a Ramist but we read ye Logick both of Aristotle and of Ramus, and within the Compass of the first year I was thought an acute disputant in that way.'[31] Another Rathmell alumnus, Renald Tetlaw, left a list of authorities used in the academy. They include Heerebroord on logic and ethics, and the same author's commentary on Burgersdyck's logic; Ramus's logic with the commentary (1640) of George Downame (or Downham), Bishop of Derry, upon it; the logic of the Aristotelian Smiglecius, the *Ars Cogitanda* of Le Clerc,[32] with Govean, Milton and others for good measure. The metaphysicians Fromenius and Barlow, the philosophers Colbert, Eustache and Descartes, and the ethics of the Cambridge Platonist, Henry More, all came under review.[33] This broad approach, and the use of some of the authors already named, was adopted by John Woodhouse at Sheriffhales,[34] James Owen at Shrewsbury,[35] and John Ker at Bethnal Green (1680?-1708?).[36]

As for the writings of Locke, whose period of exile in Holland (1683-9), where he met the Arminian Philipp von Limborch (1633-1712), is by no means insignificant, *An Essay Concerning Human Understanding* was proscribed at Oxford in 1703,[37] though it was read by some under cover. At a number of Dissenting academies, however, the *Essay* quickly became the epistemological staple, as we shall see.

Although the influence upon Dissenting academies of Cambridge men was paramount, we ought not to leave the impression that all Oxford alumni were intellectually hidebound. Matthew Warren, for example, who had been educated at St. John's College, Oxford, became tutor at Taunton academy (1670?-1759), to which town he had moved in 1687, and where he remained until his death in 1706. Of him it was written, 'Tho' bred himself in the Old Logic and Philosophy, and little acquainted with the improvements of the New, yet he encouraged his pupils in a freedom of enquiry, and in reading those books which would better gratify a love of truth and knowledge, even when they differed widely from those writers on which he had formed his own sentiments.'[38] Thus, while Franco Burgersdyck's *Logic* and traditional works by David Derodon and Eustachius de Saint-Paul were studied in class, 'Locke, Le Clerc and Cumberland were guides to [the students'] just thinking, close reasoning and enlightened views in their closets.'[39] Not indeed that all academies were beacons of philosophic light. Though a pupil of Frankland, the Independent Timothy Jollie, estimable as he was in inculcating practical divinity, 'forbad the Mathematicks as tending to scepticism and infidelity,' and gave no instruction in logic.[40] Of his Attercliffe academy (1690-1720?) it was said that 'only the old philosophy of the schools was taught there, and that neither ably nor diligently.'[41]

Joshua Oldfield (1656-1729) taught at Coventry academy from 1693, and at Southwark (later, Hoxton Square) from 1699. He had read philosophy at Christ's College, Cambridge, under Cudworth and More, and it is possible[42] that he also studied under John Shuttlewood at Sulby Academy (1680-88), a Cambridge man, among whose other students were Thomas Emlyn and Julius Saunders, later a tutor at Bedworth academy (1710?-50).[43] He also met Locke at the time of the latter's work on his paraphrases of Paul's letters,[44] and was a friend of Newton. In 1707 Oldfield published, *An Essay towards the Improvement of Reason*, in which Cartesian, Platonist and Lockean emphases are discernible. Thus, he is with the empiricists in his conviction that where things, words and notions are concerned, 'Nature seems commonly to lead men to begin with the first of these;' on the other hand his declaration that 'The first thing of which we are aware is our own awareness,' would warm a Cartesian heart; while in ethics he follows the Cambridge Platonist Henry More in according conscience the role of judging the value of notions presented to the intellect.[45] Eclectic and ambivalent Oldfield may have been, but he does at least present some of the major philosophical options which lay before philosophers as the eighteenth century opened.

After 1690 promising Dissenting students did not need to stay at home awaiting the influx of continental and Scottish ideas. Under the Common (that is, Presbyterian and Congregational) Fund (1690) and, following the failure of the Happy Union, the Presbyterian Fund (1693), to which resource was latter added Dr. Williams's Trust (1706), scholars went to study in Scotland, Holland and Halle. Of those who became philosophical tutors, Samuel Jones had been to Leiden, Samuel Benion at Glasgow, and John Aikin – Philip Doddridge's first student at Northampton[46] (1729-51) – at Aberdeen, where his thought took an Arian turn.[47] In Scotland a prominent open-minded line flowed down from Francis Hutcheson, who had been educated at James M'Alpin's philosophical Dissenting academy at Killyleagh (1690s-1724), Co. Down,[48] and who, in 1710 proceeded thence to Glasgow, where he sat under Gershom Carmichael and John Simson. The latter had studied under the orthodox Reformed theologian, Marckius (Johannes Marck), in Leiden, but was himself suspected of heresy though never deposed.[49] Carmichael, who became Glasgow's first professor of moral philosophy in 1727,[50] was poised between the older scholasticism and the new experimentalism, and it was the latter upon which Hutcheson, influenced by Locke, was to fasten. Hutcheson succeeded Carmichael in 1730, and his supporter and theological colleague, William Leechman, who had been nurtured at Edinburgh in William Hamilton's nest of moderates (and Hamilton was a friend of Simson), lectured to crowded classes in an undogmatic manner, and had himself attended Hutcheson's classes prior to his appointment.[51]

If it be true that 'By their honours ye shall know them,' then of the fifteen out of some forty Dissenting philosophy tutors who received Scottish DDs during the eighteenth century, Aberdeen awarded eleven (including one from each of its colleges to Doddridge), of which nine went to conservative or moderate thinkers, and two to theological liberals; Glasgow, at Leechman's suggestion, honoured the liberal John Taylor in 1756 (though for his Hebrew scholarship, not for his as yet unpublished critique of Hutcheson's moral theory); and Edinburgh admitted three liberals only; the first, in 1743, was Caleb Rotheram of Kendal academy (1733-53) – and this for a thesis in which 'he ably refutes the notion strongly insisted on by many sceptical writers, and somewhat incautiously admitted even by Mr. Locke, "that the probability of facts depending on human testimony must gradually lessen in proportion to the distance of time when they happened, and at last become entirely evanescent."'[52]

Two further preliminary points remain to be made. First, until Philip

Doddridge pioneered the provision of academy libraries as distinct from the tutors' personal collections,[53] students were at the mercy of their tutors' own books. Early tutors were sometimes on the run; most tutors were impecunious; and some, like Ebenezer Latham of Findern, professed a wide range of subjects, ministered to a local church, and served the district as physician. None of these circumstances was conducive to reading, let alone to building and maintaining comprehensive libraries. It is therefore all the more impressive a tribute to John Shuttlewood that his student, Thomas Emlyn, who resigned because Shuttlewood 'had very few books, and them chiefly of one sort,' went on to Oxford, sated himself in the Bodleian Library, but subsequently returned to Shuttlewood for teaching and example which were not to be found among the dreaming spires.[54]

Secondly, there is the matter of teaching through the medium of English. Among the Dissenting pioneers of the use of English in preference to Latin was Charles Morton of Newington Green academy.[55] In Scotland Hutcheson introduced the practice at Glasgow, and Leechman followed suit. When Doddridge adopted the practice his powerful example ensured that henceforth English would be the normal medium of instruction in Dissenting academies. But there resulted a serious time-lag in the provision of translated texts by continental authors. This threw the onus very much upon the tutors, who had to refer to foreign sources in their own lectures. That they sometimes did this to the point of inducing intellectual indigestion may be seen from surviving manuscripts.

II

The foundations laid, we shall proceed to note the place of place of philosophy in the eighteenth-century Dissenting academies, and the philosophical writings (excluding from this chapter those on moral philosophy) of their tutors. It may facilitate understanding and make certain inter-academy links clearer if, to use very rough categories, we think in terms of more liberal, more conservative and more theologically mixed academies. It goes without saying that the labelling of academies and divines alike is a hazardous undertaking. Some establishments and teachers were more open to 'advanced' thought with its frequent accompanying doctrinal change than others; but matters were seldom tidy, either ecclesiastically or theologically. Ecclesiastically, it by no means followed that a student entering a Presbyterian, Congregational or Baptist academy would remain within the fold, or even within Dissent. Thus, Timothy Goodwin, the future archbishop of Cashel, had studied at Samuel Cradock's academy at Wickhambrook, Suffolk (1678?-1696), where he was a contemporary of Edmund Calamy.[56] Josiah Hort, later archbishop of Tuam, was at Thomas Rowe's notable academy (founded at Newington Green *circa* 1666, and continued by Rowe at Clapham and Little Britain until his death in 1705, whose alumni also included Isaac Watts, Daniel Neal, John Evans and Henry Grove, later of Taunton Academy (1670?-1759). Again, the lay Presbyterian tutor Samuel Jones[57] of Tewkesbury academy (1708?-24) nurtured both the future bishop Joseph Butler and Thomas Secker. The latter came to Tewkesbury following studies under Timothy Jollie at Attercliffe. He 'preached as a Probationer at Bolsover, but failed to get an invitation to the pastorate.'[58] He did, however, subsequently manage to become archbishop of Canterbury. From Ebenezer Latham's Presbyterian academy at Findern (1710?-1754) emerged John Wiche the General Baptist, and Ferdinando Warner, who became an Anglican and published among other things, *A full and plain Account of the Gout . . . with some new and important Instructions for its Relief.* The work appeared in 1768, the year of Warner's death – from gout. This unhappy coincidence, as his biographer drily remarks, 'destroyed the credit of his system.'[59] Joseph Priestley, the first student under the Congregationalist Caleb Ashworth at Daventry (1752-89),[60] became the leading Unitarian of the latter part of the eighteenth century, while from the moderately Calvinistic Bristol Baptist College (1679, continuing) there issued General Baptists, Unitarians and Sandemanians.[61]

Theologically, the Congregational Fund Board's academy which, from 1752, was conducted successively at Ottery St. Mary (John Lavington), Bridport (James Rooker), Taunton (Thomas Reader) and Axminster (James Small), was decidedly evangelical,[62] as was that at Mile End under John Conder's tutelage from 1755 to 1781.[63] Indeed, with reference to the latter, Priestley wrote, 'My Aunt, and all my relations, being strict Calvinists, it was their intention to send me to the academy at *Mile-end*, then under the care of Dr. Cander [*sic*]. But, being at that time an Arminian, I resolutely opposed it, especially upon finding that if I went thither, besides giving an *experience*, I must subscribe my assent to ten printed articles of the strictest calvinistic faith, and repeat it every six months.'[64] Instead Priestley studied at Daventry, as we shall see.

Other academies were notably open and progressive – supremely the 'Athens of the North' established at Warrington in 1757. John Taylor, the first divinity tutor there, exhorted his students thus:

> I, I do solemnly charge you, in the Name of the God of Truth, and of our Lord Jesus Christ, . . . that in all your Studies and Inquiries of a religious nature, present or future, you do constantly, carefully, impartially and conscientiously, Attend

to Evidence, as it lies in the holy Scriptures, or in the Nature of things, and the Dictates of reason; cautiously guarding against the Sallies of Imagination, and the Fallacy of ill-grounded Conjecture. II, That you admit, embrace, or assent to, no Principle or Sentiment, by me taught or advanced, but so far as it shall appear to you to be supported and justified by proper Evidence from Revelation, or the Reason of things. III. That, if at any time hereafter, any Principle or Sentiment by me taught or advanced, or by you admitted and embraced, shall, upon impartial and faithful Examination, appear to you to be dubious or false, you either suspect or totally reject such principle or Sentiment. IV, That you keep your Mind always open to Evidence. That you labour to banish from your breast all prejudice, Prepossession, and Party-zeal; . . . and that you steddily assert for yourself, and freely allow to others, the unalienable Rights of Judgment and Conscience.[65]

Between the decidedly evangelical and the equally decided liberal academies were some which, according to one's viewpoint, provided a varied theological diet or emitted mixed theological signals. Thus at Daventry, according to Priestley, 'Our tutors . . . were of different opinions, Dr. Ashworth taking the orthodox side of every question, and Mr. [Samuel] Clark, the sub-tutor, that of heresy, though always with the greatest modesty.'[66] When William Bull, later tutor at Newport Pagnell (1783-1820), entered Daventry academy in 1729, four years after Priestley's departure, the staunch Calvinist found a number of Arians among his fellow students;[67] and in 1762, when Samuel Morton Savage[68] was appointed divinity tutor at Hoxton (1701-85) his colleagues were the Arian Abraham Rees[69] and the Socinian Andrew Kippis.[70]

III

As to the more liberal academies: we may turn first to that at Whitehaven (1708-1729), which was founded and conducted by the Presbyterian Thomas Dixon,[71] who had studied under John Chorlton and John Coningham in Manchester.[72] He was an honorary MA of Edinburgh University (1709) and also graduated MD from Aberdeen in 1718. From the manuscript notes of his student Henry Winder[73] we learn that Dixon made reference to Bacon, Newton, and Locke on miracles and toleration, and not least to the Locke-Limborch correspondence. Winder's notes contain references to Chillingworth's view on natural reason as the only appropriate supplement to the revelation in Scripture, and to various writers on natural religion. Among Dixon's students were John Taylor of Norwich and Warrington academy and George Benson.[74] The latter proceeded to Glasgow, where he studied under Gershom Carmichael. He paraphrased the Pauline epistles which Locke had left undone as well as the catholic epistles, but his principal philosophical contribution was *The Reasonableness of the Christian Religion as delivered in the Scriptures* (1743). In this reply to the younger Henry Dodwell's *Christianity not Founded on Argument* (1741),[75] which some evangelicals had mistakenly construed as an attack on reason designed to make way for faith,[76] Benson consciously follows Locke in title and argument, contending that 'by our reason we are to make trial of what is offered to us as a revelation from God. Otherwise how could we distinguish between the Koran of Mahomet and the Bible?'[77] 'A moral philosopher', who may have been Peter Annet or Thomas Morgan, both of whom used that pseudonym, took issue with Benson in *Deism Fairly Stated and Fully Vindicated from the Gross Imputations and Groundless Calumnies of Modern Believers* (1746).[78]

Thomas Hill,[79] under whom John Taylor completed his training, founded the academy at Findern in 1710. He required his students to read Le Clerc's *Ars Cogitandi* for logic and Fromenius for metaphysics. His successor, Ebenezer Latham, however, prescribed Carmichael, under whom Latham had studied in Glasgow following a period at James Owen's academy in Shrewsbury, and Locke on logic, but nothing on metaphysics or ethics.

With the Presbyterian Henry Grove (1684-1738)[80] we come to a more accomplished philosopher. Grove had studied under Matthew Warren, and then took further training under his uncle, Thomas Rowe, in London. Following Warren's death on 14 June 1706 the Somerset Presbyterians appointed the twenty-two-year-old Grove as his successor, and in that post he remained until he died. As early as 1708 Grove, though generally sympathetic to Samuel Clarke's Newtonian stance, was corresponding with the Anglican divine on certain points in the latter's formulation of the theistic arguments, but his first significant philosophical publication was *An Essay towards the Demonstration of the Soul's Immateriality* (1718). From this we learn that although Grove held Locke in high esteem he was by no means intellectually subservient to him. Thus, for example, in making out his case that because the soul is immortal it cannot be a system of matter, he takes issue with Locke's supposition that, had he so chosen, God could have endowed matter with the power of thought. This, in view of his determination 'to prove the existence of spiritual substances against the materialists,'[81] Grove strenuously denies, showing 'Mr. Locke not to have been infallible'[82] to his own satisfaction. The crux of his case is that '*Matter* cannot *think*; and if so, *unquestionably the soul is immaterial.*'[83] But for all his eagerness to defeat the materialists, Grove does not wish to fall into the opposite error of denying the reality of the external world. Hence his rebuttal of Arthur Collier's *Clavis Universalis: or, a New Inquiry after Truth. Being a Demonstration of the Non-existence, or Impossibility of an External World* (1713).[84] Collier holds that matter has no existence independently of its being perceived. Grove agrees with him that the immediate object of perception is not external, and that our knowledge of the visible world is by idea, not intuition. Nevertheless, 'if the world serves all the same ends both of contemplation and action, tho' knowable only by idea, as it would if it were visible, or the immediate object of perception, then its invisibility can be no reason against its existence.'[85] Grove's concluding argument is that 'God is a Spirit, and thinking doth essentially and necessarily belong to his Being;'[86] and, further, that it is not at all incredible that God should 'communicate a copy of his essence' to human beings.[87] Moreover, God can do this without any blurring of the necessary Creator-creature distinction. Which thoughts prompt Grove to end with 'an act of devotion.'

In 1730 Grove, though no lover of controversy, rose up against his fellow Presbyterian Joseph Hallett Jr., tutor at the Exeter academy (1690?-1722).[88] Hallett had argued that we can learn of the future state only from the Bible, and not at all from natural reason. This, thinks Grove, is both to undermine the admirable views of John Howe, Clarke and William Wollaston on the matter, and to imply that those who have never heard the Gospel will be annihilated. Grove argues that reason is competent to demonstrate the existence of a future state wherein people will be rewarded or punished according to their deserts. His position, he is convinced, is 'more agreeable to the doctrine of holy scripture, better fitted to wipe off all aspersions from the Perfections and Providence of God, and of greater service in disputing with the enemies of our Religion.'[89] None of which is to deny that revelation 'gives a plainer and fuller representation of the whole duty of man than was ever done by unassisted Reason'[90] – a point Grove urges against the deists. That Hallett was not altogether persuaded by Grove is clear from his pamphlet, *A Defense of a Discourse on the Impossibility of proving a Future State by the Light of Nature. With an Answer to the Reverend Mr. Grove's Thoughts on the Same Subject* (1731).

During the 1730s Grove championed the cause of *Wisdom the First Spring of Action in the Deity* (1734). This was in opposition to John Balguy who had opted for *Divine Rectitude* (1730), and Thomas Bayes who gave first place to *Divine Benvolence* (1732) construed with respect to the happiness of all. Grove argues that by giving priority to divine wisdom over arbitrary will or blind inclination, we have the view which 'best consults the honour of the divine perfections, best agrees with the universal sense of mankind, and is best adapted to answer the most difficult questions on the subject of Creation and Providence. . . .'[91]

Of Grove it was said, 'Truth in every form had charms for him, but moral truth the most, because it immediately improves the heart.'[92] Certainly his most important work was in the field of moral philosophy, and to this we shall come in the next chapter. For the present it remains only to add that in his Taunton curriculum Grove was among the first, if not the first, to separate ethics from theology. Although he asserted the religious basis of ethics and insisted, in *quasi*-Newtonian fashion, upon God's orderly governance of a morally ordered world, the time would come when others would feel free to dispense with this foundation.[93] However, while Grove was attacked by the high Calvinist John Ball of Honiton for his alleged elevation of reason above Scripture,[94] he does not appear to have been rebuked by anyone for his 'Pelagian' or 'Stoical' treatment of ethics apart from theology – unlike his contemporaries at Yale, of whom Cotton Mather wrote, 'There are some unwise things done about which I must watch for opportunity to bear public testimony; one is the employing so much time upon Ethik in College, a vile form of paganism.'[95]

Among those who had studied under Joseph Hallett Jr. at Exeter was James Foster (1697-1755). His was one of the more liberal minds, and his was one of the more interesting doctrinal pilgrimages: not only from Calvinism to Arianism, but from Presbyterian paedobaptism to believer baptist views. To these last he was converted on reading the works of the General Baptist John Gale, who baptised him.[96] He comes to our attention principally for his answer to the deist Matthew Tindal, *The usefulness, Truth and Excellency of the Christian Revelation defended against the Objections contain'd in a late Book, intitled, Christianity as old as the Creation* (1731). Foster readily grants that Christians themselves have encouraged prejudice against the faith by 'corruptions in doctrine, and gross superstitions in worship.'[97] He then explains that as between himself and Tindal,

> the dispute between us is not at all about the *supreme* and *immutable excellency* of the *religion* of *nature*, nor whether this, which is by far the *greatest and best* part of *Christianity*, be as *old as the creation*, and *as extensive as human nature*; it is not, whether it be the *chief* design of *revelation*, to explain and restore this *primitive religion* in its original purity and perfection, and to assist and promote the regular and universal practice of it; not whether *reason* be our *ultimate rule* in all

our religious enquiries, a *rule* by which *revelation itself* must be judged; for the affirmative in all these questions is admitted.[98]

Some felt that all this being conceded, there was little left to argue about; and following the publication of Foster's *Discourses on all the Principle Branches of Natural Religion and Social Virtue* (1749, 1752), the high Calvinist Baptist, John Brine, countered with a forthright *Vindication of some Truths of Natural and Revealed Religion* (1746).[99]

Thomas Amory (1701-74), Grove's nephew, biographer and editor, trained for the ministry under his uncle at Taunton, and also at the Congregational Fund Board's academy at Hoxton, London, under the learned John Eames, FRS, who was unusually a lay principal tutor of a Dissenting academy.[100] In 1725 Amory returned to Taunton as assistant tutor and, on Grove's death he assumed charge of the academy from 1738 to 1759, when he removed to London. In Alexander Gordon's opinion, 'In all his work [Amory] was a dull, honest, serviceable man.'[101] No doubt his was not an original mind, and he left no complete philosophical works for our perusal though, as we shall see, he did contribute the concluding eight chapters to Grove's *System of Moral Philosophy*. Even so, his sermons and prefaces furnish evidence of the ideas typically received and popularly communicated by the more liberal tutors, and are to that extent interesting. Thus, in his sermon delivered at the ordination of William Richards we find Amory's apologetic *credo*:

As to the great Doctrines therefore of *Natural Religion*, which the *Gospel* takes for granted, and which are the foundations of our Faith in any Divine Revelation, because these can only be proved by reasonings on the nature of things, the frame of the world, and the like; we must, by arguments of this sort, addressed to the Reason of Men, endeavour to establish in them the belief of the Being, Perfections, and Moral Providence of God; of the moral and essential differences of chracters and actions, and of a future state of recompences. . . . As all men therefore are obliged to receive these Truths, and are *capable* of discerning the evidences of them; all they, whom we would confirm in the faith of these, have a right to demand from us *rational grounds for their faith*. To require that they should believ, without good reasons, what we affirm on these heads, is to exalt ourselves into *Lords of Faith*, and degrade them to a level with *brutes*.[102]

In similar vein, Amory's preface to an address to young men begins thus: 'The main Doctrines and Duties of the Christian Religion are not only agreeable to Reason, but may be proved immediately by it: These, on Account of their Internal Evidence and Excellency, claim our Belief and Regard, as well on Account of the Revelation which delivers and enjoins them.'[103]

Here we have the characteristic emphases of the rational Dissenters: the Gospel is grounded in the doctrines of natural religion; these can be proved and commended to reasonable beings; such beings are required to, and are capable of, assent to the proofs (no noetic effects of sin here); and to refuse to offer rational grounds for faith is to tyrannize and dehumanize others. But however wide the consensus on such matters, liberal Dissenters could, as we have seen in connection with Grove and Hallett, differ in emphasis on other points. Thus in a sermon on Psalm 145: 9 entitled, 'Goodness proved to be a Divine Perfection,' Amory declares that God's goodness is demonstrated, *inter alia*, by the moral sense he has planted in us; and in a note he writes, 'In proof of this, see Hucheson's [sic] *Inquiry* concerning moral Good and Evil.'[104] Amory would thus appear to be more favourably disposed to Hutcheson than John Taylor, who will engage our attention in the next chapter.

Like Amory, John Aikin who, following training at Kibworth academy under Philip Doddridge, began to lean towards Arianism whilst at Aberdeen University, left no philosophical works. That he was a most highly regarded tutor at Warrington academy is clear, however, from the remarks of John Yates. Aikin, he says, 'Who, though little known to the world, because he was restrained by an aversion to public notice from ever being an author, possessed an union of genius, learning and eloquence, which eminently qualified his for preparing youth for the office of the sacred ministry.'[105] William Enfield was more specific concerning Aikin:

> The first object of his researches was, to discover those truths which are the foundation of moral wisdom. Subjects merely speculative he occasionally examined, either in the way of amusement, or in the ordinary course of instruction. But those questions which are intimately connected with the conduct of life, and the happiness of rational beings, he studied with a degree of attention and solicitude, which discovered a deep sense of their importance.
>
> Whilst he readily acknowledged the existence, and the powerful operation, of original principles in human nature, he was no advocate of that indolent philosophy (so well adapted to the spirit and manners of the present age) which has raised an unnatural contest between *Reason* and *Common Sense*, and instructed men to trust to their feelings rather than to their understandings. He thought it the duty of every rational being to employ his powers of reasoning and judging in the search

of truth, and to endeavour to deduce the practical rules of life and manners from such theoretical propositions as have been established by conclusive argumentation. . . .

The same rational and Christian principles, which gave him such elevation and strength of mind, likewise taught him the lessons of humility and charity.[106]

Without question Warrington's most polymathic tutor was Joseph Priestley, who also taught *gratis* at Hackney college during its declining days. Priestley touched on a wide variety of philosophical topics, sometimes in an unduly combative spirit. Thus, for example, in his first philosophical publication, *An Examination of Dr. Reid's Inquiry into the Human Mind on the Principles of Common Sense* (1774), he takes Thomas Reid to task for his epistemological appeal to the common sense of mankind, which Priestley construes as sanctioning subjectivism or psychologism – that is, the view that if I feel something to be so, it is so: a stance which reveals more about my state of mind than about what is, or is not, the case. In reply, Reid points out that for him common sense implies judgment; it is 'that degree of judgment which is common to men with whom we can converse and transact business.'[107] More generally, Reid regularly distinguishes between sensation, the condition of a percept, and extension as a percept. Priestley further faults Reid for multiplying intuited instinctive principles, and for failing to heed the principle of the association of ideas. As Priestley despairingly remarks, Reid's notions of human nature were 'the very reverse of those which I had learned from Mr. Locke and Dr. Hartley.'[108] Priestley was further indebted to Hartley for his denial of the spirit-matter dualism, while his advocacy of philosophical necessity brought him into controversy with bishop Samuel Horsley and, as we shall see in the next chapter, with his friend Richard Price.[109]

Reactions to Priestley were varied, and some were hostile. For example, bishop Horne's biographer, William Jones, remarks, 'I have often wondered secretly, why this good man [i.e. Horne] should have felt as if he was called upon to encounter a writer of Dr. Priestley's disposition. . . . That Dr. Priestley is a man of parts, a versatile genius, and of great sagacity in philosophical experiments, is well known and universally allowed: but let any person follow him closely, and he will see, that if ever there was a wise man, of whom it might be said, *that the more he learnt, the less he understood*, it will be found true of Dr. Priestley.' Indeed, as Horne said, Priestley was a man, '*who is defying all the world, and cannot construe a common piece of Greek or Latin.*'[110] There you have it. But this very English 'put-down' emanates from the camp of evangelical orthodoxy.

The most eminent eighteenth-century philosopher to be trained in a Dissenting academy, to remain a Dissenter, and to become a Dissenting tutor was undoubtedly Richard Price (1723-91).[111] He was educated in turn under the Independents Samuel Jones[112] at Pen-twyn, Vavasor Griffiths[113] at Chancefield, and John Eames in London. Time would fail to tell of his polymathic activities, and to his ethical writings we shall come in due course. But here we must refer to a puzzle surrounding his tutorial activities at the liberal Hackney College (1786-96). How much teaching did he do? Herbert McLachlan cites Thomas Belsham as saying that Price gave no lectures at all at Hackney; and his biographers as saying that Price's tutorial experience was brief. McLachlan sides with William Broadbent, a student who wrote to the *Christian Reformer* as follows: 'The good Doctor had only three pupils to attend upon him ... and gave but very few lectures at all ... both Tutor and Pupils being better pleased to fill up the lecture hours in agreeable conversation on philosophy or politics, rather than employ it in difficult and abstruse calculations.'[114] There is no good reason to doubt the accuracy of Broadbent's statement, though it is a moot point whether it reflects adversely upon the tutor's commitment or upon the students' lack of capacity for what Price could have offered, or both.

Among Samuel Jones's other students at Pen-twyn was Noah Jones (1725-85).[115] After five years under Jones he went on to the Carmarthen academy in 1742, then in the charge of the Independent Samuel Thomas (1692-1766), minister of Lammas Street,[116] whose lectures were boring and whose manner was frigid. According to James Scott,

> One of the first books which Mr. Thomas put into [Jones's] hands was Dr. Watts' Logick, which he read with great pleasure twice over. This treatise together with Mr.Locke's Essay on the Understanding taught him to think freely, and put him upon the right scent in his enquiries after truth. He applied very closely to his studies; and on Lord's Days read books of devotion and practical religion. Manton and Flavel, and honest Matthew Henry on the Psalms and Proverbs, Mr. Grove's Tracts, Dr. Evans' Sermons on the christian temper, and many Welsh books.

Jones himself recalls the Carmarthen curriculum thus:

> The various languages, and mathematics were studied here upon a comprehensive plan. The Tutors read on natural history and ethics. Puffendorf, Hutcheson, Clarke, Wollaston &c in Divinity, Pictet's Lectures on the Greek Testament. In Logic, Watts, Locke, Duncan. In Natural Philosophy, Keil, Muschenbrook, Fergusson.[117]

As I have elsewhere observed,
> This is a characteristically 'Enlightenment' bibliography – Jones's *Sunday* reading of [the Puritans] Manton, Flavel and Henry notwithstanding. It comes as no great surprise to learn that the Congregational Fund Board became uneasy with the Carmarthen tutors. Thomas was a Pelagian – possibly an Arian; and Evan Davies was suspected of guilt by association. The Board requested Davies to secede, and to form an Independent Academy elsewhere. This he refused to do. Accordingly, the Board discontinued grants to Carmarthen students in 1757. David Jardine, a pupil of Evan Davies, was charged with the task of setting up an orthodox Academy at Abergavenny.[118]

IV

Isaac Watts (1674-1748)[119] may serve as a bridge between the more liberal and the more conservative academies, for his *Logic* was widely used by tutors of all theological hues: at the more conservative Bristol Baptist and Newport Pagnell (Independent) academies, as well as at the more liberal centres at Carmarthen and Warrington. As we have seen, Watts was an alumnus of Thomas Rowe's academy, and although he never held a tutorial post his writings made a considerable impact in their day, as the best of his hymns do to this day. His philosophy is eclectic. While he has reservations concerning the encumbered condition into which scholastic logic had fallen, he does not wish to lose the discipline of orderly thought. Impressed by the empiricism of Newton and indebted to Locke, the mind-body dualism he inherits from Descartes precluded uncritical discipleship of either.

Alive to the intellectual challenges of his own day, he contends that neither atheism nor deism, for all their vaunted reasonableness, can ensure that the virtuous course is known to the bulk of humanity, and pursued by them. Divine revelation alone makes plain the path, provides the power to walk in it, and inclines the will towards godliness. This theme is reiterated in a number of anti-deistic tracts, of which the most important is, *The Strength and Weakness of Human Reason: or, the Important Question about the Sufficiency of Reason to conduct Mankind to Religion and Future Happiness, Argued between an Inquiring Deist and a Christian Divine: the Debate Compromis'd and Determin'd to the Satisfaction of both, by an Impartial Moderator* (1731). At the end of this four-part dialogue the hapless deist confesses:
> I am fully satisfy'd, that the Bulk of the *Heathen* World is in a very dark and deplorable State, and amongst those who have

lost all traditional Knowledge of divine Revelation, their own Reason is far from being sufficient in any *practical* Sense . . . to lead them to Virtue, Religion, and Happiness. Upon a just Review, I am convinced, that had I been so unhappy as to have been born amongst them, my Reasoning Powers would have been exercised to no better purpose than theirs are. . . . I begin to see there is a Necessity of some better Advantages in order to reform Mankind, and to render them wise, pious, and happy: Nor do I know how this can be attain'd, but by some favourable Discoveries sent from Heaven . . . you have *almost persuaded me to become a Christian*.[120]

The necessity of divine revelation is constantly reiterated by Watts, not least in his *Logick* (1724).[121] This observation cautions us that the *Logick* is by no means simply a manual comprising definitions, modes of argumentation and exercises. Indeed, it is innocent of the last. Like the comparable works of Le Clerc, Condillac, Wolff and others it ranges widely over epistemological and psychological matters concerning the mind's cognitive abilities and accomplishments. Among the many topics treated are perception, memory, and right judgment. Running through the work we find Watts's qualification of the logic-spinning scholastics who have preceded him. Thus, for example, having expounded the several facets of the syllogism he seeks, in a manner reminiscent of Ramus, to cut away the dross:

Now it has been the Custom of those who teach *Logic* or *Rhetorick* to direct their Disciples, when they want an Argument, to consult the several *Topics* which are suited to their Subject of Discourse, and to rummage over the *Definitions*, *Divisions* and *Canons* that belong to each *Topic*. This is called the *Invention of an Argument*; and 'tis taught with much Solemnity in some Schools. . . .

By some *logical* Writers this Business of *Topics* and *Invention* is treated of in such a Manner with mathematical Figures and Diagrams, fill'd with the barbarous technical Words *Napcas*, *Nipcis*, *Ropcos*, *Nosrop*, &c. as tho' an ignorant Lad were to be led mechanically in certain artificial Harnesses and Trammels to ind out Arguments to prove or refute any Propostion whatsoever, without any rational Knowledge of the Ideas. Now there is no Need to throw Words of Contempt on such a Practice; the very Description of it carries Reproof and Ridicule in Abundance.[122]

Again, in connection with argumentative method, Watts positions himself in relation to his scholastic predecessors who distinguished between analysis and synthesis. In the received tradition synthesis concerned the progression from the parts to the whole, while analysis was designed to resolve a species or an individual into its parts. Watts's adjudication of the matter is as follows:

> The *antient scholastick* Writers have taken a great deal of Pains, and engag'd in useless Disputes about these two Methods, and after all have not been able to give such an Account of them as to keep them entirely distinct from each other, neither in Theory or in Practice. Some of the *Moderns* have avoided this Confusion in some Measure by confining themselves to describe almost nothing else but the *synthetick* and *analytick* Methods of *Geometricians* and *Algebraists*, whereby they have too much narrow'd the Nature and Rules of Method, as tho' every thing were to be treated in *mathematical* Forms.
>
> Upon the whole I conclude, that neither of these two Methods should be too scrupulously and superstitiously pursued, either in the Invention or in the Communication of Knowledge. 'Tis enough if the *Order of Nature* be but observed in making the Knowledge of Things following depend on the Knowledge of the Things which go before. Oftentimes a *mixed Method* will be found most effectual for these Purposes; and indeed a wise and judicious Prospect of our main End and Design must regulate all Method whatsoever.[123]

Watts's primary motive in seeking to ensure clarity and orderliness of argumentation is that Christianity be ably articulated and defended.

While in general agreement with Locke's repudiation of innate ideas on the ground that they are unnecessary because God has given us the capacity of forming ideas, making judgements and acquiring knowledge, Watts nevertheless thinks that some ideas may, in a sense, be innate. Not, indeed, that they are 'actually formed in the Mind at Birth,' but in that they 'seem to have been given to the Mind by a divine Energy or Law of Union between Soul and Body, appointed in the first Creation of Man: and this Law operates or begins its Efficacy in all particular Instances, as soon as those sensible Objects occur which give occasion to these sensible Qualities and Ideas to be first perceived by the Mind.'[124]

Like his contemporary, Henry Grove, Watts challenges Locke's supposition concerning thinking matter, and in doing so reveals his indebtedness at this point to Descartes: 'Now though I never was, nor could persuade myself to be a Disciple of *Des Cartes* in his doctrine of the Nature of *Matter*... and I have many Years ago given up his Opinions as to the chief Phaenomena of the corporeal World, yet I have never seen sufficient Ground to abandon all his Scheme of Sentiments of the *Nature of Mind* or *Spirit*, because I could not find a better in the Room of it, that should be free from Objections and Difficulties.'[125] He feels that Grove and others have adequately disposed of the notion of thinking matter.

What concerned Watts more was the position taken by Locke on the nature of the human being in relation to the resurrection. Locke had proposed that 'A *Person* is a thinking intelligent Being, which has Reason and Reflection, and can consider itself as itself . . . which it does only by that *Consciousness*, which is inseparable from Thinking.'[126] Watts grants that at the present time a person's consciousness will provide assurance of personal identity, but he is concerned with the future state of the person. Thus in connection with the resurrection, while granting that a person's total number of material particles cannot be raised after death, he is nevertheless concerned to secure the resurrection of the *same* body; and this need will be met if even a few only of the material particles remain: 'For if the new-raised Body has but as many essential Atoms of the dead body in it, as the new Stalk or Ear of Wheat has of the Grain that was sowed, it is enough: And the Union of the same conscious Mind or Spirit, makes it the same Man.'[127] In conclusion, Watts adds a 'short and plain Remark':

> There are some of those who follow Mr. *Locke* and his Way of thinking in many of these Matters, who also go a Step further, and suppose the Spirit or conscious Principle in Man to lose all Consciousness when the Body dies, and that at the Resurrection God shall give Consciousness to the Person again, or make a conscious Principle to exist in the new-raised Body. Now if this be the Case, then 'tis neither the same Body nor the same Spirit that is raisd from the Dead, but a new Spirit and a new Body, which I think must necessarily be called *another Person* . . . and I am sure such a new made Creature, consisting of another Mass of Matter, and another conscious Principle, can never be justly rewarded or punished for *personal* Virtues and Vices, good or evil Actions, done in the former Life by a different Body and Spirit, *i.e.* by *another Person*.[128]

His disagreements with Locke notwithstanding, Watts regularly describes Locke as 'great' and 'judicious', though this did not prevent his having certain anxieties regarding Locke's eternal state. Thus in a lyric poem 'On Mr. Lock's [*sic*] Annotations upon several Parts of the new Testament, left behind him at his Death,' the fourth stanza reads:

> Sister of Faith, fair Charity,
> Shew me the wondrous man on high,
> Tell me how he sees the Godhead Three in One;

> The bright conviction fills his eye,
> His noblest powers in deep prostration lie
> At the mysterious throne.
> 'Forgive,' he cries, 'ye saints below,
> The wav'ring and the cold assent
> I gave to themes divinely true;
> Can you admit the blessed to repent?
> Eternal darkness veil the lines
> Of that unhappy book,
> Where glimmering Reason with false lustre shines,
> Where the mere mortal pen mistook
> What the celestial meant!'

In a footnote Watts explains, 'I invoke Charity, that, by her help, I may find him out in heaven, since his Notes on 2 Cor. v ult. and some other places, give me reason to believe he was no Socinian; though he has darkened the glory of the gospel, and debased Christianity, in the book which he calls the Reasonableness of it, and in some of his other works.'[129]

Despite the widespread use of Watts's *Logick* and the pervasiveness of arguments – especially the cosmological – for the existence of God, it does appear that from about 1730, in the more conservative academies, philosophy – especially epistemology and metaphysics – begins to take a back seat in the curriculum if, indeed, it is present at all. It is not difficult to divine the reasons for this. On the one hand there is the concern of the theologically orthodox to 'guard the Ark' against a rationalism which was turning many in an Arian, and even in a Socinian, direction. On the other hand there is the influence of the Evangelical Revival, which fostered the establishment of academies exclusively devoted to ministerial training rather than to the provision of a broad university-level education. This was the context in which Thomas Ridgley worked, and his system is the only substantial publication of its kind to emanate from this class of academies.[130]

Ridgley is thought to have been educated under the Particular Baptist John Davison of Trowbridge. In 1712 he succeeded Isaac Chauncy as divinity tutor at the Congregational Fund Board academy at Moorfields, thereby becoming a colleague of John Eames. In his *Body of Divinity*, to which reference has already been made, Ridgley is especially concerned to repudiate the charge that such doctrines as those of election, particular redemption and efficacious grace are inconsistent with 'the moral perfections of the divine nature.'[131] Against encroaching Arminianism and Arianism he intends to uphold the doctrine of the Trinity, and is concerned that some ways of explicating the eternal generation of the

Son and the procession of the Spirit have given encouragement to Arians. Alexander Gordon declares that in seeking to avoid the latter pitfall, Ridgley 'denudes' his system of those doctrines, and 'is essentially Sabellian.'[132] In fact Ridgley strove to maintain the independence of the divine persons in their personalities and their essence. How far he succeeded we need not here inquire.

More to our purpose is the position Ridgley accords to reason. To him, reason is important, but it is subordinate to revelation. By revelation we become aware of such a doctrine as that of the Trinity, and reason's task is to prove both the truth of the doctrine, and the fact that we are under obligation to assent to revealed truth: 'what is false cannot be the object of faith in general.'[133] Reason, however, yields only relative security in matters of faith, and we can be saved from being 'tossed to and fro, and carried about with every wind of doctrine' only if our hearts are established with Grace.

Ridgley's system was in use at Bristol Baptist academy under Bernard Foskett (1686-1758),[134] who had studied medicine in London, but entered the Baptist ministry. He served the Bristol academy from 1720 until his death. In 1744 his student, the high Calvinist John Collett Ryland,[135] wrote in his diary a detailed description of his proposed academic work for the year. Of particular interest to us are the following remarks:

> 1. Go thro' Dr. Watt's Logick twice. 2. Then thro' his Scheme of Ontology twice. . . . N.B. Also read quite perfectly thro' Mr. Lock's Essay on Hum. Understanding, and sometimes when Mr. Fosket requires it give an account of it. . . .
> 1. Make me Self (i.e. in God's Strength) a Perfect and Compleat Logician and Metaphysician – from Dr. Watts's 2 Treatises on those Subject – But if possible I'll excell the Dr. Watts in both those Sciences – and Correct and improve and inlarge where he'd defective. 2. Read Correct and Explain and make Remarks on Mr Locks Treatise before Mentioned. . . . Get a Large Knowledge of Moral Philosophy as founded on Reason and Scripture [on which subject Foskett used Pufendorf].[136]

Happily, Foskett's manuscript lectures on *Pneumatology* are extant.[137] He begins optimistically enough: 'Pneumatology by some stil'd the special part of Metaphysicks, by Mr. Lock a branch of Physics must be agreeable to every students Mind because it is a Discourse of Spirits.' By the time he reaches the end of page three he has announced that thinking beings are immaterial; that the fact that we are 'Ridles to our Selves' shows only that 'the Soul is derived and dependent on some other being who for wise Reasons has been pleased to limit its knowledge of itself'; and that 'We have an original Freedom of Choice, and are not blindly, determined, by Fate and Necessity.' He next pronounces upon the relation of reason and revelation: reason, despite its best efforts, cannot produce full knowledge of God. Hence 'We should receive what Revelation discovers of the divine Being, the Trinity and hypostatic union, and not with the Socinians and others object their Repugnancy to Natural Reason – for there are as great seeming absurdities in our Notions of God's Eternity, Immensity &c. which are universally own'd.'[138]

Foskett proceeds to discuss the essence and immateriality of the soul, siding on occasion with Locke, but more generally with the Cartesians, Cudworth and Grove; and then considers the nature and origin of ideas, with a reference to Mr. Leibniz. He passes to the faculties of the soul and the will, to affections and passions; to the souls ubiquity, its union with the body, and its immortality. In this last connection he again cites Grove with approval.

In his second book Foskett has essays 'Of angels' and 'Of God' separated by some blank pages. We do not need to designate Foskett an original philosopher, but at least we can say that he reflected upon many of the available theoretical options, presented both sides of the several arguments, and drew his own conclusions. In doing so he appears to have been among the most thorough of the more conservative mid-eighteenth-century academy tutors.

Foskett was succeeded by Hugh Evans (1712-81), whom he had baptized at Broadmead church, Bristol in 1730.[139] During Evans's term of office a student, Thomas Dunscombe, reported on work he had done during 1770-71. From this statement, and from a subsequent one written a year later, it would seem that while in both years Watts's *Logick* was studied, that work was the sole representative of the philosophical disciplines. Alongside it went the Baptist John Gill's high Calvinistic theology and a good deal of Hebrew and classics.[140] In 'A Catalogue of a Few Useful Books' presented to one of his leaving students in 1773, Evans recommends the following of philosophical interest: Doddridge on the evidences – 'a very valuable performance'; Boyle on natural and revealed religion; Jonathan Edwards, 'the most rational, Scriptural divine and the liveliest Christian the world has ever been blessed with,' on freewill and other topics; and, under 'Miscellaneous', Derham's *Astro-* and *Physico-heology*, Locke's *Essay*, and Watts's *Improvement of the Mind*.[141] These last are clearly 'runners up' to a substantial list of doctrinal, practical and historical works, and they reveal that Evans's disciplinary preferences were in line with those of most other tutors with conservative leanings.

As staunchly Calvinist as John Collet Ryland was his Independent contemporary Abraham Taylor (fl. 1727-40),[142] who was appointed to the Clerkenwell-Deptford academy of the King's Head Society at its inception in 1730. Indeed, Taylor was as staunchly Calvinist as John Gill, but that did not forestall controversy between them in 1732 when the latter suspected the former of lurching dangerously towards Arminianism. Taylor has left us his manuscript *Lectures on Natural and Revealed Theology*, which appear to be largely a regurgitation of Marckius, and *An Introduction to Logick, with a few Lectures on Perception, the first part of that Science*. Never averse to *ad hominem* argument, Taylor asserts: 'If we consider matters justly and impartially, we must conclude, that Adam our common parent, impair'd his intellectuals greatly by his fall. . . . '[143] Even so, the world owes a debt to Aristotle in the matter of orderly reasoning.[144] Sufficient of Taylor's manner (which was irascible) and attitudes will become plain from one further quotation:

> The Popish writers run into great confusion in endeavouring to make free thinking consistent with implicit faith in the dictates of their church; and Mr. Locke, who let his admirers say what they will of him, was no better than a Socinian in principle, and but a mean Divine for that sort, and no great friend of revelation, has interlarded his work with a great many subtleties, which tend to bring persons to have a mean and low view of what is properly mysterious. These men were certainly persons of deep thought, and penetrating genius, but their learning was very inconsiderable, and their reading was not large. This, in a particular manner, was true of Mr. Locke. Those that knew him personally were satisfied, that, as to ancient literature he was but very superficial.[145]

Thomas Gibbons (1720-85) began his higher education under Abraham Taylor, but on 3 January 1737 he addressed a letter to the King's Head Society in which he expressed his wish to resign from the course. His complaints were that Taylor taught no logic, that his introductory lectures on divinity took up too much time and were excessively concerned with classical learning, and that Gibbons was required to ask permission to leave the premises at other than stated times. The Society found in favour of Taylor, and discharged Gibbons from its care.[146]

Gibbons completed his education under John Eames and eventually, in 1754, became tutor in logic, metaphysics, ethics, rhetoric and *belles lettres* at his original *alma mater*, by this time located at Mile End. On 22 May 1754 he recorded in his diary that he had informed the governing body of his intention to teach 'Logick, Metaphysics, Ethics, Rhetorick, Stile in gener:, Pulpit Stile', and that this was approved. On 26 May

1758 he writes, 'Lectured at Mile End. Poorly in the afternoon with the head-Ach. Blessed be God that poorly as I was, I finished the last Lecture of the four years' course of lectures at the Academy, & hereby have acquired a Sett of Lectures for my whole future life, or so long as I may continue in the Tutorship.' Before we deem this unforgiveable slackness, let us recall that Gibbons was pastor for forty years at Haberdashers' Hall, and that on 1 March 1755, at a time when he felt that his pastoral work was under threat of too much lecture preparation, he wrote, 'My business as a Pastor is first to be taken care of. My Business as a Tutor is only secondary.'[147]

Gibbons wrote on a variety of subjects: numerous elegies and a book on *Female Worthies* are among his publications. But on logic, metaphysics and ethics he did not commit himself in print. His personal confession of faith at his ordination does, however, mark him as an eighteenth-century man in his starting-point, and as a traditional Calvinist in his conclusion. For he sets out from 'the Evidences derived from the Light of Nature,' adverts to the obligations of duty, but then affirms that over and above all this, 'I believe we are indebted to the Light of a Verbal Revelation from God;' whereupon he summarizes his position on the cardinal doctrines of the Reformed faith.[148]

Among Gibbons's students was Caleb Evans (1737-91), who in 1781 became president of the Bristol Baptist College in succession to his father, Hugh. Though always on the conservative side theologically, we gain the distinct impression that this institution is now being 'warmed up' by the Evangelical Revival. Thus, of Caleb Evans a student expostulates, 'Oh, how often has he in prayer, and in advice, melted over us.'[149] This calls to mind a Fletcher of Madeley rather than an Abraham Taylor. There can be no question that Evans's supreme objective was the production of godly ministers of the Word. Like many of these, and according to the candid John Rippon, he seems to have been quite effective 'off the cuff': 'He never professed himself to be a *profound* metaphysician . . . yet his mind was enriched with numerous combinations of thought, with a taste cultivated and pure, and a memory eminently accurate. Warm and occasionally rapid in manner, he sometimes succeeded more through a kind of natural felicity than previous study.'[150]

As already noted, the Abergavenny academy was established in 1757 by the Congregational Fund Board as a result of the Board's dissatisfaction with the liberalizing tendencies at Carmarthen (though it should be noted that the perceived doctrinal laxity was the product of the spirit of open enquiry fostered at Carmarthen, not of the indoctrination of students by subversive tutors).[151] Information is scare, but we learn that logic and ethics were specified in the course of instruction, but not metaphysics or epistemology. Without question the most prominent theologian-philosopher to emerge from Abergavenny was Edward Williams (1750-1813) who, for the last eighteen years of his life was principal of Rotherham Independent college. During his student days under Benjamin Davies [152] he read the works of Theophilus Gale, Ralph Cudworth and William Wollaston, and the imprint of their defences of natural religion may be seen on his own writings.[153] But how far these works were generally prescribed for study at Abergavenny, or how far Williams was prompted towards them by his own studious nature is not easy to determine. We shall meet him again in chapter five.

At Trevecca, opened on the Countess of Huntingdon's birthday, 24 August 1768, the philosophical disciplines were, with the exception of logic (Watts's) conspicuous by their absence from the list of subjects to be studied: 'Grammar, logic, rhetoric, ecclesiastical history, natural philosophy and geography, with a great deal of practical divinity and languages.'[154] But Trevecca was a special place, where evangelical Calvinist preachers were to be trained, where students and tutors alike had to subscribe to fifteen Calvinistic articles of faith, and where the entire syllabus could be set aside if Fletcher of Madeley,[155] president of the college, was seized with a concern for the students' souls:

> Languages, art, sciences, grammar, rhetoric, logic [a passing mention], even divinity itself . . . were all laid aside when he appeared in the school-room among the students. His full heart would not suffer him to be silent. He *must* speak, and they were readier to hearken to this servant and minister of Jesus Christ than to attend to Sallust, Virgil, Cicero, or any Latin of Greek historian, poet, or philosopher they had been engaged in reading. And they seldom hearkened long before they were all in tears, and every heart caught fire from the flame that burned in his soul.[156]

At the second Hoxton academy – that is, the Independent one established in 1788, Robert Simpson, who had studied under James Scott at Heckmondwike, was at the helm.[157] He was 'distinguished for his consistent and systematic theology which was in every particular Calvinistic.'[158] He taught the three 'R's': 'Ruin Redemption, and Regeneration,' and expected his students to preach with 'Animation, Affection and Application' – and, no doubt, with Alliteration. There is no evidence of philosophical studies in the Hoxton curriculum until 1803, when logic makes its appearance. Nonetheless, among Hoxton's alumni was George Payne (though he had also been a Dr. Williams scholar at Glasgow University), who went on to teach at Blackburn and Exeter

Congregational colleges, and was said to have 'a genuine gift for metaphysical speculation.'[159] Philosophy was similarly elusive at the missionary enthusiast David Bogue's Gosport academy (1780), where the Bible reigned supreme, where students were expected to have had a definite conversion experience, and in whose curriculum there is no reference to philosophy. Yet from here there emerged the historian James Bennett, who became tutor at Rotherham Independent academy (1795-182) in 1813, following the death of Edward Williams. There, among other things, he taught logic and the history of philosophy. The relevant publications of Payne and Bennett will occupy us later..

The origins of the Newport Pagnell academy (1782) are unusual in that the moving force was the Anglican evangelical clergyman John Newton who, supported by likeminded colleagues, persuaded William Bull the Independent to lead the new institution. Bull had been under Caleb Ashworth's open-minded tutelage at Daventry but, staunch evangelical Calvinist that he was, he was more than happy with the prescriptions which Newton laid down in his *A Plan of Academical Preparation for the Ministry*.[160] A letter from Newton to Bull contains the intriguing assertion: 'Many persons are seriously thinking of a new academy, on *liberal* grounds, for preparing young men for the ministry, in which the greatest stress might be laid upon truth, life and spirituality, and the least upon modes, forms, and non-essentials.'[161] At once we see that this 'liberal' academy is for ordinands only, and that piety is to be the main objective. It takes little imagination to guess what the 'non-essentials' might be, but if we are at a loss, Newton will illuminate us. In his *Plan* he declares that the Bible is his body of divinity, and that he prefers Paul's letters 'to any human systems I have seen.' He does not wish the tutor to be 'seduced by the specious sounds of candour and free enquiry.' Of the list of books recommended for study, Ashley Smith justly remarks, 'the most striking characteristic . . . is its out-datedness. These were the standard texts of fifty or more years before.'[162] Watts's *Logick* and *Improvement of the Mind* were approved for study, but of other branches of philosophy Newton writes, 'I have no great opinion of metaphysical studies. For pneumatology and ethics I would confine my pupils to the Bible.' Out, too, went the evidences, which had loomed so large at Doddridge's Northampton and Ashworth's Daventry academies: Newton had no patience for the 'needless and hurtful attempt of proving first principles.' In a letter to Newton, Bull contemplated the future with some alarm: 'I expect the time will come when [the friends of Jesus] will not dare to say anything but what may be proved by *Cicero De Officiis* or Wollaston's *Religion of Nature*.'[163] There is no suggestion, however, that future ministers needed to be equipped to address such a state of affairs should it come to pass.[164] Not surprisingly, William Bull left no philosophical remains – an achievement in which he was emulated by tutors at Gosport and other evangelical academies.

Overall, the more conservative academies founded in the wake of the Evangelical Revival with an exclusive concern for ministerial training were least hospitable to the philosophical disciplines. Their supporters thought they had seen enough of the baneful influence of rationalism upon more liberal academies and, thence, upon church life at large,[165] and we can appreciate the pressure upon tutors to produce 'sound' ministers. But are ministers adequately equipped if at least some of them cannot face the scepticism of a Hume or the materialism of a Priestley? The philosophical record of the conservative Dissenting academies and tutors is not encouraging to those who would return a negative answer to this question.

V

We turn finally to those academies which were mixed in that while generally moderate and intellectually open, and having a broad curriculum for ministerial and lay students alike, both more liberal and more conservative tendencies were found among their staffs and students.

As with the classes of academies already reviewed, information concerning the place of philosophy in the curriculum of the mixed academies is sometimes sparse. We learn, however, that at Hoxton academy (1701-85)[166] the manuscript *Institutiones Ethicae* of John Eames (who himself published nothing) was used by his pupil and successor, Abraham Rees (1743-1825), its Latin notwithstanding.[167] Rees was educated under David Jennings[168] at the Coward Trust' academy, London, and following a period as assistant there he removed to Hoxton. When that academy closed he went on to Hackney. When it ceased in 1796 he assumed pastoral charge first in Clapham, then at St. Thomas's, Southwark, and finally at Old Jewry Meeting House. He was a high Arian, and the last London minister to wear a wig when conducting worship. More importantly, he was a considerable scholar, and his great memorial is the forty-five volume work, *The New Cyclopaedia or Universal Dictionary of Arts and Sciences* (1802-40). As restrained as Abraham Taylor was pugilistic, of Abraham Rees it was said that 'The area of controversy he seldom entered. When he wished to destroy error, his plan was to inculcate the opposite truth. He aimed rather to sap than to storm the fortifications of the adversary.'[169]

Samuel Jones[170] was trained at Abergavenny under Roger Griffith[171] and at Shrewsbury under James Owen. He went on to Leiden in 1706, and on his return to England two years later he opened his academy at Gloucester, removing to Tewkesbury in 1712. For information concerning his course at Tewkesbury we are indebted to a letter from Thomas Secker to Isaac Watts. According to Secker, Jones's students were allowed 'all imaginable liberty of making objections against his opinion, and prosecuting them as far as we can.'[172] More specifically:

> Our *Logic*, which we have read once over, is so contrived as to comprehend all *Heereboord*, and the far greater part of *Mr. Locke's* Essay, and [Le Clerc's] the *Art of Thinking*. What *Mr. Jones* dictated to us was but short, containing a clear and brief account of the matter, references to places where it was more fully treated of, and remarks on, or explications of the authors cited, when need required. At our next lecture we gave an account both of that the author quoted and our tutor said, who commonly then gave a larger explication of it, and so proceeded to the next thing in order. He took care, as far as possible, that we understood the sense as well as remembered the words of what we had read, and that we should not suffer ourselves to be cheated with obscure terms which had no meaning. Though he be no great admirer of the old *Logic*, yet he has taken a great deal of pains both in explaining and correcting *Heereboord*, and has for the most part made him intelligible, or shown that he is not so.

Sadly, after a time Jones 'began to drink too much ale and small beer and to lose his temper, and most of us fell off from our applications and regularity.'[173]

Samuel Chandler, DD, FRS (1693-1766)[174] was another alumnus of Tewkesbury, to which he had come from Bridgewater academy, and whence he departed for further study in Leiden. He was a voluminous writer, whose most important philosophical works are his *Vindication of the Christian Religion* (1725, 1728), in which he attacks the views expressed by the deist Anthony Collins in his *Discourse on the Grounds and Reasons of the Christian Religion* (1724), and *Plain Reasons for being a Christian* (1730).

John Jennings (d. 1723)[175] was trained at Attercliffe under Timothy Jollie. In 1715 he opened his own academy at Kibworth, where he was the Independent minister, and removed it with him to Hinckley in 1722. His *Logica in usum Juventutis Academicae* (1721) covers ninety-eight pages, and is replete with references to Locke, whose *Essay, Conduct of the Understanding*, and *Method of Common Places* appear in Jennings's 'Syllabus librorum.' Among seventeen other works are listed Descartes's *Meditations* and *A Discourse on Method*. Unlike Jollie, Jennings favoured an extensive and inclusive curriculum, and was more than willing to introduce his students to a variety of authors. He was not, however, reluctant to adjudicate between them. Thus, for example, he refers to Malebranche's *Recherche de la Vérité*, and sides with Locke against the Frenchman's view that God communicates ideas of phenomena to the human mind directly from his own mind. Locke had argued that this would have made the creation of matter unnecessary, and that it is as conceivable that God had ordained the union of sensory perception with mind as that all ideas were in him.[176]

Jennings's most illustrious student, Philip Doddridge, declared that 'Mr. Jennings encourages the greatest freedom of enquiry, and always inculcates it as a law, that the scriptures are the only genuine standard of faith.' At the same time, 'Mr. Jennings does not follow the doctrines or phrases of any particular party; but is sometimes a Calvinist, sometimes an Arminian, and sometimes a Baxterian,[177] as truth and evidence determine him.'[178] In a letter to Thomas Saunders of 16 November 1725[179] Doddridge provides a full account of Jennings's course, from which we learn that Burgersdyck's *Logic* was dealt with in about six lectures, and supplemented by Jennings's own system, 'a great deal of which was taken from Mr. Locke.' Metaphysics appears in a list of 'Miscellanies' which includes Fortification and Psalmody, while in ethics recourse was had to Grotius, Pufendorf and Wollaston. During the eighth half year a brief historical account of ancient philosophy was given.

Doddridge was much indebted to Jennings's breadth and style of teaching in his own tutorial work at his celebrated academy at Northampton (1729-51).[180] While a student he had received advice from his friend Samuel Clark of St. Albans which he never forgot:

> I am sensible of the difficulties pneumatology has attending it. The only method of extricating oneself out of them is to see that we have clear ideas of all the terms we use, whether single, or connected with propositions, and that we take nothing for granted without sufficient evidence; and, which flows from the other two, that we do not pretend to reason upon things about which we have no ideas; that is, that we do not pretend to impossibilities. Mr. Locke's Essay is so useful to direct the mind in its researches, that methinks it should have been read before you entered upon pneumatics. . . . As to your contemplations upon the being and attributes of God, take heed of suffering your mind to rest in barren speculations. Whatever clear and enlarged ideas you attain to of the divine excellencies, see that they have proportionable effect upon the soul, in producing reverence, affection, and submission.[181]

According to Doddridge's student, Job Orton, logic was studied,[182] while ethics and pneumatology were incorporated in the divinity course, as were studies of the nature and properties of the human mind, the theistic proofs, the nature of moral virtue, natural law, the immortality of the soul, and the necessity of revelation. Orton remarks that 'In his Lectures of *Philosophy, History, Anatomy*, &c. [Doddridge] took Occasion to graft some *religious* Instructions on what he had been illustrating, that he might raise the minds of his Pupils to GOD and Heaven.'[183] Doddridge paid particular attention to the proofs of Christianity, a subject which he thought was 'more largely and accurately exhibited than in any other place of education I have ever heard of.'[184] As to teaching method, Doddridge 'referred [students] to Writers on both Sides, without hiding any from their Inspection.'[185]

As to Doddridge's own opinions: although on occasion he disagreed with Locke's interpretation of particular verses, and felt, like Peirce and Benson, that Locke erred 'in too great a fondness for new interpretations,'[186] he was in general sympathy with Locke's approach to Paul's epistles.[187] Again, he took the risk, given the ever-present scrutiny of eagle-eyed high Calvinists, of articulating a favourable interpretation of Locke's widely-suspect view that the fundamental of Christianity is that Christ is the Messiah. He grants that

> a question arises concerning the extent of these words: perhaps it may be sufficient to answer it by saying, that wherever there appeared to be such a persuasion of the dignity of Christ's person and the extent of his power, as should encourage men to commit their souls to his care, and to subject them to his government, those who professed such a persuasion were admitted to baptism by the apostles, and ought to be owned as Christians.[188]

Further, Doddridge fully accepts the position of Baxter and Locke that the Christian religion has a rational basis, and that its truth can be argued for: hence, for example, his rebuttal of Henry Dodwell's *Christianity not founded on Argument*. But that he was no slavish follower of Locke is seen from his challenge to Locke on such matters as personal identity, the liberty of indifference and miracles.[189]

While Doddridge is rightly remembered more for his hymns, his temperate theology, and his personal marrying of head and heart than for his philosophy, there is always a place for the journeyman in philosophy, who will present and digest a variety of views in an balanced manner, so that they who run may read.

Not the least of the tributes to Doddridge is the fact that his *Lectures* were used by Samuel Morton Savage (1721-19)[190] at Hoxton Academy

(1701-85), and by his pupil and chosen successor, Caleb Ashworth. Neither of these left any philosophical writings, though the former presented his case for a broad curriculum in the ordination charge he delivered to Samuel Wilton on 18 June 1766; while the latter, on taking up his tutorial work, was cautioned by Job Orton thus: 'Especially warn the students against metaphysical and philosophical prayers, but *let not your animadversions be severe, as the good Doctor's often were* [i.e. Doddridge], *when he thought they were not evangelical, which intimidated and discouraged many of his pupils. Errors that will naturally mend by years and experience should be gently treated.*'[191] There spoke a wise pastor.

Ashworth's assistant at Daventry from 1760 was Noah Hill (1739-1815),[192] who had been a pupil at Noah Jones's school at Cradley. Of Hill, Thomas Belsham said, 'of Logic and Mathematics he knew but little';[193] but another states that among the many subjects he taught were the philosophy of the human mind and moral philosophy, and that 'He was particularly clear and excellent in his mathematical lectures.'[194] Hill was succeeded by Belsham in 1771, and with reference to his logic course Timothy Kenrick wrote on 10 June 1775, 'We entered immediately after Xmas on Logic, and have now finished it; we always followed Dr. Watts's plan, except in a very few instances.'[195] When Belsham became divinity tutor in 1781 his course included logic, the doctrine of the human mind, the existence and attributes of God, the first principles of ethics, and the evidences of revealed religion.[196] Of particular importance is the fact that Belsham appears to have been the first Dissenting tutor to teach materialistic and necessarian philosophy.'[197]

A number of Belsham's manuscript lectures are extant.[198] Among these are some *Additional Lectures in Pneumatology*. These contain references to numerous authorities – especially to Locke, Clarke, Butler, Reid, Beattie and Priestley (notably to his *Abridgment of Hartley*). Part One is a defence of the doctrine of necessity, in which such matters as personal identity, the passions and isntincts, liberty and necessity, and the immateriality of the soul are discussed. The second Part concerns the being and attributes of God, and includes discussions of natural and moral evil, of Bonnet's *Essai analytique sur les facultés de l'âme* (1769), and references to Leibniz. There follow numerous blank pages, and we then come to lectures on sensation, ideas, vision, hearing, intellect – at which point the writer runs aground. Much of the material here treated appears in Belsham's major published philosophical work, *Elements of the Philosophy of the Human Mind* (1801); and further philosophical contributions are to be found in his manuscript lectures of 1805 and 1806 on *Evidences of Divine Revelation*. Here, among other things, he offers an answer to Hume's objections that events which are claimed as miracles are reliant upon human testimony, which may be faulty: 'The falsehood of Testimony in certain given circumstances is *impossible*,' Belsham confidently declares, 'viz. When the witness is neither himself deceived nor desirous to deceive others.'[199] There are references to Paine, Price, Priestley, Paley, Hartley and other moderns, and to numerous classical authors.

By 1789 Belsham, by now decidedly unitarian in his views, did the honourable thing and resigned his post at Daventry and removed to the liberal Hackney academy. He was replaced at Daventry by John Horsey (1754-1827),[200] who had been trained at Homerton and who, though not doctrinaire, remained in the middle way. He reintroduced Doddridge's lectures and although his students now comprised ordinands only, he maintained the spirit of free enquiry. In his inaugural address Horsey outlined his policy in terms which would have found the approval of more liberal tutors than he: 'It is not the design of this institution, and it is very far from my inclination, to usurp any authority over Conscience, or to cherish Bigotry or party zeal.' He continued, 'My object is not to stamp infallibility on any human system of Religion . . . but . . . to promote a Scriptural Christianity.'[201]

Horsey's manuscript lectures on logic and ethics are extant. In the former he compares various systems of logic and then expounds Watts, suitably amended and enlarged by reference to other writers. Lant Carpenter, who entered the academy in 1797, informed his mother by letter that he was giving 'very close attention to the study of the doctrine of Necessity,' and said that the works of Locke and Hartley had been read 'with great care.'[202] All of which was too much for the recently appointed classical tutor, David Saville, a Scot and a staunch Calvinist to boot. He anonymously advised the Coward Trustees that the academy was 'tinctured not a little with Socinian principles,' and Horsey was informed by a letter of 15 June 1798 that the trustees had decided to close the academy; and so it was.[203]

Thirty years later Horsey's posthumous *Lectures to Young Persons on the Intellectual and Moral Powers of Man* were published in his memory. In the preface he writes,

> The following Lectures took their rise from some peculiar circumstances attending my situation at the time when they were drawn up. Having had the honour and the felicity of presiding for the space of eight years over the Academical establishment supported by the Trustees of the late William Coward, Esq., without the slightest censure from them, collectively or individually, but receiving, on the contrary, in

the most handsome terms, repeated testimonies of their approbation, – the ninth year became exceedingly uncomfortable, by the introduction of a very unsuitable classical tutor. The connexion was in consequence dissolved, and the Academy removed to Wymondley in Hertfordshire.

The passing events of the period led to the construction of the following Work, as an exercise pleasant in itself, and a seasonable relief to the mind, under no small share of misrepresentation, and consequent unmerited censure.[204]

The theme of Horsey's lectures prompts us to turn in more detail to the contribution made by eighteenth-century Dissenters to moral philosophy.

3

The Eighteenth-Century Dissenters' Contribution to Moral Philosophy

The eighteenth-century Dissenters had their ethical roots partly in the works of Grotius, Pufendorf and others, but also in those massive Puritan bodies of practical divinity which might, as in the case of Thomas Watson's work of 1692, comprise expositions of the Westminster Shorter Catechism, the Decalogue and the Lord's Prayer. To the Puritans theology and ethics comprised an harmonious whole. The fact that God had spoken had implications for conduct. A running theme of Paul's letters: if this is what you believe, then this is how you should live, was congenial to the Puritan mind. Time-lags being as they are in intellectual history, this approach was still followed by some Dissenters in the eighteenth century, notably by the high Calvinist Baptist John Gill (1697-1771).[1]

Having expounded the entire Bible, Gill published his *Complete Body of Doctrinal and Practical Divinity* in 1769-70. His stance is clearly indicated on the first page of his Introduction:

> Doctrine has an influence upon practice, especially evangelical doctrine, spiritually understood, affectionately embraced, and powerfully and feelingly experienced. . . . Where there is not the doctrine of faith, the obedience of faith cannot be expected. . . . Doctrine and practice should go together; and in order both to know and do the will of God, instruction in doctrine and practice is necessary; and the one being first taught will lead to the other.[2]

On this basis Gill proceeds through the Christian doctrines from God to eschatology (though reserving ecclesiology for his practical chapters concerning worship), Christian virtues and practice, and private and public duties. This clearly sets him in the line of such Reformed thinkers as Witsius and Macovius, and of his fellow-countrymen William Perkins and William Ames. Thus, as Richard Muller has pointed out, Gill 'rooted himself in a theology that was far more compatible with his understanding of Christian doctrine than the Anglican theology that inhabited the English universities of his time.'[3] All of which means that the self-educated Gill, though he was contemporary enough in his polemics against deists, antinomians, Arminians and others, was not in the van of his century's ethical discussion.

More typical of the moral philosophy of the eighteenth century is the increasing divorce of moral questions from theological. Many divines came to see that it would no longer suffice to confine ethics to expositions of the Decalogue or the Beatitudes. This is by no means to say that the Dissenters (or the Anglican divines for that matter) excluded God from their ethical writings; but their tone becomes gradually less homiletic, or more technical, with the realization that intellectual challenges in ethics as elsewhere must be met on their own terms. The arguments of Hobbes and Shaftesbury served as stimuli in this respect. Concurrently, there arises the conviction that, while special revelation is by no means redundant – indeed, it is essential as acquainting people with the mind and will of God (and thus the deists are wrong), morality rests on an universal, rational basis. In view of this the recourse of many eighteenth-century moral philosophers to continental post-Reformation natural law theories and to Cicero and the Stoics is not surprising.[4] Nor, closer to home, should the influence of the Cambridge Platonist Benjamin Whichcote (1609-1683) and others be overlooded. In heady sectarian days he advocated a reasonable, ethical Christianity over against the then prevalent dogmatic scholasticism.

In the story of this transition from what we might call Puritan ethics to modern ethics, Isaac Watts (1674-1748) and Henry Grove (1683/4-1738) are 'bridge' persons. Indeed, Grove, as we saw, with no intention of disparaging divinity, separated dogmatics from ethics in his academy curriculum.[5] Unsurprisingly, those who did most to advance the cause of ethical discussion were divines of a generally open disposition. For the most part they were educated in the more doctrinally tolerant – even liberal – academies. By the end of the century some of them were distinctly radical. But even among the more open-minded there were those like John Aikin (1713-80), of whom it was said that 'His lectures on Morals and Theology, and his comments upon the Holy Scriptures, were adapted to improve the heart, as well as to inform the understanding.'[6]

What were the issues in moral philosophy tackled by the eighteenth-century Dissenters? In the turbulent politico-religious situation following the Reformation, recourse was had by Grotius, Pufendorf and others to natural law, and the resulting obligations upon rulers and ruled alike. Their works were among those read in a number of the early Dissenting academies, and their influence upon Watts, Grove and their Dissenting successors was considerable. As Sidgwick showed long ago, this emphasis upon natural law gave rise to such questions as, 'What is man's ultimate reason for obeying these laws? Wherein does their agreement with his rational and social nature exactly consist? How far, and in what sense, is his nature really social?'[7] The consideration of such questions in Britain took the form it did largely in response to the perceived threat posed by Hobbes. Indeed, Sidgwick declares that 'for two generations the efforts to construct morality on a philosophical basis take more or less the form of answers to Hobbes.'[8] Between Hobbes and the eighteenth-century Dissenters came the Cambridge Platonists, Cumberland, Locke and Clarke, all of whom in their several ways repudiated Hobbes's materialism, and his hypothesis that unless state power were concentrated in one man or assembly of men, a reversion to the state of nature would ensue in which the human life would be 'solitary, poor, nasty, brutish, and short.'[9] Further, the general tendency of these writers was away from Hobbes's reduction of the natural law to a law of self-preservation.[10] To them it was the moral basis for living, supplying common ground on which all reasonable people could stand. As Locke put it, the law of nature is 'the Will and Law of a God.' It is 'the decree of the divine will discernible by the light of nature and indicating what is and what is not in conformity with rational nature, and for this very reason commanding or prohibiting.'[11]

In the wake of Hobbes ethical discussion tended in two directions. On the one hand there were writers primarily interested in politics, economics and statecraft; on the other hand there were writers (sometimes the same ones) who, on the assumption that moral properties are objective, went in quest of an answer to the question how our moral obligations are determined. Are we indebted to intuitions of reason, or of a special moral sense? Concerning the latter, while thinkers as diverse as Descartes, Hobbes, Henry More and Locke had, in varying degrees, adverted to the human mind's passions and sentiments, it was Shaftesbury (1671-1713) who gave the cue to those – supremely Francis Hutcheson (1694-1746) – who sought, on analogy with knowledge-yielding physical senses, to ground ethics in a moral sense. Shaftesbury's methodological contribution, which grew out of his opposition to established religion and its educational institutions, lay in his determination to make the constitution of human nature, not the purposes and promises of God, central to his ethics..[12]

We shall see that while political questions could never be far from the minds of Dissenters – especially those concerning liberty of belief and worship, their moral philosophy was undergirded by the discussion of moral ends, and of the ways in which we determine our duty. Some Dissenters were in the stream of rational intuitionism flowing down from

Ralph Cudworth and Samuel Clarke, while others were indebted to, and in the case of at least one who wrote on ethics, taught by, Francis Hutcheson.[13] Yet others adopted an eclectic approach.[14]

Let us now turn to these generally neglected thinkers.[15] I shall first treat them in chronological order, and indicate some of their main concerns in moral philosophy; and I shall then consider one theme, that of freedom, which exercised them all in one way or another. As we proceed we should remind ourselves that their thinking was done at a time when the idea that the individual has a right (over against authorities whether ecclesiastical or secular) freely to exercise reason and conscience was gaining ground;[16] and when older notions – for example, that an atheist (the psalmist's 'fool' = immoral person, who says in his heart there is no God) cannot be a morally upright person – lingered strongly in many Christian minds.

I
Isaac Watts

Isaac Watts evinces a strong interest in the moral law. This emerges, for example, in a discourse on 'The perpetual obligation of the moral law, the evil of sin, and its desert of punishment.' He defines the moral law thus:

> The moral law signifies that rule which is given to all mankind to direct their manners or behaviour, considered merely as they are intelligent and social creatures, as creatures who have an understanding to know God and themselves, a capacity to judge what is right and wrong, and a will to chuse and refuse good and evil. This law, I think, does not arise merely from the abstracted nature of things, but also includes in it the existence of God, and his will manifested in some way or other, or at least within the reach of our knowledge: it includes also his authority, which obliges us to walk by the rule he gives us.[17]

This law is given in the Decalogue, and it is 'scattered up and down through all the writings of the new Testament.' It was written by God's finger on tablets of stone; it was written by God's inspiration in the Bible, and 'it is written in the hearts and consciences of mankind by the God of nature. The voice of God from heaven acclaimed this law, the voice of the prophets and apostles confirm it, and the voice of conscience, which is the vicegerent of God in the heart of man, speaks the same thing.'[18]

In a note Watts explains that the moral law comprises the natural law which arises from the natural principles of reason, and the written law given at Sinai. The natural law, which contains moral precepts addressed to all human beings, 'lies within the reach of all men whose consciences are not grossly blinded or hardened by sin;' the written law is clearer, and also contains ceremonial regulations prescribed for the Jewish people; but 'the grand requirements and the design of both these are the same. . . .'[19]

The moral law is of universal and perpetual obligation: 'It springs from the very relation of his creatures to their Maker and to one another.'[20] In answer to the question whether it is reasonable on God's part to require perfect obedience to the law from fallen humanity, Watts maintains that although human powers are vitiated, 'God continues still to demand a perfection of obedience; he cannot give an imperfect law, or a law that requires but an imperfect obedience to it.'[21] The grace of the Gospel provides 'a relief for us under our failings,' but it does not abate the demands of the law. Those saved by grace do not perfectly obey the law, yet God still requires such obedience. Indeed, 'it is one great design of the gospel to restore us again to a chearful and regular obedience to [the moral law].'[22]

It is quite clear that Watts understands that all people have the ability, by the use of their reason, to grasp the dictates of the moral law. But, in his eclectic way, he also has a place for a moral sense. He does not develop a sensationalist theory as Hutcheson did, still less does he pit a moral sense against rational intuitions; and he is by no means the first to advert to such a sense. He appeals to what he takes to be a moral experience common to, and recognizable by, all. He does this, for example, in a sermon on 'The universal rule of equity.' He here expounds Matthew 7: 12, 'All things whatsoever ye would that men should do unto you, do ye even so unto them; for this is the law and the prophets.' He writes,

> This excellent precept of Christ, carries greater evidence to the conscience, and a stronger degree of conviction in it, than any other rule of moral virtue. . . . [T]here is not much need of a reason to find it out; for we reach the proof of it from within ourselves, even from our own inward sensation and feeling. If we would know what is just and equitable to do to our neighbour, we need but ask our own inward sense, and our conscience together, what we would think equitable and just to receive from him.[23]

What is more, with this precept our Saviour, knowing the power of self-love, 'wisely takes this very principle of self-love, and joins it in the consultation with our reason and conscience, how we should carry it forward to our fellow-creatures. Thus by his divine prudence, he constrains even this selfish and rebellious principle to assist our consciences and our rational powers in directing us how to practise the social duties of life.'[24]

Impressive though the natural law is, revelation is nonetheless required. Watts makes this point strongly in a work entitled, *Self-love and virtue reconciled only by religion*. In the context of a critique of atheism and deism he writes as follows:

> It is granted, the most general rules of duty, the chief outlines and boundaries of vice and virtue, may be discovered by the reasoning powers of man, if rightly employed; but these discoveries are so few, and some of them are so feebly impressed upon the minds of the multitude, that, in many cases, they leave but a general glimmering light, and give but a doubtful direction. . . . But God, by revelation of his will in scripture, has given so bright a discovery of these general boundaries between vice and virtue, and made plain a multitude of these particular duties both by many express commands, and prohibitions, and various parallel examples, both of vice and virtue, that even the common people may learn what they are to believe, and what they are to practice, or avoid, by a far more easy and ready way of instruction. Milk-maids and plowmen, and the menest offices or capacities in the world may learn their duty here.[25]

For our final glimpse of Watts we shall turn to the question of truthfulness – a theme which concerns him greatly, and on which we find him at his most casuistical. He has eleven sermons on 'Christian morality,' all of them based on Philippians 4: 8, 'Whatsoever things are true, whatsoever things are honest, whatsoever things are just, whatsoever things are pure, whatsoever things are lovely, whatsoever things are of good report . . . think on these things.' Of these sermons, two are on 'Whatsoever things are true.' He sets out from the observation that we need both 'the furniture of the head' and the integrity of the heart[26]. Accordingly, truth encompasses veracity, faithfulness and constancy. The light of nature requires us to practise truth, but in addition we have a Gospel of truth from the God of truth. It follows that 'no circumstances whatsoever can make a lie lawful.'[27] In an appendix to the first three sermons Watts considers the question of the lie told for good ends. He illustrates his point by reference to Rahab, the harlot of Joshua 2: 4, 5, who hid the Israelite spies, told the messengers of the king of Jericho that she did not know whence they came nor whither they went, and was commended for this by Paul (*sic*) in Hebrews 11: 31. Reflecting upon this, Watts first makes it clear that an utterly unlawful action does not become lawful when performed for good ends. The law of God is not thus to be manipulated. What, then, of Rahab's commendation? Although a 'woman of evil fame in Jericho,' she had heard of God's intention to establish the Israelites in the land of Canaan, and the assisted them in their conquest of the land. For this she was approved. But 'she used a very sinful method of accomplishing this design.' Moreover, 'The timorousness of her temper was a sore temptation to her; and though she fell into a criminal action, yet God so far excused the ill conduct, as to forgive the falsehood. . . . But the lie, though it was pardoned, remains still a blemish to her character.'[28] Furthermore, 'A woman of her character, living in a heathen country, may well be supposed to have had little knowledge of the sinfulness of so beneficial a lie as that was, and no scruple about it.'[29] Watts proceeds in some detail to consider the possibility that there may be those – children, cheats and others – who may be incapable of receiving the truth, or may be deemed not to deserve to hear it. In all cases Watts urges truthfulness. Even if one should lose one's life as a consequence of speaking the truth, the advice stands. Such a person 'dies a martyr to the truth; his name shall be registered with honour among the saints of God on earth, and his soul shall have its place among the martyrs in the upper world.'[30]

Henry Grove and Thomas Amory

Henry Grove's substantial work, *A System of Moral Philosophy*, was published posthumously in two volumes by his nephew and successor, Thomas Amory (1700/1-1774) in 1749. The preface and the concluding eight chapters were contributed by Amory himself. In his preface Amory informs us that Grove used his manuscript for over thirty years in instructing youth. On his death-bed he charged Amory to ensure its publication.

Morality, says Grove, is the knowledge and practice of those things that concern human beings as moral agents. To pursue the moral path is the way to happiness, for 'the design of Morality is to unite the distracted opinions of mankind in one uniform invariable idea of happiness, to lead them to the injoyments (*sic*) in which it is to be found, and to direct to the means for the attainment of it.'[31] Virtuous practice is of paramount importance, but it needs to be grounded in good theory. No doubt not all are equipped for such philosophical work, but gentlemen, lawyers and divines should pay heed to it. It might, however, be objected, 'To examine these matters by *Reason*, when we have *Revelation* . . . is like lighting up a candle at noon-day.'[32] It is certain that revelation enables us to see our duty plainly and easily, but it is nevertheless useful for the Christian to investigate the foundations of moral goodness, and to distinguish the several virtues by right reason. Moreover, reason guards us against false ideas of God, and against irresponsible appeals to Scripture – as when people appeal to the example of Rahab when they wish to tell a lie. We also need reason to show that the general plan of the Gospel accords with it, and to help us choose between conflicting duties.

Morality is within the capacity of all who are sincere and well disposed. The scholar will give a better account of it than the mechanic, but 'Morality, being the concern of all, must be within the reach of all.'[33] The data of morality are God and man, and the fundamental duty is to know and meet our obligations. The end of morality is happiness – not absolute happiness which, owing to human degeneracy is unattainable, but 'the highest attainable by man in the present circumstances of his Being.'[34] However adverse a believer's circumstances may now be, God rewards the virtuous with an happiness in the after life, which is not fully bestowed here below.

Grove then turns upon Hobbes, who denies all natural distinctions of good and evil, yet declares that morality is capable of demonstration. He can do this, protests Grove, only because, as he says, 'we ourselves are the authors of the difference between Justice and Injustice, by the establishment of Laws and Conventions, to which moral good and evil owe all their being'[35] As for Locke's view[36] that morality is as capable of demonstration as mathematics, Grove finds the reason given for this unacceptable. Locke thinks that moral terms stand for ideas in the mind, and that we can be clear concerning these. But this, says Grove, presupposes rather than proves the certainty of morality; and we need to be able to show that 'my ideas connected with praise or dispraise, with good or ill desert, have a foundation in the nature of things.'[37] In other words, to demonstrate that one is morally obliged to act in a certain way is more than a matter of defining terms; it has to do with the deliverances of the natural law. On this basis Grove proceeds to elaborate upon the themes of happiness, human actions and passions, and the freedom of the will (to which we shall return).

Part II of Grove's work opens with a discussion of conscience. While the external, supreme and ultimate law is the law of God, 'the *internal, subordinate,* and *immediate* Rule of every man's actions is his own *Conscience.*'[38] Conscience is not a power or faculty distinct from reason, but is 'the reasoning or judicative faculty of the Mind.'[39] Thus, 'Conscience is a man's Reason or Understanding, considered in the relation it bears to his Actions, in their moral Nature, and most important Consequences.'[40] Conscience has to do both with the practical principles by which it guides its judgment of all actions, and with the actions themselves. The will of God, whether discerned by reason or revelation, is the only rule immediately binding upon the conscience. Parents, magistrates and others may bind our conscience in things indifferent and within their jurisdiction. There is a natural conscience possessed by all, and an enlightened conscience which benefits from revelation, but nevertheless has its foundation in the natural conscience. A conscience which is objectively morally good has as its object the good life; and evil conscience 'has lost more or less the sense it ought to have of the distinctions of *moral* good and evil.'[41]

As for obligation, 'The true notion of *Obligation* is a *moral Necessity* of doing actions, or forbearing them.'[42] All laws are obligatory, but what is it which gives authority to one person over another? According to Hobbes and Spinoza (as understood by Grove) it is the prerogative of the most powerful to impose their will on others in the state of nature. Against this Grove protests that the notions of authority and power are different and separable. Either can be present in a given situation without the other. Again, when Hobbes posits a state of nature in which every person is a king without subjects, he flies in the face of what everyone else has always thought, namely that 'all authority from the highest to the lowest had a proportionable degree of obligation answering to it.'[43] (Grove and his contemporaries could not easily surrender the idea of the orders of society and the duties appropriate to each in his or her station). Furthermore, Hobbes wishes to hold both that the possession of power confers the right to govern, and that some have a natural right to govern. The problem is further complicated when Hobbes declares that God's irresistible power is the foundation and source of his sovereignty. This means, says Grove, that God has a right to do whatever he has the power to do: he could rightfully damn innocent creatures. But this 'is a monstrous contradiction; for either it cannot be exercised, or the exercise of it will be incompatible with the very being of several divine Attributes. It is a contradiction to say, there is such a right but it *cannot* be exercised; for what should hinder?' Hence,

> From all that has been offered I infer, that if we can suppose this boundless right in God over his creatures, we must suppose it possible for this right to be exercised; but on the other hand it is undeniable, that the full exercise of this right would be *inconsistent* with *goodness, holiness,* and *wisdom*: wherefore I conclude, that either there are no such perfections in God, or he is possest of *no* such right.[44]

Grove proceeds to discuss the law of nations, civil and canon law, and natural law, of which he says (with indebtedness to Cicero), that it is 'the *fundamental* Law, upon which all other Laws, whether *divine* or *human* are built, and the *great fountain* of *moral truths*. . . .'[45] The law of nature requires a thing, it does not merely warrant it. More specifically,

The *Law of nature* is the *Will of God* relating to *human Actions,* grounded in the *moral differences* of things: and because *discoverable* by *natural light, obligatory* upon *all mankind.*[46]

Grove advances an *a priori* demonstration of the natural law grounded in a consideration of the divine and human natures, and then develops an argument which is partly *a priori* and partly *a posteriori*:

1. There is a *natural and essential difference* between *Virtue* and *Vice,* and those several actions and dispositions which are denoted by these two opposite terms.
2. *Natural Reason* discovers it to be the *Will of God* in this case, that every man should look upon this *difference* in the nature of things and actions, as a *Law* or *Rule,* which he is always religiously to observe, under *pain* of his *Maker's displeasure.*[47]

There follows a further rebuke to Hobbes for supposing that left to themselves people would harm one another. Cumberland, declares Grove, has capably disposed of this suggestion, and Grove draws an analogy between Descartes and Hobbes:

In order to be *certain* of *something, Des Cartes* would first have us *doubt* of *every thing*; and so Mr. *Hobbs* sets the *world* together by the ears, that he may have an opportunity to show us his art in bringing them to treat of *peace.* Both of them lead us a great way round about, only to bring us at last to the very same place where they first found us.[48]

Far from being naturally hostile to one another, human beings are lovers of beauty, and they are creatures 'formed for religion . . . God has designed the *nature* of *things* as an *interpretation* of his will. . . .'[49] God himself is just, good, merciful and true, and he 'hath shown it to be his will, that men should practise virtue, by so *forming the mind,* that *propositions* containing the *principal* duties of morality are no sooner understood, but *assented* to. . . . '[50]

The law of nature is necessary, eternal, universal and immutable. From this law are deduced our obligations to love God and our fellow creatures, and to regulate our own self-love. This leads Grove to an extensive consideration of virtues and vices: prudence, sincerity, fortitude, sobriety, temperance, justice, truth and faithfulness. With his remarks upon faithfulness his own work ends, and Amory adds his chapters.

Amory discusses the themes of restitution, deliverative justice, marriage, parental authority, government, universal benevolence and piety. In the concluding chapter he says that while this study of the principles and rules of religion and morality has focused those upon those discoverable and proveable by reason, 'we cannot conclude without acknowledging our obligations to *Revelation*.'[51] It is the fault of the deists to magnify reason at the expense of divine revelation, but they have the advantage of having been educated in an environment permeated by the Christian revelation, and are thus more advanced in their moral understanding than even the best pre-Christian writers. Hence, 'To judge aright . . . of our obligations to *Revelation*, we should consider the state of the world as *idolotrous, ignorant,* and *corrupted* to the grossest degree in their Religion and Morality, and *uncertain* as to the most important truths, when the light of *Revelation* broke forth upon them; and what would have been the probable consequences in all following ages, had not God favoured men in this extraordinary manner. . . .'[52] While reason can prove a first cause, it is from revelation that we learn the attributes of God and our obligations to him. To revelation we owe the doctrine of a moral and particular providence, a clearer perception of our duties, and the obligation to prevent self-love from blinding ourselves to the just needs of others. From revelation are likewise learned the duties which we owe to ourselves: we are not to live like beasts, but as those who are destined to be heirs of heaven. Further, revelation teaches the truths and duties of morality with authority and (with an acknowledged debt to Locke's *The Reasonableness of Christianity*) this greatly helps those who have not the leisure or ability to weigh moral matters carefully. The deliverances of revelation do not fluctuate, whereas apart from its authority a person's reason may be blinded by temptation. Again, revelation yields many noble examples for us to follow; its teaching on final rewards and punishments affords a powerful motive to virtue; and its provision of the Christian Church, with its ministry, facilitates the universal spread of knowledge concerning the truths and duties of religion.

Grove's *A System of Moral Philosophy* is the first substantial work devoted to its subject by an eighteenth-century Dissenter. For this reason, and also because of its long use in manuscript as a teaching resource in Grove's academy, I have outlined its contents in some detail. But Grove had much to say concerning morality in his other writings. Two themes to which he constantly reverts may be mentioned.

First, like many others in his time, Grove, while emphasising the conscientious rights of the individual, and also the need to maintain a proper self-love, also clearly understands that human beings live in societies. In this latter capacity they contribute to the happiness or misery of their fellow creatures. In order to increase the happiness of others Grove extols benevolence as a virtue. Once again Hobbes's doleful view of humanity is his target: 'I always imagined that kind and benevolent propensions were the original growth of the heart of man, and, however checked and overtopped by counter inclinations that have since sprung up within us, have still some force in the worst of tempers, and a considerable influence on the best.'[53] Indeed, Grove cannot conceive that the benevolent God, in creating human beings in his own image, would omit benevolence from their make-up. Reason teaches us this, but so does experience of life, as when we see examples of 'the pity which arises on sight of persons in distress, and the satisfaction of mind which is the consequence of having removed them into a happier state....'[54]

Secondly, reverting to the objective of happiness, which Grove declares is man's chief end,[55] Grove is insistent that the route to this happiness lies in loving God. In a sermon delivered at the ordination of his nephew Thomas Amory and the latter's friend William Cornish, Grove ranks the obligation to love God above any specific commands of God:

> We are obliged to love God not merely because he hath commanded us to love him, but because he hath made us capable of loving him, and both by his perfections and his benefits challenges our love. Did these not oblige us to love him as soon as we were in a condition to make any reflection on them, no subsequent command could oblige us to it. . . .
> For if there are good reasons why we should love God, now that he commands it, they must be equally reasons for love antecedent to the consideration of any command whatsoever.[56]

In his Preface to the published sermon Grove underlines the point with respect to the issue of self-interest in relation to divine rewards and punishments:

> Upon the whole, this notion which resolves all obligation into the promises and threatenings annexed to the law of God, or, which is the same thing, into the hopes and fears of men's minds raised by them, tho' it presupposes the will of God which hath enacted the law, and fixed the sanction, yet, under pretence of doing more honour to God and his law, hath in reality no respect to them at all, but terminates wholly in self-interest; whilst the other notion which asserts obligations antecedent in nature to the will of God, carries in it a tacit acknowledgement of the necessary and immutable perfections of God, and of his unmerited favour which hath bestowed being with all the privileges belonging to it: forasmuch as among these antecedent obligations, the obligation to the love of God, and a cheerful obedience to his will, is one of the principal . . . . [w]hen God and nature, reason and scripture have joined the

love of God with the hope of a reward, it is but presumption in any man to put them asunder.[57]

Grove's ethics were grounded in his conviction that we are obliged to love God and to show benevolence towards other intelligent beings. We are, moreover, under the commands of God but these, though challenging, are not the sole ground of our obedience. Specific commands apart, all reasonable people will agree that God has created us in such a way that we can love him, and this we ought to do. With this emphasis upon the primacy of the intellect over the will Grove was revealing indebtedness to Cudworth, and laying a trail which both John Taylor and, more definitively, Richard Price, were soon to follow.

John Taylor and Samuel Bourn III

The Presbyterian divine John Taylor (1694-1761)[58] was educated under Thomas Dixon at Whitehaven academy, whence he proceeded to Findern, Derbyshire, under Thomas Hill.[59] He ranged widely over the theological disciplines, being awarded the Doctorate of Divinity of the University of Glasgow in 1756 for his *The Hebrew Concordance adapted to the English Bible,* and causing much fluttering in the conservative theological dovecotes with *The Scripture-Doctrine of Original Sin* (1740), and *The Scripture-Doctrine of Atonement Examined* (1751). These sufficed to have him marked down as an Arian. Following a pastorate in Norwich (1733-57), Taylor became the first divinity tutor at Warrington academy, where he remained until his death. It fell to him to teach moral philosophy, and his writings specifically on this subject are *An Examination of the Scheme of Morality advanced by Dr. Hutcheson* (1759), and *A Sketch of Moral Philosophy* (1760). He was indebted to Philips Glover's *An Enquiry concerning Virtue and Happiness* (1751), but also feels that his conversations with Glover over a number of years contributed to the latter's work. He also owed much to *A Review of the Principal Questions of Morals* by his Presbyterian colleague, Richard Price, the first edition of which had appeared in 1757.[60] It will be convenient if we outline Taylor's ethical works in reverse order.

Taylor intended his *Sketch* as an introduction for young students to William Wollaston's *The Religion of Nature Delineated,* which was first circulated in 1722, and published in 1724.[61] According to Wollaston, the truest definition of religion is '*The pursuit of happiness by the practice of reason and truth.*'[62] As was appropriate in one suspicious of 'enthusiasm', Taylor launches forth with the assertion that 'Revelation is of no use to us, if it is not an Address to the Understanding and common Sense of Mankind.'[63] If we are firmly grounded in the principles of natural religion 'we shall be furnished with a Standard, by which to measure every part of Revelation; a Standard of the same Authority with Revelation itself.'[64] While 'The Rule of right Action lies open to every honest Mind; and all men see, or may see, the Difference between moral Good and Evil, as plainly as they see with their Eyes the Difference of Objects which are before them,'[65] the discussion of moral principles is the province of a few. The foundation of virtue 'is that principle, which being supposed, Virtue, or Action morally right, necessarily results.'[66] Such a principle should be as forceful as any demonstrated proposition of Euclid, though such demonstrations are easier in mathematics, which is not subject to prejudice. Such a principle should apply universally, and should be consistent with liberty or freedom of choice.

The rightness of an action does not depend upon the will or power of the actor; the loss or gain accruing to the actor; or upon the subsequent reflections or affections of the actor or others. The only consideration is the nature and properties of the object. Indeed, 'To know the Natures of Things, is the same as to know the Obligation to right action.'[67] Truth is the conformity of our ideas to the natures of things, and all obligations arising from truth are necessary and hence independent, eternal, universal and immutable. The obligations of truth do not depend arbitrarily upon God's will. On the contrary, 'The great God himself is necessarily under the Obligations of Truth:'[68]

> his Divine Rectitude, or Perfection of Holiness, consists in his constant and invariable Conformity to this eternal and immutable Rule of all right Action. Which indeed is no other than his own infinite, eternal and all-perfect Understanding; which Understanding is the eternal and unchangeable Law, or Rule by which He is directed in all his Actions.[69]

It is by reason that we perceive and understand the truth. Unlike the senses, reason distinguishes, compares and compounds; it implies an obligation to right action because it acquaints us with the natures of things. Freedom and agency are the same thing. A person who acts is free; one who is acted upon is not an agent. To act virtuously, or in a morally right manner, is 'to treat, or behave towards, all rational and sensible Beings, and the Things which may affect them, according to their Natures, Properties, Relations, and Circumstances, or according to the Truth, so far as known, or apprehended by any particular Agent . . . and to act in a contrary Manner is Vice, or Action morally evil.'[70] Moreover, 'All rational Beings, without Exception, are necessarily and unavoidably subject to the Obligations of Virtue.'[71] Even though a judgment is mistaken, a moral agent ought to do what he or she sincerely feels obliged to do. On occasion temptation or trial may alleviate guilt, but they do not 'lessen the general obligation to virtue.'[72]

Moral obligations cannot clash because they are founded upon truth. But although there may be more reasons for performing one duty than another, the fact that we cannot do all we ought does not nullify the several obligations. While virtuous action is necessarily free, reasonable authority may be heeded, 'as in marital Affairs, or the ordering of Children.'[73] God assists our virtuous choices without hindering our freedom, though moral agents may resist the preceptive, though not the absolute, will of God. For an action to be moral, both the ends and the means must be virtuous. (At this point Taylor appears to introduce teleological considerations into what has been largely a deontological account of morality).

Happiness, or pleasure, is essentially different from virtue: 'Happiness is a pleasing Sensation; Virtue is right Action.'[74] Happiness is a gift from God. It cannot be the foundation of virtue, though it may be a motive to it. While suffering may yield the highest degree of happiness, falsehood and vice can never yield virtue. Happiness (presumably in the sense of immediate sensations of pleasure) is not a necessary consequence of virtue, but virtue is the only ground of happiness. As an end, happiness is always subordinate to truth and reason.

The will of God is necessarily under the obligations of truth and right, and he judges all moral agents. Revelation cannot contradict or annul the obligations of natural religion, though it may introduce new obligations which do not conflict with those of natural religion.

The human conscience is not a distinct faculty, but 'the Judgment of our Minds concerning our own Actions; or it is our Apprehensions of Right and Wrong, either directing, or reflecting upon, our own Conduct.'[75] If we would be guided by conscience we must lay aside all prejudice, guard against deception, and faithfully seek the truth. We shall thus be able to act according to the light afforded to us by our capacities, opportunities, means and advantages: 'It is all we have, and all we can have at present.'[76]

It is hardly surprising, in view of Taylor's strongly rationalistic account of morality, that when he turns to examine Hutcheson's[77] moral sense he is less than content. First, however, he dissents from Hutcheson's replacement, in *An Inquiry into the Original of our Ideas of Beauty and Virtue* (3rd. edn., 1729), of self-love, interest or private advantage as the foundations of virtue, with benevolence or a disinterested goodwill to others. As we have seen, Taylor grounds virtue in the nature of things.

Next, Taylor objects to Hutcheson's appeal to a special moral sense. He quotes Hutcheson's definition that the moral sense is 'a natural determination to love and approve, or condemn and despise actions and agents, without any views of interest, as they appear benevolent, or the contrary.'[78] This sense, claims Hutcheson, is the fount of moral ideas. Apart from the instincts of benevolence and the moral sense, Hutcheson contends that we should have no perception of morality at all. These instincts, like our other senses, assert themselves antecedently to our use of reason, and independently of our wills. Reason's role is to correct wrong opinions and impressions, and to direct our good inclinations towards the end proposed by benevolence and the moral sense: that is, reason is subordinate to them.[79]

Against Hutcheson's position as thus described, Taylor counters as follows: first, Hutcheson is wrong to reduce all virtue and religion to his two favoured instincts. He gives no place to self-love, and he overlooks other virtues which we possess. Secondly, the existence of a moral sense distinct from reason may be questioned, not least because if our reason clearly shows us the nature and difference of actions, 'then there is no occasion for inventing a new sense.'[80] Hutcheson thus bases his whole scheme on 'a non-entity, the mere fiction of his own brain.'[81] Thirdly, whilst we are all aware that instincts like benevolence, sympathy and social affections are within our natures, where virtue is concerned they cannot be other than auxiliaries to reason. For as virtue is the most excellent disposition of intellectual nature, 'its principles, laws and exercise must be assigned to the chief and governing powers in such a nature,' namely, reason.[82] Furthermore, instincts have no place in the deity; if they were the ground of virtue we should be in the unfortunate position of believing that the stronger the instinct the greater the virtue, and *vice versa*; and instincts, being arbitrary and changeable provide no proper foundation for virtue. Hutcheson is quite wrong to state that reason 'cannot propose an end, a good or happiness to be pursued, nor consequently, excite to action.' On the contrary, Taylor declares, '*Reason*, which alone can judge of, and reason about, the natures and relations of things, is the *only* faculty that can distinguish between actions morally good and evil . . . and therefore is the *only* faculty, that can supply justifying *reasons* of our actions.'[83] Happiness is but one object of reason and virtue; the all-comprehending object of our minds is truth. Virtuous actions renders the agent morally praiseworthy, but one cannot be praised for possessing particular instincts.

Fourthly, benevolence and the moral sense are not true springs, standards or judges of virtuous actions; for benevolence may be weakened by self-love, and the moral sense itself is guided by the opinions and judgements we make of persons and things, and these are the work of reason. Fifthly, on Hutcheson's own account benevolence and the moral sense do not constitute an action virtuous unless they are guided by reason. Thus, lastly, although in his theory Hutcheson accords reason a role subservient to benevolence and the moral sense, he actually elevates it above them. Similarly, in Hutcheson's work on the passions we find that his rules for governing the passions are rational rules, and that they depend upon examining the true nature of objects and actions. So Taylor concludes that

> the very writing of his books confutes the principles therein advanced. It is as if he had undertaken to demonstrate that there is no demonstration. For he *reasons* at large about the nature and principles of virtue, in relation to his two instincts, in order to prove, that *reason* is no percipient nor judge of virtue.'[84]

I cannot forbear to remark here that Taylor protests too much: Hutcheson understands his moral sense to be a means of perception only, and, to mention the point that Taylor urges against him, in an admittedly developing account of ethics Hutcheson was increasingly open to consequentialism, with the attendant view that reason has to work upon the perceptions received. But however deficient his theory may be at certain points, there can be no doubt of Taylor's support of the ethical rationalism flowing down from Cudworth, Clarke and Grove, and already being given more sophisticated expression than Taylor could manage by Richard Price.

There is some evidence to suggest that one of the reasons for Taylor's unhappiness at Warrington academy was that the secretary to the trustees, the single-minded John Seddon, was a Hutchesonian in ethics, and over-inclined to meddle in curriculum matters which were, strictly, the preserve of the professors, and concerning which (as on other matters) Taylor could be equally dictatorial.[85] Interestingly, however, there is no record of any friction between Taylor and his younger colleague Samuel Bourn (1714-96), in whom we meet the third generation of Samuel Bourns in the Presbyterian ministry. His grandfather (1648-1719) ministered at Bolton, his father (1689-1754) finally at Coseley and Birmingham, while he himself served first at Rivington, Lancashire, and then as co-pastor with John Taylor at Norwich from 1754 until the latter left for Warrington in 1757.[86] Of all the Dissenting divines with whom we are concerned in this chapter, Bourn was the only one to receive a university education. He studied at Glasgow University, 'when professor Hutcheson began to add celebrity to that seminary.'[87] It would seem that there was no friction between Taylor and his younger colleague arising from the latter's tutelage under Hutcheson – though it must be remembered that Taylor had not at that time begun to teach ethics; and Bourn in his published works did not advance a moral sense theory. He did, however, have a good deal to say concerning justice and human moral agency.

In a discourse on Psalm 58: 11, 'Verily there is a God, that judgeth in the earth,' he treats of God the moral governor. The natural order, he declares, yields irrefutable evidence that it has been created by a just and good God. But God is not merely a creator and preserver of all things, he is a moral governor and judge of humanity also. This has been a puzzling truth to many when they have seen how the righteous suffer and the wicked prosper: 'These are appearances which seem inconsistent with the perfection of a divine government.'[88] However, difficulties notwithstanding, 'the arguments drawn from the whole frame of nature which lead us to ascribe infinite wisdom and benevolence to the Supreme Being, conclude equally for his perfect justice.'[89] As seen in the realms of civic and domestic government, in the desire of societies to punish their wicked members, in the reactions of the human body to excesses, and in the human conscience, the natural order reveals the divine intention to encourage virtue and punish vice. Again, the measures of divine justice are more extensive that is generally realized. People tend to look for the justice of God's providence in striking cases, overlooking the general operations of God's justice. In fact, the proof that there is a God who judges 'lies not in particular and extraordinary signs and appearances; but in the general order and constitution of the moral world, and the effects continually resulting from it; in like manner as the creative wisdom of God appears in the general frame and constitution of the material world.'[90]

Next, apparently contrary evidences are exceptions to the general rule. It cannot be denied that good people suffer in ways which are quite uncompensated. While adversity may be a school of wisdom, it is clear that not all virtue is rewarded in this life. Those noble souls who have witnessed bravely in trying circumstances have been inspired not by any 'principle in the human mind, but the *Faith* of the *Gospel*, the earnest belief of a future life and the rewards of immortality. . . . [T]he *Gospel-revelation* is abundantly sufficient to give entire satisfaction, and to support all good men under the severest trials.'[91] There is no reference to Christ's victory over suffering, sin and death as the ground of this conviction.

As God is just, so should his creatures be. In a sermon on Micah 6: 8, Bourn explains that God has shown us what is good by the light of reason, by conscience, and by the original sentiments of the heart To these he has added the verbal revelation of his will in Scripture. From all of these we learn that we are to 'do justly', as well as to 'love mercy,' and 'walk humbly with God.'[92]

Richard Price

A full account of Price's ethics would entail careful scrutiny of the degree of his indebtedness to Cudworth, Locke, Clarke, Butler – even Reid;[93] but for our present purposes a general statement of his approach will suffice to locate him among his eighteenth-century Dissenting colleagues. Price published *A Review of the Principal Questions and Difficulties in Morals* in 1758, in the wake of Hutcheson's posthumous *System of Moral Philosophy* (1755), and of Hume's *An Enquiry into the Principles of Morals* (1751). To both of these works Price found it necessary to adjust himself. He became convinced that what was morally right or wrong was not to be determined by reference to our sensations, or by recourse to utilitarian considerations, but only by reference to the characteristics of the moral acts themselves. As he put it, 'right *and* wrong, *or* moral good *and* evil, *signify somewhat* really true *of actions, and not merely* sensations.'[94] It is the work of the understanding, not of a special 'sense', to intuit an action's nature. All of which makes it clear that for Price the foundation of moral philosophy is epistemological and, when directing the reader's particular attention to the second section of his first chapter, that on 'Of the origin of our ideas in general,' he famously declares, 'If I have failed here, I have failed in my chief design.'[95]

As Price views matters, Hutcheson's position is that 'Virtue . . . is an affair of taste. Moral right and wrong, signify nothing *in the objects themselves* to which they are applied, any more than agreeable and harsh; sweet and bitter; pleasant and painful; but only *certain effects in us*.'[96] As for Locke, Price regrets that his making sensation and reflection the source of all our ideas excludes the reality that the understanding, 'or the faculty within us that discerns *truth,* and that compares all the objects of thought, and *judges* of them, is a spring of new [simple] ideas.'[97] These simple ideas of right and wrong must 'be ascribed to some power of *immediate* perception in the human mind.'[98] Price does not deny that feelings of pleasure or pain generally accompany our perceptions of moral right and wrong but, *pace* the proponents of moral sense theory, the perceptions are distinct from the feelings. How odd it would be to suppose that the moral rectitude of an action is as variable as our sensations. Indeed, if nothing were intrinsically proper or improper, just or unjust, there would be no such thing as moral obligation. In fact, however, morality is eternal and immutable: 'No will . . . can render *any thing* good and obligatory, which was not so antecedently, and from eternity; or any action right, that is not so in itself. . . . '[99] Nevertheless, when the intellectual intuition that a particular action is right is accompanied by feelings of approbation, we are motivated to perform the action in question. Indeed, 'in men it is necessary that the *rational principle*, or the *intellectual discernment* of *right* and *wrong*, should be aided by *instinctive determinations*' and our Maker has provided such aid.[100]

Price proceeds to consider the origins of our desires and affections, and of good and ill desert; and he then discusses a possible objection to his claim that morality is necessary and immutable. Does not this make morality independent of God, and as eternal and necessary as he is? Price replies that 'none have reason to be offended, when *morality* is represented as eternal and immutable; for it appears that it is only saying that God himself is eternal and immutable, and making his nature the high and sacred original of virtue, and the sole fountain of all that is true and good and perfect.'[101]

There follows a discussion of moral obligation, in which Price maintains that obligation to action and rightness of action are identical, and that virtue has a real obligatory power, antecedent to all positive laws and independently of all will. Since we are always obliged to be virtuous, virtue is a law: indeed, it is a law which rules the whole creation – 'It is the source and guide of all the actions of the Deity himself, and on it his throne and government are founded.'[102] As for God's sovereign authority, it is derived not merely from his almighty power, but from 'The necessary perfections of the Deity; the infinite excellencies of his nature as the fountain of reason and wisdom; the entire dependence of all beings upon him, and their deriving from his bounty existence and all its blessings and hopes. . . .'[103]

Price next ponders the several ways in which the term 'obligation' is used, and what he says of Hutcheson, who argues that a person's or a spectator's approval or disapproval of an action is what obliges to the performance of omission if it, is particularly interesting:

> It is not exactly the same to say, it is our *duty* to do a thing; and to say, we *approve* of doing it. The one is the quality of the action, the other the *discernment* of that quality. Yet, such is the connexion between these, that it is not very necessary to distinguish them; and, in common language, the term *obligation* often stands for the sense and judgment of the mind concerning what is fit or unfit to be done. It would, nevertheless, I imagine, prevent some confusion, and keep our ideas more distinct and clear, to remember, that a man's consciousness that an action ought to be done, or the *judgment concerning obligation* and inducing or inferring it, cannot, properly speaking, be *obligation itself*; and that, however variously and loosely this word may be used, its primary and original signification coincides with *rectitude*.[104]

The upshot is that 'What denominates an agent virtuous, and entitles him to praise, is his acting from a regard to goodness and right.'[105]

The subject matter of virtue next falls under review. Price follows Butler in denying that the whole of virtue consists in benevolence. Of paramount importance is our duty to God: 'We ought to refer ourselves absolutely to his management, rely implicitly on his care, commit, with boundless hope, our whole beings to him *in well-doing*, and *wish* for nothing, at any time, but what is most acceptable to his wisdom and goodness'.[106] Price emphasises the awesomeness of such a commitment, which emerges in such a consideration that 'Whatever our consciences dictate to us, and we know to be *right* to be done, *that* he commands more evidently and undeniably, than if by a voice from heaven we had been called upon to do it.'[107]

But if we have a duty to God, we have a duty also to ourselves. In particular, we must ensure that proper self-love does not degenerate into the indulgence of our lower principles and appetites. Again, we are charged to seek the good of others, to be grateful, truthful and just. Price grants that, owing to differing temperaments, prejudices and corruptions, there will be different perceptions of what it is to be virtuous in different societies and at different historical periods, and these will lead to disagreements. We cannot, from the principles of morality, always perfectly deduce what we should do. This leads Price to distinguish between absolute virtue, which is 'a quality of the external action or event,' and practical virtue, which 'has a necessary relation to, and dependence upon, the opinion of the agent concerning his actions.'[108] Such opinions must be conscientiously reached, and 'It is happy for us, that our title to the character of virtuous beings depends not upon the justness of our opinions, or the constant *objective* rectitude of all we do; but upon the conformity of our actions to the sincere convictions of our minds.'[109] Practical virtue presupposes liberty, and to what Price says under this heading I shall allude later. For the present it will suffice to note that Price understands that '*Liberty* and *Reason* constitute the *capacity* for virtue,'[110] and that the contemplation of an after-life is a powerful inducement to virtue. Indeed,

> the firm belief of future rewards is in the greatest degree advantageous to virtue, as it raises our ideas of its dignity by shewing us the Deity engaged in its favour, and as it takes off every obstacle to the practice of it arising from self-love, sets us at liberty to follow the good inclinations of our hearts, gives all good affections within us room to exert themselves, and engages us, by an additional motive of the greatest weight, to cultivate them as much as possible....[111]

As with virtue, so with vice. Actions are vicious only in so far as the agent knew them to be so; but voluntary ignorance is inexcusable.

Price next launches into an account of the degrees of virtue and vice, the place of trials in promoting virtue, and the essentials of a good and bad character. The nub of his case is that in human nature pre-eminence belongs to the reasonable faculty, and wickedness arises from the subversion of this original state of the mind, in which reason is deposed and appetite exalted. But 'When the intellectual and moral principle . . . is the *reigning* principle, it excludes everything irregular and immoral from the behaviour.'[112] Not, indeed, that we can become perfect; but, errors notwithstanding, this principle must be the predominant allegiance of the virtuous person. Such a person is truly happy.

On the basis of his moral theory as thus set out, Price proceeds to establish the existence of God. He first recapitulates his understanding of the basis of morality, underlining the point that when we say that we must do the will of God we mean either that this obligation is an instance of necessary self-evident truth and duty; or that if we do God's will he has the power to make us happy, while if we fail to do it he is able to make us miserable; but the latter reduces matters to self-love which, as earlier shown, is an inadequate basis for ethics. The satisfactory approach is to see that the distinctions between right and wrong, good and evil, are in the natures of things; but since all things have been created by God, these distinctions reflect God's attributes and will. God created out of goodness, but goodness, a free principle, is grounded in reason. The end of God's providence and government is happiness, but he pursues this end justly and truthfully, that is, in ways consonant with his nature. The divine benevolence, for example, is not designed to make all people indiscriminately happy, but to make the faithful, pious and upright happy. It must always be remembered, however, that all of God's attributes are aspects or manifestations of the 'supreme principle,' everlasting rectitude, or reason, which 'includes the whole of moral perfection.'[113] As for ourselves, 'this world appears fitted more to be a school for the *education* of virtue, than a station of honour to it; and the course of human affairs is favourable to it more by *exercising* it, than by *rewarding* it.'[114] But whatever suffering and inequalities may be endured here, hereafter matters will be set to rights. Meanwhile our proper course is to pursue virtue and shun vice. The work concludes, almost bathetically, with a *quasi-* actuarial calculation that since 'there is not only an *equal chance*, but a *great probability* for the truth of religion,'[115] to opt for a life of vice is utterly foolish. More characteristic of Price than this apparently prudential excursus are the following words from his penultimate chapter:

> *Beauty* and *wit* will die, *learning* will vanish away, and all the *arts of life* be soon forgot; but *virtue* will remain for ever. This unites us to the whole rational creation. . . . But what is of unspeakably greater consequence is, that it makes God our friend, assimilates and unites our minds to his, and engages his mighty power in our defence.[116]

Price thus sets his face against the sensationalism of Hutcheson, the scepticism of Hume and the several varieties of teleological ethics which were then current; and, in the wake of Cudworth and Clarke, he defends the objectivity of morals along epistemological lines. We are aware of moral principles which are self-evident to our understanding, divine in origin, and which place us under obligation. We have the capacity freely to meet, or to deny our obligations, and virtue lies in the willing fulfilment of them. Although the principles of morality originate in God, they are not expressions of an arbitrary or capricious divine will. For Price, supremely in the case of God, the intellect has primacy over the will: God ordains what is good; things are not good because God ordains them.

The Unitarian Andrew Kippis, who delivered the address at Price's interment, said that 'By his moral writings he has laboured, with distinguished ability, to build the science of Ethics on an immutable basis: and what he has advanced on the subject will always stand high in estimation, as one of the strongest efforts of human reason in favour of the system he has adopted.'[117] This judgement is more than dutiful, and not all statements made in funeral orations have stood the test of time so well. That Price was more than an armchair moralist is clear from Kippis's further remark: 'every one must admire the zeal and earnestness, and strength with which he endeavoured to lead men into pious views of God, of Providence and of Prayer, and to promote the exercise of devout and amiable dispositions.'[118] In the following month Price's friend, Joseph Priestley, similarly bore testimony: 'No person well acquainted with Dr. Price could say, that rational sentiments of christianity are unfriendly to devotion.'[119]

Thomas Belsham

Thomas Belsham (1750-1829)[120] was educated at the Daventry academy (1752-89) under Caleb Ashworth,[121] whose first student was Joseph Priestley. After a period as assistant tutor at Daventry (1771-78) Belsham accepted the call to the pastorate of the Dissenting church at Angel Street, Worcester,[122] where he served until, in 1781, he returned to Daventry as head of the academy and minister of the church in the town. His views having become unitarian, and he being a person of integrity, he resigned his post in 1789, and became divinity tutor at the academy of the rational Dissenters at Hackney (1786-96). Following the closure of the academy, he taught privately in Hackney.

Belsham's major philosophical work is *Elements of the Philosophy of Mind, and of Moral Philosophy, to which is prefixed a Compendium of Logic* (1801). He opens the ethical portion with the declaration that 'The only valuable end of existence is happiness.'[123] Virtue and vice relate to voluntary qualities. The choice of the former leads to ultimate happiness, to opt for the latter is to court ultimate misery. Involuntary natural qualities such as beauty and health are neither virtuous nor vicious. When making moral choices we sometimes have to weigh benevolence against self-love: the opposing interests of these are reconciled only if we believe in a future life. He elsewhere affirms that the obligation to altruism and self-sacrifice – even of one's life – would not be apparent or convincing if the doctrine of a future life were denied.[124] The upshot is that 'Moral agents are obliged to the practice of virtue, in interest, in reason, and by the will of God.'[125] This is underlined in a lecture to young people in which he says that 'moral and religious knowledge are as necessary to the practice, and as conducive to the perfection of virtue, as philosophical science is to the invention and improvement of the arts.'[126]

Returning now to the *Elements*, Belsham discusses the moral sense, which he defines thus: The moral sense is that faculty, affection, or state of mind, which excites an instantaneous, disinterested approbation and love of what is considered as virtue, and disapprobation and abhorrence of what is considered as vice, when perceived in ourselves or others.'[127]

The problem is, he continues, that the dictates of the moral sense in different ages and countries are diverse, and can be in conflict. We must therefore recognize that the moral sense is a complex sense, compounded of many complex feelings. For example, 'The coalescence of complacency, benevolence, and fear, produces that complex feeling which is called filial affection.'[128] To this complex idea or feeling a child is taught to apply the word 'right'; to the contrary disposition, 'wrong'. The perception of right and wrong is acquired by instruction, and the tendency to practise the former and avoid the latter is generated by discipline.

For Belsham, therefore, the moral sense is not an instinctive principle; rather, is is acquired by the association of ideas – a view to which he was led by his consideration of the writings of Locke, Hartley and Priestley. In the Preface to his *Elements* he declares that 'The doctrine of Association, opened by Locke, improved by Gay, matured by Hartley, and illustrated by the luminous disquisitions of Dr. Priestley, the author regards as established beyond the possibility of controversy, in the judgment of those philosophers who have studied, and who understand it.'[129] His moral theory is built upon this doctrine, which he defines as follows: 'Association is that law of the mind by which two or more sensations, ideas, of muscular motions are so united, that any one of them impressed alone shall introduce all the ideas and motions connected with it.'[130]

When actions which are approved by the (composite, non-instinctive) moral sense lead to the ultimate happiness of the agent, the moral sense conforms with truth; when the actions do not so lead, there is no conformity with truth. The moral sense is not infallible, and people may be misled; though in 'persons tolerably well educated' the moral sense generally conduces to virtue.[131] People are under obligation to cultivate the moral sense. It is, he repeats, fed by early impressions, and for this reason is thought by some (Clarke and Price, for example) to be instinctive; but in reality it is a sense into which we are educated. Hutcheson is equally at fault in representing 'the obligation to virtue as consisting in the impulse of this internal feeling,'[132] which is liable to err. While the pleasures and pains of the moral sense are powerful motives to practice, it remains the case that motive and obligation are distinct ideas.

Those actions have moral value which are rationally and freely chosen; indeed, 'Reason and choice are essential to the moral value of an action.'[133] But if we would find happiness, we also need just ideas of God, and knowledge of the courses of action he requires. Because people acquire erroneous sentiments as they grow up, moral agents of years of discretion have 'to review and examine closely the dictates of the moral sense, to bring them to the test of the above mentioned principles, and standards of judgment, to supply what is wanting, to correct what is erroneous, to confirm and improve what appears to be right.'[134]

Belsham then very briefly reviews the positions of Clarke, Butler, Hutcheson, Reid, Price, Wollaston, Cumberland, Rutherforth, Browne and Adam Smith. Our purposes are served if we merely note that, against Hutcheson, he reiterates his charge that the moral sense is not an instinctive faculty; while Price is faulted for his view that right and wrong are simple ideas: in fact, Belsham insists, they are 'very complex notions, formed, like all other complex ideas, by association, and by the coalescence of the component simple ideas.'[135] What we perceive to be right may not be so at all; and if it is not, we are under no moral obligation to act upon what we have perceived: 'If I believe persecution to be right, my idea in this instance is incorrect; and however *prone* I may be to act upon it, I can be under no rational or moral obligation to persecute.'[136]

Belsham next opposes Hume's view that personal merit consists in the possession of mental qualities useful to ourselves or others, and that the source of moral approbation is a natural, universal, principle of benevolence. While reason instructs us as to the tendencies of our actions, moral blame or approbation is the province of humanity. Belsham considers that Hume's definition of virtue as a useful or agreeable quality is too indefinite, and that the 'natural benevolence' or 'humanity' which produces moral praise or blame is simply another name for moral sense or sympathy, which Hume wrongly supposes to be an instinctive affection.[137]

Belsham notes the contention of other modern writers that those actions are virtuous which are useful or expedient, but, he says, these terms are ambiguous and open to misconstruction. There is and can be only one rule of right, namely, 'the tendency of an action or affection to the ultimate happiness of the agent, or what completely coincides with this, under the government of perfect wisdom and benevolence, to the greatest general good; and all distinctions between what is commercially, legally, politically, &c. right, and what is morally or theologically right, are groundless, absurd, and in practice highly pernicious.'[138]

In conclusion, Belsham offers brief reflections on the accounts of virtue given by Hartley, Paley, Cooper, Gisborne, and Godwin. His last words – in block capitals – are a reiteration of his point that 'Self-love and benevolence can only be reconciled by religion.'[139] As he elsewhere put it, 'the love of God and of our neighbour is the consummation of virtue.'[140]

II

Having introduced the moral philosophy of those eighteenth-century Dissenters who had most to say about it, we may now turn to the theme of freedom, which was never far from their minds, or those of their co-religionists at large. The discussion of 'freedom' ranged widely, and we may conveniently, albeit briefly, indicate their positions on the problem of liberty and necessity, freedom of conscience and the right of private judgment, and toleration, or the right freely to worship.

Freedom and necessity

At the beginning of our period Isaac Watts is found championing the cause of liberty over necessity. In his essay 'On the freedom of the will in God and in creatures' he first distinguishes between general or natural necessity, as when a ball rolls down a hill, and external or forcible necessity, as when a ball is thrown up a hill. With these he contrasts liberty, a term which may be applied figuratively to inanimate phenomena

– 'as free as the wind' – and animals, but is most properly applied to intellectual beings. In this latter case freedom is either natural or moral. Natural liberty comprises liberty of volition and liberty of action; moral liberty is freedom from all superior authority. Liberty of choice, or of indifference, implies 'a power to chuse or refuse, one thing or another among several things which are proposed, without any inward, or outward restraint, force or constraining bias or influence.'[141] The will's freedom may be absolute and perfect, as when there is no restraint upon it at all, or comparative, as when 'the mind has some inward reluctance or aversion to those actions which yet it wills to perform for other more prevailing reasons.'[142]

What determines the will to choose or act? This is Watts's next question. Some say that a judgment concerning the greatest apparent natural good is the operative factor To this Watts replies that this is the view of fatalists, for if such a judgment always and necessarily governed moral choice, then the will would never be free. In fact the greatest apparent natural good does not invariably determine the will. The ultimate recourse is to God's revelation of the rules of moral virtue or natural religion in the Bible. That is to say, 'in the grand lines of moral virtue and piety there are their eternal fitnesses; and our reasoning powers, when they have found out the being of a God, and our relation to him, must also acknowledge they are so far the will of God, that we are obliged to practice according to these moral fitnesses, these eternal rules of virtue.'[143] Furthermore, it is only by virtue of the self-determining power of the will that God has freedom of choice in distributing his favours to his creatures as he pleases. God does not constrain the human will so as to ensure compliance with his law, 'yet the light in which God sets the gospel before the eyes of the mind is so great, as will finally and certainly persuade the will, though not necessarily impel or constrain it.'[144] Thus are maintained both the human being's accountability and the honours due to God's grace.

Henry Grove is equally concerned to show that human beings are free agents, that is, that they are free as willing. In fact, 'Liberty is *radically* in the Will, and not in the Understanding.'[145] Perception is the act of the understanding, but the will directs the understanding to its object; indeed, the will 'commands the doing or forbearing of actions, both mental and bodily.'[146] At the same time, actions are imputable only when they are rationally decided upon, and apart from the activity of the reason, no action may properly be said to be voluntary. Without reason the will has no moral liberty.

At this point Grove launches into a critique of Locke who, he declares, treats liberty of the will as a solecism and absurdity. He agrees with

Locke that liberty is a power to act or not to act, but regrets that he added 'according to the preference of the mind'[147] which, for Locke, is not free. For this entails non-culpability, whereas, according to Grove, it is the free exercise of our will which renders us liable to praise or blame. At this point Grove invokes logic and imagination:

> [L]et us suppose a man locked into a room in company with a tempting Harlot, who imploys all her charms and cunning to draw him into sin; and that he *prefers* to stay there. I ask, whether he be free in this preference or not? If not, he is guilty of no fault therein, since no action can be culpable that is not free. If he be free, then it follows, that he has a *power to will* or *not to will* his stay; in other words, that he is free as willing.[148]

Again, Locke thinks that what determines a will in its choice is 'the greatest uneasiness it lies under.' No doubt, but the agent still has a power not to will to do something, or to will the contrary action. Because of certain concessions Locke makes, Grove will not brand him a fatalist, but his concessions, for example, that 'a man has a power to consider, or not to consider,' are not consistent with his denial of liberty to the will.[149] Although Locke's personal belief was that human beings are free moral agents, he could not see how this conviction could be squared with the omnipotence and omniscience of God. Grove's own answer to the question of human free agency and divine foreknowledge is that God foreknows free human actions as free. How can he do this? We do not know; God, he says, as if clutching at a straw, 'may have ways of knowing things wholly inconceivable to us.'[150]

Grove was not the only Dissenter to express general gratitude for Locke's contribution whilst finding him wanting at certain points. Watts queried Locke's view that it is improper to speak of the freedom of the will because it is persons who are free; Bernard Foskett criticized Locke for restricting the will to actions and excluding desire from the definition of will, whereas in fact the will first moves towards pleasure and happiness which gives rise to a thought or action as means to these desired ends; and Philip Doddridge found Locke confusing on the subject.[151]

Among Grove's more popular *Four Essays* is one entitled 'A defence of the liberty of the will.' He here attacks the 'extravagant notion' that man is a mere machine and God the master of a puppet show. As well as denying human liberty, and given that people violate rational, civil and religious laws, this would make God the source or origin of all evil, that is, 'that sin and folly are the necessary productions of infinite goodness and wisdom; which is a manifest contradiction.'[152]

For his part John Taylor is concerned, not least in his treatise upon

The Scripture-Doctrine of Original Sin, that the way in which doctrine is frequently taught militates against human freedom and responsibility. He stoutly opposes the view that Adam's guilt is imputed to his descendants: 'I see no sufficient Ground for believing more than this: that in Consequence of *Adam's* Sin, he and his Posterity were adjudged to Labour, Sorrow and Death: and that thereupon a new Dispensation, *abounding* with Grace, was erected in a Redeemer.'[153] Taylor is under no illusion that we are now in a state of innocence, but he cannot accept that a corrupt nature will, 'to the End of the World, remain in every Man so long as he liveth: Consequently, the Reformation of mankind must be impracticable with regard to the impure Spring of all Wickedness.'[154] How could we use the means of amendment if we were totally corrupt? Indeed, to believe that our nature is originally corrupted is 'highly injurious to the God of our nature, whose Hands have fashioned and formed us.'[155] Such a doctrine would encourage us to transfer our wickedness and sin to a wrong cause, Adam, whereas we ourselves are culpable when we freely sin.

Taylor returned to this theme in the *Supplement* published in 1741.[156] Against the author of *The Ruin and Recovery of Mankind* (1740) – Isaac Watts – he insists that human beings have the power to perform their duty, and this power comes from God. By contrast, the doctrine of original sin encourages the contempt of human nature: 'Brutes act by Instinct, and therefore their Regularity is no more Virtue than the regular Motions of a Clock; whereas Men are moral Agents, and act upon Choice.' If they 'misapply their nobler Powers in a Manner the Brutes are not capable of,' they are culpable.[157] 'Righteousness,' he declares, 'must be our own Choice and Act,'[158] and we are capable of making this choice. Watts referred to Taylor's *Supplement* in the preface to the second edition of his own book, but did not otherwise engage Taylor. He did, however, admit that he could not prove the imputation of Adam's sin from the Bible – something on which Taylor pounced as strengthening his own case, in a pamphlet entitled, *Remarks on such Additions to the Second Edition of the Ruin and Recovery of Mankind as relate to the Arguments Advanced in the Supplement to the Scripture-Doctrine of Original Sin* (1743). Watts was not alone in repudiating Taylor's position. To Philip Doddridge his efforts appeared as 'a vain attempt to prove that impossible, which, in fact, evidently is.'[159] Samuel Hebden came forward as a defender of the Westminster standards, pitting the sole agency of the Holy Spirit in regeneration against Taylor's view that virtue and holiness result from the human being's free choices. He maintains the federal headship of Adam, and challenges Taylor either to prove that God did not make a covenant with Adam 'as a Publick person', or else to surrender his whole scheme.[160] John Wesley, drawing heavily upon Watts's *The Ruin and Recovery of Mankind*, entered the lists with his pamphlet, *The Doctrine of Original Sin* (1757), in which he wondered whether Taylor was not overthrowing the very foundations of primitive, scriptural Christianity.

The biggest gun against Taylor, however, sounded from across the Atlantic. In the opinion of Jonathan Edwards, no book had done as much to undermine the Westminster standards as Taylor's *Original Sin*, and he set out to repair the damage. Edwards perceived that at the heart of the problem was a conflict between the increasingly fashionable individualism of the Enlightenment and notions of human solidarity. Where Taylor urged that universal sinfulness results from the free exercise of the human will, and that to invoke the concept of universal depravity is redundant and immoral, Edwards counters that if we do not posit universal depravity we cannot explain how every individual, as a matter of fact, freely chooses what is evil. His conviction is that to be morally responsible entails not moral atomism (as we might nowadays designate it), but the recognition of one's solidarity with all of humanity from Adam onwards.[161]

Richard Price is in agreement with his Dissenting forebears that liberty is the power of acting and determining, 'And it is self-evident, that where such a power is wanting, there can be no moral capacities. As far as it is true of a being that he *acts*, so far he must *himself* be the cause of the action, and therefore not necessarily determined to act.'[162] It would be absurd to suppose that '*my* volitions are produced by a *foreign* cause, that is, are not *mine*.'[163] Intelligence is a further requisite of practical morality, says Price, and intelligence presupposes liberty: we cannot conceive of a thinking, designing, reasoning being which has no liberty. Further, an agent cannot justly be said to be virtuous unless his or her actions are performed 'from a consciousness of rectitude, and with regard to it as his *rule* and *end*.'[164] The upshot is that '*Liberty* and *Reason* constitute the *capacity* of virtue.'[165] None of which is to deny that a state of virtue morally necessitates virtuous action, while a 'detestable state of wickedness implies the greatest necessity of sinning, and the greatest degree of moral impotence.'[166] But this is very different from that natural necessity which would remove an agent's liberty and with it his or her liability to praise or blame.

In the first of his *Four Dissertations* (1767) Price argues that God's governing providence is not inconsistent with human liberty or with the fact of evil in the world. But it was in discussion with Priestley (1733-1804),[167] who served for a period as tutor at Warrington Dissenting academy, that Price faced the challenge of determinism most directly.

Priestley published *Disquisitions relating to matter and spirit* and an appendix to it, *The doctrine of philosophical necessity illustrated*, in 1777. Price replied by way of a set of questions posed to Priestley, and there flowed what must surely be the among the best-tempered series of letters between two divines in the whole of the eighteenth century. These were published in 1778 under the title, *A Free Discussion of the Doctrines of Materialism, and Philosophical Necessity,* a work which runs to four hundred and seventeen pages, excluding Priestley's Introduction and an index.

In his appendix Priestley declares that Locke's chapter in his *Essay* on power is 'remarkably confused, in that Locke's general maxims imply and are consistent with philosophical necessity, while his preferred position is libertarian. In Priestley's view this confusion was cleared up by Anthony Collins in his *Philosophical Inquiry concerning Human Liberty* (1715). The debate between Price and Priestley ranged widely, encompassing materialism and the soul as well as philosophical necessity, but it is the last which bears particularly on ethics. It will suffice for our present purposes if I simply state the nub of Price's case, and the kernel of Priestley's response to it. Price explains,

Now, it should be recollected, that the whole controversy has been reduced to this short question. 'Has man a power of *agency*, or *self-determination*? Dr. Priestley has denied this. He has maintained that such a power is an impossibility; . . . that we are mistaken when we refer our actions to ourselves; that our volitions are *perfectly mechanical things*; that motives influence *exactly as weights operate on a scale*; and that there is only *one agent* in nature.[168]

Clearly such a view as Priestley's runs counter to the entire basis of Price's ethics, as we have seen. Priestley sums up his case in these words: 'As to the doctrine of *necessity*, I cannot, after all our discussion, help considering it as *demonstrably true*, and the only possible foundation for the doctrines of a *providence*, and the *moral government of God.*'[169]

Of Taylor's *Original Sin* it was said that this book 'did more than any other to emancipate the English Presbyterian Dissenters from Calvinism.'[170] Leaving on one side the question of the soundness or otherwise of this judgment, we may suppose that on the one hand Priestley would have approved the outcome specified, while dissenting from Taylor's libertarianism. On the other hand, Priestley was more than willing to commend the Calvinist Jonathan Edwards for his determinism. He does, however, allow himself the observation that 'the concurrence of the philosophical doctrine of *necessity* with the gloomy notions of Calvin appears to me to be a strange kind of phenomenon, and I cannot help thinking that had this ingenious writer lived a little longer, and reflected upon the natural connexion and tendency of his sentiments, as explained in his treatise [*On the Freedom of the Will* – which Priestley elsewhere describes as being 'in the extreme of diffuseness'[171]], he could not but have seen things in a very different light, and have been sensible that his philosophy was much more nearly allied to Socinianism than to Calvinism.'[172] Elsewhere Priestley invokes Edwards against James Beattie's critique of fatalism, concluding, 'How very different is the *common sense* of Mr. Edwards from the common sense of Dr. Beattie!'[173] He is not satisfied, however, with Edwards's way of dealing with the problem of necessity in relation to the charge that along necessarian lines God becomes the author of sin. Edwards distinguishes between God as ordering a certain state of affairs in the sense of not hindering it, and God as the positive agent in causing the state of affairs. Priestley counters that 'whatever takes places [*sic*] in consequence of [God's] withholding his special and extraordinary influence, is as much agreeable to his *will*, as what comes to pass in consequence of the general laws of nature.'[174] For him the solution is that God 'may adopt some things which he would not have chosen *on their own account*, but for the sake of other things with which they were necessarily connected.'[175]

As might be expected of one of whom Alexander Gordon said that 'There are few expositions of determinism more forcible and lucid than will be found in his "Elements",'[176] Thomas Belsham was firmly on the side of Priestley in this friendly dispute, though it must be said that he did not add a great deal to the debate. Against Benjamin Carpenter (d. 1816), an Arian Presbyterian divine who had, like Belsham and Priestley, been trained under Caleb Ashworth at Daventry, Belsham points out that 'The necessarian contends that no one can perform a voluntary action without a motive, that is, without a reason or an inclination to determine his choice; and that it is not in the power of the agent to chuse differently while the same reason and inclination continue without any variation.'[177] As for God's foreknowledge, 'Either God does not foresee future events, or philosophical liberty is not the attribute of man.'[178] At which point Belsham allows himself some crocodile tears on behalf of his worsted opponent: 'O naughty metaphysics! Thus cruelly to impale a worthy well-meaning gentleman upon the horns of a *goring dilemma*, and to leave him writhing and smarting there, without hope of relief.'[179] With which we may leave the chortling, sardonic Belsham, and this phase of our discussion, only pausing to add that in a later work Belsham sought to answer the anti-necessarian objection that under a deterministic system God is made the author of sin, by saying that while no evil can exist without the appointment of God, 'it by no means follows that God is . . . the *author*, as to be the *approver of sin* . . . or that he would even suffer it to exist in the universe, any further than is absolutely essential to the production of a greater sum of rectitude and happiness than could possibly have existed without it.'[180]

Freedom of conscience and the right of private judgment
However much they may have differed on other matters, all the divines here under review – 'conservative' and 'liberal' alike – were united in their advocacy of the rights of conscience. People are free to exercise their judgment, and are under a moral obligation to do so. Hence, for example, Henry Grove's exhortation:

> Let us maintain the freedom of Conscience, particularly against *Interest, Passion, Temper, Example,* and the *Authority of great Names. Interest* warps the judgment, for which reason we should abstract every doubtful care from *ourselves,* and judge it as if it were another's. . . . *Passion blinds* the Conscience and *hurries* it headlong. . . . *Temper* insinuates into every act of Conscience and perverts it. . . . *Example* is apt to embolden the Conscience, and *great names* to bring it in love with an *implicit* resignation.[181]

None was more keenly aware of the harm to religion which might ensue from undue deference to great names than Samuel Bourn of Coseley and Birmingham, who had trained for the Presbyterian ministry at the Manchester academy of James Coningham and John Chorlton.[182] In general terms, 'If a Man only professes to believe what another dictates, or acts only as another requires, without using his own Reason, or attending to the Dictates of his Conscience, he has nothing like a divine Faith, but substitutes a blind Obedience to Man instead of a Regard to God and Truth.'[183] More specifically, in a sermon designed to foster peace among Dissenters by encouraging them to eschew the confessional tactics of others, Bourn points out that

> It has been an antient Practise for Church Bigots, and Orthodox Zealots to make many Fundamentals in Religion, many Conditions of Salvation, which God never made so; and then to miscall, curse, excommunicate and damn those who do not believe and submit to them. We *wish* there were no like instances in any Christian Church. However, we *hope* this Anti-Christian Spirit will not haunt the Christian Church much longer. . . .
>
> [I]t is possible for good Men to believe, preach, and to impose upon Others, as *fundamental Truths*, very great Errors. . . . [Such errors include the following]: That human inventions in *Creeds* are very lawful and necessary. . . . That

private Christians and Ministers are not to have the free Use of their *own Reason*, and of the *Holy Scriptures*; but are *obliged* to understand them as their Fathers did; tho' they are *not able* so to understand them.[184]

Bourn is convinced that the imposition of trinitarian tests of faith, for example, entails the forsaking of the principle of the sufficiency of Scripture and the return to the tenets of Popery. Such tactics will, he predicts, in time 'sacrifice the Cause of Christ to infidels.' The upshot is that 'If we pay that Regard to any Body of Men, tho' the most learned Assembly in the World, which is due to *Christ* only; we make a *Christ* of these Men; they are our Rabbi.'[185]

Bourn expressed his positive point less polemically in the sermon he delivered at the ordination of his friend, Job Orton:

Sincerity in searching after, and in professing religious Truth, or christian Honesty is, as to God, the only acceptable *Orthodoxy*; in any other Sense it is either precarious or impossible. In any other Sense it signifies our Agreement to *Human Schemes*; which is only a topical and chronical Character, suited only to certain Places and Times; so that what is orthodox in one Church, or in one Age, is not so in another. But an upright Mind, a pure Conscience, a good and honest heart is the same in all ages, in all Places, in both Worlds.[186]

That John Taylor was of like mind with his Presbyterian contemporary is quite clear. He inveighs against

Protestant Popery; which, though in some respects better than Romish, is yet more inconsistent, because it renounceth infallibility, and yet imposeth and persecuteth as if infallible; rejecteth human authority, and yet in many cases pleadeth and resteth upon it; lastly, permitteth the Scriptures to be read, but not understood; or, which is all one, to be understood only in the sense of schemes formed and established by men.[187]

Taylor is dismissive of those who seek to justify their position by appealing to antiquity:

[I]f the Christian Revelation was handed down to us from the Fountain of Light with so much care and exactness, both as to matter and words, by the *Son of God,* by the *Spirit*, and by the *Apostles,* Who were the ancient doctors and bishops? Or who were the first Reformers? Or who were any synods or assemblies of divines, that they *dared* to model Christian faith into their own invented forms, and impose it upon the minds of men, in their own devised terms and expressions? Hath Christ given authority to *all* his ministers, to the end of the world, to new mould his doctrines by the rules of *human learning*, whenever they think fit? Or hath he delegated his power to any particular persons? Neither the one nor the other. His doctrines are not of such a ductile nature; but stand fixed, both as to *matter* and *words*, in the Scripture.[188]

Taylor's position on the Christian's duty faithfully to bring his or her intelligence to bear upon the things of the faith is epitomized in his eulogy, written as he looked back to the Glorious Revolution of 1688:

LIBERTY at the Revolution, O bright auspicious Day! Reared up her heavenly Form, and smiled upon our happy Land. . . . Men began freely to use their Understandings; the Scriptures were examined with more Attention and Care, and their true sense, setting aside human Comments, and especially the Jargon and Sophistry of School-Divinity, was sought after.[189]

Thomas Amory was equally concerned that people should not bring preconceived ideas to the Bible, determined to find therein 'the favourite Tenets of a Party,' for this would be to 'raise the *Heads* of *Parties*, to be *Lords of Faith* in opposition to *Christ*. . . . '[190] Like Taylor, he cites authorities which are not blindly to be heeded – the Councils of Nicea and Trent, and the Westminster Assembly among them, and repeats the now familiar charge against any who would unwarrantably add conditions of fellowship to the Gospel, 'as if [Christ] either could not, or would not, reveal important Truths in a clear and satisfactory manner, but left his Gospel in want of our improvements to render it a perfect rule of Faith.'[191] If the attempt is made to bind men's consciences, with penalties attached, 'without first convincing the Judgment, and ingaging the Conscience . . . this is not only usurping *Dominion* in the kingdom of Christ, but directly counteracting the great designs of it.'[192] But Amory did not only look back to earlier alleged authorities; he was writing at a time when the Evangelical Revival was gathering momentum, and felt it incumbent upon him to warn young people, in the preface to a published lecture, to beware of 'enthusiasm' as well: '*Whatever some may imagine, an* implicit Faith *which rests only on the* Authority *of* Parents, *or* Ministers; *or an* Enthusiastick *one which is resolvable only into some warm* Emotions, *and unaccountable Impulses* on the Mind, are, for real Excellency and valuable Effects, *no way comparable to that Truth, which is produced by an honest and impartial* Study *of the* Proofs *of* Christianity, *and a* clear *Discernment of its Evidences.*'[193] Small wonder that Amory expostulated, '*my Friends,* what Joys can equal those of a *good Conscience*?'[194] or that, on his death, Roger Flexman summed up Amory thus:

Impartial in his searches after truth, at the feet of the divine master, maintaining an inviolable regard to the sacred oracles as containing a perfect rule of faith, worship and practice, strongly attached to the interest of religious liberty, the rights of conscience, and the dispositions of unconfined benevolence and charity, he was zealous in dispensing the word of life, and training up precious and immortal souls for eternal happiness.[195]

Bourn's son, Samuel of Norwich, had no difficulty in following in his father's footsteps on the question of religious liberty. In a substantial sermon of the subject he construes Paul in I Corinthians 2 as teaching that 'every man hath an equal right to think and judge for himself: that all christians are upon a level in matters of faith and religion; and none hath a right to claim any spiritual authority and jurisdiction over others. . . .'[196] He proceeds to argue that among all Christians, 'where there is the most moderation, candour, and humanity in practice, there is also the most truth, and the least error in belief and opinion.' By contrast, 'the church of Rome is at this day the most uncharitable, domineering, and persecuting in practice, and at the same time, the most erroneous and corrupt in doctrine.'[197] Bourn cautions his hearers not to 'cover your uncharitableness with boasting and hypocritical pretensions of holding the right faith and maintaining true religion,' for 'the true faith and charity of the Gospel are inseparable: and . . . the latter is the clue by which we are to find out the former, amidst the confusion of various discordant opinions, modes, parties, and denominations.'[198]

For his part, Richard Price argues that to seek to dominate another's conscience implies that there is 'a *right* to oblige persons to *do wrong*.' In fact, 'Every man ought to be left to follow his conscience because then only he acts virtuously.'[199] To the end of his life Price urged integrity of mind and heart. In one of his later addresses he looks for the time when it will be agreed universally 'That nothing is very important except an honest mind; nothing fundamental except righteous practice, and a sincere desire to know and do the will of God;' and he expresses sorrow for those who, lost in the doctrines of the dark ages, 'have not yet felt the chearing power of a religion which makes nothing essential but an honest heart.'[200]

As might be expected, Priestley, who had, it seems, something to say on most topics, was not slow to endorse all of the foregoing sentiments. He maintains the right of free inquiry, even if it should result in the demolition of Christianity: 'should free inquiry lead to the destruction of Christianity itself, it ought not, on that account, to be discontinued; for we can only wish for the prevalence of Christianity on the supposition of its being *true*; and if it fall before the influence of free inquiry, it can only do so in consequence of its not being true.'[201] He urges Dissenters to maintain the spirit of free inquiry, and elsewhere declares (as if oblivious of the then current discussions concerning the place of creeds and the position of Scripture in Anglican circles) that it is 'from Dissenters alone, not shackled by the fetters of our universities, that free inquiry into matters of religion can be expected.'[202]

At the end of our period, in 1800, Thomas Belsham addressed the Western Society of Unitarian Christians on the subject of freedom of enquiry. His case is that 'it is the indispensable duty of all who profess faith in the christian religion, to exert their best endeavours to acquire a distinct and correct conception of revealed truth, to separate it as accurately as possible from the corruptions with which it has been debased, to arm their faith with meekness and candour, and by all fair and honourable means to communicate to others the light which they have discovered and enjoy.'[203] To Belsham's address are appended the principles of the Western society, one of which sums up the tradition we have traced from Grove to Belsham: '[W]e admit in the most unrestrained sense the right of every man to think for himself in matters of religion, and apprehend that this right extends to judging the importance of opinions as well as the truth of them.'[204]

A corollary of liberty of conscience is the right not simply to eschew imposed doctrines, but to bring a moral critique to bear upon the doctrines of others which are deemed to be repugnant and offensive to God. The eighteenth century was replete with such protests, and many of our divines were ardently engaged in such activity. Two or three examples will suffice to illustrate the point. Bourn of Coseley and Birmingham writes thus of the doctrines of election and preterition:

> I think I ought to acknowledge that there are Doctrines which I am not able to defend; and therefore I give them up: They appear to me, and I believe to most Men, inconsistent with Gospel *Declarations*, and contradictory to its whole *Design*. . . . A very good Account may be, and had been given of the many Texts which speak of *Predestination* and *Election*; without drawing in a Scheme so dishonourable to God.'[205]

John Taylor was a veritable hammer of Calvinism. He denies that Adam is our federal head, and that his sin is imputed to ourselves; that our natures were originally corrupt, this doctrine being a denial of our creation in God's image; that we have no power to perform our duty; and that the idea of original righteousness is inconsistent with the nature of things, for 'Righteousness must be our own Choice and Act.'[206] When, with reference to the deceased Unitarian, William Tayleur, Theophilus Houlbrooke uttered the following words he spoke for many on the liberal wing of Protestant Dissent:

> The Calvinistic doctrines, which represent the God of mercy as a God of Vengeance – stern and inexorable in his nature – as charging the offences of our first progenitor on each of his descendants without distinction of age – accepting as an atonement for guilt the vicarious sufferings and imputed righteousness of another – and finally and capriciously selecting some men for reward without respect to merit, and consigning others to punishment, without the imputation of crime – these, and some other doctrines which he believed to be contained in the established creed, his mind had long rejected, as equally contradictory to revelation, and repugnant to reason – as dishonouring the attributes of God, degrading the value and dignity of virtue, withdrawing from the mind its strongest motives to generous exertion, and suppressing the noblest energies of the human heart.[207]

It comes as no surprise to learn that many Calvinists resented the suggestion that their position was immoral, and made strenuous efforts to counter the accusation. Thus the Independent Thomas Ridgley set out to defend such doctrines as election, particular redemption and efficacious grace, and to show that they were not inconsistent with 'the moral perfections of the divine nature.'[208] Many others followed in his wake.

While it cannot be denied that the Arian-liberal-rational Dissenters were most vocal on the question of liberty of conscience and religion, we should not overlook the fact that more conservative Dissenters, including evangelical Calvinists, upheld the same principle, however much their doctrinal conclusions might diverge from those of their more 'advanced' brethren. In this connection it is interesting to place side by side some sentences from the confession of faith given by the Baptist Caleb Evans (1737-91), an evangelical Calvinist, at his ordination service, and the judgment of Samuel Stennett (1728-95) delivered in his funeral sermon for Evans:

> The right of private judgment, especially in matter of religion, I apprehend is the undoubted and unalienable privilege of every rational intelligent creature. It is a privilege I claim for myself, and for the use of which I am accountable only to God; and it is a privilege which I think every one *ought* to exercise, and has a right *fully* and *freely* to enjoy.[209]

> He was no bigot, he could not be such, for he well understood the rights of private judgment, was sensible of the weakness of the human intellect, and felt the difficulties of truly upright

minds on points wherein he and they could not agree.²¹⁰

At Evans's interment John Tommas said,
> He was possessed of real candour. The rights of private judgment, which he well understood, were in his apprehension sacred, But he was not indifferent to sentiment. He would with severe investigation examine and judge for himself; and when once his opinion was settled, he made no secret of it, but would preach it without reserve; and if opposed would defend it, but was still himself open to conviction.²¹¹

Another Baptist, Robert Robinson (1735-90) of Cambridge, stood foursquare for the right of private judgment:
> If to deny the right of private judgment be destructive of the nature of christianity in general, it is more remarkably so of the christianity of the reformed churches. The right of private judgment is the very foundation of the reformation [a view which is rightly queried by many Reformation scholars, who feel that it the phrase has more of a Renaissance ring to it, and also that it overlooks the religious motivation of the Reformation], and without establishing the former in the fullest sense, the latter can be nothing but a faction in the state, a schism in the church.²¹²

From the Independent side we have Jonathan Toothill's testimony to James Scott (1710-83), who established the Heckmondwike academy with a view to arresting the spread of 'Socinian darkness' in the north of England.²¹³ It appears that Scott's version of Calvinism precluded him from freely offering the Gospel to all, and that Toothill disagreed with his former teacher on this point. What is significant is one of Toothill's reasons for defying those who traduced Scott for what they regarded as a pernicious error: 'It was his *real sentiment* which he believed in his heart. Has not a man a right to declare his own sentiments? If not, what becomes of liberty of conscience?'²¹⁴

The Calvinist Dissenting divines just mentioned would have agreed with the words of George Walker, professor of theology at the New College [Unitarian], Manchester, who, in a sermon 'On the Right of Individual Judgment in Religion,' said of his Dissenting forebears:
> The principle on which they found this claim to christian liberty, on which they justified their non-conformity, and their determined resolution of disobedience to their civil rulers, is, that they must hearken unto God, and follow his directing voice, nor in opposition to this render any obedience to men. But this voice of God is not confined to the Apostles, it is extended to every Christian, and in some degree to every human being;

and what this voice declares to every individual man, the maxim and conduct of the Apostles pronounce to be his sovereign rule in religion.[215]

But this reference to Nonconformity brings us to the last aspect of the question of freedom with which we are here concerned: liberty of worship, or toleration.

Toleration, or the right freely to worship

To the Dissenters, freedom of worship, granted by the Toleration Act of 1689, was the natural corollary of freedom of thought and conscience. Fortified by the writings of John Owen from their own ranks, and John Locke[216] who, on this issue as on some others, they were pleased to regard as one of their own, they were ever watchful lest the measure of toleration granted them might be whisked away. Many of them sincerely yet also tactfully praised God for his favour and, by implication, the civil powers for their wisdom, in granting liberty of worship. Thus, for example, Isaac Watts draws a contrast between the Dissenters' condition and that of many 'scattered christians' in the 'popish nations'. He gives thanks, and I interpolate what is between his lines:

> Let us again give thanks to our God, who has so formed our civil constitution and government, at this day, that we have liberty to worship God, through Jesus Christ the Mediator, in his own appointed ways [and not as required by the monarch or parliament]; that we are not persecuted from corner to corner [as were our forebears all too recently], but in every place, we are permitted to erect synagogues for divine service, and to attend God in those ordinances [prescribed in Scripture, not by parliament], on which he has stamped his own name.[217]

Their delimitation of the rights of the civil powers where matters of religious practice were concerned did not, in most cases, land Dissenters in anarchy or republicanism. On the contrary, most of them looked back to the civil strife of the seventeenth century with dismay, and wanted no repetition of it in their own time: hence the critique by some among Old Dissent of the 'enthusiasm' of the Evangelical Revival; it was not only out of place in orderly religion, it could disturb the peace. The vast majority of Dissenters wished to be loyal to crown and country, but they also wished the church to be the church, appointing its officers and ordering its worship along scriptural lines, without impositions from the state. Thus Thomas Amory sets out from the consideration that the obligation to worship God is indispensable, and that

> To make our worship and obedience acceptable unto God it must proceed from an *inward conviction*, that what we do in

religion is required by God, and agreeable to him; and to practise any thing as religion out of deference to human authority, which we believe *not* acceptable to God, instead of qualifying us for his favour, must render us offensive to God; as it manifests that we regard men more than we do him. No magistrate therefore can have a right to compel any person to religious professions or practices, which he does not inwardly approve; because it is compelling him to disobey God, and to put himself out of his favour. *Absolute Toleration* therefore, and a *general Liberty* of *Conscience,* where persons violate not the rights of others, and propagate no doctrines destructive of society, are the unalienable right of all.[218]

Elsewhere Amory speaks of the happiness of Dissenters 'in being free from all usurpation over Conscience,' and points to 'the *goodness* of our Cause, which is the Cause of religious Liberty and genuine Christianity, and founded on the *sole* Authority of Christ to be King and Lawgiver in his own Kingdom'[219] – by which he means that, unlike the Church of England, which has one foot in Scripture and one in the constitution of the land, and a monarch as temporal head, the Dissenting churches are free to own the exclusive Lordship of Christ over his Church.[220] To this Samuel Bourn of Norwich adds the consideration that 'there are no characters in the world more opposite to each other, than those of a christian, and a persecutor,' that the true faith has never been promoted by persecution, and that in any case, 'The Kingdom of Christ is *not of this world*; and never was, nor ever can be established on the foundation of wordly principles and motives, or secured and extended by the terrors of persecution.'[221]

In his *Observations on the Nature of Civil Liberty,* Richard Price distinguishes between physical liberty, moral liberty, religious liberty, and civil liberty. He defines religious liberty as 'the power of exercising, without molestation, that mode of religion which we think best, or of making the decisions of our own consciences respecting religious truth, the rule of our conduct, and not any of the decisions of our fellow-men.'[222] Running through all the species of liberty is the idea of self-direction, or self-government. Thus, negatively, 'He ... who, in religion, cannot govern himself by his convictions of religious duty, but is obliged to receive formularies of faith, and to practise modes of worship imposed upon him by others, wants religious liberty.'[223] Here lies the seed of Price's critique of church establishments. He rests on the principle that all are equal in Christ, and that no other master is to be acknowledged but Christ himself. Civil establishments violate the rights of private judgment by imposing formularies of faith and worship; they resist free enquiry, and, by restricting the exertions of reason, they impede the improvement of the world.[224] What is the remedy? Price answers,

> It is indeed only a rational and liberal religion, a religion founded on just notions of the Deity as a being who regards equally every sincere worshipper, and by whom all are alike favoured as far as they act up to the light they enjoy, a religion which consists in the imitation of the moral perfections of an almighty but benevolent governor of nature, who drects for the best all events . . . it is only this kind of religion that can bless the world or be an advantage to society. . . . But it is a religion that the powers of the world know little of and which will always be best promoted by being left free and open.[225]

It must be confessed that while welcoming toleration for themselves, Dissenters were not always eager to accord it to all others. The political situation set Roman Catholics in a dangerous light, and many regarded them as owing allegiance to a foreign power, the Vatican. But of all those we have considered Priestley was in the van in this matter. He was for the toleration of Roman Catholics on the ground that the advance of popery need not alarm the friends of liberty.[226] He also favoured the toleration of atheists, believing that Christians should accord to atheists the same freedom which they would desire if atheists wielded political power; and he regretted that 'Mr. Locke was staggered at the thought of tolerating *Atheism*. . . .'[227] For his part, Thomas Belsham's verdict was that 'The sacred and unalienable rights of conscience extend to the adoption, the profession, and the peaceable promulgation of religious principles.'[228]

III

We have now passed in review those eighteenth-century Dissenting divines who wrote most thoroughly on moral philosophy, all but one of whom (Price) have been neglected in the general histories of ethics, and some of whom are little studied at all. While some, of whom John Gill was our main representative, were content to work in the line of the Puritans of the previous century, the more liberal divines were quicker to respond to the ethical challenges posed by Hobbes, Shaftesbury and others. Their responses entailed their answering others in their own terms, and ethics increasingly became a field of study in its own right, in some cases removed in content and sometimes in temper from the biblically-based ethical expositions of the Puritans. Steeped in natural law theory, they abominated Hobbes's materialistic construction of it, and devoted themselves to a fresh examination of the basis of ethics. To them all morality rests upon a universal, rational basis and, as Watts with his strong sense of the fitness of things insisted, the moral law is of universal and perpetual obligation.

It important to note that thus far Watts as well as divines more heterodox than he were at one with the high Calvinist John Gill who, as we saw, ordered his material after the pattern of his Puritan forebears. But if Gill made no significant ethical advances, he was by no means innocent of a rationalism no less potent than that of those generally known as rational Dissenters. If more extreme representatives of the latter tendency appeared to elevate reason at the expense of revelation, Gill's *a priori* system of biblical truth, worked out on the basis of such axioms as that God is the sovereign Lord, was in its own way quite tightly rationalistic.[229] We should, therefore, view with caution the too easy identification of rationalism with 'Arianism' or other varieties of heterodoxy. The reality is that if more liberal divines invoked reason and conscience against such apparently copper-bottomed systems as that of Gill on the ground that the would-be imposition of such systems upon believers would amount to 'Protestant Popery',[230] Gill's rationalism led him to elevate and defend the Bible (construed as he himself construed it) as the sole fount from which divine truth could be deduced. It is no accident that the subtitle of Gill's *Complete Body of Doctrinal and Practical Divinity* is *A System of Evangelical Truth deduced from the Sacred Scriptures*. The upshot is that, in their differing ways, both Gill and his heterodox contemporaries sought to reach the heart through the head.[231]

But if high Calvinists and more liberal divines were alike in deferring, in their several ways, to reason, the latter emphasized the fact that the principles of the moral law, grounded as they were in creation, were ascertainable by man *qua* man. Their advocacy on this point, coupled with the external challenges, gradually drew ethics away from theology – not least in the academy curriculum – but it by no means entailed the denial of special revelation. On the contrary, the Dissenting divines firmly believed that God makes his will known in the Bible, both in the principles and the moral examples it contains. A certain eclecticism characterizes much of their work, with moral sense and teleological considerations mingling with rationalis of varying strengths. As to teleology, some Dissenters, Grove among them, specifically designate happiness as the chief end of humanity; but, being well aware of the problem of evil and the suffering of the godly, they do not equate happiness with feelings of immediate pleasure. On the contrary, they posit an after-life during which the inequities of our present existence will be resolved, and rewards and punishments meted out as appropriate.

This important emphasis notwithstanding, the major thrust of their ethics is in the direction of rational intuitionism in the line of Cudworth and Clarke, supplemented and corrected by the deliverances of revelation. Not even Bourn of Norwich, who studied under Hutcheson, made the moral sense the major plank of his ethics, while Taylor and Price were keen to oppose Hutcheson, pointing out the vagaries of the moral sense, and arguing that a rational foundation for ethics was essential. For his part, Taylor consistently construed teleology in rational terms, stoutly contending against all comers that truth and reason, not happiness, are the supreme ends. With Belsham we arrive at an understanding of the moral sense regarded not as an instinctive principle, but as acquired by the association of ideas; it is a capacity into which we are educated, and which we are obliged to cultivate. With this suggestion we approach a socio-cultural understanding of the ways in which knowledge is acquired, which questions and supplements the options of innatism and sensationalism which were so familiar to Belsham's forebears.

Not surprisingly, the heterodox divines were quicker to detect the pitfalls in the moral sense than to heed the noetic effects of sin, to which high Calvinists frequently drew attention. But this latter theme was not only an occasion of polemics as between high Calvinists and 'liberals'; it was equally subject of sometimes heated discussion between Calvinists of various hues. For example, the question of the ability of human beings to make a free response to God's grace was treated by the evangelical Calvinist Andrew Fuller (1754-1815), like Gill a self-educated Baptist, in his work *The Gospel Worthy of all Acceptation, or the Duty of Sinners to Believe in Christ* (1785).[232] Within Baptist circles the Gillites battled it out with the Fullerites, the former stoutly maintaining that unregenerate people could not be morally obliged to put their faith in Christ, the latter insisting that while all sinners are under obligation to heed the Gospel, their sinfulness renders them morally and actually incapable of doing so unless aided by divine grace.[233]

Of all the divines here studied, it was Price, in one of his anticipations of Kant, who most deliberately advanced a moral argument for God's existence. It is notable that he did this before Kant's demolition of the classical theistic arguments was published.[234]

On the specific theme of freedom we found that on the issue of freedom over against necessity, Priestley and Belsham stood on the necessarian side, the remainder for libertarianism. They all, 'conservative' and 'liberal' alike, stood for the right of private judgment, the evangelical Calvinist Baptist Robert Robinson ill-advisedly branding this the very foundation of the Reformation. Coupled with this was their attachment to the principle of the sufficiency of Scripture – however much they might have disagreed with one another over specific doctrinal points. The more liberal Dissenters were not slow to bring a moral charge against doctrines – especially Calvinistic ones – which they felt to be morally repugnant, and insistence upon which they deemed a new popery. All – liberal and conservative Dissenting divines alike – advocated toleration, or liberty of worship, though Priestley would have opened the door wider than many of the others, admitting both Roman Catholics and atheists. While convictions concerning liberty of conscience and freedom of enquiry have clear implications for freedom of worship, it is not so clear how the discussions of freewill and determinism bear upon the more practical questions concerning liberty; in fact, for the most part the sets of discussions are conducted in parallel, and do not mutually fertilize each other. What may be more confidently affirmed, however, is that the eighteenth-century Dissenters were working with those postulates of God, freedom and immortality which Kant was to make foundational to his theism.

From these general remarks we may turn to four specific matters which are raised by the eighteenth-century Dissenting moral thinkers and merit continuing reflection in our own time. First, for Isaac Watts, as we saw, the moral law signifies a rule given to all humanity *qua* rational creatures; but its authority derives from the will of God.[235] That is to say, reason apprehends the moral law, but God obliges us to obey it. It thus appears that the ultimate foundation of the moral law is in God, and Watts assumes that all people know God. What becomes of this view in our secularized society in which many do not claim to know God, yet appear to lead morally impeccable lives? Have they misunderstood the moral situation? Or is Watts mistaken? Or are we to resort to an 'anonymous believer' view which some have construed as an incipient imperialism which knows much better than others what they are really doing?

Secondly, on the one hand, may not the claimed universality of the moral law render the appeal to revelation finally redundant – at least as the source of moral guidance if not as a motive for the moral behaviour of believers? Watts, Amory and others, we recall, argued that revelation reinforces the deliverances of the natural law in such a way that even the 'common people' may learn their duty.[236] Does the Christian revelation supply moral guidance over and above that derived from natural law? Price, for example, declares that the original signification of the term 'obligation' coincides with rectitude,[237] and that we are obliged to perform the most fitting action. But what of the idea of going beyond the call of duty? We might, for example, compare Jesus's remark concerning the apostles who merit no praise for doing their duty, with his response to the woman who anointed him with costly oil – something she was in no way obliged to do.[238] On the other hand, against believers who might say that revelation suffices, we might ask, Can Christians manage without at least a 'weak' doctrine of natural law if, in a multi-*cum*-non-religious society there is to be a basis for common ground in practical ethics? (By a 'weak' doctrine of natural law I mean one which, for example, proclaims that 'all right-thinking people' will agree that there are some things which it is good to do – relieve the hungry, house the homeless – and that such activities transcend doctrinal or other convictional boundaries; a 'strong' doctrine of natural law would be one in which a particular institution authoritatively specifies very detailed obligations which are said to have been deduced by itself from the natural law).

Thirdly, there is an interesting oscillation in Price's thought which seems to mark a dividing-line between his predecessors and his seniors and successors. As we saw, he distinguishes between absolute virtue – 'a quality of the external action or event,' and practical virtue, which concerns the agents' opinions of their actions.[239] It would thus appear that while Price's older contemporaries – John Taylor, for example – emphasised the idea that the virtuous action is that which is objectively morally right, Price takes a step in the direction of individualism with his practical concern that we do what we *think* is right, and that provided we have seriously attempted to discover the right, our action is virtuous even if wrong. In appearing to vitiate the objectivity which Price elsewhere claims, this might seem to place him at the top of a slippery slope, at the bottom of which is anarchy – a book of Judges situation in which 'everyone did what was right in his own eyes'[240] – a teleological version of Hobbes's state of nature, indeed! It was considerations such as these which prompted Kant's formulation of the categorical imperative, 'Act only on that maxim whereby thou canst at the same time will that it should become a universal law.'[241] Another way of expressing the underlying concern here is to ask, Does not rational intuitionism constitute an inevitable step on the way to an individualism in ethics which disinclines those who espouse it to accommodate the societal context in which our moral ideas are actually developed, and our lives lived?

Fourthly, it goes without saying that the question of freedom in its various forms – libertarianism *versus* determinism; freedom of thought and conscience over against authorities of various kinds; and freedom of religious expression in relation to the nature of the Church and the rights and duties of the state, remain to this day among the ethical agenda, and are discussed with varying degrees of vigour and enthusiasm.

Of those Dissenters who were in the van of eighteenth-century moral philosophy, the majority were Presbyterian divines of a liberal cast, some of whom were decidedly Arian, some, as the century proceeded, unitarian. In facing the challenges to moral philosophy flowing down from Hobbes they drew ethics ever further away from dogmatics, whilst retaining a strong conviction that God was the undergirding moral reality. With the increasing challenge to theism and, in the nineteenth century, the increase of atheism, agnosticism and humanism, the time was soon to come when most moral philosophers would be methodologically at least as far from Priestley and Belsham as they were from Gill and his Puritan predecessors. In a word, they would not be nearly so inclined to hold together the ideals of an honest mind, righteous practice and the desire to know and do God's will in the way Price recommended when he said, nothing is very important except an honest mind; nothing fundamental except righteous practice, and a sincere desire to know and do the will of God.[242]

IV

Before leaving the eighteenth century a few concluding remarks are in order. First, while information is generally scanty, the evidence suggests that where teaching methods were concerned the earlier academy tutors tended to keep their students' noses in the texts, so to speak. The emphasis was upon memorizing content and subsequently regurgitating it orally. We may not unjustifiably suppose that Toulmin's account of the procedure at Sheriffhales could easily be replicated elsewhere:

> In all lectures, the authors were strictly explained and commonly committed to memory, at least as to the sense of them. On one day, an account of the lecture of the preceding day was required before a new lecture was read: and on Saturday a review of the lectures of the five days before was delivered. When an author had been about half gone through, they went over that part again; and so the second part passed under a second perusal; so that every one author was read three times.[243]

Henry Grove pursued an intermediate course, 'confining himself to no system of divinity, but the scriptures, directing his students to the best writers on the several subjects of enquiry';[244] while Doddridge and other later tutors devised their own systems (or borrowed those of others) and worked through them systematically. To some students the systematic method had the disadvantage of either encouraging false discipleship by elevating extra-biblical authorities to undue prominence, or of inducing a scepticism on important questions prompted by the disagreement over them of acknowledged authorities.[245] But if the newer method lacked appeal for some, Strickland Gough, in 1730, lamented the time 'usually wasted in old systems of logick and metaphysicks.'[246] Perhaps the backhanded compliment paid by John Rippon to Bernard Foskett has a wider application: 'If it be conceded that Foskett's method of education was limited rather than liberal, severe rather than enchanting, employing the memory more than the genius . . . in a word, if it be granted that Mr. Foskett is not the first of tutors . . . it is a debt of honour, to acknowledge that some good scholars and several of our greatest ministers were educated by him.'[247] At least Rippon stopped short of referring at this point to a benign overruling Providence.

Secondly, into the question how the eighteenth-century academies at large compared academically with the universities of Oxford and Cambridge it would not be proper to enter, for we have not adduced evidence concerning the latter.[248] It may not be inappropriate, however, to say that our findings modify the view of such older historians as Irene Parker that where modern studies are concerned the Dissenting academies left the English universities standing.[249] For while such better endowed and relatively well-staffed academies as Warrington could afford the luxury of scientific teaching (Dalton, Priestley) and apparatus, most could not.[250] Furthermore, curriculum innovation was not a primary concern of the more evangelical academies, and some of them resisted certain aspects of it. Nevertheless, whereas many who were called upon to teach philosophy in the Dissenting academies left no published works in the field, a few made contributions of lasting interest. Among these Price is supreme (and it is not partisan to suggest that he and Butler, both of whom received their grounding in the academies, are the philosophical equals of any to have emerged from Oxford and Cambridge in the eighteenth century); Watts deserves to be more than sung, and Leslie Stephen's description of his philosophy as 'a crude amalgum'[251] is unduly biased; Grove is by no means uninteresting; and Priestley and Belsham are irrepressibly provocative. Nor are the activities of such philosophical journeymen as Foskett, Doddridge and Aikin to be despised.

Thirdly, if the fate of some of the more liberal academies suggests that victory is not necessarily with those who pay the greatest heed to reason, the relative absence of philosophy from some of the more conservative academies makes one a little concerned – if not for the faith itself, at least for the competence of ministers to offer viable defences of it when it is intellectually challenged. With hindsight we can see that there was to be plenty of scope for the construction of such defences in the nineteenth century. But, as so often, it is Richard Baxter who presents both sides of the coin without which there is no coin at all. He asks, 'What more can be done to the disgrace and ruine of Christianity, then to make the World believe that we have no reason for it?'[252] But he also wrote, 'What delights . . . there are at God's right hand, where we shall know in a moment all that is to be known.'[253] Perhaps such moderate academies as the line flowing down from Doddridge's Northampton, or Bristol academy up to Caleb Evans's time, came closest to holding the two sides together. We may suspect that according to their success or failure in this matter theological colleges and seminaries may, to this day, properly be judged.

4

Philosophy and Philosophers, 1800-1920

While a few of the eighteenth-century academies were transmogrified into nineteenth-century theological colleges – the Baptist college at Bristol and the Congregational Western academy among them – many of the eighteenth-century academies were no more. The death of tutors and paucity of funds were among the causes of the demise of Dissenting academies. It must also be said that not all of the teaching in the academies was of the highest order. Thus, for example, when Robert Brook Aspland reflected upon his father Robert's time as a student at Bristol Baptist College in the declining years of the eighteenth century, he was moved to write,

> Had the studies of the English Dissenting academies at the close of the last century been elevated and regulated by affiliation with a higher institution, possessing the power of awarding literary and scientific degrees, like the present London University, it is more than probable that they would have produced a greater number of accomplished scholars and vigorous-minded men, and that the intellectual standard of English Nonconformity would now be (as it was at the close of the seventeenth century) greatly in advance of the age.[1]

Theological disputes had taken their toll too. The fate suffered by John Horsey was shared by others. Even William Parry of the conservative Wymondley academy was charged with Socinianism – an accusation he strenuously denied.[2] Over and above all of this there was the fact that as the nineteenth century progressed it became less necessary for specifically Christian institutions to provide general higher education as the earliest academies had done. In 1826 the 'godless' institution, the University (later, University College) of London was founded, and it numbered such prominent Dissenters as Robert Vaughan and Henry Rogers among its professors; and the Scottish universities continued to receive those Nonconformist students who could make their way there.

More positively, in view of numerical growth prompted by the

Evangelical Revival, Old Dissent needed new institutions, while, as the nineteenth century progressed, the several branches of Methodism and the Welsh and English Presbyterians established theological colleges for the first time. These developments were not unrelated to a growing sense of denominational consciousness as the nineteenth century progressed, and this in turn was connected with a feeling in more forward-looking circles that Nonconformists must position themselves to meet the challenges of burgeoning centres of population and industry. Whereas the Congregationalist J. Guinness Rogers (1822-1911) described the eighteenth-century academies as 'domestic institutions'[3] (a description which fits many, but not, for example, Warrington), his fellow Congregationalist William Jay wrote of his *alma mater*, Cornelius Winter's academy at Marlborough, 'One of the advantages of a smaller academy . . . was its assuming a kind of domestic character, and associating us more with the tutor himself. A freer and more intimate access to the tutor is sadly wanting in some, yea, I fear, in all our public institutions.'[4] But the tide was against Jay. Not, indeed, that proposals to establish new centres of theological learning were assured of instant success. On the contrary, the case for a theologically educated ministry still had to be made, and that not only among those comparative youngsters, the Methodists.

Thus, for example, as part of the proceedings connected with the opening of Lancashire Independent College, Manchester, John Harris, of Cheshunt College, delivered an address entitled, 'The importance of an educated ministry', in Grosvenor Street Chapel on Tuesday 25 April 1843. While in no way denying that 'the preaching of some uneducated ministers' had been 'greatly blessed', he pointed out that God 'did not bless on account of their ignorance, but in spite of it.'[5] That this needed to be said one hundred and eighty years after the founding of Sheriffhales Academy suggests that the victory of those in favour of formal education over those who repudiated 'book learning' in favour of possession by the Spirit was hard won. It could not, of course, be denied that some learned men had proved useless in the pulpit, but as Daniel Fraser, principal of Airedale College, pointed out in 1865, 'It does not follow because some educated men fail as preachers, that it is a matter of no moment or of small moment whether those who are able to preach, and *do* preach are educated or not.'[6]

If the argument still had to be made by those of Old Dissent, small wonder that the Methodists – Calvinist and Arminian alike – had their tussles over the matter. The historian of Trevecca College informs us that 'the Welsh Calvinistic Methodist Movement had been in existence for 100 years, before a College was established';[7] while as late as 1900, 37% only of Primitive Methodist ministers had received a college education, as against 78% of Wesleyans (whose first Theological Institution was opened as late as 1835), and 79% of Congregationalists.[8]

Behind the Primitive Methodist figure there lies a concern not only for evangelization in general, but for that class of society to which the Primitives felt particularly called. At their conference in 1871, Mr. E. Brick insisted that 'young men who were so gentlemanly that they could not blend with colliers, puddlers and tinkers were not the men for our ministry. (Hear, Hear).'[9] By contrast, that man of fine taste, Robert Vaughan, the first president of Lancashire College, sadly aware that Congregationalists had the reputation of being 'a sort of rude commonwealth', hastened to reassure distinguished laymen that if they 'take their place frankly among protestant dissenters, [they] need not be apprehensive that the respect shewn to their civil rank elsewhere, will be wanting on the part of their new friends.'[10] Even before this the Wesleyan, Joseph Entwisle, had written to Jabez Bunting on 23 June 1831 to express his fear that 'Unless the improvement of young preachers keep pace with the general improvement of Society . . . the Clergy and our brethren the Dissenters will take our glory from us;'[11] and as early as 1806 the Wesleyan biblical commentator, Adam Clarke, had written, 'The time is coming, and now is, when illiterate piety can do no more for the interest and permanency of the work of God than lettered irreligion did formerly.'[12]

It should be noted that in some Wesleyan circles opposition to a theological institution was an aspect of a more general dislike of increased denominational centralization, at the hub of which was Jabez Bunting. This opposition, inspired by a desire for greater local (not least lay) responsibility, prompted the expulsion or secession of some circuits to form the Wesleyan Association in 1835.[13]

Interestingly, it was not only those on the evangelical wing of the Church who feared lest too much education might divorce ministers from the masses. A proposal that the word 'Board' be replaced by 'College' in the title of the Manchester Unitarian Home Missionary Board – an agency set up to train ministers – was defeated when the principal, John Relly Beard, argued that 'if they adopted the name of College they might increase the soreness in certain quarters.'[14]

Despite opposition and set-backs, the supporters of an educated ministry for the major Nonconformist denominations persisted, and new institutions – almost fifty of them – were founded during the nineteenth century. Indeed whether the colleges were, like those of the Baptist, Congregational and Unitarian traditions, independent of their denominations, or whether, like those of the Methodists and the Presbyterians, they were formally part of their denominational structures, they witnessed to increasing denominational consciousness. When we place together the fact that a number of academies did not survive the eighteenth century, and the fact that the nineteenth-century saw the opening of so many new theological institutions – including Methodist ones for the first time, we find the explanation of the hiatus in this study. The few continuing eighteenth-century academies apart, there was little continuity of teachers or teaching. Rather, for Old Dissent the nineteenth-century was a period of new institutional beginnings – some of these undertaken with reference to population growth in such centres as Manchester and Leeds, while for Methodism the century saw moves to inaugurate institutional ministerial training for the first time. The consequence is that the story of all the theological disciplines, not least philosophy, is not smooth-flowing across our period as a whole.

Undeterred, I shall introduce the nineteenth-century colleges by denomination, and shall seek to discover what place they gave to philosophy. The attempt is fraught with difficulty because of the paucity of information in the case of a number of the colleges. Even when philosophy is listed as a subject of study the course content is frequently unspecified. The situation becomes clearer in the case of those colleges which joined the Theological Senatus, constituted in 1879, with its common syllabus and examinations; but not all of the Dissenting colleges became members, and none of the Methodist ones did.

It is less difficult to discover the published philosophical contributions of the tutors and alumni of the nineteenth-century colleges. These, as we shall see, vary greatly in style and value. Since intellectual trends do not rise and fall in relation to our way of dividing time up into centuries, we shall not be surprised to find that many eighteenth-century philosophical interests flowed on into the following decades. It will become clear that what we nowadays regard as the traditional arguments of natural theology, and the biblical 'evidences' of miracles and the fulfilment of prophecy had their defenders until well past 1850, while concern with ethical questions persisted throughout the century. But the Romantic turn to inwardness over against 'external' proofs, which brought human experience to the fore and hastened the development of psychology, could not but influence the way in which Christian claims were made. Above all, there was the intellectual sea-change represented by the increasing reception of modern biblical criticism[15] on the one hand, and the advance of evolutionary thought on the other. The latter seemed to many to accord with that post-Hegelian immanentism by which so many philosophers, whether Christian or not, were impressed from about 1875 onwards.[16] These new intellectual impulses made their way against the background of rapid social change and population movements resulting from ever advancing industrialization. In the field of religious debate – controversy is not in some cases too strong a word – Nonconformists sniped from the sidelines at Anglican Ritualism, while, as the century wore on, the Establishment question more directly engaged their energies. During this turbulent period the Nonconformists attained their greatest ever numerical strength, and their highest degree of social prestige. With many captains of industry and commerce in their ranks they were able to command a hearing – none more so than the Congregationalist Joseph Parker at London's City Temple, whose sermons were regularly reported in the press – piracy he called it.

With ideas coming from so many quarters, not least from such continental thinkers as Auguste Comte, it is not surprising that philosophy as a discipline became more specialized as the century proceeded. The territories of logic, philosophy of science, political philosophy and aesthetics, for example, gradually became more distinct, and it became less and less likely that any one person would range over all of them. At the same time the discipline was becoming ever increasingly laicized – the examples of Edward Caird, T.H. Green and Samuel Alexander spring at once to mind. But within Nonconformity philosophy was, with very few exceptions, the preserve of the ordained throughout the period here under review.

There can be no question that between the years 1800 and 1920 there was more Nonconformist writing on ethics and apologetics than on any other branch of philosophy. As promised earlier, we shall pay particular attention to these fields in the next chapter. For the present, and at the risk of a certain jerkiness, we shall note the contributions of Nonconformists to other aspects of philosophy in the course of describing the place of the subject in the institutions in which they studied and/or taught. It will become clear that apart from fugitive reviews there was little mutual interaction on philosophical issues on the part of the Nonconformist philosophical professors and authors: the sense is rather of individual efforts than of a philosophical guild. It is not, for example, that their literary energies were consumed by contributions from Church of England philosophical writers. On the contrary, such a formative (if in many ways derivative) thinker as Coleridge is barely acknowledged by most of them. In some cases they were not thus inhibited where theological or ecclesiastical issues were concerned, but these lie outside our purview.

Congregational Colleges

We may set out from the college at Homerton, which was founded by the orthodox Calvinists of the King's Head Society shortly after the constitution of that Society in 1730. In 1801 John Pye Smith, fresh from his studies under Edward Williams at Rotherham College, was appointed tutor, assuming charge of the College in 1806. For his theological method

Smith looked back to the ejected Puritan, Thomas Goodwin; for pastoralia and homiletics he turned to Philip Doddridge; but he was also *au fait* with German scholarship, and to his theological work he added courses in physics, chemistry, geography, astronomy, psychology and rhetoric and – our primary concern here – logic, ontology and the philosophy of the human mind. The classical tutor, Thomas Hill, who arrived from Rotherham College in 1806, relieved Smith of Latin, Greek, Hebrew, Syriac, algebra and geometry. The full course covered six years.

John Daniel Morell is probably the best known of Pye Smith's philosophically inclined students. His father ministered at Little Baddow Congregational church from 1799 to 1852, and Morell early felt the call to follow in his footsteps. After Homerton he proceeded to Glasgow, where he excelled in philosophy; and thence to Bonn, where Fichte made a lasting impression upon him. In 1842 Morell began his ministry at Gosport, but in 1845, since 'his creed was hardly of the type normally associated with the nonconformity of a place like Gosport,'[17] he became an inspector of schools and an author of texts books on grammar and reading, though with continuing forays into philosophy. For a while he worshipped with Anglicans and then with Unitarians. Among Morell's philosophical contributions we find his well-received two-volume work, *An Historical and Critical Review of the Speculative Philosophy of Europe in the Nineteenth Century* (1846), *Handbook of Logic* (1855), *Modern German Philosophy* (1856), and *A Manual of the History of Philosophy* (1884).

The Homerton programme was typical of a number of others.[18] Coward College, named after its benefactor William Coward, was established in London in 1833, its student nucleus being the remnant from the academy at Wymondley (1799), a number of whose students had succumbed to Socinianism and migrated to the Unitarian Manchester New College, York. While the theological disciplines were treated in the college, arts subjects were taken at University College, London, the 'godless institution' opened in 1828, whose early professors, as already mentioned, included Robert Vaughan and Henry Rogers, subsequently the first two Presidents of Lancashire Independent College. In 1776 the *Societas Evangelica* was formed to 'extend the gospel in Great Britain by itinerant preaching.' The preachers were to be trained, and an Institution was opened for this purpose in 1778. At first lectures were given on three days per week – including lectures in logic given by John Kello, the minister at Bethnal Green for fifty-six years, who joined the staff in 1779.[19] It was not long before teaching was given on five days per week. The Institution migrated to Hoxton Square in 1791, and to purpose-built premises in Highbury in 1825. Henry Foster Burder was professor of philosophy and mathematics at Hoxton/Highbury from 1810-1830.[20] An alumnus of Hoxton, he also studied at Glasgow University, where George Payne and Joseph Fletcher – both destined to teach in Congregational colleges – were among his contemporaries. His student John Stoughton recalled that Burder was 'a methodical thinker, a great admirer of Dugald Stuart's [sic] philosophy. . . .'[21] The manuscript autobiography of another student, Alexander Stewart, is even more illuminating:

> Dr. Burder's department was the Mathematics, Mental and Moral Philosophy, Logic, *etc*. To read up for these was hard work. To this Tutor we also had to write and read essays which were criticized. . . . Dr. Burder had a clear but narrow mind, prim, stiff, and formal in all his intercourse with the students, always the gentleman but no less always the distant Tutor.[22]

Another of Burder's students, Henry Rogers, taught logic and rhetoric at Highbury from 1832-1839, though his name never appeared on the list to college tutors.[23] As we shall see, 1839 Rogers left Highbury for Spring Hill College, Birmingham, and in 1858 he became the second president of Lancashire Independent College. Precluded by a weak voice from normal pastoral duties, Rogers devoted himself to teaching (though he declined to become a candidate for the late William Hamilton's chair of logic and metaphysics at Edinburgh) and writing. Rogers was described as 'a literary man pure and simple.'[24] The subjects of his numerous essays ranged from Sunday observance to the state of the railways. His critical studies of philosophers include his pieces on Butler, Gassendi, Hume, Paley, Pascal and Voltaire in the eighth edition of *Encyclopedia Britannica*, and essays on Bacon, Descartes, Locke and others in *The Edinburgh Review*, whose most prolific philosophical writer he was. He has little patience with that 'unballasted soul', Voltaire, whom he describes as 'the glory and shame of French literature.'[25] He finds that while Bacon and Descartes were methodologically one-sided in opposite directions, and were both guilty of the same fault: they 'thought that a system of rules might be devised which would do much more than any such system can; which, in fact, would wonderfully diminish that interval which must ever subsist between a great genius and a great blockhead.'[26] Pascal is praised for his insights and precision of thought, while Leibniz, great as was his industry and knowledge, is rebuked for failing to make his monads intelligible.[27] As for Locke, Rogers seeks to rescue him from such writers as Condillac and Condorcet, who attempted to brand Locke an out and out sensationalist. Rogers will have none of it: to him Locke's insistence upon reflection brings him closer to Descartes than is commonly supposed.[28] Rogers is methodologically indebted to Butler and Paley, but he is dismissive of Hume, whom he regards as the most sceptical philosopher, the most bigoted historian. He lumps Hegel together with such 'German infidels' as D.F. Strauss, charging them with undermining the Bible's credibility. We shall return to Rogers's apologetics in the next chapter.

Rogers's successor in philosophy at Highbury was the capable John Hensley Godwin (1809-1889).[29] He studied at Highbury Independent academy (1833-1836) and at Edinburgh University (1836-1837). Following two years at Old Meeting, Norwich, he became professor of philosophy at Highbury (1839-1850) and of New Testament and mental philosophy at New College (1850-1872). As an introduction to an account of his writings it is instructive to hear his obituarist:

> The mere love of abstract truth sometimes makes a man cold, dry, unsympathising. It was not so with Professor Godwin. In his a keen analytical power, a subtile, searching intellect, was happily combined with the most tender sensibility and devout affection. . . . The broken voice, the failing uttereance, the starting tear, bore emphatic testimony to the depth of emotion within.[30]

In 1884 Godwin published his *Intellectual Principles; or, Elements of Mental Science.* Godwin understands psychology as having 'respect to the whole Spiritual nature of Man, – to Knowledge of every kind and degree, and to all the Feelings and Actions it occasions.'[31] Mental science is that part of psychology which concerns intellectual principles and every description of knowledge. Hence Godwin considers our knowledge of ourselves and of every other object, emphasizing the fact that we are conscious of spiritual facts as well as of those material facts with which our senses acquaint us. He first discusses intuitions. These are of various kinds. There are corporeal intuitions of a general kind: pressure, temperature, motion, resistance and pleasure and pain; and special intuitions such as taste, smell, hearing and seeing. All knowledge of the external world comes to us via the senses, but attention, memory and reason are also required if knowledge of material objects is to be had. Our primary perceptions are those which are intuited, and they cannot be wrong; secondary perceptions, which 'respect objects which existed before they were known by us, and which are known by others as by ourselves,'[32] are inferential, and may be mistaken. Next, Godwin introduces us to spiritual intuitions – our consciousness of our own self as a unity, and the states of feeling in which we know our selves. The previous existence of our own self is remembered; its continuance is inferred; but its present existence is an intuition. Mental capacities are inferred from conscious states of mind, and the immateriality of mind 'is simply a negative expression for what is not known' – the mind does not perceive itself as material.[33] There follows a discussion of the metaphysical intuitions of space and duration, and then of intuitions of comparison: number (unity and plurality), and relation: co-existence, position, resemblance, and subject and object.

Part Two concerns thoughts or representations.: 'Thoughts or Ideas may be defined as Mental *forms*, existing in consciousness, produced by the Mind, and *representing* what is not present in consciousness.'[34] Godwin proceeds to expound his view that thoughts or ideas may be classified according to their elements (simple/compound), their sources (in sensation or reflection), their objects (concrete/abstract, singular/common, relative/non-relative, positive/negative), and their relation to objects (true/false, adequate/inadequate, distinct/confused). He then turns to natural laws of thought: 'Natural laws, as *real facts*, are the constant connections of natural objects existing together, or following one another. As *verbal expressions*, they are general statements of such facts.'[35] According to the laws of impression, anything seen, heard, felt or done leaves an impression on the mind which, if remembered, can subsequently be thought about. Thoughts can be generated by the likeness of a present to a past experience, or by temporal or local contiguity; and 'The objects which leave the most permanent impressions on the mind are those, the remembrance of which is most desirable.'[36] Part Two ends with a discussion of the necessary laws of thought: co-existence, comprehension and exclusion, resemblance, negation and the excluded middle.

The third Part concerns beliefs and convictions. Beliefs differ from thoughts in that they have to do with evidence; and they differ from intuitions in that they may concern past, present and future ideas, and in that they are not reliant upon the presence of objects; they result from the exercise of memory and reason. Beliefs may arise from remembrance, from inference from natural connection, or from inference from apparent necessity. Of these the first are convictions of memory, the others are convictions of reason. As to the intellectual faculties, these are 'the *powers* inferred from the *states* of Mind of which we are conscious. All the *states* are transient, but the *powers* are permanent.'[37] These powers are attention, memory, abstraction, imagination, judgment and reason, and Godwin devotes a section to each. Discussions of the the association of ideas and of authority follow, in the latter of which the point is strongly made that if a claim to authority is not supported by evidence that the alleged authority has superior knowledge, or properly used abilities and opportunities above those elsewhere possessed, submission is unreasonable. Jesus, who habitually appealed to reason and conscience, spoke with the highest authority as a manifestation of the truth; and he urged people to respect reasonable authorities, but on some matters to judge for themselves. Godwin's work concludes with appendices on matter, substance and properties, and on the brain and the nerves.

In 1850 Homerton, Coward and Highbury united to form New College, London, which survived until 1977. Six professors and two lecturers now comprised the academic staff, and more specialization and greater depth of study on the part of the students was now possible. Godwin transferred from Highbury and remained until 1872, bearing the title Professor of New Testament and Mental Philosophy. Interestingly, the structure provided for the College's own faculties of arts and of theology: the policy of the former Coward College of sending arts students to University College does not seem to have been adopted, though New College students sat for the London BA degree. From 1872 to 1884 John Stoughton held the Chair of historical theology, though as we shall see he was more than adept in defending the faith in a contemporary way.[38] According to a list of 1879, the professor of logic at New was J. Radford Thomson, and logic and mental philosophy were taught in the second year. Thomson appears again as professor of moral philosophy, a first year course within the faculty of theology, while apologetics, a concurrent course, was taught by Robert A. Redford.[39] Students who matriculated in the University of London at the end of their first year had their arts course extended by one year, to include, *inter alia*, mental philosophy.[40] Not untypically, during the period of his professorship, Thomson was minister first at Mount Pleasant, Tunbridge Wells, and then at Mill Hill. It may be that additional assistance on the philosophical side was given by Robert Vaughan Pryce, nephew of Robert Vaughan and Principal of New College from 1889 to 1907, for he had taken his London MA in philosophy in 1861, and had taught the subject for eight years at Cheshunt College.[41] From 1882-1907 Hackney College students joined New College classes in mental and moral philosophy.

The college at Hackney had been founded in 1803 – a development of the work of the Village Itinerancy or Evangelical Association for spreading the Gospel in England (1796). In 1879 it had three professors, of whom George Lyon Turner taught classics, philosophy and Hebrew, though his most well-known work is his *Original Records of Early Nonconformity under Persecution and Indulgence* (1911). Among the works studied at Hackney during 1878 were McCosh's *Christianity and Positivism*, Hagenbach's *German Rationalism*, Wayland's *Moral Science*, Butler's *Sermons* and *Analogy*, and Paley's *Evidences* and *Horae Paulinae*.[42] No doubt the exposition of at least some of these fell to the competent apologist, Samuel McAll, principal from 1860-1881.[43] J.

Radford Thomson combined his work at New College with the chair of mental and moral philosophy at Hackney and New Colleges (1882-1907). The two colleges, whose students had attended classes in both institutions for a number of years, finally united in 1924.

The West Country had a tradition of migrating Congregational academies reaching back to that at Ottery St. Mary in 1752. From there the Western College removed to Bridport (1765), then *via* Taunton (1780), Axminster (1795) and Exeter (1829) to Plymouth (1845), finally reaching Bristol in 1901.[44] During the period with which we are concerned the college was first at Axminster, in the sole charge of James Small, who is known to have taught classics, mathematics and theology – and to have refused to countenance any tutorial assistance.[45] We may surmise that philosophy was not prominent in the curriculum. But in that respect a significant change occurred with the removal of the college to Exeter on Small's death, and the appointment of George Payne, who was still in charge when the college removed to Plymouth in 1845, and remained so until his death in 1848.[46] His moral philosophy will engage out attention in the next chapter.

Payne's successor as principal was Richard Alliott (1804-1863), in whose hands the philosophical work at Plymouth was secure until his removal to be president of Cheshunt College in 1857.[47] Alliott's studies at Homerton college were interrupted by ill health, but he was able afterwards to enrol at Glasgow University, of which he was made LLD in 1840. He served as assistant to his father at Castle Gate Congregational church, Nottingham (1828-1830), succeeding him in the latter year. Following a six-year pastorate at York Road, Lambeth, he became principal of Western College (1849-1856), then president of Cheshunt College (1857-1860), and finally professor at Spring Hill college, Birmingham, with oversight of Acocks Green Congregational church (1860-1863). In 1854 Alliott delivered his Congregational Lecture, *Psychology and Theology*, and this was his major work. G.B. Johnson, a former student, declared of it,

> It was the very subject to absorb him: and his treatment of it is most characteristic, – simple, unaffected, clear, logical, laborious, but utterly devoid of those illustrations or digressions which minds less capable than his of abstruse reasoning seem imperatively to demand even in such discussions as he there pursues.[48]

As might be gathered from this description, Alliott's detailed work is so closely reasoned that it defies summary. His overall intention, however, is clear enough. He makes it very clear that his starting-point in this work is psychological. He wishes to discover 'whether religion is the offspring of a distinct mental faculty' and 'whether the will (which must have to do with its production) be a self-determining power.'[49] His argument, which incorporates some perceptive criticisms of Schleiermacher's view of religion as grounded in a feeling of absolute dependence, leads him to conclude that 'Religion . . . as developed in man, is not attributable, directly or indirectly, to a separate original religious power or susceptibility'[50] – a view which leads him to counter Morell's contrary conviction. His case for denying that the will is a self-determining power turns upon the view that if it were, we should not be susceptible to divine influence, and therefore that influence could not be, as it in fact is, 'the first cause to which our religion is to be attributed.'[51] 'The will,' he continues, 'is determined by motive, including under motive the subjective feeling as well as the objective appeal to the mind'; and this truth is inseparably connected with another, namely, 'that man is righteously responsible for all his actions.'[52] As for the idea of God as first cause, independent, necessary, eternal and infinite,

> I have shown that the idea is not our own creation, that it is not innate, that is is not owing to immediate intuition nor to any revelation of reason, and that it is attainable by the simple exercise of our reasoning faculty in reference to phenomena within the sphere of phenomenal intuition.[53]

Alliott proceeds to prove to his own satisfaction that a Being actually exists who corresponds to our idea of God, and the attributes of this Being are passed in review. There follows a discussion of the internal and external evidences of Christianity, which includes further criticisms of Morell, and a rebuttal of Hume on miracles. Regarding the latter, Alliott thinks that 'In the discussion of Hume's argument, too much attention, as it appears to me, has been given to the historical question, "how man comes to believe in testimony?" The original source of his belief may be one thing, and the reason why testimony is really worthy of belief may be another and different thing.'[54] He concludes with a discussion of the inspiration of Scripture. Supposing Christianity to be of God, he argues, 'it is *probable* that a book would be written which should be so far inspired as to render the communication it contained uncorrupted and authoritative.'[55] Such a book is necessary because the truths of Christianity are not exclusively such as to carry their own evidence with them; the evidence and value of some Christian truths depend entirely upon God's own testimony.

For all his interest in psychology, it would be quite wrong to suppose that Alliott is for subjectivism in matters of faith. In a lucid address from the Chair of the Congregational Union of England and Wales, delivered on 11 May 1858, he sought to redress the balance between the subjectivism of what at the time was branded 'the new theology', or 'the negative theology', or 'Germanism', or 'spiritualism', or 'the intuitional theology', and the older distorted objectivism which gave the impression that at the heart of Christianity is intellectual assent to certain truths attested by external evidence.[56]

It is instructive to place Alliott's address alongside a sermon preached at Cross Street Unitarian chapel, Manchester, by its minister, William Gaskell, on 18 March 1883.[57] Gaskell, an MA of Glasgow University, trained for the ministry at Manchester College, York. He was called to Cross Street in 1828, and remained there until his death. He combined his ministry in Manchester with the professorship of English history and literature at Manchester New College from 1846-1853, when that college removed to London. Later he became a keen supporter of the Home Missionary College which developed into Manchester Unitarian College. At one period he deputised for Principal A.J. Scott in evening classes in logic sponsored by the fledgling Owens College. In his sermon, *The Investigation of Religious Truth,* Gaskell declares that 'God has formed our minds for the search after truth.'[58] Accordingly, we must sincerely love truth, and be eager to learn from every available source of truth. In our quest we must proceed with self-diffidence, humility, caution and moral and spiritual purity. Then, in a manner typical of many on the liberal theological wing, Gaskell urges that while not undervaluing the doctrines held by ourselves or by others, 'I have no hesitation in saying that right dispositions and habits of mind are much more important than them all.'[59] Against those who thus appear to devalue the objective, Alliott would protest that 'not only are they left without any adequate standard whereby to test the subjective, they are left without any means for producing the true subjective.'[60] As George Payne had earlier explained, the truth is the whole of divine revelation, but especially the doctrines of the Gospel. Into this truth we grow: sanctification includes the progressive illumination of the understanding, and the removal of prejudice and of remaining depravity.[61]

Returning to Alliott, we may conclude on the basis of a former student's testimony, that his teaching was appreciated by those who could acquire the taste for it:

> Though adopting a mode of lecturing which necessarily limits the area of subjects discusses, the Doctor was happy in putting in the briefest and most pungent form the material of his lectures. . . . Such a method unavoidably produced a certain dryness of style, and could be successful only when combined with the severest logic: but the enthusiasm of the Tutor soon diffused itself throughout the class, and the Doctor having

finished his subject-matter in a clear and tangible form, by Essays and Discussions with the class supplied all that seemed lacking to secure their fullest interest in the work in hand.[62] Alliott's successor at Cheshunt, H.R. Reynolds, who said that Alliott had 'made the work difficult, by his own extensive industry and varied accomplishments,' quoted another student who said, 'I consider that Dr. Alliott's lectures were quite perfect of their kind'; and for his own part Reynolds declared that 'The stimulus [Alliott] gave to the students was great, and the information he imparted to them admirably digested, and wondrously condensed, and yet so arranged as to be capable of easy reproduction.'[63] Those last words may seem ominous to all who are suspicious of rote learning and parrot-like repetitions; and as we proceed we shall receive further hints suggestive of the possibility that these practices were widespread in the nineteenth century Nonconformist colleges. It is hardly necessary to read between the lines of those who regarded Alliott with great respect to surmise that he was not a caster of spells over his hearers. If confirmation of this were needed we need look no further than a remark of Urijah R. Thomas, a student at Cheshunt under Alliott and then under Reynolds: 'with no lack of gratitude to our former president,' he nevertheless declares, 'We had had much laborious and lucid instruction in many things from the principal who has just left us and from his colleagues. But Dr. Reynolds's great and gracious personality immediately threw a spell over us such as we had not known before.'[64]

The status of philosophy in the Western curriculum is not clear for the duration of John Charlton's period as principal and theological professor (1857-1875), but his successor, Charles Chapman, who was appointed in 1875 and remained in post until he retired, aged 82, in 1910, taught logic and rhetoric in the first year of the five-year course, and mental science in the second.[65] In 1886 Thomas Macey was added to the staff to teach logic and Hebrew.[66] He, together with Chapman, removed to Bristol in 1901, where teaching was shared with the staff of Baptist College, the students reading arts subjects at the University College – from 1909, the University of Bristol – of which the two theological colleges were formally designated Associated Colleges. Western College merged with Northern College, Manchester, in 1970.

Like its southern counterparts, the Independent academy at Rotherham had predecessors stretching back into the eighteenth century: at Heckmondwike (1756), and Northowram (1783). But in 1795 the opening at Rotherham took place, and the first principal was Edward Williams, who combined his college work with the pastorate of Masbro' chapel.[67] Williams was a leading theologian of the time who did much to move scholastic Calvinism in a moderate direction; he was a prolific writer, and widely-read in a number of fields. This was just as well, since in addition to teaching logic and moral philosophy in the second year of the four-year course, he was also responsible for sacred criticism, mathematics, rudiments of natural philosophy, composition – especially of sermons, ecclesiastical history, theology and instructions in pastoral care.[68]

Three principals later, we find F.J. Falding in charge.[69] He was an alumnus of Rotherham, and had also been a Dr. Williams scholar at Glasgow, where he took his MA in 1845. Following pastorates in Wellington, Shropshire, and Bury he returned to the College as tutor in 1850, and was made Principal eighteen months later. Falding was especially interested in Hegel, and one of the students to whom he communicated this enthusiasm was Bertram Smith who, in partnership with his fellow student Francis Wrigley, went on to exercise a notable ministry at Salem, Leeds from 1891 to 1929.[70] Falding remained at Rotherham until 1888, in which year the college united with Airedale College to form the Yorkshire United Independent College at Bradford. The report of the college for 1883 shows that in the preceding academic year the course in philosophy covered Locke and Berkeley, Leibniz, Plato and the Platonists, while that in logic was concerned with propositions, syllogisms and fallacies. The report includes the findings of the external examiner, Mr. W. Crosbie of Brighton. He found something to commend in each of the six logic papers examined, but went on to say that 'My complaint, if I must complain, is not that there is carelessness, but rather paucity of knowledge. . . . Knowing something of the competency of the beloved teacher, and of the pains he takes, and considering the somewhat elementary character of the examination, every Student ought to have been in the first division.' In fact, two only were thus placed. As for philosophy, three students deserved special praise, and apart from careless orthography, all ten of them would have passed 'in the first division, though exhibiting different degrees of excellence.'[71] Meanwhile, Firth College, the predecessor of the University of Sheffield, had begun classes in January 1880. Some Rotherham students had taken arts courses there, while others had gone to Edinburgh or Trinity College, Dublin; but it was decided that as from 1884 all students would take arts courses at Firth College. This relieved the college staff, and pleased those laypersons who regularly quibbled at the amount of time spent by theological teachers on 'pagan' learning.[72]

It was in 1884 that Elkanah Armitage (1844-1929) was called to the pastorate of Doncaster Road Congregational church, Rotherham – a position he held jointly with a professorship in the college there. He had taken his BA at Owens college, Manchester, and a first class degree in moral sciences at Trinity college, Cambridge. Following a short course at Lancashire Independent college under Henry Rogers he was ordained and inducted at Waterhead, Oldham, where he served from 1872 to 1884. Although he did not publish much, he was *au fait* with philosophical developments and unimpressed by some:

> The search after the absolute, if by that term be meant something which is out of all relations, is the search for the Void, and not for Truth and Reality. That which is true and real is true and real *for somebody*; it stands in relation to their perceptive minds. Indeed, *it is the relative alone which is real*, and *the realities of religion are all relative to the percipient souls of men.*[73]

Following Armitage's death his successor at Bradford, E.J. Price, prepared his text, *The Riddle of Life; or, the Testimony of the Soul*, for publication, completing it from notes and filling gaps as necessary. Here Armitage ponders the supremely important questions, 'What can I know about myself? and, What ought I to do?'[74] He argues that neither science nor mechanistic philosophy can provide a complete account of humanity. *A priorism* fails because it yields an intellectualist abstraction of form from matter, while rationalism mistakenly treats the intellect as if it were 'a distinct faculty, capable of acting apart from all others, and of judging them.'[75] It also overlooks empirical, including societal, influences upon consciousness, and forgets that what we call rational standards have been devised by us from experience. He is thus led to draw a sharp distinction between the God of religion and the god of rational philosophy: 'experience knows nothing of the Infinite and the Absolute.... It is concerned with God as He enters into relations with men, and it knows Him in those relations.'[76] When agnostics fault Christians for believing in a God of whose properties as they exist outside of ourselves nothing can be known, they simply show that they have missed the point. Our conceptions are phenomenal and relative, and God is real in the only way anything can be real to us. He is known in the venture of faith, and this is a matter of active and practical choice, not merely of rational assent. Christians believe that in Christ they have seen 'into the very heart of the eternal.'[77] Whatever we may make of his philosophical position, there is no doubt that Armitage, highly regarded for his sincerity and integrity, made a considerable impression upon generations of theological students: 'How he captured our vagrant souls, as we wandered through the mazes of philosophical difficulty,' exulted one.[78]

Like its sister college at Rotherham, Airedale Independent College traced its roots to Heckmondwike and Northowram.[79] Following the closure of Northowram pressure mounted for a college in the north of the populous West Riding, and Idle Independent Academy was opened in 1800 under the Northumbrian William Vint, a noted itinerant despite his lack of oratorical skills.[80] In 1826 'Airedale' was substituted for 'Idle' in the college's name, and in 1834 the institution removed to new premises at Undercliffe. Ten days later Vint died, and Walter Scott succeeded him.[81] Scott taught philosophy as well as divinity, biblical criticism and Hebrew. In 1841 the college became affiliated with London University, and in 1848 a benefaction enabled the appointment of Henry Brown Creak, who took charge of philosophy.[82] He was succeeded by William Campsall Shearer, who taught philosophy, but principally New Testament, until 1902.[83] As early as 1865 Scott's successor, Daniel Fraser, was arguing for the separation of arts and divinity, and for study of the former to be undertaken in universities, and to precede theological study.[84] He listed a number of areas in which students in the Congregational colleges could not, in ordinary circumstances, be expected to be proficient. He did not think, for example, that they could 'Be so familiar with Philosophy as to know how to trace the influence of Metaphysical Theories on Theology and of Theological Systems on Metaphysics.' But he did expect that by their end of their course students would 'Be so familiar with Logic and Metaphysics as to be prepared for a careful and discriminating acquaintance with schools of Philosophy.'[85]

Fraser's successor was A.M. Fairbairn, whose apologetic writings will concern us in the next chapter. He was an errand boy before the age of ten, an auditor at some classes in the University of Edinburgh, but a non-graduate; trained for the ministry under James Morison of the Evangelical Union; a prominent preacher; passed over for the chairs of moral philosophy at Aberdeen and St. Andrews, and later the first principal of Mansfield College, Oxford.[86] Fairbairn arrived in Yorkshire at a challenging time. Principal Fraser was bypassed when a new college building was opened in Emm Lane, Bradford, in 1877, and resigned. Fairbairn, the last of thirteen ministers to be approached, had to satisfy Yorkshire folk that he was up to the job. He taught apologetics and philosophy and, in addition, historical and dogmatic theology, and New Testament exegesis, introduction and theology. Like Fraser, he powerfully argued the case for 'arts-before-divinity', the governors of the College acquiesced, and from 1884 most Airedale students read arts in Scotland (by-passing the fledgling universities at Leeds and Sheffield) – in accordance with Fairbairn's conviction that philosophical studies provided the best foundation for divinity.[87] In 1886 Fairbairn was called to Mansfield, and fresh talks with Rotherham were initiated which led to the union of Airedale and Rotherham to form the Yorkshire United

Independent College in 1888. Dr. Falding of Rotherham became principal, and he was succeeded in 1892 by the theologian David Worthingston Simon, who had been successively principal of Spring Hill College, Birmingham, Mansfield's predecessor, and of the Theological Hall of the Scottish Congregational Churches, Edinburgh.[88]

On 24 August 1768 Selina, Countess of Huntingdon, opened her college for the training of evangelical preachers at Trevecca. Following her death in 1791, the college removed to Cheshunt, where it was publicly opened on 24 August 1792. Piety rather than philosophy had prevailed in the minds of its early teachers, but with the passage of time a more typical curriculum was developed. Thus, for example, we find Joseph Sortain delivering *A Lecture Introductory to the Study of Philosophy* in 1838. He declares that in teaching the students he will use the method of Bacon to discover, and that of Aristotle to demonstrate. In addition to logic, he will deal with mental philosophy and rhetoric; and his hope is that he will cultivate, and not merely inform, the minds of his students. With reference to their calling, he relates philosophy and preaching by declaring that demonstration is required in the latter.[89] Sortain had studied at Trinity College, Dublin, and was an alumnus of Cheshunt. *Circa* 1851 he published *The Life of Francis, Lord Bacon*.[90]

Sortain's friend, Richard Alliott, brought his philosophical skills with him from Plymouth, serving as Cheshunt's president from 1857 to 1860, and in 1879 we find logic, the philosophy of mind and ethics, and the history of philosophy being taught by R. Vaughan Pryce who, as we saw, proceeded to New College in 1889. The 'exit' essay title in philosophy for 1879 was 'Anselm – philosopher, theologian, monk, and statesman.'[91]

Like most of its English counterparts, the Congregational college at Brecon had a migratory pre-history, beginning with academies at Abergavenny (1757), and thereafter at Wrexham, Llanfyllin and Newtown, finally settling at Brecon in 1837. In 1842 Henry Griffiths was appointed senior tutor. He had studied at University College, London, under Augustus de Morgan; had held pastorates on the Isle of Wight and at Stroud; and was the author of a number of books on philosophy and religion.[92] He returned to pastoral charge in 1853, and was succeeded at Brecon by John Morris, who remained in post until his sudden death in 1896. The 1879 *Calendar* shows that Morris was teaching philosophy as well as theology and Hebrew.[93] In 1899 Thomas Rees, an alumnus of Cardiff, and with a London MA in philosophy (and later a PhD for his book on *The Holy Spirit*) assumed responsibility for divinity at Brecon, and when he became principal of Bala-Bangor Independent College in 1909 his place at Brecon was taken by David

Miall Edwards.[94] Miall Edwards, who had studied at Bala-Bangor Independent College and then under Fairbairn at Mansfield College, wrote a number of theological works in Welsh, but his main philosophical writings were in English: *The Philosophy of Religion* (1924) and *Christianity and Philosophy* (1932). The former ran to a number of editions, and was translated into Japanese by a Buddhist priest.[95]

Turning now to Lancashire, we find that the energetic William Roby, minister of Grosvenor Street chapel, conducted a theological academy there from 1803 to 1808. Moral philosophy was on the curriculum and, of the students it is reported that 'Logic formed an eminent part of their studies, and they were required, not only to read and understand Watts [Isaac Watts, *Logic*, 1724], but to form an abstract of the whole work for themselves.'[96] Roby's academy closed following the removal from Manchester of its benefactor, the cotton merchant Robert Spear, but Roby continued to teach some students, among them Robert Moffat of Africa. Between 1811 and 1813 an academy was conducted at Leaf Square, Manchester, where four theological students only were trained and, funds failing, the institution passed into private hands.[97]

A third start for Congregational theological education in Lancashire was made in September 1816, when the first probationer student of Blackburn Independent Academy enrolled.[98] The location was determined by the committee's wish to engage as principal Joseph Fletcher, who was then ministering in Blackburn.[99] Fletcher covered Intellectual Philosophy in thirty-eight lectures based on the systems of Reid, Stewart and his own teacher Mylne. George Payne occupied the theological chair from 1823 to 1829, when he removed to Exeter. He was succeeded by Gilbert Wardlaw, who had previously served for three years as classical tutor.[100] To Wardlaw's apologetics we shall come in due course. He resigned in 1843, not wishing – partly on account of failing eyesight – to remove to Manchester, the pull of which rapidly growing hub of commerce and industry was proving irresistible to most of those concerned with ministerial training.[101]

Robert Vaughan was appointed the first president of Lancashire Independent College, and logic fell within his purview (though his chair at University College, London, had been that of modern history). Of Vaughan it was written

> Dr. Vaughan identified himself so thoroughly with literary movements [he founded and edited *The British Quarterly Review*] and was so desirous especially of securing high intellectual culture for the Dissenting ministry, that it was generally supposed that he was a distinguished scholar himself. But this he certainly was not. . . . The truth is, he never had the

opportunity of regular scholastic discipline, not even of so much as the Dissenting Academy of his early years would have afforded. . . . What an active and powerful brain and incessant diligence could do to overcome the disadvantages arising from want of early training, was done. But everyone knows that it cannot supply deficiencies in the minutiae of scholarship.[102]

This may explain the uneasiness of some students who transferred to Manchester from Blackburn, where they had had the most patient and thorough grounding in all things scholastic from Gilbert Wardlaw. It also reminds one of Fairbairn – both he and Vaughan could conjure up ever-broadening vistas, and both had the rolling cadences to match.

The classical tutor from 1849 to 1855 was Robert Halley, against whose teaching of classics the students rebelled, but whose logic class was recalled by Robert Bruce in the following terms: 'I always look back with pleasure, and a grateful sense of profit, to the hours we spent in that class, conducted largely on the conversational or Socratic method, professor and students discussing together the merits and views of Thompson, Whately, and Mill. . . .'[103] Bruce further notes that 'a thorough and genuine examination' was held, in contrast to the 'pious fraud' which occurred in other classes, where questions were set from a list of questions previously seen by the students. Following Vaughan's resignation in 1857, there came Henry Rogers, who served as president until 1869, and continued to teach until 1871. As we have seen, his interests were broad, and he was an acute observer of the philosophical scene.

James Muscutt Hodgson was appointed in 1875, and at first his duties were somewhat miscellaneous within and without the college; but in 1882 he was installed in the chair of the science of religion and apologetics, and there he remained until he became principal of the Theological Hall of the Scottish Congregational Churches in 1894. We shall meet him again in the following chapter. Meanwhile George Lyon Turner was appointed to teach philosophy and church history in 1880, and remained until 1889, complaints about his teaching in 1884 notwithstanding. By now most of the arts courses were taken in Owens College, the predecessor of Manchester University, while in the theological course apologetics and philosophy were taught in the first year, apologetics, philosophy and science of religion in the second, and philosophy of religion in the third.[104]

Hodgson was succeeded in 1894 by Robert Mackintosh, who had been minister at Dumfries since 1890. He was appointed to teach ethics, sociology and apologetics, later adding philosophy of religion. Mackintosh devoted his deep knowledge, fluent pen, sharp intellect and sardonic humour to the College until he retired in 1930.[105] A self-styled 'refugee' on theological grounds from the Free Church of Scotland to the more open waters of Congregationalism, he was educated in Glasgow under Edward Caird (from whose idealism he largely departed). With his books, *From Comte to Benjamin Kidd* (1899) and *Hegel and Hegelianism* (1903) and his articles – notably his full entry on 'Theism' in *Encyclopedia Britannica* (11th edn., 1910-1911) – Mackintosh ranged widely over the history of philosophy, making incisive remarks as he went. Thus, for example, in admitting both sensation and reflection, Locke, we are told, showed himself to be 'a double-minded or half-hearted philosopher.'[106] As for more thoroughgoing empiricists, Comte, who does not regard metaphysics as disproved but only as outmoded, and who will not be called an atheist or a materialist, 'will neither say "yes" nor "no." But he is filled with scorn for those who say "yes," for he is perfectly and dogmatically assured that we have no right to dogmatise."[107] Spencer fails to show how organization, consciousness and history are deducible from his formula of 'growing complexity'.[108] The intuitionism of Reid and others 'finds its chance in the misadventures of empiricism;'[109] while Kant broke from intuitionalism 'by substituting *one system of necessity* for the many necessary truths or given experiences from which intuitionism takes its start.' However,

> Kant's idealism is incomplete. On one side, the world we know by valid processes of thinking cannot, we are told, be the real world. Or, beginning from the other side; neither the reality which ideal thought reaches after, nor yet the reality which our conscience postulates is the valid world of orderly thinking. The great critic of scepticism has diverged from idealism towards scepticism again, or has given his idealism a sceptical colour, mitigated – but only mitigated – by faith in the moral consciousness.[110]

As for Hegelianism, its great problem is that it 'understands all mysteries.' The fact is that 'We must be in earnest in establishing a distinction between Divine and human consciousness. We must make the difficult assertion of the limitation of human knowledge and human experience.'[111] Above all, we must not follow 'those mystics or idealist philosophers who, with many kind compliments, dissolve the personal Redeemer into an abstract principle, once more betraying the Son of Man – with a kiss.'[112]

The irony in the fact that idealism, which was supposed to unify all, presented numerous faces to the world of thought was not lost upon Mackintosh:

> [I]n the name of ultimate reason – Professor Bradley gives us

a Pantheistic Absolute, and no human immortality; and Dr. McTaggart gives us an eternal society of interrelated spirits, and no absolute being as such; and Professor Royce gives us God and immortality, but without mention of Christ; and Professor Taylor [whose later position was significantly different from that here described by Mackintosh] finds that Royce's arguments are vitiated by reliance upon the relational form of thought, and himself gives us a fighting chance of immortality, and an Absolute that cannot be called personal or a self. Such differences do not prove that idealism is barren; but surely they prove that idealism is no case to claim a monopoly of certainty. Dim movements of faith may be wiser than this shrill logical debate.[113]

Nevertheless Mackintosh was prepared to see some good in idealism:

Idealists in a sense, we believe that Idealism is the effective reply to scepticism; but, however contemptible the position may seem to a higher soaring reason, we think that this wisdom gives us the half, not the whole. We *know* a love which *passes knowledge*. We know it; the sceptics are wrong, and Idealism may help us to prove that they are wrong. But it *passes knowledge*. The philosophical dogmatists are no less in the wrong.... Knowledge teaches us many short-cuts; but a short-cut which should supersede the significance of life has no charm to dazzle us.[114]

In a later work Mackintosh proposes that idealists and realists band together

in damning the torrent of extremely clever rhetoric which is the whole ascertainable achievement of the Pragmatist movement.... The idealist emphasis may be 'we *know* reality' and the realist emphasis 'we know *reality*'; but both forms of assertion will be uttered in vain if Pragmatism is allowed to shut us down. Yet, for as much as ... Pragmatism has found it necessary to acknowledge, among other 'practical' interests which sway the mind, a possible interest in knowledge for knowledge's own sake – why, Pragmatism has refuted itself; Pragmatism has committed suicide; and we need not permit its full-blooded rhetoric to detain us any longer.[115]

Many of the aphorisms sprinkled through Mackintosh's writings are well worth pondering, and it is not difficult to envisage some of them as assertions to be discussed in examination papers. For example, 'Butler fears profoundly that there must be a just God who will punish us. Kant hopes, with tolerable strength of conviction, that there may be a just

God who will reward us.'[116] As to the existence of God, Mackintosh reviews the traditional theistic arguments and finds that Kant's demolition of the ontological, cosmological and teleological 'proofs' is successful. But Hegel's transformation of the arguments into 'reflections on the course of rational thought in man' substitutes intellectualism for the moral process which is Christianity.[117] Miracles, he thinks, may be signs to the believer, but they do not constitute evidence capable of convincing a sceptic. Nevertheless we may not altogether dispense with natural theology. Though incomplete, it may lead people to the threshold of revelation. Indeed, 'If there were nothing in this world which made it look like God's world, faith would be too utterly a paradox.'[118] But in Christ God addresses us personally: he is the heart of God's moral revelation; 'But all moral revelation is twofold – a revelation of grace and of duty; a revelation of moral forces above us, and of moral obligations resting on us.'[119]

It remains only to add that in 1904 Lancashire College, like its neighbouring theological colleges of other denominations, played a significant part in the constitution of the Faculty of Theology of the University of Manchester.[120]

Finally we come to Spring Hill College, Birmingham, founded in 1838 through the generosity of the Mansfield family, whose name is perpetuated in Spring Hill's successor college at Oxford. Henry Rogers was invited to become the first holder of the chair of intellectual philosophy, and he took up his duties in 1839. His text books were Dugald Stewart's *Elements of the Philosophy of the Human Mind*, and Whately's *Elements of Logic*. Rogers so enthused his students that the ablest proceeded to the London MA – generally in philosophy, ethics and political economy – even though this entailed the curtailment of their theological course. In addition to philosophy, Rogers taught English language and literature (the subjects he had professed at University College, London, from 1836-1839), English history, and mathematics. He left Birmingham for Lancashire Independent College in 1858. Following Rogers's departure, Richard Alliott was called from Cheshunt College, and he taught philosophy at Spring Hill from 1860 until his death in 1863, when he was replaced by George Bubier, who served until he died in 1869.[121] With the arrival as principal of David Worthingston Simon in the latter year, the teaching of philosophy received a new lease of life. The subject was placed within the department of dogmatic and general theology and philosophy, within which the following courses were given: philosophy of revelation and general apologetics (one of five theological courses) and three philosophy courses: outline of the science of man; psychology, ethics and logic;

and history of philosophy.[122] In 1884 Simon proceeded to Edinburgh, thinking that his departure would advance the removal of Spring Hill to one of the ancient university centres, thereby taking advantage of the 1871 legislation which opened the portals of Oxbridge to Dissenters. Thus Mansfield College, Oxford, was opened in 1886, Fairbairn having charge of philosophy and much else besides.[123] Fairbairn was followed in 1909 by William Boothby Selbie, who had been Mansfield's first student, and who, in addition to his biography of Fairbairn, published a number of popular books as well as more substantial works on Schleiermacher and psychology of religion.[124]

We have now considered the Congregational colleges in which philosophy was most likely to have been taught. It should, however, be noted that elementary philosophy was taught such in other short-lived and/or short-course venues as those at Cotton End, Bedfordshire (1840-1874) where the evidences of Christianity were covered;[125] Cavendish Theological College (1860-1863), Manchester, the inspiration of Joseph Parker, whose aim was to produce 'earnest and powerful preachers,' and who justified his shortened course on the ground that 'the King's business requireth haste' – but not so much haste that there was no time for philosophy, Christian evidences and logic, taught by J.B. Paton, who went on to become the first Principal of the Nottingham Congregational Institute (1863), later named Paton College after him;[126] and the Bristol Theological Institute, established in 1867 with the same objectives as its Nottingham sister, where Christian evidences were taught until its union in Plymouth with the college there in 1891.[127] Mention should also be made of the Bala College, begun at Llanuwchllyn in 1841 and continued at Bala from 1842, with Michael Jones as its first principal. On his death in 1853 his son, Michael Daniel Jones, succeeded him, resigning in 1892 in order to facilitate the formation of the Bala-Bangor College in Bangor. Philosophy is listed as a subject taught at Bala in 1879.[128]

Before leaving the Congregationalists mention must be made of a significant and fruitful area of cooperation between a number of their colleges: the constitution of the Senatus Academicus. We have seen that as the nineteenth century wore on the Congregational colleges increasingly sought to refer their students to newer institutions of higher education for their arts courses. Not indeed that this found universal favour, as a writer in *The Congregational Magazine* for 1844 made clear: 'We think that the connexion of our colleges with the University of London, and the path which that connexion had opened to literary honours, present strong temptations to certain minds to be more anxious about philosophy than about divinity.'[129] But such attempts to stem the tide did not avail. On the contrary, the success of the arts experiment in raising standards prompted Henry Roberts Reynolds, president of Cheshunt College to contemplate cooperative work in theology to the same end. Indeed, he thought this a religious as well as an academic necessity, as he made clear at a conference of delegates of the Congregational colleges and institutes in January 1865:

> The Colleges will fail of their purpose, and will be deservedly superseded by other and more spiritual organizations, if they cease to supply to our vacant Churches, godly, energetic labourers, and men who in the pulpit can, in the spirit and with the word of Christ, attract the wayfarer, convince the doubter, and console the broken heart. At the same time, the demand of all earnest and thoughtful men at the present day comprehends more than this. The controversies which are closing round the Church, and engaging the most active minds in the Europe of this generation, in a war to the knife with our holy Christianity, demand that we, as well as other sections of the Church, should furnish our contingent to the great army, which is prepared to fight the battle for the truth as it is in Jesus Christ.[130]

Reynolds therefore proposed the formation of a Senatus Academicus comprising the staffs of participating colleges, which would organize courses and examinations at the levels of Licentiate, Bachelor and Fellow, the work to be examined by formally appointed external examiners.[131] Reynolds was, however, before his time, and not all of the colleges were ready to move in the direction proposed. However, thirteen years later, at a meeting of professors from seven English Congregational colleges held at New College on 15 March 1878, it was decided to proceed, and the Senatus was established, with the two levels of Associate and Fellow, in 1879. Fairbairn was prominent in holding himself aloof from the venture. In an article of 1881 he argued that the the curriculum of the Senatus was too narrow and its standards too low – though he did deign to serve as an examiner in 1883.[132] By 1899, however, he had undergone a change of heart, for he told the assembled delegates at the second International Congregational Council of the 'wonderful change' which had come over the English Congregational churches in connection with the training of the ministry, and as evidence of this he noted that 'The colleges, apart from Mansfield, have federated themselves into a *senatus academicus*, and hold common examinations, testing all the choicest men reared in their respective borders.'[133] Eventually colleges of other denominations joined the Senatus, though T. Vincent Tymms, president of Rawdon Baptist College from 1891 to 1904, was more concerned to encourage original thought among his students than to prepare them for examinations; but his college, which had applied for membership of the Senatus in 1881, continued in membership until the organization was disbanded. For an opinion opposite to Fairbairn's original conclusion we may cross the Pennines where concerning the presidency of Edward Parker at Manchester Baptist College (1877-1898), it was said that 'the necessities of the "Senatus Academicus" work, widened the range of the themes he discussed and taught, and added greatly to the tone and extent of the work done.'[134] With hindsight, A.J. Grieve, principal of Lancashire Independent College and noted for meticulous scholarship, declared that the Senatus, 'by maintaining a high standard gave its diplomas of A.T.S. and F.T.S. very real worth.'[135] By 1885 eight Congregational, two Baptist and one Presbyterian college were involved in the work of the Senatus, while in its last year of operation, 1901, nine Congregational (including that in Melbourne, Australia), seven Baptist and one Presbyterian colleges were members. It is noteworthy that none of the Methodist colleges was associated with the Senatus, and no Methodist minister held the ATS or FTS.[136] When recalling his college days at Didsbury (Wesleyan) College from 1892 onwards, J. Ernest Rattenbury noted that 'the tutors discouraged pursuit of university degrees.'[137]

The panel of examiners of the Senatus Academicus was interdenominational, many of them were from Scotland, all of them were reputable and some of them were distinguished. Examiners in philosophy included Robert Adamson of Manchester, Edward Caird of Glasgow and Oxford, Robert Flint of Edinburgh, and J.S. Mackenzie, then of Cambridge and subsequently of Cardiff; while the list for apologetics included A.B. Bruce of Glasgow, Robert Flint, James Iverach of Aberdeen, and James Orr of Edinburgh and subsequently of Glasgow.[138]

We may sample the apologetics and philosophy questions set for 1884. The apologetics paper for the ATS includes twenty-four questions, of which not more than ten were to be attempted in three hours:

7. A numerous school of modern philosophers and scientists affirm that the order and adaptations of the universe afford no proof that they have originated in Intelligence. Refute this position. . . .
10. Give an account of Hume's attack on Miracles, and of the ways in which it has been met by Apologists.

The ATS paper on the psychology of the intellect (cognitions) comprises fifteen questions – no more than eight to be attempted – including the following:

9. We have no difficulty in forming a conception of a golded mountain, but we are unable to conceive of two straight lines inclosing a space. How do you account for this difference?
13. 'The essential characteristic of Thought is the comprehension of a thing under a general notion or attribute' (Hamilton). Examine this view, with more particular reference to the nature of Reasoning.
14. Discuss the nature of the distinction between Knowledge and Belief.

The ATS paper on the history of pre-Socratic philosophy contains eighteen questions of which not more than ten are to be attempted. Three of the questions require the translation of texts in Greek, while a further four require a reading knowledge of Greek. Other questions include:

6. 'Like is known by like.' 'Like is known by unlike.' To whom do you assign these opposed dicta? Consider their significance.
11. The system of Empedocles, it has been said, is entirely eclectic. Discuss the relation of its fundamental positions to those of preceding systems.
17. Can you point to any contributions towards a logical theory among the pre-Socratic speculations?[139]

Clearly, apart from the last (atypical) question quoted, which invites a blunt 'Yes' or 'No', these questions are designed to stimulate thought, and they invite candidates to use, and not simply to regurgitate, knowledge they have acquired. The fact that candidates are asked to attempt so many questions in three hours does, however, give one pause. Nevertheless between 1880 and 1901 511 candidates gained the ATS, and eleven the FTS. These figures, coupled with the academic respectability of the enterprise, lent weight to the arguments of those who were pressing the University of London to inaugurate a Faculty of Divinity. As S.W. Green pointed out, 'The new University had attained its purpose of being non-sectarian only by being entirely non-theological.'[140] A First Scriptural Examination, open to graduates, had been introduced in 1839, and a Further examination was possible after the lapse of one year, but every examiner had a veto on all questions, and no question could concern doctrinal matters of dispute among Christians.[141] The success of the work of the Senatus Academicus showed up the inadequacy of this arrangement, and pressure was brought to bear for the recognition of theology as a fully-fledged university discipline. The objective was attained in the reconstituted University of 1900, when the Faculty of Theology held its first meeting on 20 November of that year. The Senatus Academicus having served its purpose, it was disbanded, and henceforth seven of its constituent colleges became divinity schools of London University until, in some cases, more local universities established faculties or departments of theology, or welcomed Nonconformists into those they already had.[142]

Baptist Colleges

It is with a certain relief that we leave the complex story of philosophy in the many Congregational colleges and turn now to the Baptists, whose institutions were fewer in number but in other respects comparable with those of their fellow Dissenters. Their oldest continuing college is that in Bristol, founded in 1679. John Ryland, appointed principal in 1792, was destined to lead the college through the first quarter of the nineteenth century.[143] He taught Hebrew, Greek, Latin, theology, church history, sacred antiquity, rhetoric and logic. During his time twenty students found their way to the universities of Aberdeen, Glasgow and Edinburgh. Ryland was succeeded by T.S. Crisp,[144] whose most distinguished philosophical student was Thomas Spencer Baynes. Baynes did not enter the ministry; instead, following studies under William Hamilton in Edinburgh he engaged in literary work, finally becoming professor of logic, metaphysics and English literature at the University of St. Andrews. He was an editor of *Encyclopedia Britannica* (9th edn.), and among his many publications is one on the dialect of Somerset.[145] Two of his works concern William Hamilton: *An Essay of the New Analytic of Logical Forms* (1850), to which he added an historical appendix; and a paper on Hamilton in *Edinburgh Essays by Members of the University* (1857). The latter concludes with a paean of praise:

> the whole procedure of philosophy hitherto, has been either an assumption of principles, a criticism of principles, or at most, a capricious and immethodical appeal to facts. To Sir William Hamilton belongs the glory of having finally abolished this vicious system, by expounding with philosophical rigour and minuteness the nature and conditions of the one true method; – fixing the point of departure for philosophy in the facts of inward experience, and converting the appeal to Consciousness, hitherto at best so partial, fluctuating and contradictory, into a scientific instrument of the utmost precision.[146]

In 1841 Bristol College and its sister college at Stepney became affiliated with the University of London, the Unitarian James Martineau being among their prominent advocates.

During the 1840s two alumni of Bristol Baptist College published text books in logic. John Leechman, who also studied at Glasgow University, succeeded William Carey at Serampore college, India, from 1832 to 1837. Ill health forced his return to pastoral charge at Irvine, Scotland. He published *Logic: Designed as an Introduction to the Study of Reasoning*, which reached its fourth edition in 1845. In a straightforward way he covers terms, judgment and reasoning – syllogisms, fallacies and the like; and then considers the laws of evidence, and the connection of logic with grammar and rhetoric. For this work he was awarded the honorary degree of LLD by Glasgow University in 1859.[147]

Leechman's fellow-Baptist, Joshua Taylor Gray, tutor at Stepney from 1850 until his death in 1854, was also educated at Bristol Baptist College. He was in pastoral charge in Cambridge, then kept schools in London before moving to Wellington Street church, Hastings in 1849. His first book was *Immortality, Its Real and Alleged Evidences* (1843), and in 1845 he published his *Exercises in Logic*. This comprises brief definitions followed by exercises for practice. He explains that some of the exercises on which students are invited to comment 'are designed for the especial use of *theological* students'[148] – and in his hands some of these become vehicles for Nonconformist polemics:

15. The divine law bids us obey secular magistrates:
    Bishops are not secular magistrates:
    The divine law does not bid us obey bishops.
18. We ought to believe Scripture:
    Tradition is not Scripture:
    We ought not to believe Tradition.
20. If Abraham was justified, it must have been either by faith
    or by works:
    He was not justified by faith (according to James) nor by
    works (according to Paul):
    Abraham therefore was not justified.[149]

In 1846 F.W. Gotch, an *alumnus* of the College, returned to Bristol from Stepney College, where he had taught philosophy and science for four years, to teach logic and rhetoric, classical languages and geography.[150] He succeeded Crisp as principal, and was himself followed by James Culross, whose subjects included Christian evidences, in 1883.[151] William J. Henderson became principal in 1894.[152] During his tenure of the position the Congregational Western College arrived in Bristol in 1901, and joint teaching was immediately arranged. Thenceforward, for the rest of the period with which we are concerned, philosophy was taught by the Congregationalists – from 1909 within the context of the new University of Bristol.

Next in order of seniority is the General Baptist College conducted briefly by Stephen Freeman, and then by John Evans, first at Hoxton and then at Islington from 1795-1818.[153] On Evans's resignation the college had a peripatetic life until it settled in Nottingham as the Midland Baptist College. Earlier strife over matters Calvinist and Arminian being by then subdued, it united with Rawdon College in 1919.[154]

Rawdon College, Leeds, had its origins in Horton College, Bradford, founded in 1804. Its first principal was William Steadman,[155] who 'could shake a sermon from the sleeve of his coat,' and who managed affairs single-handedly until in 1816 he was joined briefly by Jonathan Edwards Ryland, son of the Bristol principal.[156] A longer-serving colleague was Benjamin Godwin, whom we shall meet again in the next chapter. He remained until 1836.[157] The objectives of Horton College included one to the effect that students 'shall be instructed in English Grammar, if necessary, the learned languages if from their age or previous acquisition there be any rational prospect of success, Logic, Rhetoric, the elements of Composition, Theology, etc.'[158] Steadman was succeeded by James Acworth, who served from 1836 to 1863.[159] During his time, in 1849, the college removed to Rawdon, and in 1852 he was joined by S.G. Green.[160] The course was lengthened to five years, and in 1852 the college became affiliated with London University.

The most significant philosopher at Rawdon was William Medley, who taught there from 1869 to 1908.[161] An MA of London University, he pursued further studies at Göttingen under Ewald, and at Geneva under Merle d'Aubigné. He then embarked upon his life's work at Rawdon Baptist College. His influence was widespread, and he is said to have been 'like a fragrance which you cannot analyze,' and 'possessed of a kind of holy merriment.'[162] His major, somewhat repetitive work, *Christ the Truth. An Essay towards the Organization of Christian Thinking* (1900), is directed to thoughtful Christians who may from time to time find that their spiritual and intellectual ideas and emotions are like cross-currents, or are even mutually antagonistic. His objective is to show that truth 'must at last find its consummated meaning in that highest form of absolute trust of which our nature is capable, viz., trust in a Person.'[163] He cautions that the intellect has its rights, and 'they are losers who deny or disparage them. Yet those are greater losers still who would make the measure of their compass the measure also of the meaning and substance of the Religion which approaches us on every side of our nature, and claims us at the centre of our being.'[164] The truth he has in mind is not simply cerebral: 'it is of that moral and spiritual order which requires for its apprehension the *movement* of life: it must be *entered into*.'[165] On this basis Medley passes in review logic, science, philosophy, aesthetics and ethics, showing how each, though important in its place, leaves us short of the highest expression of truth. Thus, logic concerns the validity of inference, and cannot guarantee, and is not concerned with, truth; the role of science is to investigate causal sequence in the natural order; philosophy is confined to the realm of the intellect; the 'satisfactions of Art . . . are addressed only to certain provinces of the spirit's life';[166] but in ethics, where truth and beauty are applied to character, 'we are on the confines of that widest realm which includes all others that we have traversed.'[167] Truth in its highest form is thus seen to be personal, and its highest expression is Jesus Christ: 'It is, therefore, Truth in a Person, which on its authoritative, imperative side is the Supreme Will, that claims our own will when Duty meets us. Duty, like truth, meets us "in Jesus".'[168]

When T. Vincent Tymms, whose apologetic contribution will concern us shortly, came as principal (1891-1904), Rawdon was unusually strongly placed among the denominational colleges in those allied disciplines.[169] In 1885 the curriculum included logic, inductive logic, apologetics, ethics (if the tutors think fit), mental and moral philosophy, history of philosophy, and Christian ethics.[170] In 1915 Rawdon became affiliated with the University of Leeds.

The Baptist College at Abergavenny was founded in 1807, and led until his resignation in 1836 by Micah Thomas. Its particular objective was to equip Welsh-speaking candidates in English, partly in order that they might benefit from a wider range of reading, and partly with a view to the evangelization of English speakers. Thomas faced a good deal of opposition, much of it inspired by the belief that he was inclined to Arminianism (among his 'sins' was his stated preference for Wesley's Scripture *Notes* to those of the high Calvinist John Gill – fighting talk indeed!). The standard history of the college refers to sermon class, and to instruction in various subjects – even in minerology, galvanism and meteorology – but not to philosophy.[171] Following Thomas's resignation the work of the college was continued at Pontypool under Thomas Thomas.[172] As time passed, and with the anglicisation of South Wales proceeding apace, it could be assumed that more college entrants could handle English, and this enabled more time to be devoted to other aspects of the curriculum. The addition of George Thomas to the staff in 1841 facilitated this. But the curriculum was largely biblical, doctrinal and linguistic, with considerations of Puseyism, Mormonism and other Nonconformist entertainments thrown in. A student did, however, present a paper on 'The principles of moral philosophy' to the Annual Meeting of the college.[173] In 1871 W. Mortimer Lewis was appointed to teach a great variety of subjects including logic, metaphysics and moral philosophy[174] William Edwards, principal of the college at Haverfordwest, was called to succeed Lewis, and he remained in post until 1925.[175] Edwards taught philosophy, moral science, using Wayland's text, and logic, using the introductions of Morell and Jevons. Among works studied with the senior class in 1885 was G.P. Fisher's *The Grounds of Theistic and Christian Belief*.[176] In Edwards's time the college joined the Senatus Academicus, and this further shaped the curriculum.

Philosophy does not appear to have featured significantly at the Baptist academies established at Haverfordwest in 1839 (though presumably Edwards taught some philosophy there between 1880 and 1889) and at Llangollen in 1862. Of these the former removed to Aberystwyth in 1894, but in 1899 it united with its sister at Pontypool to form the South Wales Baptist College, where increasingly close relations were developed with the University College of South Wales (1883); while, in the wake of the establishment of the University College of North Wales in 1884, the latter removed to Bangor in 1892.[177]

The Baptist Academical Institution was opened at Stepney in 1810, and of its early tutors Solomon Young, who taught mental philosophy among other things, was the most gifted philosophically. Of him it was said that 'there was, perhaps, no valuable metaphysical work in any language accessible to Mr. Young which he had not made his own by a discriminating perusal. No man, however, more steadily thought for himself.'[178] A memorandum of 1828, drawn up by W.H. Murch and Samuel Tomkins, principal and tutor respectively, specifies that logic and a course on the evidences of divine revelation are to be taken in the first year, mental philosophy in the second, and moral philosophy in the fourth.[179] Among the external examiners was John Hoppus, professor of the philosophy of mind and logic in the University of London, with which university the college became affiliated in 1841. At this period, students read Whately's *Rhetoric*, James Mill's *Analysis of the Phenomena of the Human Mind*, and, later, Sidgwick's *Methods of Ethics*. Joshua Taylor Gray, whose books on immortality and logic have already been noted, was on the staff from 1851 to 1854. In 1856 the college removed to Regent's Park, and thence it carried its name to Oxford in 1927. In 1889 it joined the Senatus Academicus, and in 1900 it became a divinity school of the University of London.

In 1844 Henry Dowson minister of Westgate, Bradford, a strict-communion Baptist whom some had hoped would have become principal of Rawdon College, became the first president of the Baptist college at Bury, Lancashire.[180] Founded as a closed-communion institution, its curriculum excluded classical studies (except for a voluntary Latin class, the purpose of which was to assist the students' comprehension of the

English language) and mathematics, on the ground that these were dissuasives from focused theological study. There were, however, lectures on logic and mental science, and on Christian evidences, in which 'the whole of the first part [of Butler's *Analogy*] was studied and digested.'[181] The study of languages, however, gradually became more prominent. In 1873 the college moved to Manchester, and ten years later it joined the Senatus Academicus. In 1885 J.T. Marshall was the tutor in biblical languages, philosophy and mathematics, and we find that in the first year courses were given in apologetics and logic, in the second, in apologetics, and in the third, in philosophical and ethical systems.[182] The college subsequently became an associated college of the Faculty of Theology of the University of Manchester.

In 1856 C.H. Spurgeon founded his Pastor's College, later renamed after himself.[183] The celebrated evangelical Calvinist preacher was on the one hand concerned with the huge task of evangelizing the masses crowding into the English cities, and on the other hand persuaded that the existing colleges were less than ardent in their Calvinism. As he picturesquely put it, 'Too many ministers are toying with the deadly Cobra of "another Gospel", in the form of "modern thought".'[184] This might seem a recipe for a reactionary curriculum, but by 1881 Spurgeon was expecting that a full course would include eleven subjects, among them mental and moral science, metaphysics and casuistry.[185] But the college's priorities were elsewhere; it did not join the Senatus Academicus; and its historian, remarking on the testing of rote learning as late as 1916, concludes that 'Academically, Spurgeon's College was far behind the other London colleges, whose teaching methods and examination questions had been profoundly influenced by the university.'[186]

Unitarian Colleges

The same could not be said of the Unitarian college which inherited the best educational traditions from Old Dissent, and made its peripatetic way from Manchester (1786) to York (1803), to Manchester again (1840), to London (1853), and finally to Oxford (1889), where it continues as Harris-Manchester College. No injustice is done to any of the other colleges with which we are concerned if it is granted that philosophy fared at least as well in Manchester College as anywhere else. In 1798, at the threshold of our period George Walker, minister at Nottingham, but previously a tutor at the Warrington academy (1757-1786) was appointed professor of theology in succession to Thomas Barnes. The prospectus of that year lists his duties thus:

Logic and Metaphysics, Ethics or Moral Philosophy, including the principles, character and history of Civil Society, to which will be annexed a view of the laws and constitution of Great Britain. Natural and Revealed Religion; comprehending their history and evidences. Critical Lectures on the New Testament. Composition. Superintendent of Academical Disputations and of excercises in Elocution.[187]

Charles Wellbeloved became principal on the removal of the college to York in 1803. He was highly esteemed, though, as he told the chairman of the college committee, a serious illness in 1807 prevented him from covering his desired syllabus without additional assistance. His plan included the philosophy of the human mind and logic, and moral philosophy and jurisprudence with a view of the English government during the first three years of the course, and (for divinity students only) the evidences of natural and revealed religion.[188] From 1809-1827 William Turner taught logic and metaphysics among other things, and, with certain reservations, he was a necessarian in the line of Hartley, Priestley and Belsham.[189] Turner was succeeded as philosophy professor by William Hincks, who remained in post until 1739, and who introduced the students to the mental philosophy of the English and Scottish schools, as well as to major German and French philosophers.[190]

In 1740 the college returned to Manchester, and James Martineau, then ministering in Liverpool, became professor of mental and moral philosophy and political economy,[191] and later principal (in London) from 1869 to 1885. Concurrently, the college curriculum was reordered so as to meet the matriculation requirements of the University of London. Martineau was trained at Manchester College, York, where the philosophy tutor was William Turner, a determinist in the line of Hartley. As an indication of Martineau's general approach in philosophy we may note his description of the task of mental philosophy as being

> to note and register, according to some natural order, all the phenomena of the mind; to detect the occasions of their first appearance; to analyse their composition; to determining the laws of their succession; to estimate the value and proper direction of the several faculties, as instruments for the discovery of truth, the invention of beauty, and the increase of happiness.[192]

Martineau wrote a number of expository-*cum*-critical studies, including those of Lessing, Comte, Whewell, Hamilton, and John Stuart Mill.[193] A larger work is Martineau's *A Study of Spinoza* (1882), in which Spinoza is faulted for positing a substance out of which all is to proceed, but which is yet absolutely divorced from all predicates: all that can be said of it is that it is. In Martineau's opinion this is no basis for theism. To an account of his ethical theism we shall come in the next chapter.

Among Martineau's colleagues was J.J. Tayler, who taught church history and Christian evidences, and who was principal from 1853-1869. In the latter year he was succeeded by James Drummond, who was principal from 1885-1906. When the elderly Martineau's duties were reduced in 1875, Charles Barnes Upton was appointed to assist in mental and moral philosophy and logic. Upton had been Martineau's student at Manchester New College, London, where, as Hibbert Scholar, he graduated BA and BSc of London University. Following a pastorate at Toxteth Park, Liverpool (1867-1875), he returned to his *alma mater*, where he taught until 1903. In 1905 he published *Dr. Martineau's Philosophy: a Survey*, in which he both reveals his indebtedness to his teacher and finds him wanting at certain points. In particular, there is, he feels an epistemological block in Martineau's thought, for on the one hand he holds that we know God in the way in which we know other objects – that is, by inference; but on the other hand, and supremely when his theme is worship, Martineau asserts the immediacy of our experience of God.[194] Upton was followed by Lawrence Pearsall Jacks, author of urbane books on a variety of topics and editor of the *Hibbert Journal*, who remained in post until 1931 – for the last sixteen years as principal.[195]

On reading the story of the Unitarian Home Mission Board institution in Manchester, one is conscious of being in the orbit of English Unitarianism at its most evangelistic. Established in 1854, with John Relly Beard, a fellow-student of Martineau's at Manchester College, York, as its first principal,[196] the institution set about training preachers and church planters; but, although Beard published in the field of apologetics, as we shall see, philosophy as such does not seem to have featured strongly in the early years. However, T. Elford Poynting, theological tutor from 1874-1878, had a keen interest in mental and moral philosophy, and with the appointment in 1894 of J.E. Manning as tutor in Old Testament, Hebrew and philosophy, the discipline received due attention.[197] Manning died in 1910, and was succeeded in the following year by S.H. Mellone (1869-1956),[198] a theologian of some note, with strong interests in philosophy and psychology. Mellone had taken his London BA in 1890, and after further training at Manchester New College, he was Hibbert Scholar from 1894 to 1897, during which time he secured the DSc of Edinburgh and the MA of London. Following ministries at Holywood, Co. Down, and St. Mark's, Edinburgh, he became principal of the Unitarian College, Manchester (1911-1921). According to the curriculum in operation during the First World War, Mellone taught the history of Christian doctrine under the auspices of the University of Manchester, and some New Testament, in addition to the philosophy of theism with special reference to the works of Martineau and William James; psychology for ministers and teachers; landmarks in the history of ethics; and critical history of English philosophy.[199]

Mellone came to the attention of his philosophical peers in 1897, with the publication of his DSc thesis, *Studies in Philosophical Criticism and Construction: A Summary of the Problems of Philosophy*. He dedicates his book to Andrew Seth (later Pringle-Pattison) of Edinburgh, and expresses his indebtedness to James Ward and C.B. Upton, his first teacher of philosophy. He draws upon Bradley and Bosanquet for logic and metaphysics, and on Green, Martineau and Sidgwick for ethics. He reviews the several branches of philosophy from the standpoint that our knowledge of nature, phenomena and God turns upon our knowledge of the nature of humanity. Hence will, feeling and thought must all be given their due place in our intellectual construction. He proceeds along broadly Hegelian lines, whilst recognizing that we must allow for degrees of reality and truth: 'Our Ideals are the immediate self-revelation of the Absolute *for us*; but they are not, therefore, abstractly identical with the existence of the Absolute *for itself*.'[200]

Three more of Mellone's many works may be noted. To him we owe one of the most widely-read, if not one of the most adventurous or exciting, works in logic: the *Introductory Text Book on Logic* (1903), which reached its twentieth edition in 1945, by which time he had also published *Elements of Modern Logic* in 1934. *The Dawn of Modern Thought. Descartes, Spinoza, Leibniz*, was published in 1930. Here Mellone finds that 'the contrast between the monism of Spinoza (qualified by his assumption of the *conatus* as the secret of individuality) and the pluralism of Leibniz (qualified by his assumption of the "pre-established harmony")' bequeaths us a difficult and apparently inconclusive task of reconciliation. But we should be inspired by the seventeenth-century rationalists not 'to fetter the speculative impulse which is inherent in the higher races of mankind.' On the other hand, the rationalists' underlying confidence in clear and distinct ideas as the criterion of truth, raised by Locke and others, opened the way to a fresh speculative impulse, and to 'a more adequate analysis of the foundations of knowledge.'[201]

The history of the Presbyterian College, Carmarthen, goes back to 1689 and the academy conducted by Samuel Jones of Brynllywarch, Glamorgan.[202] It is a tale of many locations, doctrinal disputes and personal squabbles. It was, however, continuously at Carmarthen from 1796 until in 1979 it and the Congregational Memorial College, Brecon, entered into a co-operative arrangement in Swansea (whither the latter had removed in 1959), a situation perpetuated in Aberystwyth from 1980 onwards.[203] Apart from references to Locke, the place of philosophy in the curriculum during most of the nineteenth century is not easy to determine. It is known that in 1823 an examination was conducted in philosophy, and that the intellectual atmosphere was favourable to free enquiry. By now a number of the tutors had liberal theological views even if they were Congregationalists, and the college retained its old designation 'Presbyterian' even when its teachers from that tradition became Arian or Unitarian. In 1828 a four-year curriculum was devised which included first year logic, but no other philosophical courses.[204] In the eighteen-forties the college became associated with the University of London, and by 1847 it was possible to appoint a third tutor, and to add mental and moral philosophy to the curriculum.[205] From 1862 until his death in 1884 these were taught by William Morgan, a Congregational minister and champion of political and religious liberty.[206] From 1900 to 1938 the Congregationalist Evan Keri Evans taught philosophy at Carmarthen. He had been a student under, and then assistant to, Edward Caird in Glasgow, and in his early thirties was appointed professor of philosophy at Bangor. Ill health prompted his resignation from the chair and his removal to Carmarthen, where he also ministered at Priory Congregational Church.[207] The college became associated with the University of Wales during the early years of the twentieth century.[208]

The Welsh Presbyterian College

In 1842 the Welsh Presbyterians (Calvinistic Methodists) opened their college at Trefeca, a place steeped in associations with their early leader, Howel Harris (1714-1773).[209] The first principal was David Charles, who taught philosophy, among other things, until he became minister at Abercarn in January 1863. The second principal, William Howells, also taught philosophy until he retired in 1888. The subject then became the brief of the third principal, D. Charles Davies, 'a powerful thinker whose mind exhibited marked gifts of analysis and synthesis,' who died in 1891. Owen Prys taught philosophy from 1890. He had graduated first class in moral sciences at Cambridge, and had assisted Robert Adamson at Owens College, Manchester. In 1906 he removed with the college to Aberystwyth, where the institution united with its sister college at Bala to form The United Theological College, and he retired in 1927.[210]

Methodist Colleges

The resistance to formal theological education among the Arminian Methodists, to which reference was made at the outset, was sufficiently overcome for their Theological Institution to open its doors (in fact, the rented building of the old Hoxton Academy) in 1835. A curriculum had been drawn up in the previous year, and included in the list of subjects, of which 'As many' are to be taught 'as shall be found suitable and practical' are logic, and philosophy. The first theological tutor was John Hannah, among whose subjects was apologetics, while his colleague, Samuel Jones, taught philosophy and logic as well as classics, geometry and algebra.[211] The progress of the Institution was encouraging, and plans were made to leave Hoxton and to develop a northern and a southern branch in new locations. Thus Didsbury College opened in Manchester in 1842, and Richmond College in London in the following year. Hannah continued at Didsbury until his retirement in 1867, when he was succeeded by William Burt Pope, Methodism's most notable theologian, who himself was succeeded by Marshall Randles in 1886 until his retirement in 1902. Of Randles it was said that 'he was a great man with the brain of a philosopher and the heart of a child, but handicapped by the limitations of his early education and a technique long out of date. His logic was as remoseless as that of Calvin. If his premises were granted, his conclusions seemed irrefutable, but it must be admitted that his premises were often challengeable.' Of this period the same writer said, 'We were behind the times theologically, and lived in strange ignorance of what was transpiring in the world of thought.'[212] Randles was followed in 1902 by R. Waddy Moss, who had been assistant tutor (1871-1872) and classical tutor (1888-1901), and was principal from 1913 until his retirement in 1918, and the church historian John Smith Simon, who also ventured into apologetics, was principal from 1901 to 1912.[213] From 1905-1909 philosophy was in the hands of Frederic Platt, while between 1910 and 1915 it was taught by Charles L. Bedale.[214]

At Richmond College philosophy fell within the brief of those responsible for biblical literature and classics until 1920 – George G. Findlay among them (1875-1881),[215] when Eric S. Waterhouse was appointed to a philosophical Chair. During our period, however, we find that, according to a report of 1845, senior students were required to undergo weekly tests on Butler's *Analogy*, to master the principles of leading philosopers, and to undertake 'syllogistic practice'; and all of this amongst a myriad of other courses included a number of languages and even optics and manual astronomy. As a friendly memorialist observed, 'no educationist can believe that this grandiloquent report of studies represented anything but a veneer of studies.'[216]

Alfred Barrett,[217] house governor from 1858 to 1868, was an early, somewhat swashbuckling, Wesleyan writer on philosophy. He published a *Discourse on the Modern Mental Philosophy* in 1850. This is largely concerned with the views of Morell, whose indebtedness to

Schleiermacher is noted. Barrett welcomes Morell's advocacy of direct perception over against ideas and impressions – as advanced by Plato, Aristotle, Descartes, Malebranche, Locke, Berkeley and Hume; and regards Reid as leading the way to a sounder epistemology. He further welcomes Morell's emphasis upon an intuitional consciousness, and his agreement with Schleiermacher that the earliest phase of our religious consciousness is a feeling of dependence. However, Morell is charged with failing to rely upon the plenary inspiration of Scripture to explain the biblical facts he adduces. Accordingly, Barrett defends plenary inspiration (distinguishing it from mechanical dictation). In relation to the Bible, 'unsubmissive speculation' denies the necessity of regeneration; extravagantly assesses intuitional genius; 'spiritualises' doctrine so that it will not conflict with science, and will accord with the general prevailing mentality; changes 'the Gospel summons from an authoritative requirement into an apology; or what is even lower, an *argumentum ad hominem*'; and detaches the history of Christ's personal ministry from his entire mediatorial history. Small wonder that people in this situation cast about, devoid of the Holy Spirit, not knowing what ails them.

Probably the most competent pre-1920 philosopher on the staff at Richmond was William Theophilus Davison,[218] who served from 1883 to 1891, when he went to Handsworth College. He returned to Richmond in 1905, and was principal from 1909 to 1920. He is said, somewhat opaquely, to have 'encouraged his students in the new ways of thought.'[219] Davison wrote on a variety of topics, and his ethics will concern us in the next chapter.

Two further Wesleyan colleges remain to be mentioned: Headingley, established in Leeds in 1868, and Handsworth, opened in Birmingham in 1881. With the exception of his six-year sojourn at Richmond, George G. Findlay devoted the his working life to Headingley, serving there from 1870 to 1919. On his return from Richmond in 1881 he joined a strong team which included John Shaw Banks, appointed in 1880, as theological tutor: 'a man of massive learning, one who wrestled not merely with a few books, but with libraries.'[220] Apart from W.T. Davison who, as just noted, interspersed his Richmond periods with thirteen years at Handsworth, there was no staff member of philosophical note, and we may suppose that the elements of philosophy and logic were taught in these two colleges as in their older sister institutions.

For the 'pre-history' of the college of the Methodist New Connexion we must turn to one of the prominent ministers of the day, Thomas Allin, who in 1835 began to take prospective ministers into his home for training. This tradition was continued by William Cooke and James Stacey, until at last, in 1863, Ranmoor College, Sheffield, was opened with Stacey as principal.[221] For the first two years he had the assistance of Samuel Hulme, but for the next thirteen years he was in sole charge of the familiar miscellany of subjects. Of Stacey's philosophy class a former student wrote:

> Incidentally in his lecture, the doctor drops the name of a philosopher, or of some philosophic system. A student, in the quarter of an hour at the end of the lecture allowed for questions, makes an enquiry about the philosopher or his system of thought. Then would be given us a glimpse of the greatness of the man we had for a tutor. With uttermost ease, in phrase clear as light at noontide, he would give us an outline of the philosopher's system . . . all with such fulness of knowledge, such wideness of outlook, such aptness of illustration, as amazed the gazing students ranged around.[222]

In 1876 Stacey passed the principalship to William Cocker, who inherited the teaching of mental and moral philosophy and logic. In 1886 Cocker was succeeded by T.D. Crothers, among whose delights was Butler's *Analogy*.[223] At this time the course included apologetics, ethics and social problems, and logic. When Crothers retired in 1898, moves were made to ensure that the theological education given was abreast of the latest developments in theological thought, though it was not until 1910 that it became possible to offer the majority of students a three-year course.

The United Methodist Free Churches opened their theological college in Manchester in 1871, and during the 1890s the Bible Christians began to use their school at Shebbear for individually-tailored courses for ministerial candidates. Richard Pyke was among those who were trained in this way – a preparation which he found 'slender and inadequate.'[224] The Bible Christians were on the point of taking more formal steps when, in 1907 the New Connexion, the United Methodist Free Churches, and the Bible Christians came together in the United Methodist Church. This enabled Bible Christian candidates to study at Manchester and, after a period of trans-Pennine shuttling by the staff, Ranmoor was closed in 1919 and the work consolidated in Victoria Park, Manchester. The philosophical disciplines taught were logic, social philosophy, moral philosophy, metaphysics, and Christian and comparative ethics. By now the Manchester teachers were playing a full part in the Faculty of Theology of the University, and there was increasing co-operation with Hartley Primitive Methodist College. For those matriculated students (the majority) who could not afford the time required to read for Manchester's postgraduate BD, the London External BD course was available. Following Methodist union in 1932, Victoria Park and Hartley united as Hartley Victoria college in 1934.[225]

Turning now to the colleges of the Primitive Methodist Church, we find that in 1863 a school was opened in Elmfield House, near York, which, under the principalship of John Petty (1865-1868), gradually veered in the direction of a training school for ministers.[226] Thus was the way paved for the opening in 1868 of a Theological Institute in Sunderland. The following subjects appear in the early curriculum: 'Arithmetic, Grammar, English History, Church History, Primitive Methodist History and Rule, Geography, Logic, Rhetoric, Mental and Moral Science, Theology, Semonizing, Biblical Literature and Exegesis, and Elocution.'[227] All of these subjects, be it noted, were at first in the hands of one man, the principal, William Antliff, who served from 1868 to 1881, and was joined by Thomas Greenfield in 1877.[228] The growing importance of Manchester, and the increasing reputation of Owens College, prompted the removal of the college to that city, where the first students were received in 1881, and its name became Hartley College in 1906, following the benefactions of Sir William Hartley of jam fame. The early students studied Wayland's *Moral Science*, Jevons's *Logic*, and Whately's *Rhetoric*, but philosophy was not taught by a specialist until the layman Atkinson Lee was appointed in 1908. A graduate of Cambridge University, he had been lecturing at the University College, Aberystwyth, and remained at Hartley until 1947. From 1920 to 1950 he taught philosophy in the University of Manchester. In 1946 he published his *Groundwork of the Philosophy of Religion*, which indicates that his interests were more in the phenomenology of religion than in the then current challenge of logical positivism, and the swelling tide of analytical philosophy.

The Presbyterian Church of England College

We come finally to the college of the Presbyterian Church in England, which Church united with the English Synod of the United Presbyterian Church to form the Presbyterian Church of England in 1876. Lectures – including a course in logic – began to be given in Exeter Hall, London in 1844, and thereafter the college had a number of homes until, after considerable debate and some dispute, it removed to Cambridge in 1899, and was named Westminster College.[229] Peter Lorimer (1812-1879), educated at Edinburgh University and ordained in 1936 as minister of Colebrook Row church in Islington, was appointed the first professor of biblical criticism and Hebrew in 1845. In 1878 he became the first principal. He was not averse to straying from the particular duties of his chair, and we shall note his apologetic contributions in due course. William Chalmers taught apologetics from 1867, and was principal from 1880 until his retirement in 1888. During this period the college became affiliated with the Senatus Academicus, though its curriculum of 1885 makes no mention of philosophical disciplines other than apologetics – which seems surprising given the Scottish origins and/or education of its professors.[230] Chalmers was followed by W.G. Elmslie, who taught Old Testament and apologetics, but he died in the following year, aged forty-one. He was succeeded in the chair of Old Testament and apologetics by John Skinner, who became principal in 1908, and resigned in 1922. J. Oswald Dykes became principal in 1888, and remained until his retirement in 1907. He was succeeded by John Wood Oman, regarded by many as the outstanding Nonconformist philosophical theologian of his generation.[231]

Conclusion

On the basis of the evidence (some of it scanty) presented in this chapter, we may tentatively conclude that while philosophy was generally represented in the Congregational, and in most of the Baptist, colleges, the subject enjoyed its greatest degree of stability in the Unitarian institutions. It featured in the curriculum of the Welsh Presbyterian College at Trefeca, but appears to have been more spasmodically present in Methodist colleges, some of whose tutors taught so many disciplines over so short a period of overall study that one cannot but suspect a plethora of 'outlines', and a measure of rote learning issuing in regurgitation during examinations.[232] The Scottish intellectual heritage of the college of the Presbyterian Church of England ensured that due attention was paid to apologetics. The curriculum of the Theological Senatus, though at first viewed askance by Fairbairn, and by Tymms, whose college nevertheless participated in the scheme, undoubtedly ensured the regular teaching of philosophy and apologetics, as well as competent, interdenominational, external examining. The number of questions to be attempted in the examination papers, however, raises once more the spectre of the regurgitation of notes rather than the reflective utilization of knowledge acquired. For all that, the Senatus paved the way for the new faculties of theology at the beginning of the twentieth century, and with these the Methodist colleges, though not in membership of the Senatus, became fully involved.

As for the miscellaneous philosophical works noted in this chapter, it must be said that while, no doubt, the logic handbooks of Leechman, Gray and especially of Mellone proved useful to students, their authors cannot be said to have advanced the discipline in any significant way, nor did they set out to do so. Of those who discussed philosophers ancient and modern, Martineau is careful, Rogers elegant, and Mackintosh pungent. That close reasoner, Richard Alliott, impressed by the psychological interest and an early English critic of Schleiermacher, nevertheless eschewed subjectivism and, while carrying forward *a posteriori* natural theology in the line of Paley, was equally opposed to any objectivism which would suggest that Christianity is at heart a matter of intellectual assent to truths externally attested. Godwin's *Intellectual Principles*, though bearing the marks of psychological reflection, is largely descriptive and devoid of extended engagement with his peers. Towards the end of the century, when philosophical idealism was prominent in some quarters Elkanah Armitage clearly distinguished the God of religion from the Absolute of philosophy, thereby revealing himself at a considerable intellectual remove from Mellone, whose thinking followed broadly Hegelian lines in metaphysics, a dash of rationalistic epistemology notwithstanding. In William Medley's *Christ the Truth* we have both a confession of faith and an inkling of rising personalism in philosophy.

While the miscellaneous works just referred to are, together with a number of others mentioned in this chapter, of interest in themselves and as examples of the philosophizing of their century, it cannot be said that any of them thrust philosophical thinking into a new mould – which is by no means to say that none of their work merits discussion today. How did the Nonconformist philosophers fare in ethics and apologetics? To this question we now turn.

5
Nonconformist Contributions to Ethics and Apologetics, 1800-1920

I : Ethics

Edward Williams

By way of showing that interest in moral philosophy on the part of Nonconformists by no means waned with the turn of the eighteenth century, we may set out from Edward Williams. As we have seen, he was an alumnus of the academy at Abergavenny, and he later became an honorary DD of Edinburgh University. He held pastorates at Ross-on-Wye (1775-1776); Oswestry (1777-1791), to which town the Abergavenny academy migrated in 1782 so that he could be its principal; and Carrs Lane, Birmingham (1792-1795). In the latter year he began his ministry at Masbro', Rotherham, combining it with the principalship of the Congregational college in that town. Near the beginning of our period we find him gloomily assessing the present state of moral science. He understands moral science as 'a sure and exact knowledge of virtue and vice, as to what they are in themselves, from whence they spring, and to what they tend, respectively, as their ultimate results';[1] and he regrets that few writers on morals discuss virtue, and even fewer, vice. Moral science thus compares unfavourably with physical science, which from the time of Bacon onwards has been making progress; and, as the works of Reid demonstrate, mental science, the laws of which have more in common with those of the physical sciences, has also advanced. But 'the freedom which belongs to the doctrine of our active powers is more remote from the notion of cause and effect in physics than the laws by which the intellect is governed.'[2] The mere observation of phenomena will not tell us what ought to be. If we wish to gain demonstrative evidence in moral science the only way is by setting out from axioms, for these, 'whether perceived intuitively or learned from Divine revelation, are in morals what experiments or observed phenomena are in physics.'[3] Morals imply obligation; obligation implies a law; a law implies a Moral Governor, namely, God – Williams's primary axiom from which all else is developed.

Among Williams's *Dissertations* is one on liberty and necessity. He here carefully distinguishes between active power, which is all from God, and principles – good or evil, in accordance with which we act or refrain from acting. Because he does not observe this distinction, Reid's account of moral actions is deemed contradictory. For Reid holds that liberty is active power derived from God; but this, says Williams, implies a necessitation of that power while it continues: 'Therefore, Dr. Reid's notion of liberty itself is, that it is the offspring of necessity; while at the same time he maintains it is a fundamental principle that it is subject to no necessity, which is a direct contradiction.'[4] The underlying fault is the attribution of good and evil to the same source. No doubt all actions are willed, but good and bad actions are willed according to different principles; they do not flow from the same source: 'To admit diversity of effects without a corresponding diversity of causes, is the same thing as to admit an effect without an adequate cause; which is subversive of all reasoning, and of common sense.'[5]

In further elucidation of necessary agency Williams argues necessary that the supreme being is, with reference to natural acts, the only proper agent in the universe. Created agents are subject to necessity in various ways – for example, they are subject to divine influence in making moral choices, to the connection between the disposition and the act, and to the connection between the act and its consequent. However, 'in all acts morally evil the soul is passive in reference to that necessity of dependence which is inseparable from a created nature, which may be called passive power, without which the existence of moral evil would be impossible.'[6] If there were only one agent, the supreme being, in the universe human beings would not be moral agents, and there would be no evil in bad volitions, but only in their effects. But we are moral agents, and the notion of passive power, coupled with that of morally free choice best preserved God's status and ours.

We may note in passing that Williams's views on passive power drew a response from William Parry who was trained at Homerton and, after suplying the pulpit at Gravesend, held the pastorate at Little Baddow, Essex, from 1780-1799. He became principal of Wymondley (Congregational) Academy in the latter year, and remained there until his death in 1819.[7] He finds Williams's views on passive power confusing, contending that to maintain, as Williams does, that God leaves people to a conjunction of passive power and moral freedom, which combination is the cause of moral evil, 'gives a harsh and unwarrantable view of the Divine character.'[8]

Williams discusses moral inability (with reference to the writings of

Jonathan Edwards), moral evil (God is not the author of sin), and virtue and vice (under which heading strictures are levelled the Baptist Robert Hall's treatment of Edwards). Dissertations on war and the internal evidence for Christianity are followed by a final piece (in what is an unfinished work) on justification. Here is presented Williams's conviction that 'The rule of moral government in reference to justification is that we believe on our Lord Jesus Christ as the end of the law of righteousness.... An endeavour to set up our own obedience instead of the righteousness of Christ is rebellion against the authority of God, and undervaluing His wisdom and grace. None deserve condemnation more than those who reject the only remedy [for moral evil and the human predicament].'[9]

George Payne

One of the most substantial of Nonconformist works on moral philosophy is George Payne's *Elements of Mental and Moral Science; designed to exhibit the Original Susceptibilities of the Mind* (1828), which ran to four editions. Payne was educated at Hoxton academy and Glasgow University, of which he was MA and, in 1828, in recognition of his *Elements*, LLD. Following an assistantship at Salem, Leeds (1807-1808) and pastorates at Fish Street, Hull (1808-1812) and Albany chapel, Edinburgh (1812-1823), he became theological tutor at Blackburn Independent academy (1823-1829), and president of Western College, Exeter/Plymouth (1829-1848).[10]

Payne's emphasis throughout is upon morals, and upon the way in which our thoughts on that subject (and on theology) are modified by the views we entertain regarding the nature and laws of the mind. Indeed, 'Mental philosophy is the anatomy of human nature. How is it then possible to exhibit the rationale of morals if we are ignorant of this species of anatomy?'[11] He agrees with Thomas Brown against Reid that consciousness is not a distinct power of the mind; he is with Locke against innate ideas, and with Dugald Stewart in holding that apart from sensations the mind would have no knowledge of its own existence. He argues that moral rectitude is 'the correspondence or harmony of our affections, and conduct, with the various relations we sustain.'[12] In connection with pleasure and desire, Payne dissents from the view of Richard Price, and from Brown who follows him. Price and Brown claim that objects afford pleasure because they have been desired; in fact, counters Payne, 'Certain sensations are by nature agreeable; their return is desired, and desired *because* it is agreeable.'[13]

The first task of moral science is to ask what is our duty, why is it our duty, and how may we know that such and such is our duty? He first argues for the essential difference between right and wrong. Brown's theory of morals, he complains, proceeds on a practical forgetfulness of the distinction what is/what ought to be. Not all passions are right – hence the need of a moral rule to try their rectitude. On Brown's principles, indeed, 'there might be virtue in a nation of atheists' – a possibility which Payne contemplates with horror.[14] On Brown's theory it would be impossible for us to say that a man who thinks he does no wrong may in fact be guilty. Payne insists that 'there is a moral obligation to actions which is totally independent of the state of feeling of the agent.'[15] Butler is found wanting insofar as he says much about the role of conscience in approving virtue, but does not stay to explain the nature of either conscience or virtue.[16] Virtue is thus referred to conscience or the moral sense. Again, 'The assertion of an essential difference between right and wrong, is opposed to the sentiments of those who maintain that the consequences of actions impart to them their moral character – or, in other words, who place the foundation of virtue in utility.'[17] Having ruled out positions he deems unsatisfactory, Payne proceeds to argue that 'rectitude . . . is the conformity or harmony of [man's] affections with the various relations in which he has been placed, – of which conformity the perfect intellect of God, guided in its exercise by his immaculately holy nature, is the only infallible judge.'[18] Against Price and Brown, who say that there is a difference between right and wrong because we perceive it so, Payne pits the objective, revealed, law of God. Nor does Jonathan Edwards escape: his view that virtue consists in love to being is denounced as the invocation of the abstract, and, in its generality, overlooking the fact that all obligations rest upon particular relations. In a word:

> Rectitude is conformity to relations. Now the relations of man to his Maker – the relations of man to his fellow-man – may be seen by reason even unenlightened by revelation. . . . There is, then, a natural morality . . . as well as a natural theology.[19]

Nevertheless, the Bible, which came from God, 'presents us with a more full and perfect disclosure of truth and duty, than can be derived from any other source.'[20] But this must not encourage us to agree with those 'theological moralists' who ground rectitude in the command of God. For while 'The Divine command is, indeed, the source of obligation . . . it is not . . . the source or foundation of virtue. Rectitude is the source of the command; the command is not the source of rectitude.'[21] The divine command is to be heeded, and the divine claim upon us is to be honoured. Those who fail here are immoral and bad.

In a later paper, presented to a Literary and Scientific Society in Exeter, Payne discusses 'Conscience – its nature and claims.' His definition of conscience, if not unproblematic, is carefully qualified and clear:

> *conscience is a power or faculty or susceptibility of the mind, distinct from all others, in the sense in which any of the mental faculties can be distinct from the rest, rendering it capable of experiencing powerful emotions of self-approbation or self-condemnation, when, on the retrospect of our actions, they are regarded by us as right or wrong.*[22]

He underlines the point that his definition 'restricts the operations of conscience to to ourselves, and withdraws it altogether from what is usually called the intellectual part of our nature.'[23] Conscience, that is to say, does not have the role of passing judgment upon our own actions or those of others. The mind determines the difference between right and wrong actions; conscience, having its seat in the emotions, expresses approval or disapproval. This, he claims, follows the natural order of events: we determine that something is right or wrong, and then we approve or disapprove of it. The theory of Henry Grove, the eighteenth-century Dissenting academy tutor at Taunton and ethicist, to the effect that conscience is not a power or faculty of the mind, but is simply 'reason or understanding considered in the relation it bears to [a person's] actions in their moral nature and most important consequences' is, accordingly, 'obviously incorrect.'[24] For 'An emotion can never be traced to the reason or judgment. The intellect can no more give us feelings, than the sensitive part of our nature can give us notions or ideas.'[25] Payne recognizes a certain similarity between his own position and that of Hutcheson, for we do have a susceptibility for moral emotion. But Hutcheson intended his account as an explanation of the origin of our moral ideas, and this Payne reserves to the intellect. Furthermore, he agrees with Thomas Brown that the emotions of self-approbation or remorse which arise when we contemplate our own actions are not on all fours with those which arise when the actions of others are in view; for in the former case we feel what Brown calls 'a dreadful moral regret' which is lacking in the latter. Thus it is that 'Our hearts may be broken by the delinquencies of others, but conscience condemns only ourselves.'[26]

Why has God, the Moral Governor, endowed us with conscience? God first reveals his will in the Bible, calls us to voluntary obedience, and connects happiness with obedience and misery with disobedience. The function of conscience is to 'impel to the discharge of duty.'[27] Payne concludes with an appeal especially directed to his younger hearers, that they never silence the voice of conscience.

Francis Augustus Cox

Very different in tone and content is Francis Augustus Cox's contribution to a series of thirteen lectures to Socialists and others, delivered under the auspices of the Christian Instruction Society.[28] Cox was educated at Bristol Baptist College and gained his MA at Edinburgh University. He supplied the pastorate at Cambridge for a year, and then entered upon a forty-year ministry at Mare Street, Hackney. He was active in social reform, and a pioneer of London University, of whose inaugurating committee he was secretary, and whose first librarian he became. On 4 December 1839 he delivered his lecture on *The Nature and Design of Moral Government*. Basing himself upon Psalm 66: 7, Cox takes it as evident that there is a God by whom the world was created; and that we have physical and mental faculties, and that we must die. As the Psalm says, the rebellious exalt themselves against God's creative power and moral government. Expanding upon God's moral governorship, Cox explains that God is sovereign: the world is not at the mercy of caprice. Moreover, God's government is irresistibly powerful, universal in extent, essentially benevolent and, since its present operation is modified by Adam's Fall, such as to place human beings on probation. Wilful departure from God's law is a source of human misery — misery which can be alleviated only by returning in love and obedience to God. The greatest human exercise of benevolence is to make God's claims known, and to call people to return to him. Since God has graciously revealed his will, we should do well to heed it.

In the course of his address Cox defined Socialists as those who say that we can know nothing of God. In his opinion, therefore, atheists remove a major buttress against wanton immorality. This led to a challenge to Cox from the floor of the meeting: What part of Robert Owen's system yields the conclusion that Socialists set out to demoralize society? The question was ruled out of order and Cox was relieved of the necessity of justifying or withdrawing what was clearly deemed an inflammatory charge.[29] It was certainly a tendentious one; for while Robert Owen (1771-1858), whose 'socialism' was an amalgam of communal self-help and co-operative business methods in face of social deprivation, undoubtedly believed that all religions were morally deficient, his efforts were directed towards character-building and the development of self-sufficient communities.

Ralph Wardlaw

We must now direct our attention north of the border, to Ralph Wardlaw (1779-1853),[30] uncle of Gilbert and friend of George Payne, Joseph Fletcher and Henry Foster Burder. Having gained his MA (Glasgow), he trained in Selkirk for the ministry (1795-1800) at the Theological Hall of the Associate Secession Church under George Lawson, who served as professor from 1787 until his death on 21 February 1820.[31] Influenced by James and Robert Haldane, and at a time when the church-state question was being widely discussed, Wardlaw became a Congregationalist in 1801, and after serving briefly in Perth and Dumfries, he was ordained and inducted to the pastorate of Albion (later West George) Street church in 1803. There he remained until he died, combining his ministerial duties with the chair of systematic theology in the newly-founded Glasgow [Congregational] Theological Academy from 1811 to 1853.

Wardlaw wrote against Socinianism and, above all, against church-state establishments. Many of his sermons were printed, and he also wrote hymns, a few of which are used to this day, and compiled a hymnal. He produced a number of moderately Calvinistic theological works, in which his indebtedness to Edward Williams, Andrew Fuller and Archibald McLean is clear. Of Wardlaw the philosopher, W.L. Alexander,[32] Wardlaw's former student and successor as professor of theology, declared,

> The most prominent feature of Dr. Wardlaw's mind lay in his rare powers of analysis and ratiocination. His intellect was eminently dialectic and diacritical. . . . His peculiar work was that of the philosopher and the critic. . . . His power of analysis was great. . . . To this power and this love of analytical investigation he added comprehensiveness of survey and sagacity of decision. . . . His view was penetrating, but it was also extensive.[33]

Wardlaw's most significant philosophico-theological work is *Christian Ethics; or, Moral Philosophy on the Principles of Divine Revelation* (2nd edn., 1834). Delivered in 1833, this is the first of the series of Congregational Lectures. Wardlaw grants at the outset that his title presupposes the existence of God and the authority of the Scriptures. Indeed, God 'evidently lies at the foundation of all religious principle, – of all moral obligation. Deny a God, and you annihilate both.'[34] He further assumes that human nature is fallen, and regrets that in overlooking this fact philosophy, as frequently taught, is 'in many of its principles, unbaptised and covertly antichristian.'[35] He denies that a scheme of virtue can be deduced from the present state of (depraved) human nature, and faults a number of ethical systems – those of Aristotle, the Stoics, the Epicureans, Hutcheson, Hume, Cudworth, Clarke, Price, Adam Smith and the utilitarians – for failing to pay due heed to this deficiency: '[I]f human nature be in a state of depravity, conscience, directly or indirectly, must partake of that depravity.'[36] In all of this we see that Wardlaw's stance is not only at the opposite pole in ethics to that of his eighteenth-century, theologically 'advanced' predecessor, John Taylor, for example, but that it also places him at some distance from his moderate Calvinist friend, George Payne.

Although he speaks of Butler with great respect, Wardlaw subjects his views to extensive criticism, regretting that Butler overlooks the fact that 'What we are accustomed to call the *natural* state of man, is, in truth, the most *unnatural* the mind can conceive:- inasmuch as there can be nothing more directly at variance with the essential and immutable *nature of things*, than that an intelligent creature should be in a state of alienation from his Creator.'[37] Moral principles, he insists, may be found only in the divine nature, and this is sufficiently revealed to us in the Bible, our only sure guide to moral truth.

In his discussion of moral obligation Wardlaw insists that our conduct must be regulated by the will of God, the Supreme Governor. His will is 'the immediate rule of duty and ground of obligation,' but it is not 'capricious and arbitrary', for it conforms to those principles of rectitude which subsist in God's nature.[38] Rightly understood, morality and religion are identical, for to love God is to keep his commandments (I John 5: 3). While there is, indeed, a proper self-love, 'love to God *merely* for what we receive from him *is not love to God at all.*'[39]

Wardlaw works towards his conclusion, registering his dissent from certain views of Timothy Dwight, William Paley and Jonathan Edwards as he goes. His conviction is that the Christian gospel not only reforms but regenerates, and deals with the root of all evil. By it we are restored to fellowship with God, and are thus enabled to love both God and neighbour – especially those of 'the household of faith.' He looks forward to the extension of the reign of Christ, to the resurrection of the just, and to 'the happiness of A SINLESS WORLD.'[40]

Although Wardlaw's *Christian Ethics* ran to a number of editions, not all were persuaded by his argument. A reviewer queried Wardlaw's basic notion that because of depravity human beings cannot be assured regarding the fundamental truths which natural theology has traditionally been supposed to teach. For if we can but have faith in those truths, 'the *evidences* of that faith have no power of affecting our minds, except through the medium of those very powers whose authority has been previously thrown aside . . .' and thus we land in scepticism.[41] To this criticism Wardlaw replied in the preface to the third edition of his book (1836). He did not, he says, contend that reason is so depraved that human beings cannot appreciate the grounds on which the truths of natural religion rest. Were that the case we should not be accountable. Rather, his view was that reason labours under the impediment of depravity and so is led to wrong conclusions.

To Alexander, this was one concession too many:

> For it appears from this reply, that all he intended to assert was, that natural reason and conscience are *liable* to be perverted in their decisions on moral questions. But if this is all he means to teach, then we may observe, in the first place, that his doctrine is one which the adherents of nearly all the theories on which he has animadverted, would at once admit as perfectly compatible with their principles; and in the second place, that as the alleged liability affects our reason and conscience only in the way of perverting their decisions, this can have no bearing upon the *foundation* of moral distinctions, but will operate exclusively on our practical determination and application of the *standard* or *rule* of morals.[42]

Again,

> If moral disorder unfit a man for ascertaining aright the truths unfolded by the hand of the Creator in the constitution of the moral universe, will it not equally unfit him for ascertaining aright the truths unfolded by the word of the Creator in the Scriptures?[43]

These criticisms notwithstanding, Alexander declares that

> Nothing, I think, can be more admirable and convincing than [Wardlaw's] proof that the only foundation of moral truth is to be found in the divine essence; and if he had contented himself with affirming the effect of depravity in leading men to set aside the dictates of conscience, whether instructed by the law of nature or by the written law of the Bible, instead of asserting man's inability to read the one law while he admits his ability to read the other, his moral system would, in my humble judgment, have been complete and unassailable.[44]

Thomas Jackson

Turning from Scottish Congregationalists to an English Wesleyan, we find that Thomas Jackson took it upon himself to distinguish between Christianity and moral philosophy in favour of the former. Jackson was an autodidact, of whom it was written, 'Without brilliant parts and without educational advantages he applied himself with all his heart to the improvement of such talents and opportunities as were granted to him, and with the Lord's pound he gained ten pounds.'[45] After serving numerous circuits, Jackson was appointed tutor at the southern branch of the Theological Institution at Richmond. Here he remained from 1842 until ill health forced his resignation in 1861.

In *The Duties of Christianity Theoretically and Practically Considered* (1857), Jackson undertakes to propound 'the system of duty that Christianity recognises and enforces.'[46] In the course of doing this he draws this distinction: 'Moral philosophy attempts to ascertain the duties of men from what is called the light of nature and of reason; whereas Christianity places before us a system of duty as a matter of direct revelation from God.'[47] Although moral philosophers hold that we discover the will of God by considering those actions which we feel to be morally wrong or right, in practice they are frequently at a loss concerning the appropriate course of action; their decisions lack authority, and are at the mercy of depraved passion.[48] The truth is that moral philosophy is chiefly useful as an introduction to Christianity. Christianity places us directly before God's revelation in the Bible, and from this source – especially from the Decalogue and the teaching of Jesus, we draw ample moral guidance.

Further contrasts follow: moral philosophy regards humanity as a work of God; Christianity regards persons as fallen and depraved creatures. Moral philosophy says nothing of forgiveness and hence 'calls upon mankind to discharge all the duties of religion and morality, under the power of a depraved conscience.'[49] Moral philosophy assumes that people have power to perform their duty, but Christianity declares that their ability comes from the grace of God through Jesus Christ. Moral philosophy derives its motives from the reason and fitness of things; Christianity from the redeeming mercy of God. Moral philosophy teaches us to discern the will of God in the constitution of nature, while Christianity directs us to 'the will and glory of Christ in His mediatorial office and character.'[50] Finally, the teleology of moral philosophy is temporal, that of Christianity is eternal. His foundations laid, Jackson proceeds to discuss the nature of prayer; self-government; marriage and family life; masters and servants; civil rulers and subjects; and Christians in relation to civil rulers and society at large.

John Howard Hinton

A further alumnus of Bristol Baptist College and the University of Edinburgh comes next to our attention. John Howard Hinton, MA (Edin.) held pastorates at Haverfordwest (1816-1820) and Hosier Street, Reading (1820-1837), thereafter residing first in Reading and then in Bristol. He was secretary of the Baptist Union (1837-1866), and a voluminous writer.[51] In ethics as in theology, Hinton had a good deal to say concerning human responsibility: indeed, so keen was he to uphold this that some on the Calvinist wing of the Baptist movement were highly suspicious of him as one who, they thought, played down God's saving initiative and the regenerating work of the Holy Spirit. Hinton argues strenuously for the six elements which, in his view, constitute human responsibility, 'namely, that action should be independent, intelligent, and free; that man should be competent to what is required of him, should act in view of sufficient motives, and experience an adequate impulse.'[52] Theological hackles were raised when Hinton explained that 'God, having endowed mankind with faculties for acting independently of himself, exercises within the sphere of that action no predetermining power over their conduct.' To any who may think that this flew in the face of God's ordination of the ungodly to perdition, Hinton retorted,

> I do not hold this sentiment, which, however, is too common. I see neither necessity nor warrant for believing that God has predestinated any man to destruction. It is enough in this respect that he has ordained general principles, the operation of which accomplishes, without personal predestination, the punishment of transgressors.[53]

In *Elements of Moral Philosophy* Hinton discusses first the principles of the discipline and then their relation to practice. He briefly sketches moral theories through history, and then considers the moral properties of human nature. He notes that some moral philosophers have had recourse to a moral sense, others to education, imitation and habit. These he regards as different interpretations of the fact that 'every man of sound mind does approve certain actions, and disapprove the contrary;' and whether moral judgments are instinctive or acquired makes no difference to that fact.[54] He then returns to his theme that 'Moral agency implies free agency,'[55] and acknowledges a debt to Jonathan Edwards's writings on the will. The sphere of ethical activity is constituted by those relations in which human beings (who are not insulated) find themselves. These relations require corresponding conduct, and they constitute the foundation of virtue. But whence comes the obligation of virtue? From God, who commands what is right 'because he knows it to be suitable to the relations he has established, of which, and the duties which flow from them, his whole preceptive will is declaratory.'[56] As for the motives to virtue, 'To a mind rightly constituted and free from evil bias, the fitness of actions to existing relations will be a motive of no small power.'[57] In addition, God has established the connection between virtue and happiness, vice and misery, and, as moral governor, has promulgated his law. As to the practice of the moral life, our duty towards universal being is (following Edwards on virtue) encapsulated in the concept of benevolence. Hinton then discusses in turn our relations to God, the connubial relation, the parental relation, and social relations.

George Lyon Turner and John Hensley Godwin

The Congregationalist George Lyon Turner was educated at Cheshunt College. Following a pastorate at Long Melford, Suffolk (1868-1870) he became tutor at Hackney College (1870-1880) and then professor at Lancashire Independent College (1880-1889). On resigning his chair he returned to pastoral charge at Algernon Road, Lewisham (1890-1903). Best known for his historical researches, Turner also had psychological interests, and these emerge in his wide-ranging study, *Wish and Will: an Introduction to the Psychology of Desire and Volition* (1880). He deals with ethical issues briefly in chapters XII and XIII. He discusses freedom and necessity, and the self-determining power of the will, with reference to Hobbes, Locke, Bain, Mill, M'Cosh, Kant and Edwards – whose anti-Arminian argument is deemed to be 'pure logomachy.'[58]

In 1885 Turner's fellow Congregationalist, J.H. Godwin, published a companion volume to his *Intellectual Principles* under the title, *Active Principles; or, Elements of Moral Science*. He sets out from the conviction that if we wish to know what is best for us – and everyone does wish to know this – we must have some understanding of our selves and our surroundings. Emotions, desires and affections are of primary importance in self-understanding, and the most serious errors are made by those who focus upon part of human nature as if it were the whole. For example, by embracing presuppositions which deny their own personality and run counter to the common sense of humanity, agnostics and materialists cannot acknowledge the personality of anyone else: 'If the personal I, the conscious Self, is a delusion, nothing can be known.'[59] On this basis Godwin proceeds to examine the nature of moral science. Just as knowledge begins with sensations which are transient but goes on to intelligence, so feelings, which are also sensory, go on to emotions and affections, which are as enduring as intelligence. Emotions and affections are 'the chief sources of human happiness, and the prime motives of human action.'[60] They are subject to control, they depend upon habitual conduct, and their regulators are reason and conscience. Narrowly construed, moral science concerns dispositions and actions 'which result from reflection, and show the character of the agent as apprehended by Conscience';[61] but in a broader sense moral science comprehends all the sources of voluntary action, and hence encompasses the study of mental feelings and volitions.

We thus move in Part One to an analysis of the simple emotions of joy, grief, surprise and wonder. There follows a discussion of propensities and passions: desires, aversions, hope and fear; and of social affections, including those which are pleasant and attractive, such as benevolence, gratitude and compassion, and those which are painful and repulsive, such as anger and resentment, jealousy and contempt. Following a declaration that 'The feelings which are natural, proper and useful, when directed to others, must be equally so when directed to Self,'[62] Godwin discusses the reflexive affections: self-love, self-esteem and shame. The religious affections of fear, adoration, gratitude and faith are next under review, and then we turn to the 'indefinite affections' of beauty and sublimity – terms which are extended by association and sympathy from the objects to which they are first applied to those which are entirely intellectual and moral. As to the relation between the beautiful, the true and the good, Godwin argues that we err if we draw inferences from one to another as if they were of the same class: 'Beauty is not the same for all persons, times, and places, like Truth; nor is it, like Good, comprehensive of the whole nature of any being. . . . The less beautiful may have more of the real and permanent God, compared with which the highest known Beauty is not worthy of any regard.'[63]

Part Two concerns volitions. The will, says Godwin, like all mental faculties, is known only by inference, but choice – exercises of will – is directly known. He discusses the objects of choice: ends and means; and the motives of choice: feelings, judgments, previous volitions – which, though they are the natural causes of volitions, are not necessarily connected with their consequents. But the idea of volition raises those of liberty and necessity, and Godwin presents arguments for both of these, concluding in favour of libertarianism. He contends that those who seek to demonstrate the necessity of moral actions commit the fallacy of *petitio principii* by presupposing that there is no difference between natural events and moral actions – something of which Jonathan Edwards, no less, is guilty. His 'Logic is quite certain when the Psychology is very doubtful.'[64] For 'Volitions are not like involuntary movements, the *effects* of previously existing *causes*; nor are all Motives commensurable, – similar in nature and in their mode of operation. The Necessity which belongs to all Nature does not include the Will of man.'[65] After all, 'They who can choose what is good, must be able to choose what is not good.'[66]

In Part Three Godwin discusses moral perceptions and sentiments on the basis that these are built upon natural good and right. Whereas what is naturally good is so before it is known and chosen, what is morally good is the object of free choice. Similarly, natural right, in the sense of fitness for some end, is a concept learned by children before they are capable of choosing moral ends. This leads to a consideration of moral right and good in which Godwin analyses the nature of virtue, and the special virtues: prudence, industry, temperance, courage, gratitude, compassion benevolence, respectfulness, justice and veracity. He next turns to the special vices, which are the contraries of the foregoing: imprudence, indolence, and so forth. His conclusion is that 'What is Morally good is not so because it is commanded, but it is commanded because it is good. And what is Morally bad is not so because it is forbidden, but it is forbidden because it is bad.'[67] Conscience is 'the capacity of knowing what is *morally* right and wrong. . . . Conscience is a form of Intelligence, as well as sensibility.'[68] It is indicative, therefore, as showing what is right and wrong; it is attractive as drawing us to the best; and it is imperative: 'It speaks to command and threaten, as well as to invite and persuade.'[69] Its deliverances can, however, be disregarded or resisted. Hence, 'If our *faculties* are properly exercised, and all available *evidence* is duly considered, then the voice of Conscience is the voice of God; but not otherwise.'[70] Godwin's book ends with a fairly brief discussion of moral judgments, moral discipline, and moral theories. As to the first, he argues that 'The dispositions and actions which are Virtues, in those by whom they are possessed, are Duties and Obligations, in relation to those to whom they are due. . . . All duties and obligations to others, become, with religious knowledge, duties and obligations to the creator and Governor of all; and the disregard of these is Sin. . . . Duties are not based on Rights; but both depend on what is Morally Right, in relation to individuals, to society, and to the Supreme Ruler.'[71]

In the context of moral discipline Godwin declares that 'The appearance of Jesus Christ on earth has changed the moral history of the world. His personal influence is the highest and best, to be found in any age or country.'[72] Evils have come from Christianity, but none from Christ, and 'All who have received Him as their Teacher, Leader, and Saviour, have found that a Divine influence comes to them, as they seek to learn of Him and to follow Him.'[73] The moral theories passed in swift review are those which turn upon self-interest – a basis contrary to the consciousness of humanity; utilitarian theories, which do not take us to the heart of morality, for while we are pleased when we have done something because it is useful, we approve of doing what is right; personal and intuitional theories, which do not suffice because, for example, 'The simple command of Conscience, the categorical imperative of the Practical Reason, has alone little power, and no moral authority';[74] and theological theories, which, while they should not claim that apart from religion there can be no morality, nevertheless rightly claim that the latter is sustained by the former, and that 'Whatever is known to be the Divine Will, is known to be Morally Right'[75] – a conclusion which begs a huge question.

James Martineau

The ethical contribution of Unitarian James Martineau is among the weightiest and most thorough to emerge from the Nonconformist stable. Martineau was, as we have seen, a student of William Turner at Manchester College, York. He was reared on Hartley's necessarianism and influenced by its continuation in the writings of Joseph Priestley. This teaching was mediated *via* Thomas Belsham's work of 1801, *Elements of the Philosophy of the Human Mind*, which Turner used as a text book from 1809 to 1827.[76] On completing his training Martineau assisted at his old school in Bristol for a year, and then in 1828 he was called to the Presbyterian church at Eustace Street, Dublin. In 1832 he began his ministry at Paradise Street chapel, Liverpool, and in 1840 added a tutorship at Manchester New College, Manchester, to his duties.[77] But even as he began to pass on the determinism in which he had been reared he was, under the influence of Wordsworth, Coleridge and F.D. Maurice, thinking his way out of it. As he wrote, 'The change of view was very inconvenient to me.'[78] He had to rewrite his lectures, and there were no suitable text books. But the deliverance of spirit which he felt made it all worthwhile: 'It was an escape from a logical cage into the open air.'[79] The predominant cause of the change of views was 'the irresistible pleading of the moral consciousness.' This 'drove me to rebel against the limits of the merely scientific conception. . . .'[80]

Thus was Martineau led to develop his ethical theism. In the course of so doing he was bound to ponder the relation between religion and ethics, and this he did in an inaugural lecture delivered at Manchester New College, by then in London, of which he was the principal. He recognizes that the Roman Catholic Church has always understood that

> the right guidance of life is inseparable from the functions of religion. On the other hand, Luther, denying all religious value to Morals, flung them, as a mere matter of police into the hands of the civil magistrate. And the first volume of the 'Congregational Lectures' instituted almost half a century ago was written to prove that Christianity repudiates Ethics as *ab initio* impossible to the vitiated reason and conscience of a fallen nature. The study thus ignominiously cast out to the 'infidel,' he in his turn is very ready to pick up, all the more from its being unencumbered with theology.[81]

To Martineau, 'Ethics treat of the right-ordering of Personal Relations, so far as these may be made better or worse by our will.'[82] Ethics, he argues, concern 'the entire ground of *character*,' and this being so,

> if in our character there be a part which has reference to the Infinitude which surrounds our life, a system of thought, a type

of feeling, which omits this part and treats it as though it were not, can be but a truncated moral structure, resembling the whole much as a Gothic Hôtel de Ville resembles a cathedral without its transepts and its towers.[83]

Our conscience admits us into a personal relation with the living Spirit of God, and with this the authority of duty becomes transcendent and divine; the scope of duty becomes co-extensive with the area of the will; the moral life is regarded in its cosmic dimension, and its enthusiasm is 'intensified by the consciousness of its Divine Source.'[84] Thus religion, concerning as it does the supreme personal relation, completes and transfigures ethics.

These ideas underlie Martineau's *Types of Ethical Theory* (1885). He here works his way through the positions of Plato, Descartes, Malebranche, Spinoza, Comte, the utilitarians and hedonists, Cudworth, Clarke, Price, Shaftesbury and Hutcheson, with a view to maintaining his libertarian position, to upholding conscience as the fount of moral insight, and to denying the validity of all theories which find the rightness of an action in its consequences or in intellectual intuitions. In 1890 Martineau followed up with *The Seat of Authority in Religion*, in which, over against Church and Bible, he sets up conscience as 'the very "Seat of Authority" of which I was in search.'[85]

William Theophilus Davison and George G. Findlay

With two of the Wesleyan Fernley Lectures our review of Nonconformist moral philosophy may fittingly close. Forced by adverse circumstances to relinquish his scholarship to Exeter College, Oxford, Davison spent thirteen years in circuit ministry. He was appointed classical tutor at Richmond College in 1881, subsequently becoming professor of Biblical literature and Hebrew. In 1891 he removed to Handsworth College as theological tutor, and then became connexional editor in 1904. A year later he returned to Richmond College as theological tutor, and became principal in 1909. He retired in 1920. His Fernley Lecture, *The Christian Conscience. A Contribution to Christian Ethics*, was published in 1888. Setting out from the conviction that 'The very power of forming a judgment on our own life differentiates man from all other orders of being on earth,'[86] he proceeds to show that the study of conscience has a threefold value. It is valuable in apologetics, which has neglected the study of humanity in favour of the question of God, because 'if the spiritual nature of man be once demonstrated and admitted, the way is clear for a line of argument from which we are otherwise excluded.'[87] It is valuable for theology, which has, at least in Britain, neglected conscience or consigned it to ethics – an especially unfortunate state of affairs where evangelical theology is concerned. And conscience's practical importance as the guide of life cannot be overestimated. After providing a brief history of the idea of conscience, Davison turns to the question of the genesis of the natural as understood by (then) current science. In effect he argues for a division of labour: the evolutionary scientists must till the physical soil, but of any attempt to account for the human conscience on the basis of the struggle for existence among the most favoured brutes it must be said 'that the whole chain of evidence, if it be supposed to be drawn from history, is purely imaginary.'[88] The evolutionary theory mistakenly points to the mechanical origin of moral ideas, and is determinist in character.

Davison next discusses the basis and character of the natural conscience. It is, he declares, essentially cognitive, and Kant, with his emphasis upon the unconditional nature of obligation, is applauded for delineating 'the only true foundation of morals for man.'[89] But Kant does not help us at the point of practice. Duty is to be done for duty's sake – but what, in real life, is to be done? Having found hedonism wanting, Davison finds the true guide of conscience in the will of God: conscience serves a higher authority. Hence (how different from Payne's restriction of conscience to the emotion) 'the judgment of conscience is always more or less accompanied by feelings – feelings which are quite inseparable from the judgment, and which condemn or acquit in a peculiar and characteristic way, constituting an atmosphere altogether different from the *lumen siccum* in which a purely intellectual judgment is delivered.'[90] The way in which conscience points beyond itself suggests that religion cannot be left out of account when analysing it.

On the other hand, 'much mischief has been done by the attempt to prove the entire dependence of moral knowledge upon revelation.'[91] Natural morality and the natural conscience are to be vindicated, not repudiated, for 'God has "not left Himself without witness" among men, all direct revelation apart.'[92] The fact remains, however, that 'personal man implies a personal God.'[93] So to Davison's case for the view that 'the Christian religion meets the demands, satisfies the needs, fulfils the aspirations of the human conscience.'[94] In all of this Christianity's ability to renew, and not simply to instruct, the conscience is of much importance. It does this by describing the evil and consequences of sin, and by proclaiming forgiveness through the Cross of Christ. Moreover, the offer is not of forgiveness upon condition of repentance, as Martineau and others teach: 'Christianity offers to man an Atonement.'[95] The conclusion is that 'The natural conscience becomes transformed into the Christian conscience when the revelation of God in Christ is accepted as final and authoritative.'[96]

The Fernley Lecture of George G. Findlay, an alumnus of Richmond College, who gave most of his working life to Headingly College, is entitled, *Christian Doctrine and Morals viewed in their Connexion* (1894).[97] He recognizes that he is writing in an intellectual environment in which the current of unbelief is strong, so that we cannot say as Henry Wace said twenty years before that 'the obligation of the more conspicuous principles of Christian morality is accepted by all the writers with whom we have practically to deal.'[98] Our current situation resembles that which Butler faced, and it has to be shown that religion is the parent of the highest morality, and that Christian creed and Christian conduct are one. Findlay thus discusses the doctrines of the fatherhood of God, the incarnation of the Son, the indwelling of the Spirit, the atonement for sin, the resurrection of the body, the coming judgment and eternal life with a view to showing their ethical implications.

Clearly, with the works of Davison and Findlay, we stand at a crossroads. They point in one direction towards a host of manuals of Christian ethics, some of which have little relation to moral philosophy as such: these I cannot here unearth.[99] In another direction they point towards Christian apologetics, and to this varied field we now turn.

II: Apologetics

Of all the broadly philosophical branches of enquiry, apologetics engaged more writers than any other in the nineteenth century, and yielded the largest published output and the most extensive secondary literature.[100] It would be impossible, and highly repetitive, to describe every article, tract and book issued by Nonconformists in defence of the faith, but the following selection will sufficiently indicate the diversity of contributions, ranging from the scholarly and measured to the popular and polemical, which appeared under this broad heading.

If, in the early decades of the century and, in the person of Henry Rogers, for example, lingering into its second half, the apologetic methods of Butler and Paley, and the 'evidences' of miracle and the fulfilment of prophecy were formative, a change of style and a burgeoning of apologetic activity becomes evident following the publication of Darwin's *The Origin of Species* in 1859. Motivated by the perceived need to counter increasingly vocal exponents of naturalism, materialism, humanism, agnosticism, atheism and secularism, many Nonconformist (as well as other) philosophers turned their attention to the defence of the faith. It is not too much to say that in the second half of the nineteenth century a veritable apologetic 'industry' developed with products ranging from the most sophisticated to the most polemical and even scurrilous.

At the farthest remove from scurrility (and hysteria), A.M. Fairbairn spoke for many when, in a lecture delivered at the opening of the 1878 session at Airedale College, he declared,

> The conflict of Faith in our day is most arduous and fell. It lives surrounded by great potential enemies. Science cannot publish her discoveries without letting us hear the shock of their collision with the ancient Faith. The political philosopher seeks to show how the State can live and prosper without religion; the ethical thinker how right can exist and law govern without God. A philosophy that denies the surest and most necessary religious truths works in harmony with a criticism that resolves into mythologies the holiest religious histories. A large section of our literature, including some of the finest creations of living imagination, interpret Nature and man, exhibit life and destiny from the standpoint of those who have consciously renounced belief in God and can find on earth nothing divine but humanity. Our working men listen to theories of life that leave around them only blank material walls, within them no spiritual reality, before them no higher and larger hope. With so many forces inimical to faith at work in our midst, men find it easier to assume an attitude of absolute antagonism either, on the one hand, to Faith, or, on the other to Knowledge. There is a so fine simplicity in such an attitude that the simplest person can hold it and feel himself both strong and safe. Yet that position alone is secure and permanent where the man can say, 'Faith and reason are alike sons of God, and have alike the right to be and to be honoured. The realities of the world are truths of God; the truths of God are realities of the spirit; and all that has its being in Him must be perfect and harmonious as Himself.'[101]

Robert Aspland

But let us retrace our steps to the turn of the eighteenth century. There we meet Robert Aspland, whose spiritual pilgrimage is of particular interest. He began among the Baptists, though they increasingly suspected his doctrinal soundness; he forsook Calvinism whilst at Aberdeen University, left the University and became an Arian. He accepted preaching appointments as invited, whilst working in his father-in-law's business. Pastorates followed at Newport, Isle of Wight (1801-1805), Norton, Derbyshire (a few months in 1805), and finally forty years at Hackney. In 1802 he left Arianism in favour of the simple humanity of Christ, and in 1812 he opened Hackney Unitarian Academy, which survived until 1818.[102] In a sermon on *The Power of Truth*, delivered in 1815, Aspland makes clear his conviction that the truth has nothing to fear from doctrinal openness. He defines truth as 'the conformity of our ideas to things themselves;' it is 'right reason'.[103] Revealed religion 'is pre-eminently truth, truth of greatest moment and influence.'[104] Even though human beings are imperfect, truth will prevail, and humanity is being led 'perpetually to higher degrees of improvement.'[105] A sign of the omnipotence of truth is that erroneous doctrines, once believed by Christians, have been exploded because they were at war with common sense, civil and religious liberty, and social happiness. He proceeds to recommend apologetic activity to his congregation:

> In spite of all the outcry concerning the tendency of rational religion to scepticism, I cannot help suspecting their Christian faith to be in greatest danger, who either never study the true evidences in behalf of our religion, or who estimate their faith by frames and feelings, impulses and raptures, or who are met and stopt in their inquiries by phrases which common sense must not handle, doctrines into which reason must not penetrate, and by articles and creeds which must not be tied to the Scriptures. It is among those who are unprepared for our enemy that he makes the greatest havoc.[106]

This powerful passage, which contains many of the Unitarian bogeymen, also rests upon the early Unitarian commitment to the principle of the sufficiency of Scripture.

George Redford and James Bennett

In 1821 the Congregationalist George Redford, an alumnus of Hoxton Academy and Glasgow University who ministered at Uxbridge (1812-1826) and Angel Street, Worcester (1826-1856), published a work the argument of which is sufficiently indicated by its title: *The True Age of Reason; or A Fair Challenge to Deists. A candid Examination of the Claims of Modern Deism, containing a Demonstration of the Insufficiency of Unassisted Reason to lead Mankind to Virtue, to Happiness and to God.*[107] In the 'Advertisement' he finds it satisfactory to observe that deism's revival 'is at least accompanied by no accessions of talent or learning,'[108] and brands deism 'the least defensible of any of the forms of infidelity. There is no middle place between Revelation and Atheism.'[109] Deists make much of God's benevolence, but nowhere is this more clearly seen than in the Bible, which they reject; indeed, the probability is that a benevolent God would reveal himself as, in fact, he has done in the Scriptures. In answer to the deist claim that reason is all and revelation redundant, Redford points out that the deists' first principles – for example, that there is one God – are themselves derived from revelation. Again, the deists assert immortality, but this too is beyond the competence of the religion of reason to ascertain, and hence their embracing of the belief is inconsistent with their own method. The appeal to human opinion is as nothing compared with the authoritative revelation of the mind of God in the Bible. After all,

> the writings of the philosophers are characterized by *doubt*, *uncertainty*, and *imbecility*; while revelation is harmonious, clear, decisive, and unambiguous, and what is more – *efficient* to lead man to the highest ends of his being. These facts will justify me in saying, that, in point of useful, consolatory knowledge, the humblest cottager in a Christian land, stads upon higher ground, and takes an infinitely wider range, than either Socrates or Plato.[110]

In 1847 Redford, himself a Member of the Royal College of Surgeons, published an apologetic work of quite a different kind: *Body and Soul*. The book, he declares, is for those 'who are sometimes mystified or shallowly enlightened by the confident explanations of materialists, over-chemical chemists, phrenologists, and mesmerists, and not for finished students of anatomy and physiology.'[111] Interesting as indicating the state of medical science at the time, the book is innocent of theology.

Redford's Congregational contemporary, James Bennett, was trained at Gosport Academy (1793-1796), and served at Romsey (1796-1813) and, concurrently with the principalship of Rotherham Independent College, at Masbro', Rotherham (1813-1828). He then removed to Silver Street, London (1828-1860).[112] Best known as an historian, he nevertheless prescribed *An Antidote to Infidelity* in 1831. This contains his discussion of the external evidences for Christianity; a larger, undated second edition includes also the internal evidences, and to this volume I now refer.

Bennett begins by defending miracles. He refers to Hume's view that miracles are an appeal to testimony against experience, and replies:

> Hume says, his experience tells him that the laws of nature are not altered. But his experience could tell him of nothing before he was born; nor of what happened since, except on the very limited spot where he stood. As to all that occurred prior to his existence, or as to all that was occurring, in other parts of the world, while he was speaking or writing, he could know nothing except – by what? by testimony. That very testimony he was attempting to disparage. So that, after all, he knew that the laws of nature were not frequently altered, only by testimony.[113]

Having disposed of Hume to his own satisfaction, Bennett turns to the external proofs of divinity from revelation. These proofs are miracles; such facts as the existence of the Jews, the Sabbath, Passover, Sunday as the day of worship, the Lord's Supper; and fulfilled prophecy. In passing, he challenges the deists, who contend that the Christian Sabbath is an invention of a later age, to celebrate the resurrection of the more recently deceased Thomas Paine – and even offers them Friday or Thursday on which to do it.

The internal evidences are supplied by Scripture and endorsed by the moral government of God to which the Bible testifies. From this source we have accurate information concerning ourselves as created and fallen. And in addition there is the influence of divine revelation upon beievers: they experience peace, and their lives are productive of virtue, piety and holiness. Finally, Bennett argues that all attempts to prove the Bible false fail.

Benjamin Godwin

Benjamin Godwin of Horton Baptist Academy was early in the field against atheism.[114] He had a colourful youth, running away to sea at the age of fifteen, seeing action in the Napoleonic wars, and then becoming a lay evangelist in the Forest of Dean and Cornwall. He had no formal ministerial training, but was called first to Dartmouth and then to Great Missenden. From there he went to the joint post of classical tutor at Horton, and pastor of Sion chapel, Bradford. He was for antislavery, against Robert Owen, active in popular education and the peace movement, and founder of the influential *Bradford Observer*. He subsequently became secretary of the Serampore Mission (1836-1838) and minister at New Road, Oxford (1838-1845). In 1834 he delivered a course of lectures to laypeople – especially to working men – in Bradford. This was published as *Lectures on the Atheistic Controversy*, and republished in 1853 in a revised and enlarged form as *The Philosophy of Atheism Examined, and compared with Christianity*. He argues that atheism is not in harmony with human nature's belief in an invisible power; it is forbidding in its moral aspect – not least as the fount of revolutions; and it cannot show that matter had a beginning without a maker, or that it is eternal and produced all things. He then launches a cosmological argument for God's existence, discusses his nature and attributes, and finally contrasts atheism and Christianity, especially in connection with humanity's origin, morals and happiness. Christianity wins.

Edward Higginson

Edward Higginson was an alumnus of Manchester College, York, who held pastorates at Bowl-Alley Lane Chapel, Hull (1828-1846), Westgate Chapel, Wakefield (1846-1858) and High Street Chapel, Swansea (1858-1876). During his last pastorate he also served as tutor at Carmarthen Presbyterian College, the principalship of which he was offered in 1875. According to Alexander Gordon, 'in his own denomination he ranked among its conservative scholars,'[115] but in his apologetic contribution on miracles, published in 1842, he attempts a new approach to the question. He disclaims any intention of repeating the old-style apologetic use of miracles, but cautions anti-supernaturalists against thinking that because that approach is outworn, there can be no appeal to miracles at all. He feels that too many Christian writers have given miracles not too prominent, but too early, a place in their argument. Miracles properly take their place at the argument's conclusion, when the alleged revelation has been found credible in itself: 'We do not believe Christianity true because of its miracles; but we believe its miracles true, because they are part of that Christianity which commends itself to our intellectual and moral approval.'[116] To deny the credibility of miracles is to charge Jesus with fraud or self-deception. A miracle is not an uncaused effect, it is 'an effect for the production of which the laws of Nature are not adequate'[117] and is produced by a power above nature. Against Hume he contends that miracles 'are just as fit as any other facts to be made the subjects of testimony,'[118] and he points out that 'a special and unexplained cause' may supersede 'an ordinary and understood agency, without being incompatible with it.'[119] It is necessary to take account of the occasion of any alleged miracle, and if the occasion calls for divine interposition we shall find that there is perfect harmony between nature and miracle. Christ's miracles were dignified and benevolent, and some of them were 'pointedly suggestive of the human hope of immortality.'[120] His miracles could never have 'gained general credence, in opposition to authority and interest.'[121] They were open to inspection, performed publicly, and remembered from the time of their actual occurrence. The miracles of Jesus exhibit his credentials, but were performed without any parade or boasting; to him they were the works of his Father.

Richard Alliott

In 1844 Richard Alliott delivered a discourse at York Road chapel, Lambeth, entitled, *On the Evidences of Christianity*. He was prompted to do this by the fact that 'Infidelity prevails in this parish to a fearful extent; numbers have already been led astray by the sophistry of the sceptic. . . .'[122] He discusses the authorship of the books of the New

Testament; the evidence for the credibility of the historical facts they record; and the proofs that the religion taught in the New Testament is of God. Under this last heading his proofs are first, the miracles performed by Christ and his apostles. His definition of miracle is traditional (and question-begging): 'To indicate the special interference of God an effect must be not merely a wonderful occurrence but one contrary to the established laws of nature.'[123] His second proof is the fulfilment of prophecy, and his third concerns internal evidence: we learn that God's revelation is not merely in the book of nature, but is especially adapted 'to the peculiar circumstances and wants of mankind, and this it assuredly is.'[124] He concludes by expressing the hope that in face of the evidence any unbelievers present will have their confidence shaken, and all believers will be confirmed in the faith.

On another occasion Alliott presented an undated *Lecture on the Moral Evidence of Christianity*. This type of evidence does not yield strict demonstration, but it is 'fully satisfactory to every sincere enquirer after truth.'[125] Moral evidence does not force assent, or necessarily exclude doubt, and it admits of degrees of strength. In a general sense all of Scripture constitutes moral evidence, but in a special sense moral evidence is one species of biblical evidence, and it is this sense on which he concentrates. He first infers that the Bible is moral in character and tendency from the description is gives of God's nature. If some object that that Bible reveals a sometimes capricious God, he replies that we do not know all of God's motives. As to the charge that God is unjust, – on the day of reckoning all apparent injustices will be addressed. And as to the alleged cruelty of God: if his punishments are seen in context that charge evaporates. Secondly, he infers that the Bible is moral in character and tendency from the preceptive parts of Scripture. The moral demands are lawful and, moreover, powerful motives to obey are supplied – for example, gratitude to God for the free gift of purchased salvation. The third inference is from the Bible's representation of the Gospel dispensation: pardon leads to holiness of life; the atonement exhibits the tremendous evil of sin; and the Gospel requires faith and repentance. He ends in hymnic mode:

> What if we trace the globe around,
> And search from Britain to Japan,
> There shall be no religion found
> So just to God, so safe for man.[126]

III

As we move towards the middle of the nineteenth century we begin to breathe a different air. In the wake of the assaults of Hume and Kant, the older natural theology, and the older appeal to internal and external evidences, though not, as we shall see, entirely supplanted, are supplemented by concerns, fostered by the Romantic movement, with psychology and religious experience; and there is an increasing desire to defend the Christian position against the increasingly prevalent 'isms' of materialism, agnosticism, atheism and, later, positivism.

Four Congregational apologists

Gilbert Wardlaw's writings exemplify the experiential thrust in apologetics. He graduated in the University of Glasgow and trained for the ministry at the Congregational Hall in Glasgow. His periods as tutor at Blackburn Independent Academy (1821-1823) and then as principal (1830-1843) were interspersed with a pastorate at Albany Street Congregational Church, Edinburgh. On leaving Blackburn he became a school teacher. In his 1849 work on *Experimental Evidence a Ground for Assurance that Christianity is Divine* he laments that evidence of this kind has been inexplicably neglected. When considering the divine origin of the Christian's experience the following possibilities confront us: first, that Christian experience is directly produced by divine regenerating power; secondly, that it results from the external means of Bible and church institutions which operate rationally upon human minds without supernatural influence; thirdly, that it results from the combination of the two former possibilities. He argues for the third option.

Just over twenty years later Wardlaw published *The Leading Christian Evidences*. By now, although primarily wishing to establish the faith of Christians, he is more concerned than before with Christianity's antagonists. His method is to ask first 'what kind and amount of evidence ought to be expected in a revelation from God'?[127] He then discusses the internal, experimental and historical evidence for the truth of Christianity.

With Henry Rogers we find ourselves in the presence of one in whom the apologetic method of Butler through Paley lives on; he is thus less methodologically 'modern' than some of his contemporaries.[128] But we also find ourselves in the presence of a literary man who is not above achieving his apologetic ends by having recourse to satire, allegory, and the pungent turn of phrase. The briefest account of *The Eclipse of Faith* (1852) will demonstrate the point. In this book Rogers replies to Francis

Newman's *Phases of Faith* (1850). By now Newman was sceptical of historic Christianity, and Rogers cannot understand how he can marry this scepticism with his persistent determination to remain a theist. Newman appears, thinly disguised, in the book as Fellowes. He has rejected external revelation but remains an intuitionalist theist. For this he is rebuked by the sceptic Harrington, and by Mr. B. (Henry Rogers). In a brilliant piece of writing Mr. B. recounts a dream in which all the pages in all the world's Bibles become blank, and people resort to memory by way of rediscovering the word of God. They all remember what suits them best: 'Undertakers said there was a "time to mourn"; and comedians that there was a "time to laugh"; young ladies innumerable remembered that there was a "time to love"; and people of all kinds that there was a "time to hate"; every body knew that there was a "time to speak", but a worthy Quaker reminded them that there was also a "time to keep silence".'[129] Such is the predicament of one who is content with a bookless revelation and intuitions of the divine. Later in the book we have a brilliant satire of the sceptical biblical criticism of D.F. Strauss (1805-1874) whose objective in *The Life of Jesus* (1835) was to extrude all supernaturalism from that life. Along Straussian lines Harrington determines to prove that 'Papal aggression is impossible.' A record of events c. 1850, concerning Catholic Emancipation, is discovered eighteen hundred and fifty years on (that is, after a period of time equalling that which separates Strauss from the New Testament writers), and is given Straussian treatment. It is first contended that all the names in the record are allegorical. Thus there never was a Cardinal Wiseman: 'In all probability the name was selected just in the same manner as Bunyan in his immortal Pilgrim's Progress . . . has chosen "Worldly Wiseman" for one of his characters.'[130] As for the two Newmans (Francis and John Henry),

> In all probability the names were suggested to the somewhat profane allegorico-satirical writer by that text in the English version, "put on the Newman," the new man of the *spirit*. We are almost driven to this interpretation, indeed, by the extreme and ludicrous improbability of two men – brothers – brought up in the same university, gradually receding, *pari passu*, from the same point in opposite directions, to the utmost extreme; one till he had embraced the most puerile legends of the middle ages, the other, till he had proceeded to open infidelity.[131]

Francis Newman, less than enchanted by Rogers's book, replied in an appendix to the second edition of *Phases of Faith* (1853). He felt that Rogers had treated sacred things with unbecoming levity. Rogers, in his *Defence* of 1854 retorted that he was not aware that Newman's views were sacred, and confessed that he had suppressed many 'most deserved sarcasms', and deleted many more, from his reply.[132]

In a later work, *The Superhuman Origin of the Bible* (1873), Rogers argues that 'the Bible is not such a book as man would have made if he could; or could have made if he would.' He wishes to show sceptics the difficulty they are in if they persist in positing a human origin of the Bible. He proceeds with indebtedness to Paley, but with no reference to rising modern biblical criticism which was not unconnected with the resignation of Robert Vaughan from Lancashire Independent College – which vacancy, as we saw, Rogers himself filled.[133]

Edward Miall was trained for the Congregational ministry at Wymondley academy, and served pastorates at Ware (1829-31) and Bond Street, Leicester (1831-40).[134] He then became a crusader for the disestablishment of the Church of England and, in 1852, Member of Parliament for Rochdale. He published his *Bases of Belief* in 1853. The work reached its third edition by 1861. It falls into four parts. Miall first considers 'The Phenomenon' – Christianity as a fact for moral good in the world. It is a spiritual power inseparably associated with both the teaching and the mediatorial role of Jesus Christ. In Part Two he discusses 'The Revelation' from the point of view of its objective. Neither the human being nor the material universe can awaken that spiritual life which reflects man's true nature. Hence the revelation in Christ – a revelation which is not repugnant to human reason. The shape of the argument at this point is that 'Facts lead us back to a cause whence they sprang – that cause presents itself to our notice as a professedly peculiar manifestation of the Deity to man. We look at it, and discover that it marvellously corresponds with what our nature and position required, in order to the development of our being, considered in its religious aspect.'[135]

Part Three concerns 'The Seal' – God's authentication of his revelation. In this sealing miracles are prominent, and in this connection Miall faces up to Hume's sceptical account of such phenomena. He argues first that Hume flies in the face of the fact that many have believed in miracles through time and hence Hume, unphilosophically, fails to generalize his theory from that fact: 'Mr. Hume undertakes to lay down for us the law of rational belief, either as *it is*, or as it *ought to be*. If the former, where is his induction of facts? If the latter, where is his authority?'[136] Secondly, Miall takes Hume to task for claiming that miracles are unreliable as evidence because we have to rely upon the testimony of others, which may be mistaken, whereas concerning matters of empirical fact we are not thus at risk. But, counters Miall, we rest our belief of many empirical facts upon the testimony of others [thereby bypassing a possible Humean objection to the effect that, testimony apart, there is a distinction to be drawn between facts which are currently or in principle empirically verifiable and alleged facts which are not]. Be that as it may, Miall holds that 'our belief in miracles will represent not alone our dependence on the veracity of human testimony, but the response of our reason to the purpose for which the miracles were professedly wrought.'[137] Nor can the sceptic who wishes to argue, for example, against the reality of medieval ecclesiastical miracles on the ground 'either that they had no purpose, or a bad one,' deny that 'congruity of purpose in supernatural displays of power is an element, and a proper element, in our belief of them.'[138] The upshot is that 'Mr. Hume has either mistaken or misstated the origin of human belief. It is a primary, not a secondary process of the mind. It is prior to experience, not a result of it. An act of belief, like an act of love, springs out of a felt congruity between an innate tendency, and an external object.'[139]

Finally, in Part Four, 'The Record', Miall sets out to show that the miracles of Jesus cohere with his mission, and to both the Bible affords a sufficient and reliable testimony. Miall rests his case, confident that he has met modern scepticism on the basis of 'facts which nobody can dispute, and on philosophical principles which few will venture to deny.'[140] He has sought 'not so much to supply proof, as to point out the kind of proof admissible, and to be regarded as reasonable and satisfactory.'[141]

Like Henry Rogers, Robert Vaughan, who had studied privately under William Thorp, minister of Castle Green Congregational church, Bristol, turned his attention, in his lofty, bombastic, way, to scepticism in a general lecture of 1855/6. Vaughan had held the pastorate of Angel Street, Worcester (1819-1825) and Horton Street, Kensington (1825-1843), combining the latter, from 1834, with the professorship of modern history of University College, London. His service as president of Lancashire Independent College (1843-1857) was followed by two further pastorates separated by some years of literary work: Uxbridge (1857-1860) and Torquay (1867-1868). In his lecture of *The Credulities of Scepticism* he declares that an out and out philosophical sceptic would not dare to live by his beliefs: indeed, his whole life refutes them. Moreover, if all our faculties are liars, reasoning is at an end. As for popular scepticism, the eighteenth-century deists, for example, rejected Christianity because it had not done everything, and professed faith in the light of nature though it has done nothing. By way of an attack on the credulities of contemporary spiritualists he comes to his conviction that the Christian revelation does not preclude the possibility of scepticism, because free assent to it is required. He ends with a declaration that systems antagonistic to Christianity will not destroy it. They will, however, 'ensure eternal vigilance and action, and . . . bring out that true Christian manhood, which in God's good time will prove to have been the manhood destined to rule over all the nations.'[142] So there!

James Acworth

James Acworth studied at Bristol Baptist College, and was a graduate of Glasgow University. Following a ministry from 1823 in Leeds, he became, in 1835 successor to William Steadman as principal of the Baptist Academy, Bradford, and went with it on its removal to Leeds as Rawdon College in 1859. There he remained until retirement in 1863. In 1856 he published a lecture on *The Internal Witness to Christianity*. He sets out from the fact that 'Miracles, prophecies, and intrinsic moral excellence are ordinarily adduced as the main proofs of the divine origin of Christianity.'[143] But another important witness is that specified in I John 5: 10: 'He that believeth on the Son of God, hath the witness in himself.' By 'believer' Acworth does not mean those who give intellectual assent to the propositions of Christianity, or those who observe 'just so many of the requirements of the Christian system as education, custom, example, interest, or convenience may render beneficial, agreeable, or easy, but no more.' He means, one who 'gives himself up wholly and unconditionally to the sovereign commanding sway of Jesus Christ.'[144] Such, even now, have eternal life, and nothing can shake this confidence.

As for sceptics, 'Every semblance of our appeal to experience in matters pertaining to religion is forthwith scouted by them as visionary, enthusiastic, fanatical and hypocritical.' They may be 'firmly attached to experiment and induction in enquiries relating to the phenomena of nature', but they will not apply these methods 'in relation to a far higher and more interesting character.'[145] Pardon, peace, fellowship, holiness and the hatred of sin are all aspects of the Christian experience. If unbelievers ask how they can know that believers are governed by such feelings, let them look at their lives and, if there are no ulterior motives, take the testimony as valid. The inward attestation of which he speaks is common to all believers; inexpensive – you do not even have to buy books!; ever present; inaccessible to injury of any kind; and one which 'affords undeniable evidence of personal interest in the blessings of salvation.'[146] It is important that believers use the appointed means to maintain their faith. As for those whose hearts are hardened, 'who ever (Oh, may he seriously lay to heart the startling question) who ever hardened himself against Him and prospered?'[147]

John Relly Beard

In markedly different style John Relly Beard, the first principal of the Unitarian ministerial training institute in Manchester, addressed some letters to a young man in a state of indecision. His objective is to show, in an expository rather than an antagonistic way, that religion is congenial to the human mind. Indeed, that the mind's true utterances are 'mere reflexes of God's voice, as put forth by his Spirit, whether in the accents of man's higher nature, the impressions of the universe, the declarations of Science, the great lessons of History, the general burden of the Bible, or the truly human and truly divine life of Christ.'[148] In the course of his letters he criticises Strauss, and contends that the historical evidence of Christianity lies on the same basis as that of any other historical phenomenon. In a manner which seems more than a little circular he says, 'As a science, religion is the appeal of God's Spirit to the congenial spirit of man, in the exciting in man's mind of ideas and the communication of truths which, approving themselves to the God-given inner light, are known to be true in a manner altogether peculiar to themselves.'[149]

In 1868 Beard published *A Manual of Christian Evidence*. Firmly within his sights here is J.E. Renan, whose sentimental book, *La Vie de Jésus*, in which all supernatural aspects of Jesus's life are excised, was published in 1863. In Beard's opinion, Renan's anti-supernaturalism disqualifies him for the task of writing Christ's life. For his part, Beard defends the miracles, sets the biblical view of man and God over against materialism and, with examples drawn from ancient and modern authors, argues that God bears witness to himself in history, science, the New Testament and Jesus Christ.

Henry Batchelor and Samuel McAll

Two rebuttals of atheism by Congregational ministers must now engage our attention. Henry Batchelor was trained for the ministry at Newport Pagnell Academy, and it appears that his enthusiasm for the public advocacy of causes was discerned early: his studies were terminated when he gave a lecture to the Anti-State Church Society without first seeking the permission of the professors. In 1858, now minister at Nether, Sheffield, he delivered three public lectures on *The Logic of Atheism*. His initial provocations were the lectures delivered in Sheffield by the secularist G.J. Holyoake, but he took the opportunity to deliver a comprehensive blow to atheism. The materialist Holyoake means by 'evidence' the evidence of the senses, yet even he can say, 'something *must* have existed from eternity.' In this he is quite inconsistent, for 'Eternity is a very big notion to get into a man through the tiny openings of his five senses.'¹⁵⁰ He proceeds to argue that it is a fact of our mental experience that mind is distinct from body. Furthermore, 'Our reason obliges us to believe that nature, with all its unutterable wonders, was complete in a mind before it was realized in matter.'¹⁵¹ Batchelor proceeds *via* a step-by-step demolition of Holyoake's case to his conclusion: 'To deny man's spirituality, man's intellectual and moral belief in God, man's religious capacity, man's responsibility, man's sinfulness, and man's forecasting of immortality, is as philosophically unallowable as to deny man's passions, senses, and limbs.'¹⁵² The truth is that both mind and matter exhibit 'the will, purpose, and continued design of an almighty Spirit. . . .'¹⁵³ All of which met with a most favourable review in *The Eclectic*, which assures us that Batchelor ably demolishes the atheist and 'His own arguments are fireproof. . . . If the fabric is sound, the colours are brilliant.'¹⁵⁴

That the passage of the years did not blunt Batchelor's gift for spirited advocacy is clear from his published address on *Rationalism: the Immediate Peril of the Free Churches* (1891). Ranging widely, he finds three types of religion prevalent in England: 'Rationalism, or the religion of man; Sacerdotalism, or the religion of the priest; Apostolical Christianity, or the religion of God.'¹⁵⁵ Since he declares that 'Rationalism is Christianity iced; sacerdotalism is Christianity veiled and draped, and its lineaments disguised beyond recognition, in Judaic and Pagan attire,'¹⁵⁶ it comes as no surprise to find him advocating the apostolic Christianity of the Cross, or lamenting the displacement by some theologians of the atonement in favour of the incarnation. His complaint against the rationalists is that, in ruling out of consideration matters which they think *ought* not to be, or which they cannot embrace within their presuppositions, they overstep the boundaries of properly rational enquiry. To him the movement of most eighteenth-century English Presbyterians from trinitarianism through Arianism to Unitarianism stands as a dire warning to those late nineteenth-century Congregationalists who elevate reason beyond its proper station.¹⁵⁷

The Sceptic's Credulity; or, the Logic of Atheism by Samuel McAll, principal of Hackney Theological Seminary, is among the most elegantly written apologies to have fallen within our purview. McAll was trained at Rotherham College, and after a pastorate at Hallgate, Doncaster (1829?-1843) he succeeded Richard Alliott at Castle Gate church, Nottingham (1843-1860). He became principal of Hackney Congregational College in 1860, remaining until retirement in 1881. His apology was first published during his ministry in Nottingham, and was a response to the fact that 'Great efforts were making at the time to diffuse through the Manufacturing Towns atheistical opinions, under the name of Secularism and Socialism. It was common for Christian Ministers to be publicly challenged to defend their principles.'[158] This work represents his defence. He rests mainly on the design argument, flowing down from Paley, and before him from John Howe, and he writes especially for the young.

He encourages his readers not to imagine that because the Christian system is attacked it is necessarily doubtful. He points out that no personal ill-will is borne towards sceptics; that their differing from Christians is not an offence; and that the advocates of religion are not so enthusiastic for controversy as some would suggest. Again, we should not infer from the great number of apologetic works that 'the cause of divine truth is thought to be in jeopardy. . . . The sure foundation does not give way.'[159] He proceeds to consider the sorry condition of the youthful atheist, who denies a truth almost universally accepted and, as a result, is suspected by his fellows – even becoming 'a kind of *outlaw*.'[160] Some say that they simply do not attempt to account for the existence of the universe, they simply marvel at it; but when believers adduce arguments from design they inconsistently repudiate them. Undeterred, McAll proceeds with his teleological argument on the basis that theism 'resolves itself into a few very plain axioms – that every effect must have an adequate cause; that an act pre-supposes a competent agent; and that a plan evinces the pre-existence of a mind to contrive it.'[161] Even if materialism could be established, it would not wreck theism, for since materialism asserts that intelligence results from the mutual action of non-intelligent substances, we could still ask, 'who brought the several particles together, in the proportions, and in the relative positions, necessary to produce it?'[162]

There is a popular and ignorant form of atheism which assumes that the universe has been from eternity. But this is to embrace 'a creed which contains, at least, quite as much mystery as ours. He believes in everlasting NATURE; we believe in ONE who is Himself "The everlasting God, Were all the nations dead."'[163] More learned varieties of atheism are no more satisfactory. The atheism of ancient Greece, where 'It was gravely taught that the universe was the result of a fortuitous concourse of atoms – driven by a force, no one knew from whence, and tossed together as the wildest chance would have it' with the result that we have order and beauty and not chaos, is incredible. Equally unacceptable is the atheism

> with which some of the German metaphysicians bewilder their fellow men, and probably bewilder themselves also. When you ask for an explanation of the existence of the universe, you do not expect to be called to define the abstract idea of "existence".

> You do not expect to be sent back into the depths of your own consciousness to settle the point, whether you yourself exist. Nor can you, at the bidding of these philosophers, throw away half a life-time in scrutinizing the import of that little pronoun "I". A plain subject is not to be mystified after a fashion so dreary as this. . . . Let us be thankful if, instead of such philosophy, we possess a scantling, at least, of common sense.[164]

In McAll's opinion, the most prevalent form of atheism at the present time is that associated with the idea of Development. While this "theory" (his emphasis) may be held in association with belief in an intelligent first cause, it frequently is not; in which case it becomes the false doctrine that 'matter has *power* to *act* independently.'[165] This he stoutly denies, and with it any idea that there can be transmission between species – a view which is 'perfectly gratuitous and unsupported.'[166]

Finally, McAll asks whether atheistic principles tend to immorality, or weaken 'the principal constraints upon the evil propensities of the heart.'[167] Not surprisingly, he opts for the latter possibility. The supposition in the term 'atheism' is that the world has no moral Governor or Judge. What, then, may check moral degradation? The end of general happiness? 'But nothing is more common than to hear the sensual and impure say, that their favourite vices are such as to hurt none but themselves;'[168] and even if they could be disabused of this view they could still seek first their own enjoyment. As for materialists, believing as they do that character is necessarily regulated solely by a person's physical make-up, they must hold that 'to attribute to any part of human conduct either virtue or vice, is as absurd as to assign moral qualities to the changes of the tide, or the movements of a clock.'[169] The moral teaching of socialism is no better, for here human beings are regarded as the passive creatures of circumstance, and all must act as well as they can. Sin, then, becomes misfortune rather than fault, and moral leniency results. Then there is the maxim, 'Follow nature.' This too is a recipe for licence: 'To be true to nature in the sense intended by those words, is to make light of the marriage relation, and thus to destroy the foundation of domestic peace, and the very bond of society.'[170] Modern atheists are thus in a line flowing down from such 'leading infidels' as Lord Herbert and Hobbes; and the more recent cruelties which were perpetrated when France was ruled by atheists should give us pause. But at least, it might be said, atheism does not persecute as Christianity has done. McAll admits the stains on Christian history, but he suggests that 'Religion may be the *pretext*, where ambition, jealousy, or mercenary interest is the cause.'[171]

As compared with atheism the advantages of Christianity are great. It assures us of general and special providence, and of the hope of immortality. It offers redemption by Christ – something the necessity of which many atheists deny. Certainly 'He who came "to seek and save the lost" will not obtrude His offices on those who are unwilling to receive them.'[172] For their part, Christians are secure, and their 'tomb will be hallowed by the pure and refining associations which belong to the "memory of the just".'[173] This concluding contrast between the atheist and the Christian is reinforced finally by a quotation in which 'the Infidel and Philosopher' Voltaire wishes he had never been born; and from 'the devout and learned' Halyburton who declared, 'Blessed be God that ever I was born.'[174] McAll does not need further to specify on which side he would prefer his readers to be.

IV
A tribe of tractarians

We now reach a period in which a number of publishers and societies were developing series designed to defend the faith and, presumably, to turn a profit. Among the latter we find the Christian Evidence Society, which sponsored John Stoughton's lecture on *The Nature and Value of the Miraculous Testimony to Christianity*. Stoughton was one of Congregationalism's wise men. Educated at Highbury College and University College, London, he served at Windsor (1832-1843) and then at Kensington from 1843 to 1875. From 1858 to 1868 he edited *The Evangelical Magazine*, and from 1872 to 1884 he was professor of historical theology at New College. In his lecture he first makes plain that the Bible nowhere defines miracles in relation to physical laws: they are not spoken of as violations, suspensions, interferences or contradictions of law. The New Testament miracles are depicted in relation to Christ the redeemer. They are '*signs*, – replete with an ulterior meaning, and testifying to the character and work of Him through whom they were accomplished.'[175] With this approach, which makes Stoughton a harbinger of many biblical theologians of the 1950s, we move away from the traditional definition of miracles as breaches of the natural law. Accepting that a miracle is a sign, the point is, he continues, 'to dwell upon the religious significancy of its occurrence first to the witnesses, and next to ourselves.'[176] While the Bible exhibits the normal constancy of nature, miracles have another and a higher purpose. When appeal is made to miracles it is not suggested that the natural order remains other than constant; hence if science pronounces miracles impossible, it steps outside of its province. Indeed, 'The assaults on what is miraculous can be carried on only with metaphysical weapons.'[177]

Positivism, when it is consistent, cannot contradict the supernatural, but can only leave it an open question. Moreover, if we opt for universal physical necessity we find that 'the warfare which assails miracles, threatens to destroy all ideas of freedom and moral responsibility.'[178] We may agree with Hume that miracles are contrary to common experience, but to deny that they are 'contrary to human experience, taken in the widest point of view, is to beg the question at issue. . . .'[179] The supreme objective of the biblical signs is to authenticate revelation 'by means of evidence corresponding with its own supernatural origin and character.'[180]

In 1872 Henry Allon lectured for the Christian Evidence Society on the supernatural character of Christianity. Trained at Cheshunt College, Allon became assistant at Union Congregational Chapel, Islington in 1844, and pastor in 1852. There he exercised a distinguished ministry until his death in 1892. He was twice called to the Chair of the Congregational Union of England and Wales (1864, 1881), and from 1866 to 1874 he was joint editor, and from 1874 to 1886 editor of the *British Quarterly Review*.[181] Allon clearly has modern historical method and idealist attempts to transmute Christianity into a system of ideas within his sights. He grants at the outset that 'The historical character of Christianity subjects it to peculiar and crucial tests.'[182] While the moral and metaphysical tests of dogma hold pride of place, 'no intellectual arguments can prevail over indubitable experiences.'[183] This should not, however, dissuade us from appealing to the historical and scientific external evidence of Christianity's truth, for 'It is morally impossible to save the dogma of Christianity and sacrifice its history. . . . [I]f the Christian history be discredited, both its dogma and its moral authority are invalidated.'[184] It is true that religious sentiment is the most powerful force in human life, but strength of sentiment does not by itself yield a conclusive argument, for there are false religions. Historical claims must be tested by historical science, and if the proof of Christianity does not have the exactness of mathematical or scientific proof, it is characterized by strong probability. He proceeds to mount a cumulative argument: Christianity and the life and teaching of Christ have to be accounted for, as do the New Testament, and the growth and expansion of the faith. He concludes that Christianity is either of God, or 'it is historically and structurally a series of marvels unique in the world's history; a miracle greater than its assumed supernaturalism itself.'[185]

The Religious Tract Society was particularly active in the field of popular apologetics, and among the writers of its series of *Present Day Tracts* was the Congregationalist John Radford Thomson. Educated at New College, London, he was an MA of London University, and he also spent a year at the University of Edinburgh. Following an assistantship at East Parade, Leeds (1857-1859) he was pastor at Heywood (1860-1862), and then for one year a tutor at Cavendish College, Manchester. He removed to Mount Pleasant church, Tunbridge Wells (1863-1881), and finally to Mill Hill (1883-1888). In addition, from 1872 to 1903 he was a tutor at New College, and from 1882-1907, professor of mental and moral philosophy at New and Hackney Colleges. In *Modern Pessimism* (n.d.) Thomson deems that world view a revival of oriental Buddhism, and criticizes its modern representatives, Schopenhauer and von Hartmann. Pessimism is metaphysically flawed because it postulates 'blind, unconscious Will' as 'the prime, all-controlling power of the Universe;'[186] belief in God is more reasonable than belief in the unconscious will; it is not the case that volition is evil and productive only of misery; in fact the enjoyments of life outweigh its ills; according to Christianity the world's evil is not irredeemable; Christianity offers hope not least to sufferers; and 'When all men are drawn unto Christ by the attractive power of His Cross . . . then shall the Will of the Holy Father be done on earth as in Heaven!'[187] In *The Witness of Man's Moral Nature to Christianity* (n.d.) Thomson discusses the human being's moral nature and the way in which it corresponds with the leading revelations of Christianity. Conscience accords with Christianity; our highest aspirations after perfections are encouraged by Christianity; and the Christian doctrine of immortality assures us that these aspirations will finally be satisfied. He grants that his argument is one of probability only, and that it is cumulative in form, but it is sufficient to justify 'a cordial and practical acknowledgement of its claims.'[188] *Utilitarianism* was Thomson's subject in 1885. He briefly expounds the views of Bentham, Mill, Sidgwick and Spencer, and contests the view that pleasure is the standard of right. He argues that utilitarianism can give no account of the moral imperative, duty, conscience, contending that we discover the right by examining the moral order discernible in the universe, and by pondering the character of the divine Ruler. Finally, Christianity, as a response to God's love, supplies a motive far stronger than hedonism ever could, and grants the glorious prospect that 'in Thy right hand there are pleasures for evermore.'[189] Two years later Thomson tackled *Auguste Comte, and 'The Religion of Humanity'*. He outlines Comte's positivism and the nature of the Positivist Church, and then sets out to show that religion of humanity is atheistic and idolatrous. Human beings are not to be worshipped; positivism has no moral authority over human conduct, and has a deficient understanding of immortality. On all these points Christianity is shown to be superior.

Not to be outdone, the Methodist publisher Charles H. Kelly also issued a collection of apologetic tracts under the title, *What is Christianity?* (n.d.). R. Waddy Moss, who spent fifteen years in circuit work and thirty-one years at Didsbury College, contributed an undated pamphlet, *Is Man a Machine?* The short answer is 'No', because human beings are self-governing and self-determining 'units' in a community of like 'units', all of which are 'under the gracious control of a supreme God.'[190] Further, human beings are moral agents endowed with freedom, and neither the appeal to heredity nor to the environment in which a person lives succeeds against this fact. By contrast the determinist can offer no hope of improvement to human beings. The Bible asserts human moral freedom, and with it the help of God. Nothing is more important than that human beings freely respond to the call of Christ.

A further contribution to Kelly's series is that of John Scott Lidgett. An MA of the University of London, Lidgett served Wesleyan circuits for fifteen years, and then maintained a notable ministry in the Bermondsey Settlement from 1890 to 1949.[191] He held high office in a number of ecclesiastical circles, and wrote numerous books. His lecture is entitled, *Spiritual Discernment, its place in Christian Evidences*. Lidgett is by no means nonplussed by the need to restate the faith, for restatement is needed only when the old is criticized as outworn. The pervasive legacy of Thomas Aquinas must now yield in face of modern Christian thinking which brings experience to the fore. Indeed, 'The primary facts of Christianity are facts of spiritual experience.'[192] Spiritual discernment does not mean the acceptance of abstract propositions about God and the world; or that Christians have a means of understanding over and above reason. Rather, 'It means the apprehension and acceptance by the Christian of certain relations as real, and the finding in these relations that which his reason tells him is and must be the meaning of the world.'[193] The Christian experience is one of salvation, satisfaction, peace, liberty and power, and Christians must show how this experience bears upon 'all the other facts and relations of human life.'[194] Moreover, this faith-confirming experience is the experience of a community, and it turns upon the filial spirit: 'The Christian consciousness stands for the apprehension of a relationship, which answers the question of the reason, satisfies the needs of the heart, and indefinitely raises the moral stature of character and life.'[195] The revelation of God as the source of all, the fact of the historic Christ – ideas concerning these are confirmed by Christian experience. Then 'The general philosophical, historical, and moral arguments in support of Christianity come in from all sides to support the primary evidence contained in the Christian consciousness itself.'[196]

Lidgett further developed his apologetic approach in *The Christian*

Religion, its Meaning and Proof (1907). He here shows himself alive to the widespread feeling that the Christian evidences of the past were built upon inadequate intellectual foundations. In particular, they fail 'to give satisfaction to the spiritual consciousness of Christian believers by giving an adequate account of the grounds of their certitude.'[197] Indeed, they are 'alien to the mind and chilling to the faith of the intensest Christian faith.'[198] Spiritual experience is not so lightly to be discarded. Further, the current philosophical emphasis upon unity, affinity and continuity between God, man and the world must not be permitted to blur those necessary distinctions upon which spiritual experience depends. Neither exaggerated intellectualism on the one hand nor exaggerated personalism on the other will suffice: 'There is need . . . of renewed effort so to bring out the relation of the Christian consciousness to the world of reality and truth, that it may become increasingly manifest that it contains within itself the only means of rational interpretation of the whole.'[199] Thus motivated Scott Lidgett provides an extended treatment of the history and objectives of the evidences, of Christianity as the absolute religion, and of the proofs of the Christian religion. In the course of his exposition he, in a manner typical of his times, ranks the 'ethnic' religions in such a way that Christianity comes out on top, counters naturalism and agnosticism, discusses the theistic argument from design, and concludes with chapters on humanity, redemption and God.

The Congregationalist A.M. Fairbairn contributed a paper on *The Miracles of Christ* to Kelly's volume. Fairbairn, who was trained for the ministry at the Evangelical Union Hall, Glasgow, and who attended some classes at Edinburgh University, ministered at Bathgate (1860-1872), then studied in Berlin for a period, returning to the pastorate of St. Paul Street, Aberdeen (1872-1877). From thence he was called to be principal first at Airedale College, Bradford (1877-1886) and then at Mansfield College, Oxford (1886-1909). In the course of his account of miracles he finds Darwin wanting. He quotes the last sentence of *The Origin of Species*: 'If you give me one or a few forms, I will show you how from those poor germs the wondrous furniture of earth has, while time has gone cycling on, been all developed and evolved.' What Darwin asks for, declares Fairbairn, is nothing less than the whole mystery of creation; he asks for a created universe so that he can explicate the processes within it. As for Hume, on his principles he has no right to the concepts of order, nature and law, while Huxley's materialism leave no room for the ethical. But Fairbairn knows himself as a moral man, and he has dealings with God. The only way this is possible is through the supernatural; and the reality of the supernatural involves the possibility of miracles.

In 1878 Fairbairn's subject for the autumn meeting of the Congregational Union was 'How to meet the un-Christian and anti-Christian teaching of the day.' He first makes it clear that he has no quarrel with science as such. The spheres of science and Christianity differ: 'Science is the real, but theism the ideal interpretation of the universe.'[200] But scientists overstep the mark when they oppose to Christianity what are in fact metaphysically-grounded views. Thus, 'Evolution, as a scientific theory, has nothing in it inimical to religion; but evolution developed into a mechanical theory of creation, or the making of nature by nature, is simply evolution translated into a metaphysical doctrine or hypothesis, and forced, perhaps, sweetly unconscious of its change, to attempt problems impossible to science, though possible to philosophy.'[201] What really disturbs is '(1) Teaching that negatives the intellectual and moral bases and contents of Christianity; and (2) teaching that discredits the character of its sacred literature, and the reality of its sacred history.'[202] In addressing such teaching our problem is that, unlike Butler *contra* the deists, we do not share the basis premisses of our antagonists: 'Christianity believes that there is a personal God, and that man is an immortal and responsible being; but the teaching opposed to it affirms either that there is not God, or that He cannot be known, and that man is a congeries of sensations, held structurally together, due to the interplay throughout vast ages of growingly complex organisms and their environments.'[203] Much anti-Christian teaching is not anti-religious – positivism, for example, extols the worship of humanity – and it is ethical in spirit. Such teaching can be met only by constructive teaching. Christians must show 'that the Christian is the most rational theory of the universe, of nature and mind, of man and history.'[204] In fact, 'what we need is a system as constructive, sublime, and comprehensive as Calvinism, but more generous – an interpretation of the universe through our higher idea of God.'[205] We must develop, he continues, those elements in Christianity 'that can satisfy the nobler aspirations and more reverential feelings of man,'[206] and we must make the ethical element of Christianity active in individual, social and political life. He then pleads for teachers of this kind of Christianity.

The rhetorical utterance of the apologetic *bon mot* (rather than detailed apologetic argument) came easily to Fairbairn, and in many of his books he is found in this mode. Thus, in one place he declares, 'a true theology can never be built on a sceptical philosophy, and . . . only the thought which trusts the reason can truly vindicate faith in the God who gave it.'[207] He denounces that variety of naturalistic thought which 'estimates a man solely by his worth to the community, is proud of him only as he has the strength that can be victorious in the struggle.'[208] Again, like many in his generation, he felt it necessary to challenge Herbert Spencer's way of merging his *a priori* understanding of force, the cause of creation, with evolution, the method of creation.[209] To a greater extent than many of his contemporaries, Fairbairn shows himself open to the views of the major faiths of the world, though, typically for his time, he ranks them in pyramid fashion in such a way that Christianity is at the apex: 'a system whose crown and centre is the Divine Man, is one which does justice to everything positive in humanity by penetrating it everywhere with Deity.'[210] In *The Philosophy of the Christian Religion* (1902) Fairbairn seeks to explain religious through nature and man, and then to construe Christianity through religion.[211] The underlying conviction is that 'The Incarnation . . . is the very truth which turns nature and man, history and religion into the luminous dwelling place of God.'[212]

Peter Lorimer

To Peter Lorimer of the English Presbyterian college we owe two essays in apologetics. He was educated at Edinburgh University and ordained in 1836 as minister of Colebrook Row church in Islington. In 1845 he was appointed the first professor of biblical criticism and Hebrew in the Presbyterian College, and in 1878 he became the first principal. In 1873 he addressed a group of young men on the subject, 'Disbelief in Christian miracles proved to be unscientific.' He points out that on the continent, disbelief in miracles is generally associated with pantheism, and he names Spinoza and Strauss as culprits. At home, by contrast, the attack upon miracles is in the name of science; but since theology's 'chief objects of contemplation lie above and beyond the sphere of nature and sensible things; its methods of inquiry are, on all subjects of revealed religion, totally different from those of physical science; and equally different are its kinds of evidence and proof from those with which the mind of the physicist is habituated.'[213] Yet both pantheists such as Strauss and Baur, and theists such as Theodore Parker and Francis Newman rest upon the sanction of inductive science in their anti-miracle stances. This is supremely true of Baden Powell in his contribution to *Essays and Reviews* (1860). Powell rests upon the immutability or infallibility of universal order, and it is odd that one so firmly in the line of Bacon should reach an anti-supernaturalistic conclusion which Bacon 'would have repudiated with his whole soul.'[214] Powell's axiom, Lorimer argues, rules out a good deal of contrary evidence from the start and, with a certain relish, he invokes John Stuart Mill's definition of fallacies of generalization in support of his case. Experience cannot afford the necessary conditions for establishing such generalizations by a correct induction, and among such fallacies 'are *all universal negatives* – all propositions that assert impossibility.'[215] He further quotes Mill against Hume:

> A miracle is no contradicton to the law of cause and effect; it is a new effect supposed to be produced by the introduction of a new cause. . . . All, therefore, which Hume has made out is that no evidence can prove a miracle to any one who did not previously believe the existence of a being or beings with supernatural power, or who believed himself to have *full* proof that the character of the Being whom he recognises is inconsistent with his having seen fit to interfere on the occasion in question.[216]

Lorimer calls Isaac Taylor, William Hamilton and Campbell Fraser in support, and concludes:

> There is no reason, then, why we should allow any philosophical *prestige* to men of such an order of intellect [i.e. the Powells of this world], when they lay down dicta and utter oracles beyond their proper province; and especially should we beware of the fallacy of transferring the character of certainty which belongs to the physical truths which they expound to the statements in which they may be pleased to indulge themselves upon the fields of metaphysics and theology.'[217]

In 1876 Lorimer gave a lecture under the auspices of the Christian Evidence Society. Here his case is that Christianity is the perfect religion because it is 'perfectly adapted to all the deeper needs of the human heart.'[218] These deeper needs are moral and religious. The conscience, that inner law of righteousness, needs an authority above itself; it needs peace with God. The human heart needs a full and adequate object of love, and strength to persist in self-denial and self-sacrifice in the service of God and humanity. Christianity supplies the above needs, and such a religion is a supernatural gift of God – its origins cannot be accounted for upon natural principles. That these needs can be met is known both intellectually and experimentally. As for currently proposed alternatives: the anti-faith position of Strauss, Comte's worship of humanity, Mill's humanist religion of simple duty, and Tyndall's recourse to the creative faculties of the human mind – none of them can become a religion of the heart.

James Martineau

We now return to the nineteenth century's most distinguished Unitarian philosopher. We have already introduced Martineau's ethics, and noted his claim that our human nature cries out for a divine source of its moral aspirations. The other plank of his theistic apology must now be mentioned: the argument to God from our intellectual demand for a first cause. There are hints of his position in his lecture of 1874 on *Religion as affected by Modern Materialism*. The sciences, he argues, are concerned with the question, How? Religion's concern is with the question, Whence? There need therefore be no conflict between them. The problem is that scientists such as Tyndall require so much of matter. Indeed, 'Such extremely clever Matter, – matter that is up to everything, even to writing Hamlet, and finding out its own evolution, and substituting a molecular plébiscite for a divine monarchy of the world, may fairly be regarded as a little too modest in its disclaimer of the attributes of Mind.'[219] The truth is that 'On the hypothesis of a Mindless universe,' there is 'a fatal breach between the highest inward life of man and his picture of the outer world.'[220] We may not erect a dualism of reason which deals with things material, and the imagination which deals with things spiritual; rather we must recognize a duality in the functions of reason itself, 'according as it deals with phenomena or their ground, with law or with causality, with material consecution or with moral alternatives, with the definite relations of space and time and motion, or with the indefinite intensities of beauty and values of affection which bear us to the infinitely Good.'[221] This is the theme pursued at much greater length in Martineau's *A Study of Religion* (1887).

Eustace Rogers Conder

To Eustace R. Conder we owe the Congregational Lecture for 1877.[222] Conder was the great-grandson of the Dissenting academy tutor, John Conder, the grandson of the bookseller and map engraver, Thomas Conder, and the son of Josiah Conder, author, editor and bookseller.[223] Eustace was educated at Spring Hill College, Birmingham, where Henry Rogers, to whom he pays a warm tribute in the Preface to his Lecture, was among his teachers. Following a pastorate at Skinner Street, Poole (1844-1861), Conder served with distinction at East Parade Congregational Church, Leeds, from 1864 to 1892, becoming Chairman of the Congregational Union of England and Wales in 1873.

Conder's Congregational Lecture is entitled, *The Basis of Faith. A Critical Survey of the Grounds of Christian Theism*. Its particular interest from our point of view lies in its comprehensive marrying of arguments drawn from standard natural theology with the biblical 'evidences' of prophecy, miracle and the life and ministry of Jesus. To these are added a concluding chapter in which, in then modern fashion, Conder discusses 'the voice within' – conscience and the claims of morality. The strategy as thus described is in keeping with the author's view that it is impossible to draw any sharp line of scientific definition, fencing off the province of Natural from that of Revealed Theology. As matter of fact, the faith of the majority of believers in God does largely rest upon the Bible, and especially on the teaching of Christ and his Apostles. In a comprehensive estimate of the evidence, therefore, the testimony of Scripture claims to be as carefully examined as that of the Physical Universe, or that of man's conscience and moral nature.[224]

Reflecting upon the then current intellectual climate, Conder declares that 'If Theism can produce convincing evidence, Pantheism, Atheism, and Agnosticism vanish of necessity.'[225] The desired evidence, as hinted in his Preface, flows along two lines:

First, we may assume the scientific attitude, and attempt the inductive method. Disclaiming all regard to preconceived opinion, we may array in order the facts of nature, including those of human nature and history; and may inquire to what conclusion these facts in their complexity, their harmony, and even their disorder and mystery, point. What theory of the universe will fit the facts? What hypothesis will carry us furthest in explaining its mystery? Secondly, we may assume a less imposing attitude – the historical and judicial. We may inquire by what evidence, supposing God to exist, His existence could be certified to us; and we may examine how far such evidence is actually forthcoming, and what are the grounds on which, in point of fact, our faith rests.[226]

Following the former approach first, Conder pays particular attention to teleological considerations. Writing when he did, he could hardly avoid what he calls the hypothesis of evolution. He finds that the idea of evolution as 'an imaginary history of the process through which the universe has passed from the beginning to the present time,' is 'not inconsistent with Theism, or even with Christianity'; whereas the notion that evolution affords 'an adequate theory of the universe, superseding the belief in a Creator' is 'inconsistent with fact,'[227] because 'PROCESS is not CAUSE.'[228] As to moral purpose: here Conder runs up against John Stuart Mill, 'a lover of truth, and an accurate (though narrow) thinker',[229] whose *Three Essays on Religion* had been posthumously published in 1874.[230] To Mill's complaint that Nature regularly performs wicked feats, and is thus 'pitiless' and 'merciless' and so cannot be the creation of a good God, Conder replies that these are attributes of personal being, which Nature is not. Nature's course is, however, just in the sense of impartial: cause and effect are constant. Moreover, 'It is not true – it is the reverse of the truth – that we blame men as wicked when their acts and works produce suffering in the same manner as suffering is produced by storms and earthquakes. We blame men only when harm is done of set purpose, or through culpable negligence; and there is no harmful purpose or negligence in Nature.'[231]

Conder concludes the first part of his enquiry by reaffirming his conviction that the unity of nature is an intellectual or moral, a spiritual, unity: 'it is a unity of plan, law, harmonious relation, beauty, significance, and moral purpose;'[232] and it is a unity which necessarily implies 'a Mind in which the end was foreseen from the beginning.'[233]

The second, shorter, part concerns revelation. Conder discusses God's self-manifestation in prophecy and miracles, briskly repudiating Hume's definition of 'miracle' as a violation of the laws of nature. This, he thunders,

> is false or misleading; not merely as presenting the repulsive incongruity of a transgression by the Creator of his own laws, but as foreign to the true idea of a miracle; involving, moreover, and enormous and unnecessary assumption utterly void of proof.[234]

He is convinced that it can be shown '*A priori*:– If God exists, as the Bible claims to reveal Him, miracles are possible. *A posteriori*:– If the miracles recorded in the Bible are historically true, God exists.'[235]

Conder passes to the life and teaching of Jesus, emphasising the authenticating significance of the Resurrection. It is, indeed, 'vital to the story of Jesus, which without it sinks into ruin and absurdity.'[236] There is, finally, 'the voice within' which reaches out for God's revelation, and testifies, as no doctrine of the evolution of moral sentiments ever can, to 'the sovereign authority of moral law.'[237] Conder's concluding hope is that all who are open to the truth will agree that 'GOD IS, and has revealed Himself to man. Knowledge of Him is the crown of all knowledge; His love the supreme good; our relation to Him the key to human life, here and hereafter.'[238]

William Medley and Thomas Vincent Tymms

In 1879, at the autumnal session of the Baptist Union, William Medley of Rawdon Baptist College, Leeds, read a paper entitled, *Our Attitude in relation to Religious Opinion and Belief*. It was a reassuring word. Amidst many speculative difficulties 'the main clue after all is furnished by the reverent, lowly, and obedient heart.'[239] Certainly science and its discoveries are not to be feared, and it must be remembered that scientific method is not of universal application. On the other hand, the Bible is not an instructor 'in any of those subjects in which the need for Divine communication to man did not exist.'[240] Medley proceeds to suggest that 'an essential condition of all safe progress and enlargement in theological opinion is the maintenance of fulness of life in the soul,'[241] and he concludes with the caution that public worship is not the place for apologetics, but for showing the people Jesus, who is the only Saviour, the same yesterday, today and for ever. With conscious acknowledgement to Medley, Benwell Bird pursued the theme further, though with an emphasis more theological and ecclesiastical than apologetic, in his paper to the Baptist Union, *The Changes passing over religious thought, and the spirit in which we should meet them.*[242]

A more substantial work of apologetics was offered by another Baptist in the same year. Thomas Vincent Tymms was trained at Regent's Park Baptist College. Following pastorates at Berwick-on-Tweed (1865-1868), Accrington (1868-1869) and Downs Chapel, Clapton (1869-1891) he was called to Rawdon College, where he served until 1904. Apologetics was his *forté*, and his most notable contribution was *The Mystery of God*, the fourth edition of which was published in 1890.

Tymms's aim is to consider the chief current intellectual hindrances to faith. In so doing he is guided by a distinguished Queen's Counsel, who whispered to him, 'I win my cases by admissions.'[243] Hence his policy: 'I have not contended for all that I believe, but by making occasional loans to the other side, have striven to show that the Christian faith will not be injuriously affected if many current controversies are ultimately decided in a way that the majority of Christian advocates neither desire nor expect.'[244] He further cautions his readers that 'The life of faith is not a mere assent of the intellect to certain propositions, and it therefore cannot be produced by logic. But faith must needs include some convictions which may be put into propositions, and either be denied or affirmed by the reason.'[245]

Tymms first examines materialism, with reference to the views of Huxley, Tyndall, Spencer and others. His case is that 'Against the theory of evolution as representing an order of progress, no Christian need have a word to utter; but on the other hand, as a theory of origins, it has not a word to say for itself. It cannot account for motion, and it cannot account for life, and it cannot tell you what is the real substance of the primary form of matter, or even prove against an Idealist that matter itself exists.'[246] The materialist has access to no facts which are incompatible with the Christian claim that 'By faith we understand that the worlds have been framed by the word of God . . .', or with Christ's teaching that 'He who made the heavens and the earth is the Father of a spiritual nature in man, and has been pleased to afford us some knowledge of Himself.'[247]

Pantheism is next considered. Tymms defines it, and discusses the

Greeks, Buddhism and Spinoza who, 'Instead of beginning with the observed order of nature and the human mind which observes, and so reasoning up towards the unity it is the business of philosophy to discover, . . . started with a definition of God, and then had to make the facts of the universe fit with that arbitrary assumption.'[248] In the wake of Spinoza, Hegel, albeit unintentionally, did much further to diffuse panethistic ideas. He proceeds to discuss the views of Seeley, for whom nature does not so much define God as constitute him, and concludes that

> To call everything God is only playing with words. Call the universe matter or mind, designate the universal substance as fire, water, motion, thought, mud, dust, or God, and it makes no practical difference. If it be only one thing, and so including ourselves, it is grinding out an evolution which no one directs or judges, and which cannot be modified or controlled – all notions of liberty are Maya.[249]

From such an inexorable conclusion, the only refuge is faith in God – notwithstanding that the 'beauty and desirability of such a faith is no sure evidence of its truth.'[250]

The next chapter, on Theism, contains a lengthy discussion of Mill's *Essay* on that subject, parts of which Tymms brands, 'ingenious trifling'.[251] For Tymms, the facts of the universe point to a First Cause, and 'the facts of consciousness and the observed order of nature indicate that this First Cause must be possessed of the attributes of Wisdom and Volition, which can only belong to a Living God.'[252] The barbs of the most honoured critics of theism leave this conviction intact. At this point some believers in God stop. But others go on to embrace the deliverances of revelation, and do so not least because without it theism has no answer to the problem of pain, so clamantly raised by Mill. So also in regard to the mystery of evil. In both cases a revelation is morally necessary 'if the Creator's goodness is to be sustained.'[253] The Bible is God's instrument of revelation, and Tymms argues that despite the Bible's character as an 'earthen vessel', it nevertheless carries heavenly treasure. At the heart of Scripture is Christ, and, with reference to Renan and Strauss, Tymms examines the person of Christ, finding him to be the fulfilment of prophecy; and the resurrection, concerning which he submits: 'the only two alternatives . . . are either to dismiss the whole matter from our minds as a mystery upon which we decline to bestow any further attention; or to accept the resurrection as a fact of history, and with it Christ's superhuman claims, and the Bible of which He is the central theme as a God-provided book, and its teachings and counsels as the guide of life.'[254]

In his concluding chapter, 'The Life of Faith', Tymms examines some of the dissuasives to faith, of which one is the difficulty people have with the miraculous. He grants that 'The winking of a Madonna and the liquefaction of the blood of St. Januarius are no more to be disproved on abstract grounds of physical impossibility than the resurrection of Christ,'[255] but attempts to draw the sting of the problem by saying that 'Only for the greatest purposes can we suppose that the Almighty will think it wise or needful to interpose some exceptional act of will within the ordinary course of nature.'[256] Miracles need to be morally, and not just physically possible, and events claimed as miraculous can be judged by their effects. Again, some are inclined to mistake faith for credulity – and in this they have sometimes been encouraged by the churches themselves. But the churches should not turn themselves into spurious authorities in this way. The authority of Christ makes a rightful appeal to private judgment and to the individual conscience, and throughout the New Testament people are addressed as reasonable beings. Yet again, people need to be disabused of the notion that faith is intellectual assent to the truth of adequately proved propositions. In fact, 'The only faith to which moral value is ascribed is that personal trust in God which distinguished Abraham. . . .'[257] While people are perfectly entitled to a spiritual faith without the necessity of passing through a course in apologetics, if a person has doubts concerning the historical evidences upon which the Christian faith is built, those doubts do need to be addressed. As for those – including the 'Hellenic Matthew Arnold' – who would opt for virtue rather than dogma, the question is, 'How shall vicious men be made virtuous?'[258] Faith in Christ counteracts tendencies towards positive evil, and 'exalts the whole idea of duty by connecting the work of each passing hour with the interests of eternity, and by bringing the powers of the world above and of the world to come to reinforce the ordinary motives to rectitude.'[259] Finally, faith 'commends itself as giving completeness and grandeur to our intellectual conceptions of the universe.[260] For whereas 'Physical science can only regard other worlds as lonely islands in an untravelled ocean of ether,' faith in the moral order of the cosmos enables us to regard them as 'many mansions' of one great house, and 'the human race as one of many tribes in the cosmic Israel of God, all journeying towards one Holy Hill of beatific vision, and all destined to worship in an Eternal Temple which shall be a house of praise for all worlds, when the Mystery of God now darkly working shall be finished, "according to the good tidings which He declared to His servants the prophets."'[261]

Tymms's reference to Mill's posthumous *Three Essays on Religion* (1874) calls to mind the considerable flurry of responses which that work elicited from far and near, and from philosophers and theologians of all stripes. Among the respondents were the Congregationalist Joseph Parker and the Unitarians Henry Shaen Solly and C.B. Upton.

Joseph Parker

Joseph Parker, the Northumberland stonemason's son, attended some lectures at University College, London, and was put through his homiletic paces over a period of nine months by John Campbell of Whitefield's Tabernacle, Moorfields. After an assistantship under Campbell was was called to Banbury (1853-1858) and thence to the important Cavendish Chapel, Manchester (1858-1869). In the latter year he removed to Poultry Chapel, London, for whose growing congregation the City Temple was built and opened in 1874. There Parker reigned until 1901.[262] His critique of Mill's *Essays* takes the form of a thinly veiled allegory, and finds him at his most teasingly rumbustuous. The tract is entitled, *Job's Comforters: Scientific Sympathy*, and in it he presents Job as a suffering Christian who is 'comforted' by Huxley the Moleculite, who assures him that the cause of his distress is 'entirely molecular'; Tyndall the Sadducee, who explains that even though Job's children have returned to dust, they will thereby 'contribute somewhat to the nourishment of animals and plants', and so assist 'the chemic economy of nature'; and Mill, who wonders why it matters so much that Job's children should live for ever – far better to 'Reform the sanitary arrangements of the country' so that people may live happier lives now. Against all of this Parker pits the view that there are depths of human need which the learned men, no matter how valuable their knowledge in its own sphere, cannot reach. God is the ultimate donor of understanding, and he will reveal himself not to their knowledge, but to their simplicity.[263]

Henry Shaen Solly and Charles Barnes Upton

Henry Shaen Solly, a graduate of London University, was trained for the ministry at Manchester New College under Martineau and James Drummond.[264] He held five Unitarian pastorates, and was deeply interested in geology and archaeology. In his review of Mill's *Essays* he contends that Mill was made a sceptic by his abhorrence of the obsolete and false phrases used by orthodox Christians, and his attachment to an obsolete empiricist philosophy. Liberal Christians have outgrown both, and understand the importance of conscience as the voice of God, and of a faculty of spiritual discernment. Mill cannot admit these, and hence, however noble the ideals of his Religion of Humanity may be, it will fail in practice.[265]

Upton's extended review of Mill's *Essays* is more closely analytical.

Against Mill's dramatic raising of the problem of evil in its most acute form, namely, that of the inequitability of nature's distribution of unmerited suffering, Upton protests that while the benign aspects of nature confirm our faith, the partial absence of such signs do not destroy faith, for faith does not originate in nature. In the paper of 'The utility of religion' Mill wrongly characterizes religion as a system of rewards and punishments believed to be guaranteed by miracles, while in 'Theism', with its less provocative attitude towards religious hope, it seems to Upton as if there is in Mill a liberal Christian struggling to get out, yet for ever imprisoned because of a stunted intellectual upbringing at the hands of his father, James, who adopted an areligious stance where his son's nurture was concerned.[266]

In 1893 Upton delivered his Hibbert Lectures on *The Bases of Religious Belief* (1894). With many an echo of his teacher Martineau, he sought a rational ground for theism in the common self-consciousness of humanity.[267]

James Muscutt Hodgson

The Congregationalist James Muscutt Hodgson was educated at the University of Glasgow, and later a DSc of Edinburgh, he was trained for the ministry at Lancashire Independent College. Following a pastorate at Uttoxeter (1866-1875) he taught at Lancashire College (1875-1894), and then became principal of the Scottish Congregationalists' Theological Hall in Edinburgh (1894-1916). Hodgson was among many who, during the second half of the nineteenth-century, elevated faith and experience into apologetic starting-points. It would, indeed, seem that the psychological strain running through his work was given a practical expression unique among Nonconformist professors. For a student writes that Hodgson

> was very genial and we all liked him. He had rather remarkable mesmeric gifts. We had no evidence of them in our classes, though I was told that occasionally – quite unconsciously – he had mesmerised people while he was preaching. But on one occasion, when he had invited some people to his house, he mesmerised one of us, a Welshman, and succeeded in making him preach part of a sermon in Welsh.[268]

Hodgson describes his *Philosophy and Faith* (1885) as *A Plea for Agnostic Belief*. The subtitle offers the clue to his approach: where knowledge fails, faith suffices. In his own words:

> the aim of the present paper is, *first*, to enquire to what extent the contents and objects of Religious Faith do or do not lie within the boundaries of possible Knowledge, and do or do

not present the indispensable conditions of Knowledge; and, *second*, to indicate the impossibility of surrendering that 'unqualified assurance' in which we revel respecting them, in spite of its condemnation by Scientists and Rational Philosophers as 'a belief void of justification.'[269]

He briefly indicates the way in which 'reason' has been used and, for his present purpose, regards it 'as solely a faculty of Knowledge,'[270] thereby restricting its operations to the phenomenal sphere. Philosophy is 'the systematic application of Human Reason to the arrangement and explanation of the various elements of experience and history.'[271] Thus conceived, philosophy may stand in one of four relations to religion:

1. Reason is absolutely incompetent to examine the deliverances of revelation.
2. Philosophy is the only instrument by which we may apprehend, interpret and be certain of divine and spiritual things.
3. The sole function of philosophy is to expose our religious convictions as psychological illusions.
4. Since the essential convictions of religion come to us 'from some other source and through some other medium, the business of Philosophy is simply, reverently to attempt to set forth the relations of the elements of our Religious Faith to the conceptions and inferences with which Reason and experience themselves have furnished us, and to trace as afar as possible the harmony and compatibility of the contents of our Faith with those of our Philosophy.'[272]

Hodgson repudiates the first approach as entailing a blind acceptance of authority, whether ecclesiastical, or of the kind exemplified by Thomas Chalmers's view that 'The authority of every Revelation rests exclusively upon its external evidences.'[273]

Options two and three are rationalistic or gnostic in assuming that 'the supreme and final test of truth and reality is to be found in the Understanding and Reason.'[274] In this connection he adversely criticizes Wolff, Schleiermacher, and such post-Hegelian philosopher-theologians as John Caird.[275] The third possibility is that adopted by sceptics and positivists. The fourth position is that of the Christian agnostics. They are Christian believers but philosophical agnostics. They accept 'the fundamental facts and presuppositions of Theism, Ethics, and Revealed Religion without the evidence of Reason, prior to and independent of its existence, and yet as being sanctioned by, at least, as valid and indisputable a guarantee as that by which Reason itself can sustain and enforce its own axioms or inferences.'[276] Indeed, faith takes us deeper than reason ever could. Reason cannot explain the sense of obligation, neither can it demonstrate the credibility of revelation. Our faith in God's reality rests upon psychological factors: the intuitions of power, constancy, intelligence, substance, personality, dependence, and morality. Furthermore, of the three kinds of certitude – empirical, logical and intuitional – only the last affirms the existence of real being, objective or subjective. Hence, 'Our only warrant . . . of the Real, and the Absolute is the universal and inevitable instinct of Faith.'[277] Hodgson developed his position in two further works. In *Theologia Pectoris: Outlines of Religious Faith and Doctrine, Founded on Intuition and Experience* (1898) he denies that purely objective systems will comprise 'the sole or primary warrant of any of the ideas or propositions of spiritual or religious truth,'[278] and accordingly sets out from the nature and actual state and needs of humanity. Finally, in *Religion – The Quest of the Ideal* (1911) he seeks to show that 'the essentials of religion are not dependent upon an intellectual formulation of the conclusions of reflective thought upon spiritual realities,'[279] because religion springs from roots in the spiritual nature of humanity. Again, he deprecates and repudiates the appeal to 'an authority from without which is assumed to be independent of the instincts, convictions, and impulses of human personality. . . .'[280] But he does not wish 'to deny or undervalue the objective revelation of the Divine, or the provision of redeeming grace and power which God has made to meet the needs and satisfy the quest of the soul as it realizes its actual condition and its natural aspirations towards a better and ideal state.'[281]

The waning of apologetics and the First World War
Apologetic works continued to appear in the first two decades of the twentieth century (we have already noted some contributions of Scott Lidgett and Fairbairn), but, even before Barth's theological revolution, one gains the impression that the period of greatest apologetic activity is passing: perhaps because the faith's enemies were not so challenging; perhaps because perceived threats such as those emanating from science or biblical criticism were generally felt to have been dealt with; perhaps because insofar as opponents reiterated older agnostic or atheist positions, the the need and the desire to repudiate them along familiar lines became less clamant. Robert Mackintosh produced *A First Primer of Apologetics* in 1904; in the same year the Wesleyan John Smith Simon of Didsbury College published a quaint lecture he gave on behalf of the Christian Evidence Society entitled, *Wesley or Voltaire?* Simon places his protagonists in the same ring, but it is hard to not feel that Wesley is given the weighted gloves. Be that as it may, Simon invites his audience in Manchester's Central Hall to choose between them. Voltaire had 'an

immoral connexion with a married woman' whereas Wesley was 'a pure-hearted man' [who neglected his wife?] Voltaire's views contributed to revolution, whereas Wesley's views reformed a nation and the Evangelical Revival 'did much to save this country from a revolution similar to that which devastated France' [a position which many latter-day church historians would seriously qualify if not repudiate].

Another Wesleyan, E.S. Waterhouse, then in circuit ministry but afterwards principal of Richmond College, whose major works appeared after 1920, published *Modern Theories of Religion* in 1910. This is a critical review of modern religious philosophy from Schleiermacher to Rashdall, coupled with an attempt to construct a religious philosophy of an empirical basis, and to vanquish such substitutes for such as philosophy as positivism, pessimism and nescience.

A work of 1913 calls for a little more comment. In that year the Congregationalist A.E. Garvie published his *A Handbook of Christian Apologetics* in Duckworth's widely-circulated series. Garvie studied for a year at Edinburgh University and then went into business for four years. He entered Glasgow University in 1885, graduating four years later. He trained for the ministry under Fairbairn at Mansfield College, Oxford. Following pastorates at Macduff (1893-1895) and Baltic Street, Montrose (1895-1903) he became professor at Hackney and New College (1903-1907), principal of New College (1907-1920), and principal of Hackney and New College (1920-1933). His *Handbook* is interesting in two respects. First, he dedicates it to the memory of Edward Caird 'by one of his students who, although led to abandon his philosophy, yet cherishes his teaching as a most precious possession.' Secondly, there is a less pugilistic air about the book than we have found in some other writings in this genre. Garvie neither swashbuckles like a Rogers nor pontificates like a Fairbairn. Indeed, 'In accordance with his idea of the task of Apologetics as commendation rather than defence, less attention has been given to meeting objections than to presenting the attractiveness of the Christian Gospel.'[282] Following an introductory chapter Garvie discusses reason and revelation, inspiration and miracle, the Lord Jesus Christ, the Christian salvation, the Christian view of God, the Christian view of humanity, the Christian ideal and the Christian hope.[283]

Finally, we may note a powerful contribution of P.T. Forsyth, *The Justification of God* (1917). Following five Congregational pastorates Forsyth became principal of Hackney College in 1901, and remained in office until his death in 1921.[284] While Forsyth did not rule the apologetic task out of order, and himself entered the lists with such lesser works as those on monism, evolution and miracles,[285] his principal aim was to defend the faith within the Church by opposing those liberal theologians who had, he thought, sentimentalized God's love by neglecting the holiness of it. As he wrote, 'The greatest issue for the moment is within the Christian pale; it is not between Christianity and the world. It is the issue between theological liberalism (which is practically unitarian) and a free but positive theology, which is essentially evangelical.'[286] Nevertheless, in his theodicy of 1917 he addressed the problem of evil with a godly defiance reminiscent of Bunyan's attitude towards hobgoblins and foul fiends. In the traumatic days of World War I he defends the Christian faith against those who would deny the God of love in view of the rampant horrors of war. His case is that precisely because God's love is holy, righteous love and human sin is as dire as it is, grievous disturbance is explicable – even to be expected. But in view of the victory of the Cross there is a practical answer to the problem – that is, an answer which fortifies believers for life's struggle and gives them hope, even though it does not answer the theoretical question, Why does righteous Job suffer? As he wrote, 'We do not see the answer, we trust the Answerer, and measure by Him. We do not gain the victory; we are united with the Victor.'[287]

V

We have now reviewed a considerable variety of Nonconformist contributions to ethics and apologetics. As to ethics, it is clear that while a number of writers – Edward Williams and F.A. Cox among them – emphasised God's moral governorship of the universe, few made human depravity their starting point to the degree that Ralph Wardlaw, more analytically, and Thomas Jackson, more popularly, did. We have further seen that those who contributed more substantial works frequently adjusted their thoughts to those of their predecessors, though the earlier ones, well versed in Hutcheson, Reid, Price and Butler though they were, do not seem to have dwelt upon Kant to the degree that, later, W.T Davison, for example, did.

The growing interest in the ethical implications of religious experience and psychological factors became evident in the works of Gilbert Wardlaw, G. Lyon Turner and J.H. Godwin. While such authors did not in their ethical works deal directly with rising utilitarianism as much as might have been expected (though, as we have seen, apologetic tracts were devoted to the topic), it is hard not to read Godwin's strongly deontological emphasis, for example, as anything other than an implicit rebuttal of Bentham and his heirs. Again, while some writers confined their attention to the more theoretical aspects of ethics others, among whom J.H. Hinton is prominent, ranged widely over family and social ethics as well. None did more to place his moral philosophy at the service of his theism than James Martineau.

By the end of our period the ethicists are much more likely to side with Davison in holding that 'much mischief has been done by the attempt to prove the entire dependence of moral knowledge upon revelation,'[288] than with Ralph Wardlaw's problematic elevation of human depravity. Of course, this difference in emphasis is an aspect of a wider scene which depicts on the one hand the gradual dilution of Calvinism and the advent of Social Gospel views which tended to focus upon more cheerful features of the human condition, and to conceive of God paternally – sometimes to the point of genial sentimentality. It would take us too far afield to paint this scene here.[289]

Turning to apologetics: from the evidence supplied it is clear that the nineteenth-century Nonconformists cut a wide swathe, and that their manner ranged from the more learned, through the gently teasing, to the swashbuckling. The Unitarian Robert Aspland was by no means alone in the early years of the century in urging the advancing of the Christian evidences in preference to resorting to 'frames and feelings, impulses and raptures;' and the Congregationalist Henry Rogers was resolutely engaged in this task even as biblical scholarship was making the older appeal to miracles and the fulfilment of prophecy ever more problematic; and as fresh challenges – evolutionary thought, positivism, naturalism, agnosticism and the like – required to be faced. Such are the time-lags in intellectual history, further evidence of which is supplied by the fact that as late as 1821 George Redford was still in hot pursuit of the deists. The attacks by Hume and Kant upon the traditional theistic arguments did not deter some, including Benjamin Godwin and Samuel McAll, from continuing to propound them; Eustace Conder appealed eclectically to ancient and modern apologetic methods, while to Gilbert Wardlaw, in modern fashion, religious experience was of particular importance.

What especially characterized the second half of the nineteenth century was the plethora of popular apologetics contributed by divines of all the Nonconformist denominations, aided and abetted by religious publishers intent upon circulating their tracts as widely as possible. By this means atheism, agnosticism, materialism, positivism, rationalism, pessimism, John Stuart Mill, utilitarianism, all received their come-uppance – at least as far as the pamphleteers were concerned. There was, in addition, a growing perception that the traditional arguments for God's existence could no longer count as demonstrative proofs; that miracles were better regarded as signs to the believer than as evidence capable of convincing the sceptic; and, the peril of psychologism notwithstanding, that serious heed must be paid to the witness of religious experience.

As for evolutionary thought, while very few Nonconformist divines meddled with the details of the scientific *theory*, in a climate of post-Hegelian immanentism spiced with Romantic optimism in human powers, the evolutionary *theme* appealed to many.[290] Indeed, to the Congregational theological liberal, T. Rhondda Williams, 'Evolution is still a hypothesis, but it is *the* hypothesis which is now used in every department of investigation . . . the use made of it at present is such that no man who wishes to serve his age in the interests of the Kingdom of God can afford to ignore it.'[291] Perhaps so; but some Christians were disturbed – at least until their theological leaders reassured them that since the theory of evolution did not yield an account of origins, but only of method, it could be annexed to the Christian doctrine of providence as suggesting the way the Creator went to work. As A.E. Garvie, in the wake of his teacher Fairbairn, put it, 'Evolution is God's method of creation of the world and man, and it is no leas the method of His revelation, for a communication beyond the capacity of man to receive and respond would be idle and vain. We may say that human development is by divine education.'[292] Thus by arguing that the theory of evolution concerned not origins, but a process, and by baptizing it in the name of God's providential method of working, most late nineteenth and early twentieth-century Nonconformist theologians felt able to accommodate the theme to their current understanding of the Bible in ways which some of their forebears would have found astounding. There can be no doubt, however, that theologians such as Fairbairn and Garvie – not to mention biblical scholars like the Primitive Methodist A.S. Peake and the Congregationalist W.H. Bennett – did much in their own right, and through those they sent out to pulpits across the land, to forestall the shriller aspects of evolutionary debate which were heard so stridently in America, and of which echoes are heard to this day.

With hindsight it may not unfairly be suggested that the second half of the nineteenth century was the hey-day of apologetics in terms of both quantity and variety. In view of the plethora of intellectual challenges which confronted them and the numerically-inspired confidence which undergirded them, it is not surprising that many Nonconformist philosophers felt called to address a printed word to those willing to devote their attention to the disputed questions of the day. Whether any of the writers was as influential over time as Butler, for example, may perhaps, without any disrespect to respected professors or journeyman pugilists (however lively), be doubted.

6

Epilogue

This attempt to portray the place of philosophy in the Dissenting academies and Nonconformist theological colleges from 1689 to 1920, and to review the philosophical contributions of their professors and alumni is almost complete. We have seen that the position of philosophy in the curriculum varied in accordance with the interests of the professors, the number of disciplines each had to cover, and the overall length of the several courses – from one to six years. The professors' published works vary in quality as one would expect; but given the constraints under which they worked, and the educational disadvantages which some of them strove so hard to overcome, it is a tribute to their persistence that we have been able to unearth so many useful contributions.

We should not forget that some of the authors considered were, by choice or circumstance, polymaths who published in a number of fields of enquiry. It would have been interesting to have sought links between their philosophical stances and their other scholarly interests. This, however, would have taken us too far afield, as would an account of surrounding Anglican thought. In this latter connection it may simply be declared that there was much more cut and thrust between Church of England writers and Dissenters and Nonconformists on questions of doctrine, church order, and church and state than ever there was over philosophical questions. Indeed, it is hard to resist the feeling that there was more commerce on philosophical questions between the Dissenters of the eighteenth century than there was between Nonconformists of the nineteenth century.

While it is noticeable that none of the eighteenth-century Dissenting philosophers became fully fledged Hutchesonians, it is not insignificant that some of the most substantial nineteenth-century works come from those who received at least part of their education in Scotland: Mellone on logic, Mackintosh on historical/critical studies, Alliott on mental philosophy, Payne on moral philosophy, and Hodgson on apologetics. But those who were educated in Scotland were sufficiently independent to think their own thoughts. Thus, for example, Robert Mackintosh largely broke from the idealism of his teacher Edward Caird, and Reid never had the impact upon nineteenth-century English and Welsh Nonconformists that he had upon American Presbyterians of the same century.

Notable among those who were trained in their own colleges are J.H. Godwin, Rogers, Martineau, Medley, Tymms and Davison. But wherever, and to whatever degree, they were trained, it is clear that their extra-establishment situation did not prevent a number of the Dissenting and Nonconformist professors from keeping abreast of philosophical discussions at large. Indeed, in some cases, as in Grove's separation of ethics from dogmatics in his Taunton curriculum, and Price's anticipations of Kant they were pioneers.

Throughout the period students were put through their logical paces, and among many of the professors interest in ethics was strong – particularly so in the eighteenth century; while in the nineteenth century the apologetic interest grew increasingly intense as many intellectual currents, friendly and hostile, had to be reckoned with. Into this reckoning were fed insights from the newer psychology and the concomitant recourse to religious experience.

It has not been possible to enter into detailed discussion with the authors noted herein, nor was it necessary, for a good deal of the work is ephemeral, and some of it is amateurish. Some indication of the value of the published offerings has, however, been presented at the end of chapters three to five. Viewing the period as a whole, Isaac Watts, Henry Grove and Richard Price stand out in the eighteenth century as, in his interestingly different way, does John Gill; while in the period 1800-1920 George Payne, Richard Alliott, James Martineau and Robert Mackintosh rise above the crowd: Henry Rogers, too, if literary grace be added to the criteria. All of these are historically interesting in their own ways and, while none of them can justifiably be followed slavishly in the twenty-first century, they can all at certain points illuminate present-day philosophical discussion.

No doubt where Nonconformist life and witness are concerned philosophy, like Septuagint studies or Cromwelliana must ever be kept in perspective. Of Richard Alliott it was said that 'Even to his acute and philosophic mind, nothing appeared so precious as the simple yet glorious statements respecting the love of God to a sinful and dying world.'[1] This attitude was almost certainly shared by all of those whose work we have reviewed. But it did not adversely affect their literary endeavours: on the contrary, it inspired them. It has thus been possible with this book to fill a gap in the history of philosophy, and to erect a modest memorial to those who taught and philosophized 'without the gate.'

Notes

Notes to Chapter 1
Introduction
pages 9-16

1. For the texts of these Acts see Henry Gee and William John Hardy, *Documents Illustrative of English Church History*, London: Macmillan, 1896. For a brief study of Dissenting life under the adverse legislation, for the patchy way in which the laws were enforced, and for the sufferings of the Dissenters, see Alan P.F. Sell, *Commemorations. Studies in Christian Thought and History*, Calgary: University of Calgary Press and Cardiff: University of Wales Press, 1993, ch. 5.
2. For a convenient summary of the statutes see H. Hale Bellot, *University College London 1826-1926*, London: University of London Press, 1929, 5-6. See further, Peter Searby, *A History of the University of Cambridge*, III, Cambridge: CUP, 1997.
3. See Alan P.F. Sell, *Church Planting. A Study of Westmorland Nonconformity*, (1986), Eugene, OR: Wipf & Stock, 1998, 27; [T.G. Crippen], 'Richard Frankland and his academy,' *Congregational Historical Society Transactions*, II, 1905-1906, 242-249. For the history of the academies at large see Irene Parker, *Dissenting Academies in England*, Cambridge: CUP, 1914; EEUTA; J.W. Ashley Smith, *The Birth of Modern Education: The Contribution of the Dissenting Academies 1660-1800*, London: Independent Press, 1954; David L. Wykes, 'The contribution of the Dissenting academy to the emergence of rational religion,' in Knud Haakonssen, ed., *Enlightenment and Religion. Rational Dissent in Eighteenth-Century Britain*, Cambridge: CUP, 1996 – though beware his opening remarks on the work of others.
4. See John Medway, *Memoirs of the Life and Writings of John Pye Smith, DD, LLD*, 1853, 75-76.
5. By 1810, however, the following complaint could be voiced: 'The grand error in almost every dissenting academy, has been the attempt to teach and to learn too much.' See *The Monthly Repository*, V, 1810, 560.
6. Thomas Barnes, *A Discourse delivered at the Commencement of the Manchester Academy, September fourteenth, one thousand seven hundred and eighty six*, Warrington: W. Eyres, [1786], 14. In view of his position

as thus quoted it is strange that it should have been said of Barnes that he questioned the value of philosophy for ministers of religion (*The Monthly Repository*, V, 410) – the more so since he taught it to ordinands and lay students alike. See his *Discourse*, app. II, 7-8. It would seem that Barnes's efforts to inculcate correctness and elegance did not bear fruit. He resigned in 1798, quite unable to maintain discipline. See H. McLachlan, *English Education under the Test Acts*, 260. For Barnes (1747-1810) see further DNB; Barbara Smith, ed., *Truth, Liberty, Religion. Essays Celebrating Two Hundred Years of Manchester College*, Oxford: Manchester College, 1986, *passim*.

7. On this matter he was opposed by Joseph Priestley (1733-1804) (*The Theological and Miscellaneous Works of Joseph Priestley*, ed. J.T. Rutt, reprinted Bristol: Thoemmes Press, 1999, XX, 303-330), who had taught at Warrington academy from 1761-67; by Mrs. Barbauld – Anna Laetitia Aikin (1743-1825), daughter of the Warrington tutor John Aikin (1713-80) – in her *Remarks on Mr. Wakefield's Enquiry*, 1792; and by William Parry (1754-1819) who, from 1799 until his death served as principal tutor at the evangelical Wymondley Academy. See his *A Vindication of Public and Social Worship, containing an Examination of the Evidence concerning it in the New Testament, and of Mr. Wakefield's Enquiry into its Propriety and Expediency*, 1792. The literature on Priestley is extensive, but for him, Aikin and his daughter (and his son John [1747-1822], who also taught at Warringdon) see DNB. Priestley and Aikin Jr. are in DECBP. For Parry see DNB; DNCBP; DWB.

8. Quoted by H. McLachlan, 'The Old Hackney College, 1786-1796),' UHST, III pt. 3, October 1925, 193; idem, EEUTA, 34.

9. *Memoirs of the Life of Gilbert Wakefield*, by himself, 1792, 353. For Wakefield see also DNB; EEUTA; H. McLachlan, *Warrington Academy, its History and Influence*, Manchester: The Chetham Society, 1943; P. O'Brien, *Warrington Academy 1757-86, its Predecessors and Successors*, Wigan: Owl Books, 1989; William Turner, *The Warrington Academy* (reprinted from *The Monthly Repository*, 1813-15), Warrington: Library and Museum Committee, 1957.

10. Ibid., 355.

11. See, for example, DTLC, ch. 22; idem, *Commemorations. Studies in Christian Thought and History*, (1993), Eugene, OR: Wipf and Stock, 1998, ch. 4; *The Dissenting Witness, Yesterday and Today*, the Annual Protestant Dissenting Deputies' Lecture, 2001, London: Protestant Dissenting Deputies of the Three Denominations, 2002.

12. See Alan P.F. Sell, *Philosophical Idealism and Christian Belief*, Cardiff: University of Wales Press and New York: St. Martin's Press, 1995.

13. In 1875, for example, the Congregationalists were maintaining ten theological colleges staffed by thirty-nine tutors. The total student enrolment was 277. Not surprisingly, the denominational papers from time to time carried articles querying the poor stewardship of resources which this situation seemed to imply.

14. The factors noted in this paragraph should prompt caution regarding the exaggerated claims made for academy tuition by some older writers – even

that the academies outshone Oxbridge in the quality and range of education provided (see below, ch. 2, n. 143). The truth would seem to be that Oxbridge was by no means altogether an educational black hole in the eighteenth century; that the best academy tutors could hold their own with scholars elsewhere; that mediocre provision could be found in both the academies and the universities; and that while some academy tutors – notably Henry Grove, Richard Price and Joseph Priestley – made advances in their disciplines, and while Isaac Watts's *Logic* was used until well into the nineteenth century, most academy tutors were more or less competent journeymen. For the Oxford side of the story see R. Greaves, 'Religion in the University,' and J. Yolton, 'Schoolmen, logic and philosophy,' in L.S. Sutherland and L.G. Mitchell, *The History of the University of Oxford. V. The Eighteenth Century*, Oxford: Clarendon Press, 1986.
15. The following Nonconformists in this category spring at once to mind: W. Donald Hudson (Baptist) at Exeter; John H. Hick (Presbyterian/United Reformed Church) at Birmingham and elsewhere; John Heywood Thomas (Congregational/United Reformed Church) at Manchester, Durham and Nottingham; and David A. Pailin (Methodist) at Manchester. The present writer has, in a vagrant career, drifted in and out of institutions secular and ecclesiastical.
16. For example, Paul Helm and Roger Trigg.

Notes to Chapter 2
Philosophy and Philosophers: The Eighteenth Century
pages 17-54

1. For some examples see DTLC, ch. 11.
2. For Northern College see Elaine Kaye, *For the Work of Ministry. A History of Northern College and its Predecessors*, Edinburgh: T. & T. Clark, 1999.
3. See further, T.C. Pfizenmaier, *The Trinitarian Theology of Dr. Samuel Clarke*, Leiden: Brill, 1997; cf. the review of this book by Alan P.F. Sell in *Enlightenment and Dissent*, XVIII, 1999, 270-75.
4. For whom see DNB; Lardner is in DECBP.
5. See Alan P.F. Sell, DTLC, ch. 5; C.G. Bolam, *et al.*, *The English Presbyterians*, London: Allen and Unwin, 1968; Ian Sellers, 'The Old General Baptists 1811-1915,' *The Baptist Quarterly*, XXIV, 1971, 30-41, 74-88.
6. See DTLC ch. 5.
7. For Towgood see DNB; DTLC ch. 7. For Price see further below.
8. J. Taylor, *A Narrative of Mr. Joseph Rawson's Case: or, an Account of several Occurrences relating to the Affair of his being excluded from Communion with the Congregational Church in Nottingham*, 2nd edn., 1742, 13. See further DTLC, ch. 7.
9. For Killingworth (1699-1778) see DNB.
10. Robert Aspland, *Bigotry and Intolerance Defeated; or, an account of the late Prosecution of Mr. John Gisburne, Unitarian Minister*, Harlow, 2nd edn., 1811, 9. For Aspland (1782-1845) see DNB; DNCBP; R. Brook Aspland, *Memoir of the Life, Works and Correspondence of the Rev. Robert*

Aspland, of Hackney, London, 1850.
11. Ibid.
12. Geoffrey F. Nuttall has accustomed us to speaking of 'Arminianism of the head' in contrast with 'Arminianism of the heart.' See his 'The influence of Arminianism in England,' in *The Puritan Spirit*, London: Epworth, 1967, 78. The rationalistic Arminians were indebted to Arminius (1560-1609) for their commitment to toleration and free enquiry, if not necessarily for every doctrine they espoused. The evangelical Arminians proclaimed the universal message of God's saving grace as freely available to all who would (as they could) claim it. See further, Alan P.F. Sell, *The Great Debate. Calvinism, Arminanism and Salvation*, (1982), Eugene, OR: Wipf and Stock, 1998, ch. 1. Lest we too quickly conclude that all Independents were Calvinists, we should remember their broadly Arminian minority which includes John Goodwin (1594?-1665) who found Calvinism 'fretting to my bowels' (*Redemption Redeemed*, 1651, ix); and Caleb Fleming (1698-1779), who refused the laying on of hands, and declared that he would 'recommend [the New Testament writings] to the people in the sense in which he would from time to time understand them' (W. Turner, *Lives of Eminent Unitarians*, 1840, I, 282) at his Presbyterian ordination, and subsequently regarded himself as an Independent. For Goodwin and Fleming see DNB. Goodwin is in DSCBP.
13. Brine (1703-65), Gill (1697-1771) and Wesley (1703-91) are in DNB, and the literature on the last is vast. For Gill see further ch. 3.
14. Concurrently, a debate was raging in Church of England circles over the publication in 1690 of William Sherlock's *Vindication of the Doctrines of the Trinity and of the Incarnation*. He was accused, notably by Robert South, of tritheism. As a result of reading Sherlock's book the Dissenters William Manning and Thomas Emlyn adopted, respectively, Socinian and Arian views. For Sherlock (1641-1707), South (1634-1716), Manning (1633?-1711) and Emlyn (1663-1741) see DNB. Sherlock and South are in DSCBP; Emlyn is in DECBP.
15. Whitefield replied to Wesley in a letter of 10 October 1741, for which see his *Journals*, London: The Banner of Truth Trust, 1960. See further, DTLC, ch. 2; idem, *The Great Debate*, ch. 3.
16. See DTLC, ch. 2; Alan P.F. Sell, '*The Gospel its own Witness* : deism, Thomas Paine and Andrew Fuller,' forthcoming in a *festschrift* for Allison A. Trites, Macon, GA: Mercer University Press.
17. See Alan P.F. Sell, *John Locke and the Eighteenth-Century Divines*, Cardiff: University of Wales Press, 1997, 206-29.
18. See J. Priestley, *Theological and Miscellaneous Works*, XVII; cf. XVIII, 553-5.
19. See further, Peter Byrne, *Natural Religion and the Nature of Religion*, London: Routledge, 1989; Robert Flint, *Anti-Theistic Theories*, Edinburgh: Blackwood, 6th edn., 1899, 443.
20. For a fuller account of the philosophical context in which the eighteenth-century divines worked, and for more detailed treatment of some of the issues to be noted in what follows, see Alan P.F. Sell, *John Locke and the Eighteenth-Century Divines*.

21. T. Ridgley, *A Body of Divinity: wherein the Doctrines of the Christian Religion are Explained and Defended*, (1731), New York: Robert Carter, 1855, 9-23. For Ridgley see further below.
22. *A Sermon preached at the Ordination of the Rev. Mr. John Notcutt at the Meeting-House in Green-Street, Cambridge, on July 22, 1735 by William Ford. With the Charge then given him by the Revd. Mr. Tobias Wildboar; and Mr. Notcutt's Confession of his FAITH*, 1735, 25. For references to similar examples see DTLC, 37-40. Notcutt subsequently became a Socinian and left the ministry for business. He died in 1778.
23. A. Vos, *Aquinas, Calvin and Contemporary Protestant Thought*, Washington, DC: Christian University Press, 1985, 91, quoting Aquinas, *Summa Theologiae*, 2a2ae. 1, 4 ad 2m.
24. G. de Broglie, 'The vraie notion thomiste des 'praeambula fidei',' *Gregorianum*, XXXIV, 1953, 341-89.
25. *The Logike of the Moste Excellent Philosopher P. Ramus Martyr*, London, 1574, 7.
26. Ibid., 10.
27. Ibid.
28. See J.D. Eusden, 'Ames,' DBSCP and references. For Perkins (1558-1603) and Ames (1576-1633) see DNB. Perkins is also in DBSCP. See also, Donald K. McKim, *Ramism in William Perkins' Theology*, New York: Peter Lang, 1987.
29. For Tallents and Frankland see DNB; EEUTA. For Woodhouse see EEUTA. For all three see CR; FAE.
30. Irene Parker, *The Dissenting Academies of England*, [1914], reprinted New York: Octagon Books, 1969, 75-6.
31. *Extracts from the Diary and Autobiography of the Rev. James Clegg*, ed. Henry Kirke, Buxton, 1899, 21.
32. Jean Le Clerc (1657-1736), born in Geneva, became a Remonstrant and taught philosophy and *belles lettres* at Amsterdam. On Limborch's death he became professor of church history there.
33. See *Lancashire and Cheshire Wills and Inventories at Chester*, ed. J.P. Earwarker (Chetham Society, N.S. III), 1884, 192-3. Concerning the less familiar authors in this list: the *Ethica* of Eustachius de Saint-Paul (1573-1640) was pubished at Cambridge in 1654; Andreas Froman's *De anima in genere* was published in Jena in 1620; the *Logica Elenctica* of Thomas Goveanus was published in Dublin in 1683; the *Logica* of the Pole, Martinus Smiglecki (d. 1619?) appeared in 1618.
34. J. Toulmin, *An Historical View of the State of the Protestant Dissenters in England*, Bath, 1814, 225-30.
35. 'An Account of the Dissenting Academies from the Restoration of Charles the Second,' DWL MS 24.59.25. For James Owen (1654-1706) see DNB; DWB; EEUTA; FAE.
36. See Samuel Palmer (Ker's pupil), *A Defence of the Dissenters Education in their Private Academies*, 1703, 4-6. Palmer was replying to Samuel Wesley's *A Letter from a Country Divine, concerning the Education of Dissenters in their private Academies*, 1703. Wesley, who conformed in 1688, had been a student under Charles Morton at the Independent Academy

at Newington Green. Ker (1639-1723) had studied under Thomas Doolittle (1632?-1707), a Cambridge man, at Islington academy. For Doolittle and Ker see EEUTA; FAE; for the former see CR; DNB.

37. For the fluctuating fortunes of Locke in one Oxford college see E.G.W. Bill, *Education at Christ Church, Oxford 1660-1800*, Oxford: The Clarendon Press, 1988, 300. See also Alan P.F. Sell, *John Locke and the Eighteenth-Century Divines*.
38. Thomas Amory in his Preface to Henry Grove's *Posthumous Works*, 1745, I, xiv. For Warren (c.1642-1706) see CR; DNB; DSCBP; EEUTA; FAE.
39. J. Toulmin, *An Historical View*, 230 ff.
40. 'An Account of the Dissenting Academies,' 33.
41. *Cambridge History of English Literature, IX: From Steele and Addison to Pope and Swift*, Cambridge: CUP, 1912, 333. For high praise of Jollie's 'divine enthusiasm' see the remarks of his pupil, Benjamin Grosvenor in Giles Hester, *Attercliffe as a Seat of Learning and Ministerial Education*, London: Elliot Stock, 1893, 34-5. See further, K.W. Wadsworth, *Yorkshire United Independent College*, London: Independent Press, 1954, 29-33. Derek Linkens, 'Timothy Jollie and the Attercliffe Academy,' *The Banner of Truth*, no. 173, February 1978, 22-8. For Jollie (1659?-1714) see DNB; EEUTA; FAE.
42. The possibility is mentioned by Alexander Gordon in FAE, but not in his DNB article on Oldfield. For Oldfield see further DSCBP; EEUTA.
43. For Shuttlewood (1632-89) see CR; DNB; EEUTA. For Saunders (fl.1680-1730) see EEUTA; FAE.
44. So Walter D. Jeremy, *The Presbyterian Fund and Dr.Daniel Williams's Trust*, London: Williams & Norgate, 1885, 104.
45. J. Oldfield, *An Essay towards the Improvement of Reason; in the pursuit of Learning and Conduct of Life, 1707*, Introduction, para. 11; I.i; II.ix para. 7.
46. Not 'At Kibworth' as stated by H. McLachlan, EEUTA, 213.
47. For Benion (1673-1707/8) see EEUTA. For Doddridge (1702-51) see DEB; DECBP; DNB; EEUTA; J. van den Berg and G.F. Nuttall, *Philip Doddridge(1702-1751) and the Netherlands*, Leiden: Brill, 1987; M. Deacon, *Philip Doddridge of Northampton 1702-51*, Northamptonshire Libraries, 1980; G.F. Nuttall, ed., *Philip Doddridge 1702-51*, London: Independent Press, 1951; idem, ed., *Calendar of the Correspondence of Philip Doddridge, D.D. (1702-1751)*, London: HMSO, 1979.
48. See H. McLachlan, *Essays and Addresses*, Manchester: Manchester University Press, 1950, 169-171.
49. See further, H.M.B. Reid, *The Divinity Professors in the University of Glasgow*, Glasgow: Maclehose, 1923, ch. 6; Henry F. Henderson, *The Religious Controversies of Scotland*, Edinburgh: T. & T. Clark, 1905, ch. 1. Carmichael (1672-1729) and Simson (1668?-1740) are in DNB; the former is in DECBP, the latter in DSCHT. For Hutcheson see further below.
50. For the Scottish philosophical heritage see John Veitch, 'Philosophy in the Scottish universities,' *Mind*, II, 1877, 74-91 and 207-234. See also the admirable article by Martin Fitzpatrick, 'Varieties of candour: Scottish and English style,' *Enlightenment and Dissent*, VII, 1988, 35-56.

51. For Leechman (1706-85) see DECBP; DNB; DSCHT; H.M.B. Reid, op.cit., ch. 8.
52. So William Turner, *Lives of Eminent Unitarians*, I, 364. See further, Alan P.F. Sell, *Church Planting*, 39-41 and references. For Rotheram (1694-1752) see DECBP; DNB; EEUTA.
53. See the New College MS L185 at DWL. This is a notebook which contains (101-5) 'A Catalogue of Books given to the Academical Library [at Daventry/Northampton] with the Names of the Donors.' The list contains Watts's *Logic*, but nothing by Locke. See further, Geoffrey F. Nuttall, 'The New College, London, Library,' in his *New College, London and its Library*, London: Dr. Williams's Trust, 1977.
54. See Alexander Gordon, *Addresses Biographical and Historical*, London: The Lindsey Press, 1922, 80.
55. For Morton (1627-98) see CR; DNB; EEUTA; FAE.
56. For Cradock (1680?-1719) see DNB; EEUTA.
57. For Jones (1681?-1719) see DECBP; DNB; DWB; EEUTA.
58. So Giles Hester, *Attercliffe as a Seat of Learning and Ministerial Education*, 31.
59. Quoted in DNB. For Latham (1688-1754) see EEUTA; H. McLachlan, *Essays and Addresses*, ch. 9.
60. For Ashworth (1722-75) see DNB; EEUTA.
61. See further W.D. Jeremy, *The Presbyterian Fund*; Geoffrey F. Nuttall, 'Welsh students at Bristol Baptist College, 1720-1797,' *Transactions of the Honourable Society of Cymmrodorion*, 1978, especially 181 and appendix.
62. For Lavington (d. 1764), Rooker (1728/8-80), Reader (d. 1794) and Small (d. 1834) see DTLC, ch. 11; EEUTA.
63. For Conder (1714-81) see DEB; DNB; EEUTA.
64. J. Priestley, *Memoirs of Dr. Priestley*, 1805, 16.
65. Quoted in J. Taylor, *A Scheme of Scripture Divinity*, London, 1762, Preface, vi-vii. See further, DTLC, ch. 7.
66. J. Priestley, *Memoirs*, 18. For Clark (1728-69) see EEUTA; G.E. Evans, *Midland Churches*, Dudley, 1899 (but beware of confused dates).
67. For Bull (1738-1814) see DNB; EEUTA.
68. For Savage (1721-91) see DNB; EEUTA.
69. For Rees (1743-1825) seeDECBP; DNB; DWB; EEUTA
70. For Kippis (1725-95) see DECBP; DNB; EEUTA.The financial consequences of undue theological variety within a given institution could be severe, as when 'The Independents almost entirely deserted the [Carmarthen] Academy from 1759 to 1779, because of the theological views of the tutors.' See H.P. Roberts, 'The history of the Presbyterian academy Beynllywarch-Carmarthen,' UHST, IV no. 4, October 1930, 345.
71. For Dixon (1680?-1729) and Whitehaven see DECBP; DNB; EEUTA; H. McLachlan, *Essays and Addresses*, 131-146.
72. For Chorlton (1666-1705) and Coningham (1670-1716) see DNB; EEUTA.
73. To be found at Harris-Manchester College, Oxford. For Winder (1693-1752) see DNB.
74. For Benson (1699-1762) see DNB.

75. For Dodwell (1705?-84) see DECBP; DNB.
76. Among those not deceived were Philip Doddridge and John Wesley. See Alan P.F. Sell, *John Locke and the Eighteenth-Century Divines*, 68-9
77. G. Benson, *The Reasonableness of the Christian Religion*, London: J. Noon, 1743, 158. In 1746 Benson published a second edition with an appendix in which he replied to his critics.
78. For Annet (1693-1769) and Morgan (d. 1743) see DECBP; DNB.
79. For Hill (d. 1720) see DNB; EEUTA.
80. For Grove see DECBP; DNB; DTLC, ch. 6; EEUTA; Alan P.F. Sell, 'Introduction' to *Henry Grove: Ethical and Theological Writings*, Bristol: Thoemmes Press, 2000. References are to this edition.
81. H. Grove, III, 176.
82. Ibid., 210-11.
83. Ibid., 203.
84. For Collier (1680-1732) see DECBP; DNB.
85. H. Grove, op.cit., III, 179.
86. Ibid., 233.
87. Ibid., 234.
88. For Hallett (1691?-1744) see DNB; EEUTA.
89. H. Grove, op.cit., III, 243-44.
90. Ibid., 245-6.
91. Ibid., IV, 141.
92. Thomas Amory in 'Memoir of the Rev. Henry Grove,' *The Protestant Dissenter's Magazine*, III, March 1796, 82.
93. See further DTLC, ch. 6.
94. See John Ball, *Some remarks on a new way of preaching*, 1736.
95. Quoted by G. Stanley Hall, 'On the history of American college textbooks and teaching in logic, ethics, psychology and allied subjects,' *Proceedings of the American Antiquarian Society*, N.S. IX, 1894, 147.
96. For Foster see DECBP; DNB. For Gale (1680-1721) see DNB.
97. J. Foster, *The Usefulness, Truth and Excellency of the Christian Revelation*, iii.
98. Ibid., 4-5.
99. For Brine (1703-65) see DNB; Alan P.F. Sell, *The Great Debate*, 77-80.
100. For Eames (1686-1744) see DECBP; DNB; EEUTA.
101. A. Gordon in DNB.
102. T. Amory, *A Sermon preached at Lewin's-Mead, Bristol, at theOrdination of the Reverend Mr. William Richards, May the 22d. 1751*, London [1751], 12.
103. Idem, *Christ the Light of the World . . . a Sermon preached at the Young Men's Lecture at Exon, Thursday, September 11, 1735*, London, 1735, iii.
104. Idem, *Twenty-Two Sermons*, 1766, 39 n.
105. John Yates, *A Funeral Discourse, occasioned by the death of the Rev. Dr. Barnes, preached at Cross-Street Meeting House in Manchester on Sunday 15th July 1810*, Liverpool, 1810, 43.For Yates (1755-1826) see Walter Wilson MS A.12.10-14 at DWL; *The Monthly Repository*, 1826, 693. Trained at Warrington, he ministered at Gildersome, Yorkshire (1776-7) and Kaye Street, Liverpool (1777-1823). I cannot suppress the observation

that, a few fugitive articles apart, Yates's words could have been written of my own teacher of Christian doctrine, the greatly loved and respected George Phillips (1893-1967) of Lancashire Independent College, for whom see CYB 1968, 440.
106. William Enfield, *A Funeral Sermon, occasioned by the death of the late Rev. John Aikin, D.D., Professor of Divinity at the Academy in Warrington*, Warrington, 1781, 8-9, 12.
107. *The Works of Thomas Reid, D.D.*, ed. W. Hamilton, Edinburgh, 1846, 421.
108. J. Priestley, *Works*, III, 33. I dallied longer in this thicket in DTLC, ch. 15.
109. For David Hartley (1705-57), Samuel Horsley (1733-1806) and Thomas Reid (1710-96) see DECBP; DNB.
110. W. Jones in his *Life* of Horne prefixed to the latters *Works*, 1809, 145, 148. For Horne (1730-92) see DNB.
111. For Price see DECBP; DNB; EEUTA; D.O. Thomas, *The Honest Mind. The Thought and Work of Richard Price*, Oxford: Clarendon Press, 1977; and the present writer's review in *Philosophical Studies* (Dublin), XXVI, 1979, 305-10; D.O. Thomas, J. Stephens and P.A.L. Jones, *A Bibliography of the Works of Richard Price*, Aldershot: Scolar Press, 1993.
112. For Jones (fl. 1715-64) see DWB; H.P. Roberts, 'Nonconformist academies in Wales 1662-1862,' *Transactions of the Honourable Society of Cymmrodorion*, 1930, 55-6. He is not to be confused with Samuel Jones of Brynllywarch academy or Samuel Jones of Tewkesbury academy.
113. For Griffiths (d. 1741) see DWB.
114. H. McLachlan, 'The Old Hackney College,' 190 and references.
115. For Jones see DTLC ch. 12. Shortly before his death Jones wrote a memoir of his life, which came into the possession of the Reverend S. Jones of Wolverhampton, who made it available to James Scott. Scott edited it and filled it our with his own comments and independently-gathered information. The Scott MS is held by Messrs. Haward and Evers, Solicitors, of Stourbridge, who kindly granted me permission to publish extracts from it.
116. For Thomas see DWB; EEUTA; G.D. Owen, *Ysgolion a Cholegau yr Annibynwyr*, Abertawe, 1939, ch. 3.
117. N. Jones; see Joshua Wilson MS I. 27 – New College, London, MSS at DWL.
118. DTLC, 375. For Davies (1694?-1770) see DWB; G.D. Owen, op.cit., ch. 3. For Jardine (1732-66) see DWB.
119. For Watts see DECBP; DNB; A.P. Davis, *Isaac Watts*, London: Independent Press, 1946. Chapter 6 concerns Watts's philosophy. It is entertaining but not definitive. See also Andrew Pyle's Introduction to the reprinted edition of a selection of Watts's *Works*, Bristol: Thoemmes Press, 1999.
120. I. Watts, *The Strength and Weakness of Human Reason*, London, 1731, 280; reprinted 1999.
121. See I. Watts, *Logick*, 1725 edn. reprinted 1999, 414-17.
122. Ibid., 458-60.
123. Ibid., 514-15.
124 I. Watts, *Philosophical Essays on Various Subjects*, 1842, reprinted 1999, 102.

125. Ibid., 119.
126. Quoted ibid., 300.
127. Ibid., 194.
128. Ibid., 194-5.
129. I. Watts, *Horae Lyricae*, 1834, reprinted 1999, 163-4.
130. For Ridgley see DNB; EEUTA.
131. T. Ridgley, *A Body of Divinity*, I, vii.
132. A. Gordon's DNB article on Ridgley.
133. Ibid., 145.
134. For Foskett see DEB; EEUTA; *Bristol Baptist College. 250 Years 1679-1929*, published by the College, [1929], 17-19, with portrait facing p. 17; Norman Moon, *Education for Ministry. Bristol Baptist College 1679-1979*, published by the College, 1979; Roger Hayden, 'The contribution of Bernard Foskett,' in William H. Brackney and Paul S. Fiddes, eds., *Pilgrim Pathways. Essays in Baptist History in Honour of B.R. White*, Macon, GA: Mercer University Press, 1999, 189-206.
135. For Ryland (1723-92) see DNB.
136. Ryland's complete programme is in BQ, II, 1924-5, 249-52. Samuel Pufendorf (1632-94), following Grotius, developed a doctrine of natural rights grounded in reason (as opposed to rights grounded in the God-given Decalogue) in his *De jure naturae et gentium*, 1672.
137. I am grateful to the former principal of Bristol Baptist College, the Reverend Dr. J.E. Morgan-Wynne, and to the former librarian, Stella Reed, for granting me access to the College's manuscript collection.
138. B. Foskett, MS on *Pneumatology*, 4.
139. For Evans see DEB; DWB; EEUTA. Foskett was minister at Broadmead as well as principal of the College.
140. See Stephen A. Swaine, *Faithful Men; or, Memorials of Bristol Baptist College, and some of its most Distinguished Alumni*, London: Alexander & Shepheard, 1884, 78, 124. See also Norman Moon, *Education for Ministry. Bristol Baptist College 1679-1979*, Bristol: Bristol Baptist College, 1979.
141. Quoted ibid., 129-33.
142. For Taylor see DNB; EEUTA.
143. A. Taylor, *An Introduction to Logick*, 1739, 12 (MS at DWL).
144. Ibid., 33.
145. Ibid., 43-4.
146. For this episode see John Waddington, *Congregational History, 1700-1800*, London: Longmans, Green, 1876, 266-7.
147. See the extracts from Gibbons's diary in CHST, I, 328, 384, 380. Beware of McLachlan's broken quotation and reference at p. 177 n. 6 of EEUTA. He here misquotes the third quotation above, conflates it with the first, incorrectly places both in 1755, and wrongly locates both on p. 328. Gibbons's Diary is in the Congregational Library at DWL.
148. See T. Gibbons, *A Sermon preached at the Ordination of Mr. Thomas Gibbons, October 27, 1743. At Haberdashers' Hall, London. By John Guyse, D.D. Together with an Introductory Discourse by Richard Rawlin. Mr. Gibbons's Confession of Faith. And an exhortation to him by Thomas*

Hall, 1743, 17, 19.
149. Quoted by S.A. Swaine, *Faithful Men*, 123.
150. J. Rippon, *A Brief Essay towards an History of the Baptist Academy at Bristol*, 1795; in idem, *The Baptist Annual Register*, II, 445.
151. See D. Elwyn Davies, 'Education and radical Dissent in Wales in the eighteenth and nineteenth centuries,' UHST, XIX no. 2, April 1988, 96.
152. For Davies (1739?-1817) see DWB.
153. See *Congregational Magazine*, April 1821.
154. See Gareth Davies, 'Trevecka (1806-1964),' *Brycheiniog*, XIV, 1971, 46. See further, Geoffrey F. Nuttall, *The Significance of Trevecca College 1768-91*, London: Epworth Press, 1969.
155. For Fletcher (1729-85) see DEB; DNB; Patrick Streiff, *Reluctant Saint? A Theological Biography of Fletcher of Madeley*, Peterborough: Epworth Press, 2001.
156. [A.C.H. Seymour], *The Life and Times of Selina, Countess of Huntingdon*, II, 1840, 102. Presumably we must take this statement at face value, for it would surely be a sign of an unsanctified mind to suspect that the students were engaged in derailing the president from the syllabus – the oldest trick in any student's book.
157. For Simpson (1764-1817) and Scott (1710-83) see DEB; K.W. Wadsworth, *Yorkshire United Independent College*, London: Independent Press, 1955; E. Kaye, *For the Work of Ministry*, Edinburgh: T. & T. Clark, 1999.
158. *The Monthly Repository*, XIII, 1818, 66.
159. So his DNB article.
160. J. Newton, *Works*, 1808, V, 59-100. Newton's *Plan*, dated 14 May 1782, was first printed in 1784.
161. Josiah Bull, *Memorials of the Rev. William Bull*, 1864, 102. My italics. For Bull (1738-1814) see DNB.
162. J.W. Ashley Smith, *The Birth of Modern Education. The Contribution of the Dissenting Academies 1600-1800*, London: Independent Press, 1954, 231.
163. Letter of December 1786, *Memorials*, 162.
164. In fairness, it must be noted that the reading prescribed for the theological parts of the course was diverse, mystics and hyper-Calvinists alike being studied (and corrected as necessary).
165. See further DTLC, ch. 5.
166. For which see EEUTA; Arthur D. Morris, *Hoxton Square and the Hoxton Academies*, privately printed, 1957.
167. For Rees see DECBP; DNB; DWB; EEUTA.
168. For Jennings (1691-1762) see DNB; EEUTA.
169. Thomas Rees, *Address delivered at the Old Jewry Chapel in Jewin Street, on Saturday, the 19th day of June, 1825, over the body of the late Rev. Abraham Rees, D.D., F.R.S., &c., &c., previously to his interment in Bunhill Fields*, London: Longman, 1825, 49. Abraham and Thomas Rees were not related.
170. For Jones (1681?-1719) see DECBP; DNB; DWB; EEUTA.
171. For Griffith (d. 1708) see DWB; EEUTA.
172. The quotations are from Secker's letter, reprinted in Thomas Gibbons,

Memoirs of the Rev. Dr. Isaac Watts, D.D., 1780, 351, 348-9.
173. See further, William Davies, *The Tewkesbury Academy*, Tewkesbury: W.J. Gardner, [c. 1905].
174. For Chandler (1693-1766) see DECBP; DNB; EEUTA; Robert M. Burns, *The Great Debate on Miracles from Joseph Glanvill to David Hume*, Leisburg, PA, 1981; John Stephens, 'Samuel Chandler and the Regium Donum,' *Enlightenment and Dissent*, XV, 1996, 57-70.
175. For Jennings see DNB; EEUTA.
176. J. Locke, *Works*,ed. Bohn, 1854, II, 457, 421.
177. After Richard Baxter; otherwise, 'neonomianism': the view that by the Holy Spirit's enabling, the elect are able to fulfil the new law inaugurated by Christ. See further, Alan P.F. Sell, *The Great Debate*, 31-33.
178. Letter of Doddridge to Samuel Clark, [22] September 1722. See Geoffrey F. Nuttall, *Calendar of the Correspondence of Philip Doddridge*, no. 35. The nineteenth-century Congregational historian, John Waddington, recounter of so many insightful anecdotes, cites this sentence to show that 'The instruction [Doddridge] received at [Kibworth] was diversified, but not calculated to form a sound theologian or an efficient minister.' See his *Congregational History 1700-1800*, 273. This simply shows that one person's openness is aother's indecisiveness. Certainly Doddridge was praising Jennings for his method; more partisan contemporaries would have denounced him for it.
179. DWL MSS 24.179.4 (copy); cf. G.F. Nuttall, *Calendar*, no. 190.
180. See further, A. Victor Murray, 'Doddridge and education,' in Geoffrey F. Nuttall, ed., *Philip Doddridge 1702-51*.
181. Clark to Doddridge, 3 October 1721, in J.D. Humphreys, *Correspondence and Diary of Philip Doddridge*, 1829-31, I, 39.
182. See Doddridge's shorthand MS, 'An Abstract of the References in our Lectures of LOGICK,' New College, London, MS L95, at DWL.
183. J. Orton, *Memoirs of the late Reverend Dr. Philip Doddridge*, Shrewsbury, 1766, 89ff. Cf. Doddridge's *Works*, 1802-5, IV, 253-4. For Orton (1717-83) see DEB; DNB; EEUTA.
184. Quoted by J.W. Ashley Smith, *The Birth of Modern Education*, 138; cf. 139.
185. J. Orton, op.cit., 101.
186. P. Doddridge, *Works*, V, 473.
187. See J.D. Humphreys, op.cit., I, 428.
188. Idem, *A Course of Lectures on the Principal Subjects of Pneumatology, Ethics, and Divinity: with reference to the most considerable Authors on each Subject*, 1763, lect. 172. For the context of this debate see Alan P.F. Sell, *John Locke and the Eighteenth-Century Divines*, ch. 6.
189. Idem, *Works*, IV, 321-3, 341, 543.
190. For Savage see DNB; EEUTA.
191. Quoted by J. Waddington, *Congregational History 1700-1800*, 496.
192. For Hill see DTLC, 378.
193. J. Williams, *Memoirs of the late Reverend Thomas Belsham*, 1833, 78. For Belsham (1750-1829) see also DECBP; DNB.
194. *The Monthly Repository*, X, 1815, 186.

195. Quoted by H. McLachlan, EEUTA, 158. The Kenrick Letters are at DWL, and are reprinted in UHST, III, IV, 1923-6, 1927-30. For Kenrick (1759-1804) see DNB; EEUTA.
196. See J. Williams, op.cit., 224-5.
197. So J. Drummond and C.B. Upton, *Life and Letters of James Martineau*, London: Nisbet, 1902, II, 258 (not 252 as given in EEUTA, 162).
198. I am grateful to Principal Ralph Waller of Harris Manchester College, Oxford, and to Dr. Joanna Parker, formerly librarian there, for granting me access to the Belsham and other manuscripts.
199. T. Belsham MS, *Evidences of Divine Revelation*, Lect. V.i.
200. For Horsey see EEUTA.
201. The address was delivered on 8 January 1790. Copy at DWL.
202. R.L. Carpenter, *Memoirs of the Life of the Rev. Lant Carpenter, LL.D.*, Bristol, 1842, 26, 25.
203. See further EEUTA, 167-8.
204. J. Horsey, *Lectures to Young Persons on the Intellectual and Moral Powers of Man; the Existence, Character and Government of God; and the Evidences of Christianity*, London: Samuel Leigh, 1828, xiii-xiv. The lectures were written for the young people of Horsey's only pastorate: Castle Hill, Northampton, where he served from 1797 until his death in 1827. As we shall see, towards the end of his tenure the charge of Socinianism was urged against William Parry, tutor at Wymondley from 1799 to 1819.

Notes to Chapter 3
The Eighteenth-Century Dissenters' Contribution
pages 55-104

1. For Gill see DNB; BDEB; Alan P.F. Sell, *The Great Debate*, 127 and *passim*; Timothy George, in Timothy George and David S. Dockery, eds., *Baptist Theologians*, Nashville: Broadman Press, 1990, ch. 4; George M. Ella, *John Gill and the Cause of God and Truth*, Eggleston, Co. Durham: Go Publications, 1995; Michael A.G. Haykin, ed., *The Life and Thought of John Gill (1697-1771). A Tercentennial Celebration*, Leiden: Brill, 1997.
2. J. Gill, *Complete Body of Doctrinal and Practical Divinity*, (1769-70), Grand Rapids: Baker Book House, 1978, vii.
3. Richard Muller, 'John Gill and the Reformed Tradition,' in Michael A.G. Haykin, op.cit., 68.
4. See further, Knud Haakonssen, *Natural Law and Moral Philosophy*, Cambridge: CUP, 1995.
5. See further DTLC, ch. 6.
6. William Enfield, *A Funeral Sermon, occasioned by the Death of the late Rev. John Aikin, D.D. Professor of Divinity at the Academy in Warrington*, Warrington: W. Eyres, 1781, 17.
7. Henry Sidgwick, *Outlines of the History of Ethics for English Readers*, (1886), London: Macmillan, 1949, 163.
8. Ibid., 169.
9. T. Hobbes, *Leviathan*, ch. 13, in William Molesworth, ed., *The English*

Works of Thomas Hobbes, London: John Bohn, 1839, III, 113; cf. ch. 17 and VII, 73.

10. Cf. Hobbes: 'The right of nature, which writers commonly call *jus naturale*, is the liberty each man hath, to use his own power, as he will himself, for the preservation of his own nature. . . .' *Leviathan*, ch. 14, op.cit., 116.

11. J. Locke, *An Essay concerning Human Understanding,* ed. Peter H. Nidditch, Oxford: Clarendon Press, 1975, I.iii.6; idem, *Essays on the Law of Nature*, ed. W. von Leyden, Oxford: Clarendon Pess, 1954, 111.

12. See further, Isabel Rivers, *Reason, Grace, and Sentiment. A Study of the Language of Religion and Ethics in England 1660-1780*, Cambridge: CUP, II, 2000, 151, 236.

13. The traffic in philosophical and theological ideas between the Dissenters of England and Wales and Scotland with its Presbyterian predominance is of considerable importance in the eighteenth century. Respected Dissenters were fairly frequently honoured by Scottish universities. Among those here mentioned the following had Scottish DDs: Ridgley (Aberdeen), Watts (Aberdeen and Edinburgh), Taylor (Glasgow), Gill (Aberdeen), Amory (Edinburgh), Doddridge (Aberdeen), Price (Aberdeen), Evans (Aberdeen); Priestley was LLD of Edinburgh.

14. Of these last Joseph Butler is the most prominent. However, he rules himself out of consideration here because, although educated under Samuel Jones at the Dissenting academy in Tewkesbury, he conformed to the Church of England, proceeding then to Oriel College, Oxford. See DNB.

15. Of those to be discussed Price alone is referred to in Sidgwick's *History of Ethics*, and in Alasdair MacIntyre's *A Short History of Ethics*, London: Routledge & Kegan Paul, 1967. None of them is mentioned by J. Philip Wogaman, *Christian Ethics: A Historical Introduction,* London: SPCK, 1993.

16. For a harbinger of this argument see Richard Overton, *An Arrow against all Tyrants or Tyranny*, 1646. For Overton see DNB. Not, indeed, that eighteenth-century Dissenters would follow Overton at all points: in 1643 he published *Man's Mortality*, in which he declared it a fiction that at death the soul goes either to heaven or to hell. We are not, he contended, condemned or saved until the resurrection of all.

17. I. Watts, *The Works of the Rev. Isaac Watts, D.D.*, Leeds: Edward Baines, 1800, I, 576. In this chapter all quotations from Watts are drawn from this edition.

18. Ibid., 577.
19. Ibid., 577-8 n.
20. Ibid., 578.
21. Ibid., 580.
22. Ibid., 585.
23. Ibid., 376.
24. Ibid., 382.
25. Ibid., II, 367.
26. Idem, Sermon XXI, *Works*, I, 240.
27. Ibid., 246.
28. Ibid., 256.

29. Ibid.
30. Ibid., 261.
31. H. Grove, *A System of Moral Philosophy, by the late Reverend and Learned Mr. Henry Grove, of Taunton. Published from the Author's Manuscript, with his latest Improvements and Corrections by Thomas Amory*, London: J. Waugh, 1749, I, 3. Reprinted Bristol: Thoemmes Press, 2000 as vols. V and VI of *Henry Grove: Ethical and Theological Writings*.
32. Ibid., 11.
33. Ibid., 25.
34. Ibid., 37.
35. Ibid., 40, citing Hobbes, *De Homine*, c. 10.
36. J. Locke, *Essay*, III.ii.16.
37. H. Grove, op.cit., 42.
38. Ibid., II, 2.
39. Ibid., 7.
40. Ibid.
41. Ibid., 57.
42. Ibid., 66.
43. Ibid., 76.
44. Ibid., 78.
45. Ibid., 117.
46. Ibid., 122.
47. Ibid., 127.
48. Ibid., 133.
49. Ibid., 139, 145.
50. Ibid., 150.
51. T. Amory in H. Grove, *A System of Moral Philosophy*, II, 588.
52. Ibid., 590-91.
53. H. Grove, *Four Essays on Beneficence, Benevolence, Novelty, and the Human Soul*, 1714. In *Works*, 1747, IV, 305.
54. Ibid., 308.
55. H. Grove, *A System of Moral Philosophy*, I, 3. The claim was earlier made in Grove's 1714 essay on the human soul, *Works*, IV, 330.
56. H. Grove, *A Sermon preach'd at the Ordination of the Rev. Mr. Thomas Amory, and Mr. William Cornish, at Taunton, Somerset, Oct. 7, 1730...*, in Grove's *Works*, I, 470-71.
57. Ibid., London: R. Hett, 1731, xiv-xv.
58. For Taylor see DNB; BDECP; Alan P.F. Sell, *Dissenting Thought*, ch. 7; G.T. Eddy, *Dr Taylor of Norwich: Wesley's Arch-heretic*, Peterborough: Epworth Press, 2003.
59. For Dixon (1680?-1729) see DECBP; DNB; EEUTA; for Hill (d. 1719/20) see DNB under Hill, Thomas (1628?-1677?).
60. For Glover (d. 1745) see DECBP; Walter Wilson, *History and Antiquities of Dissenting Churches and Meeting-houses in London, Westminster and Southwark*, 1808, I, 124. For Price see below.
61. For Wollaston (1660-1724) see DNB; DECBP.
62. W. Wollaston, *The Religion of Nature Delineated*, 1724, 52.
63. J. Taylor, *A Sketch of Moral Philosophy; or, an Essay to demonstrate the*

Principles of Virtue and Religion upon a New, Natural, and Easy Plan, London: J. Waugh, 1760, 6.
64. Ibid.
65. Ibid., 7.
66. Ibid., 8.
67. Ibid., 16.
68. Ibid., 26.
69. Ibid., 28.
70. Ibid., 50-51.
71. Ibid., 53.
72. Ibid., 69.
73. Ibid., 72.
74. Ibid., 79.
75. Ibid., 101.
76. Ibid., 102.
77. For Hutcheson (1694-1746) see DNB; DECBP.
78. J. Taylor, *An Examination of the Scheme of Morality advanced by Dr. Hutcheson, late Professor of Morality, in the University of Glasgow*, London: J. Waugh, 1759, 6.
79. Thomas Amory seems to have been more inclined towards the moral sense view. Thus, in a sermon of Psalm 145: 9, entitled 'Goodness a divine perfection,' he announces that God's goodness is confirmed to us by the moral sense he has implanted in us; and in a footnote he invokes Hutcheson's *Inquiry* in support. However, he nowhere develops a detailed theory which takes the moral sense as its starting-point. See T. Amory, *Twenty-Two Sermons*, 1766, 39..
80. Ibid., 15.
81. Ibid., 18.
82. Ibid., 21.
83. Ibid., 29.
84. Ibid., 47. Pp. 48-64 of Taylor's work comprise the quotations from Hutcheson's *Inquiry* and *An Essay on the Nature and Conduct of the Passions and Affections. With Illustrations on the Moral Sense*, 1728, which are refuted in Taylor's text.
85. See W. Turner, *Warrington Academy 1757-1786*, 30; H. McLachlan, *Warrington Academy, Its History and influence*, 45; DTLC, 198. For Seddon (1727-90) see DNB.
86. For all of these Bourns see DNB. For Samuel (1689-1754), to whom reference will be made later, see DNB; DTLC, ch. 7.
87. Joshua Toulmin, *Memoirs of the Revd. Samuel Bourn, for many years one of the Pastors of the United Congregations of the new Meeting in Birmingham and of the Meeting in Coseley*, Birmingham: Belcher, 1808, 124.
88. S. Bourn, *A Series of Discourses on the Principles and Evidences of Natural Religion and the Christian Revelation. And on some Practical Subjects*, London: R. Griffiths, 1760, 156.
89. Ibid., 158.
90. Ibid., 177.

91. Ibid., 185.
92. See S. Bourn, *Fifty Sermons on various Subjects, Critical, Philosophical, and Moral*, Norwich: R. Beatniffe, 1777, I, 91 ff.
93. See, for example, Henri Laboucheix, *Richard Price as Moral Philosopher and Political Theorist*, Oxford: The Voltaire Foundation at the Taylor Institution, 1982; John Stephens, 'The epistemological strategy of Price's *Review of Morals*,' *Enlightenment and Dissent*, V, 1986, 39-50.
94. R. Price, *Review*, Preface to the first edition, 4. Page references are to the edition of D.D. Raphael, Oxford: Clarendon Press, 1974.
95. Ibid., Preface to the first edition, 3. But Price never elevates knowledge at the expense of virtue. As he said in a sermon, 'There is always a *greatness* in knowledge; but, when separated from virtue, it is the greatness of a demon.' See *The Nature and Dignity of the Human Soul. A Sermon preached at St. Thomas's, January the First, 1766. For the Benefit of the Charity-School in Gravel-Lane, Southwark*, London: A. Millar, 1766.
96. Ibid., 15.
97. Ibid., 18; cf. 38. However, a number of scholars have noted that Price nowhere justifies the assumption on which his case depends, namely, that actions have natures.
98. Ibid., 41.
99. Ibid., 50.
100. Ibid., 62.
101. Ibid., 89.
102. Ibid., 109.
103. Ibid., 113.
104. Ibid., 117.
105. Ibid., 123.
106. Ibid., 143.
107. Ibid., 146.
108. Ibid., 177.
109. Ibid., 179.
110. Ibid., 184.
111. Ibid., 196.
112. Ibid., 220.
113. Ibid., 253.
114. Ibid., 257.
115. Ibid., 274.
116. Ibid., 266.
117. Andrew Kippis, *An Address delivered at the Interment of the late Rev. Dr. Richard Price on the twenty-sixth of April, 1791*, 1791, 8.
118. A. Kippis, *An Address delivered at the Interment of the late Dr. Richard Price on the twenty-sixth of April 1791*, 1791, 8-9.
119. J. Priestley, *A Discourse on the occasion of the Death of Dr. Price: Delivered at Hackney, on Sunday, May 1, 1791*, 1791, 20.
120. For Belsham see DNB; DECBP; John Williams, *Memoirs of the late Rev. Thomas Belsham*, 1833; Alexander Gordon, *Addresses Biographical and Historical*, London: The Lindsey Press, 1922, 283-310.
121. For Ashworth (1722-75) see DNB. He had trained at Daventry's predecessor

academy, Northampton, under Philip Doddridge.
122. Among illustrious ministers who served here in the nineteenth century are Robert Vaughan, who became the first President of Lancashire Independent College, Manchester, in 1843, and George Redford, who went there in 1826 on a stipend of £500 p.a. – not much below what the present writer received there in the 1960s.
123. T. Belsham, *Elements*, London: J. Johnson, 1801, 369.
124. T. Belsham, *A Summary View of the Evidence and practical Importance of the Christian Revelation*, London: R. Taylor, 1807, 198. He had earlier made the same point in *Knowledge the Foundation of Virtue. A Sermon addressed to the Young Persons who attend at the Gravel Pit Meeting, Hackney*, London: J. Johnson, 1795, 19.
125. Idem, *Elements*, 382-3.
126. Idem, *Knowledge the Foundation of Virtue*, 6.
127. Idem, *Elements*, 384.
128. Ibid., 386.
129. Ibid., iii.
130. Ibid., 22.
131. Ibid., 390.
132. Ibid., 391.
133. Ibid., 392.
134. Ibid., 415.
135. Ibid., 423.
136. Ibid., 424.
137. Belsham refers to Hume's *Essays*, II.ix, app. 1.
138. Ibid., 433.
139. Ibid., 447.
140. Idem, *Knowledge the Foundation of Virtue*, 24.
141. I. Watts, 'On the freedom of the will in God and in creatures,' *Works*, III, 555.
142. Ibid., 556.
143. Ibid., 568.
144. Ibid., 575.
145. H. Grove, *A System of Moral Philosophy*, I, 194.
146. Ibid., 195.
147. Ibid., 197-8, citing J. Locke, *An Essay concerning Human Understanding*, II.xxi.8.
148. Ibid., 199.
149. Ibid., 200-201.
150. Ibid., 217.
151. See further, Alan P.F. Sell, *John Locke and the Eighteenth-CenturyDivines*, 132-7.
152. H. Grove, *Four Essays*, 375.
153. J. Taylor, *The Scripture-Doctrine of Original Sin proposed to Free and Candid Examination*, London, 1740, 166.
154. Ibid., 167.
155. Ibid., 249.
156. In this paragraph and the next I draw on DTLC, 247-249.

157. J. Taylor, *A Supplement to the Scripture-Doctrine of Original Sin, &c., containing some Remarks upon two Books, viz. The Vindication of the Scripture-Doctrine of Original Sin, and The Ruin and Recovery of Mankind*, 1741, 75.
158. Ibid., 162.
159. Quoted by Alexander Gordon, *Addresses Biographical and Historical*, London: The Lindsey Press, 1922, 195.
160. S. Hebden, *Baptismal Regeneration Disproved; The Scripture Account of the Nature of Regeneration explained; and the absolute Necessity of such a Change argued from the Native Corruption of man since the Fall; In a Discourse on John 3: 5, 6. With remarks on some Passages in a late Book against Original Sin; and an Appendix Relating to Three different false Descriptions of Regeneration delivered in some Modern books*, 1741, 34.
161. See Jonathan Edwards, *The Great Christian Doctrine of Original Sin Defended*, in his *Works* (1834), reprinted Edinburgh: The Banner of Truth Trust, 1974, I, 146-233. See further David Weddle, 'Jonathan Edwards on men and trees, and the problem of human solidarity,' *Harvard Theological Review*, LXVII, 1974, especially 158-169.
162. R. Price, *Review*, 181.
163. Ibid., 182.
164. Ibid., 184.
165. Ibid.
166. Ibid., 210.
167. For Priestley see DNB; DECBP
168. R. Price in *A Free Discussion of the Doctrines of Materialism, and Philosophical Necessity*, London: J. Johnson, 1778, 340-41.
169. J. Priestley in ibid., 411. In some respects the libertarian/necessarian debate between Price and Priestley mirrors the debate between the high and evangelical Calvinists and the evangelical (as distinct from the rational) Arminians. Their question was (to put it in a crude nutshell): In the matter of our salvation, does God do all, or do we freely cooperate with him? The Calvinists stood for the former alternative with a view to honouring God's sovereignty; the evangelical Arminians took the latter route with a view to maintaining the dignity of human beings created in God's image. For an attempt to venture into this hornet's nest see Alan P.F. Sell, *The Great Debate*.
170. See UHST, III, 228.
171. Ibid., IV, 257.
172. Ibid., III, 8-9.
173. Ibid., 95-97.
174. Ibid., 513.
175. Ibid. It should not be supposed that Edwards's position on freedom and necessity was admired only by some on the side of Rational Dissent. On the contrary, the Baptists, John Sutcliff, John Ryland, Robert Hall and Andrew Fuller, for example, were among a number of other evangelicals indebted to Edwards. See Alan P.F. Sell, *The Great Debate*, 85-86. Nor was recourse had to Edwards on this subject only. For indications of some other aspects of his contribution to the thought of eighteenth-century

English divines see idem, *John Locke and the Eighteenth-Century Divines*, *passim*.
176. Alexander Gordon, *Addresses Biographical and Historical*, 308.
177. T. Belsham, *Letters upon Arianism, and other Topics in Metaphysics and Theology, in reply to the Lectures of the Rev. Benjamin Carpenter*, London: J. Johnson, 1803, 42. For Carpenter see George Eyre Evans, *Midland Churches. A History of the Congregations on the Roll of the Midland Christian Union*, Dudley: *Herald* Printing Works, 1899, *passim*.
178. Ibid., 46.
179. Ibid., 47.
180. Idem, *Discourses, Doctrinal and Practical; delivered in Essex Street Chapel*, London: R. Hunter, 1827, II, 102.
181 H. Grove, *A System of Moral Philosophy*, II, 61.
182. For this Bourn (1689-1754) see DNB; DTLC, ch. 7.
183. S. Bourn, *A Vindication of the Principles and Practice of the Protestant Dissenters*, London: J. Robinson, 1748, 130-31. Cf. ibid., 126-7.
184. Idem, *The True Christian Way of striving for the Faith of the Gospel. A Sermon preached to a Congregation of Protestant Dissenters, Ministers, and Private Christians, at their Yearly Meeting at Dudley in Worcestershire. On May 23rd 1738, being Whitsun-Tuesday*, London: J. Robinson, 1738, 9-14.
185. Ibid., 23. In a postscript to the printed sermon Bourn declares that 'It is just Ground both of Wonder and Lamentation' that this sermon, designed to promote peace, should have caused a commotion. I should love to know whether he had a twinkle in his eye when he made this ostensibly innocent remark.
186. Idem, *A Charge delivered at the Ordination of the Reverend Mr. Job Orton; at Shrewsbury, September 18. 1745*, Birmingham: T. Warren, 1745, 41. For Orton (1717-83) see BDEP; DNB; EEUTA.
187. J. Taylor, *A Defence of the Common Rights of Christians; and of the Sufficiency and Perfection of Scripture, without the aid of Human Schemes, Creeds, Confessions, &c.*, (1737), London: The British and Foreign Unitarian Association, 1839, 14.
188. Idem, *A Further Defence*, ibid., 41-2. How similar the attitude to Scripture to that of latter-day fundamentalists; how different the doctrines proclaimed by the latter from those of the eighteenth-century Arian divines.
189. Idem, *A Narrative of Mr. Joseph Rawson's Case*, 2nd edn., 1742, 9. See further, Alan P.F. Sell, *Dissenting Thought and the Life of the Churches*, ch. 7.
190. T. Amory, *Ministers not Lords over the Faith of Christians, but Helpers of their Joy. A Sermon preached at Lewin's-Mead, Bristol, at the Ordination of the Reverend Mr. William Richards, May the 22d. 1751*, London: J. Waugh, [1751].
191. Ibid., 17.
192. Ibid., 18-19.
193. Idem, *Christ the Light of the World; or, the Principal Improvements made in Religion by Christianity. Represented in A Sermon preached at the Young Men's Lecture at Exon, Thursday, September 11, 1735*, London: R. Hett,

1735, vi.
194. Idem, *Ministers not Lords over the Faith of Christians*, 24.
195. R. Flexman, *A Crown of life, the gratuitous Reward of the faithful Christian: A Sermon preached at the Old Jewry, July 10. 1774. On occasion of the Death of the Rev. Thomas Amory, D.D. who died June 24, in his seventy-fourth year*, London: J. Buckland, 1774, 35. For Flexman (1707-95) see DNB.
196. S. Bourn, *Discourses on Various Subjects* [see Bibliography], London: R. Griffiths, 1760, II, 431.
197. Ibid., 438-9.
198. Ibid., 441-2.
199. R. Price, *Review*, 180 n. Cf. idem, *The Vanity, Misery, and Infamy, of Knowledge without suitable Practice; represented in a Sermon preached at Hackney, November the 4th, 1770*, London: J. Buckland, 1770; D.O. Thomas and W. Bernard Peach, *The Correspondence of Richard Price*, Durham, NC: Duke University Press and Cardiff: University of Wales Press, 1983, I, 179.
200. Idem, *The Evidence for a future period of Improvement in the State of Mankind, with the Means and Duty of promoting it, represented in a Discourse, delivered on Wednesday the 25th of April, 1787, at the Meeting-House in the Old Jewry, London, to the Supporters of a new Academical Institution among Protestant Dissenters*, London: H. Goldney, 1787, 38, 55. The academy in question was that at Hackney, where Price himself was a tutor.
201. J. Priestley, *The Importance and Extent of Free Inquiry in Matters of Religion: a Sermon preached before the Congregations of the Old and New Meeting of Protestant Dissenters at Birmingham, November 5, 1785*, in *Works*, XV, 78.
202. Idem, *The proper Objects of Education in the present State of the World represented in a Discourse, delivered on Wednesday, April 17, 1791. At the Meeting-House in the Old-Jewry, London; to the Supporters of the New College at Hackney*, in *Works*, XV, 431.
203. T. Belsham, *Freedom of Enquiry, and Zeal in the Diffusion of Christian Truth, Asserted and Recommended in a Discourse delivered at Bristol, July 9, 1800, before the Society of Unitarian Christians, established in the West of England, for Promoting Christian Knowledge and the Practice of Virtue, by the Distribution of Books*, London: G. Woodfall, 1800, 2-3.
204. Ibid., 46.
205. S. Bourn, *The True Christian Way*, 20.
206. J. Taylor, *A Supplement to the Scripture-Doctrine of Original Sin*, 162. Taylor's views famously attracted the attention of Jonathan Edwards. See David Weddle, 'Jonathan Edwards on men and trees, and the problem of solidarity,' *Harvard Theological Review*, LXVII, 1974, 155-175.
207. T. Houlbrooke, *A Sermon occasioned by the Death of William Tayleur, Esq., delivered at a Meeting of Unitarian Dissenters, in Shrewsbury upon the fifteenth day of May, 1796*, Liverpool: J. M'Creery, 1796, 17.
208. T. Ridgley, *A Body of Divinity wherein the Doctrines of the Christian Religion are expounded and defended. Being the substance of several*

lectures on the Assembly's Larger Catechism, London, 1731, iii.
209. *A Charge and Sermon, together with an Introductory Discourse, and Confession of Faith, delivered at the Ordination of the Rev. Mr. Caleb Evans, August 18, 1767, in Broad-Mead, Bristol,* Bristol: S. Farley, 1767, 14.
210. Samuel Stennett, *The Mortality of Ministers contrasted with the Unchangeableness of Christ: in a Sermon, occasioned by the Decease of The Rev. Caleb Evans, D.D., Who departed this Life Aug. 9, 1791, in the 54th Year of his Age. . . . To which is added the Address delivered at his Interment, by the Rev. John Tommas,* London: Rivington and Marshall, 1791, 29. For Stennett see DNB; BDEB.
211. J. Tommas, ibid., 53-4.
212. R. Robinson, *Arcana: or the Principles of the late Petitioners to Parliament for Relief in the Matter of Subscription,* Cambridge: Fletcher & Hodson, 1774, 33; cf. 40. My comment in square brackets. For Robinson see DNB; BDEB.
213. For Scott see BDEB; K.W. Wadsworth, *Yorkshire United Independent College,* London: Independent Press, 1954, 34-55. For Toothill (1743?-1826), who ministered for fifty-eight years at Hopton, Yorkshire, and whose wife, unusually, was the daughter of his own foster-mother see James G. Miall, *Congregationalism in Yorkshire. A Chapter in Modern Church History,* London: John Snow, 1868, 280-81.
214. J. Toothill, *The Foundation of the dying Christian's Triumph, in the Prospect of Nature's Dissolution. A Sermon, preached, Feb. 2, 1783, at Heckmondwike in Yorkshire; on occasion of the Death of the Rev. Mr. James Scott, late Pastor of the Church, and Tutor to an Academy at that Place,* Huddersfield: J. Brook, 1783, 29.
215. G. Walker, *On the Right of Individual Judgment in Religion. A Sermon preached at Chewbent [sic], Lancashire, on the 25th June, 1800, at the Annual Provincial Meeting of the Ministers of the Presbyterian Persuasion,* Manchester: J. Johnson, [1800], 2.
216. See J. Owen, *Indulgence and Toleration Considered,* 1667; *A Peace-Offering in an Apology and Humble Plea for Indulgence and Liberty of Conscience,* 1667; *An Account of the Grounds and Reasons on which Protestant Dissenters desire their Liberty,* 1670, all in William Goold, ed., *The Works of John Owen,* (1850-3), London: The Banner of Truth Trust, 1968, XIII. For Locke's influence on this matter see further, Alan P.F. Sell, *John Locke and the Eighteenth-Century Divines,* 163-7.
217. I. Watts, *Works,* III, 167.
218. T. Amory in H. Grove, *A System of Moral Philosophy,* II, 525.
219. Idem, *Ministers not Lords over the Faith of Christians, but Helpers of their Joy,* 28.
220. See DTLC, ch. 22; Alan P.F. Sell, *The Dissenting Witness: Yesterday and Today,* forthcoming
221. S. Bourn, 'On religious liberty,' in *Discourses on Various Subjects,* II, 435, 437.
222. R. Price, *Observations on the Nature of Civil Liberty,* 1776, in D.O. Thomas, ed., *Richard Price, Political Writings,* Cambridge: CUP, 1991, 22.

223. Ibid.
224. See R. Price, *Observations on the Importance of the American Revolution*, 1785, in D.O. Thomas, ed., op.cit., 130-32.
225. Ibid., 133. Cf. idem, *A Discourse on the Love of our Country*, 1789, ibid., 176-96.
226. J. Priestley, *An Essay on the First Principles of Government*, in *Works*, XXII, 64-5.
227. Idem, *Various Observations relating to the Dissenters' application to Parliament for Relief from certain Penal Laws*, in *Works*, XXII, 478; cf. 68-76.
228. T. Belsham, *The Rights of Conscience asserted and defined, in reference to the modern interpretation of the Toleration Act*, London: J. Johnson, 1812.
229. See further, Frank Louis Maudlin, 'Truth, heritage, and eighteenth-century Baptists,' *Baptist Quarterly*, XXXV no. 5, January 1994, 211-28. It is thus no accident that the twentieth-century Calvinistic rationalist philosopher, Gordon H. Clark, thought highly of John Gill's content and method. See, for example, his *Biblical Predestination*, Nutley, NJ: Presbyterian and Reformed Publishing Company, 1966, ch. 6.
230. For a further example of this attitude see John Taylor, *A Further Defence of the Common Rights of Christians*, 1738, 78.
231. See Gregory A. Wills, 'The spirituality of John Gill,' in Michael A.G. Haykin, ed., *The Life and Thought of John Gill (1697-1771): A Tercentennial Appreciation*, Leiden: Brill, 1997, 203-4.
232. See *The Complete Works of the Rev. Andrew Fuller*, London: Holdsworth and Ball, 1831-2, II. For Fuller see DNB; BDEB.
233. See A. Fuller, 'On moral inability,' in *Works*, V, 672-5; cf. II, 68-73. See further, Alan P.F. Sell, *The Great Debate*, ch. 3.
234. See R. Price, *Review*, 253 ff. Cf. Kant, *Critique of Pure Reason*, (1781), trans. Norman Kemp Smith, second impression, London: Macmillan, 1980, 495-524 (Transcendental Dialectic, Bk. II, ch. 3, sections 3-6), for the classical arguments. For Kant's moral argument see his *Critique of Practical Reason*, (1788), trans. T.K. Abbott, *Kant's Theory of Ethics*, 4th edn., 1889, 220-229 (Bk. II, ch. 2, section 5).
235. I. Watts, *Works*, I, 576.
236. See, e.g. ibid., 376.
237. R. Price, *Review*, 117.
238. Luke 17: 10; Matt. 26: 7 ff.
239. R. Price, *Review*, 177.
240. Judges 21: 25.
241. Kant, *Fundamental Principles of the Metaphysic of Ethics*, trans. T.K. Abbott, London: Longmans, Green, 10th edn., 1926, 48. It may be suggested that Kant is better at envisaging unfortunate possibilities of moral disarray – hence his invocation of universalisability – than at supplying a criterion for determining the right action in a given situation.
242. R. Price, *The Evidence for a future Period of Improvement in the State of Mankind*, 38.
243. J. Toulmin, *An Historical View*, 228. On the other side of the Atlantic, at

Yale, the recitation of memorized material constituted a prominent classroom activity, and was prescribed in regulations of 1720 and 1726. See G. Stanley Hall, 'On the history of American college text-books and teaching,' 144. There are clear resemblances between the teaching method employed in the earlier academies and the old Scottish system of regenting; on which see John Veitch, 'Philosophy in the Scottish universities,' 82-5. Veitch finds regenting a deficient method where philosophy is concerned: 'The teaching of Philosophy by means of approved books is better than none; but it is not a good arrangement. Its tendency is to make little demand either on the research or the power of active thought of the teacher, and thus to repress originality' (ibid., 83). Hence also the philosophical barrenness of the English universities, whose burgeoning [in 1877] philosophical life is not owing to native influences, but to foreign inspiration and individual force' (ibid., 84).

244. *Protestant Dissenter's Magazine*, III, 1796, 83.
245. See *The Monthly Repository*, VIII, 1813, 168.
246. [S. Gough], *Enquiry into the Causes of the Decay of the Dissenting Interest*, 1730, 43.
247. J. Rippon, 'Essay on Bristol Academy,' in his *Register*, I, 345-51.
248. For the philosophical record of one Oxford college see E.G.W. Bill, *Education at Christ Church Oxford*, 263-8, 297-307.
249. See I. Parker, *The Dissenting Academies*, 132 ff. See further, E.J. Price, 'The Dissenting academies. A neglected chapter in the history of English education,' CHST, XI no. 1, April 1930, 38-51; EEUTA, 26-7, and *passim*; J.W. Ashley Smith, *The Birth of Modern Education*, ch.5. Among those who have sought to modify the claim is Nicolas Hans, *New Trends in Education in the Eighteenth Century*, London: Routledge & Kegan Paul, 1951, 54-62.
250. This point is confirmed by O. Lewis in an unpublished Open University MPhil dissertation, *The Teaching of Science in English Dissenting Academies 1662-1800*, 1989. Lewis found that the teaching of science was absent from almost half of the academies. But, with reference to the brighter spots we may note John Gascoigne's admission that although Cambridge reigns supreme in mathematics during the eighteenth century, and although some Dissenting academies had little place for science, by the end of that century 'Dissenting academies with their close links with provincial society were generally more responsive to . . . changes in scientific interests than the universities.' See his *Cambridge in the Age of Enlightenment. Science, Religion and Politics from the Restoration to the French Revolution*, Cambridge: CUP, 1989, 282; cf. 8. The Dissenters' influence upon and contribution to the learned life of provincial towns should not be overlooked where the fostering of scientific interests and the disseminatin of scientific knowledge are concerned. See, for example, Diana Harding, 'Mathematics and science education in eighteenth-century Northamptonshire,' *History of Education*, I no. 2, 1972, 139-59. It is important to understand that where science was present in the curriculum of the academies it was not there simply or primarily for educational or utilitarian purposes. The undergirding motive was theological, as the speech

of Thomas Barnes, quoted above, reminds us. God had supplied two 'books' – the Bible, and nature; and both were to be studied devoutly. Hence the emphasis throughout the century upon the cosmological and teleological arguments for the existence of God. For an account of another 'modern' subject see Yusef Azad, 'The limits of university: the study of language in some British universities and academies 1750-1800,' *History of Universities*, VII, 1988, 117-147.
251. L. Stephen, *History of English Thought in the Eighteenth Century*, New York, 1927, II, 386.
252. R. Baxter, *The Saint's Everlasting Rest* (1650), 1651 edn., unpaginated Preface to pt. II, dated 2 April 1651.
253. Ibid., pt. iv, 224.

Notes to Chapter 4
Philosophy and Philosophers: 1800-1920

1. R.B. Aspland, *Memoir of the Life, Works and Correspondence of the Rev. Robert Aspland*, London: E.T. Whitfield, 1850, 52. Aspland senior proceeded to Aberdeen University from Bristol, and there he forsook Calvinism for Arianism. In 1802 he left Arianism for 'the simple humanity of Christ.' Ibid., 123. For both Asplands see DNB.
2. See *Evangelical Magazine*, 1818, 172; EEUTA, 171-2.
3. J.G. Rogers, *An Autobiography*, London: James Clarke, 1903, 68. For Rogers see also DNB.
4. George Redford and John Angell James, eds., *The Autobiography of William Jay*, (1854), Edinburgh: The Banner of Truth Trust, 1974, 47. See further W. Jay, *Memoirs* of Winter, London: Williams and Smith, 1809, 253. For Jay (1769-1853) see also DEB; DNB.
5. J. Harris, *The Importance of an Educated Ministry: A Discourse preached preparatory to the Opening of the Lancashire Independent College*, [1843], 29. For Harris (1802-1856) see DNB.
6. D. Fraser, 'The minimum of education which our colleges ought to furnish, and which all college-educated ministers should be expected to possess,' in *Minutes of the Proceedings of a Conference of Delegates from the Committees of the Theological Colleges and Institutes connected with the Congregational Churches of England*, London: Jackson, Walford and Hodder, [1865], 8. He did not, however, encourage his students to take arts degrees through the University of London. See K.W. Wadsworth, *Yorkshire United Independent College*, London: Independent Press, 1954, 115. For Fraser (1820-1902) see Lucy A. Fraser, ed., *Memoirs of Daniel Fraser. . . . Half-a-Century of Educational Work*, London: Percy Lund, 1905; CYB, 1903, 175-176.
7. W.P. Jones, *Coleg Trefeca 1842-1942*, Llandysul: Gomer Press, n.d., 64.
8. Kenneth D. Brown, 'Nineteenth-century Methodist theological college principals: a survey,' PWHS, XLIV pt. 4, May 1984, 96.
9. Quoted by G.E. Milburn, *A School for the Prophets. The Origins of Ministerial Education in the Primitive Methodist Church*, privately published, [1981], 6. Though (p. 7) the same writer quotes *The Primitive*

Methodist Magazine, 1864, 466-467 where an (significantly?) imaginary conversation dares to begin thus: 'If some of the holy and honoured men who accomplished such wonders during the Connexion's infancy were living amongst us, with the acquirements they then possessed, would their zeal and piety alone atone for their lack of education? . . . [U]nless we meet this state of things . . . we shall have the mortification of seeing the intelligent part of our people, the young especially, deserting our ministry for one of higher attainments and better qualified to "teach".'

10. R. Vaughan, *Congregationalism: or the Polity of Independent Churches, viewed in relation to the State and Tendencies of Modern Society*, 2nd edn., revised and enlarged, 1842, 197, 200. For Vaughan (1795-1868) see DNB. For a more than ordinarily insightful memoir see *The Congregationalist*, VI, March 1877, 129-148.
11. See W.R. Ward, *Early Victorian Methodism*, Oxford: OUP, 1976, 14. This motive seems to have more to do with the market-place than with the virtues of theological education.
12. Adam Clarke in a letter of 16 June 1806, quoted by W. Bardsley Brash, *The Story of Our Colleges 1835-1935*, London: Epworth Press, 1935, 16. For Clarke (1760-1832), see BDEB; DMBI; DNB.
13. See *The Story of Our Colleges*, ch. 2; Oliver A. Beckerlegge, *The United Methodist Free Churches*, London: Epworth, 1957, ch. 1. For Bunting (1779-1858) see BDEB; DMBI; DNB; W.R. Ward, ed., *The Early Correspondence of Jabez Bunting*, Camden 4th series, 11, London: Royal Historical Society, 1972; idem, *Religion and Society in England, 1790-1850*, London: Batsford, 1972.
14. Quoted by Mortimer Rowe, *Unitarian College, Manchester. A Centenary Address*, privately printed, 1954, 5.
15. See further, Alan P.F. Sell, *Theology in Turmoil. The Roots, Course and Significance of the Conservative-Liberal Debate in Modern Theology*, (1986), Eugene, OR: Wipf and Stock, 1998, ch. 2.
16. See further, ibid., ch. 1; idem, *Philosophical Idealism and Christian Belief*, Cardiff: University of Wales Press and New York: St. Martin's Press, 1995.
17. So the DNB biography of Morell (1816-1891) by A.R. Buckland. See also DNCBP.
18. For the older colleges see EEUTA. For Homerton see T. H. Simms, *Homerton College 1695-1978* [Simms sets out from Homerton's predecessors], Cambridge: The Trustees of Homerton College, 1979. For Smith (1774-1851) see BDEB; DNB; J. Medway, *Memoir of the Life and Writings of John Pye Smith*, London, 1853; Alan P.F. Sell, *Commemorations. Studies in Christian Thought and History*, (1993), Eugene, OR: Wipf & Stock, 1998. For Hill (1784-1813), trained at Rotherham and appointed to Homerton in 1806, see EEUTA, 182-184.
19. For Kello (1750-1827) see J.A. Jones, *Bunhill Memorials. Sacred Reminiscences of Three Hundred Ministers and other Persons of Note, who are Buried in Bunhill Fields, of every Denomination*, London: James Paul, 1849, 121-123.
20. So DNB; however CYB, 1866, 239, states that Burder (1783-1864) was tutor from 1807-1829.

21. J. Stoughton, *Reminiscences of Congregationalism Fifty Years Ago*, London: Hodder and Stoughton, 1881, 14. For Stoughton (1807-1897) see DNB; DNCBP; CYB, 1898, 204-6; *John Stoughton. A Short Record of a Long Life*, by his daughter [Georgina King Lewis], London: Hodder and Stoughton, 1898.
22. 'Life at Hoxton College 1820-1823. Being part of the autobiography of Alexander Stewart, written for his children,' CHST, XV no. 2, April 1946, 77-8.
23. For Rogers (1806-1877) see DNB; DNCBP; DTLC chs. 17, 18; R.W. Dale, Memoir of Rogers prefixed to the 8th edn. of *The Superhuman Origin of the Bible*, London: Hodder and Stoughton, 1893.
24. *The Congregationalist*, VI, 1877, 624.
25. H. Rogers, 'Voltaire,' *Encyclopedia Britannica*, 8th edn., XXI, 1860.
26. Idem, *Essays from the Edinburgh Review*, III, 1855, 73.
27. Ibid., I, 190.
28. See further ibid., 88-194; DTLC, ch. 18.
29. For Godwin (1809-1889) see CYB, 1890, 143-5; DNCBP.
30. CYB, 1890, 144.
31. J.H. Godwin, *Intellectual Principles; or, Elements of Mental Science*, London: James Clarke, 1884, v.
32. Ibid., 46.
33. Ibid., 56-57.
34. Ibid., 78.
35. Ibid., 99.
36. Ibid., 111.
37. Ibid., 210.
38. For Stoughton (1807-1897) see BDEB; CYB, 1898, 204-206; DNB; DNCBP; *John Stoughton DD. A Short Record of a Long Life, by his daughter* [Georgina King Lewis], London: Hodder and Stoughton, 1898.
39. Thomson, who entered New College as a student in 1851 and died in 1918, has no CYB obituary, but he is in DNCBP ; for Redford (1785-1860) see BDEB; CYB, 1861, 230; DNB; DNCBP.
40. *The Calendar of the Congregational Colleges of England and Wales. Including the Countess of Huntingdon's College at Cheshunt*, printed for the editor, S. Newth, 1879, 18-20.
41. For Pryce (1834-1917) see CYB, 1918, 146-147.
42. Ibid., 65. For Turner (1844-1920) see CYB, 1921, 119f.
43. For McAll (1807-1888) see CYB, 1889, 198; DNCBP.
44. See J.C. Johnstone, 'The story of Western College,' CHST, VII, 1916-18, 98-109. For references to some of the early teachers see DTLC, ch. 11. See also Elaine Kaye, *For the Work of Ministry. A History of Northern College and its Predecessors*, Edinburgh: T. & T. Clark, 1999.
45. For Small (1759-1834) see *Evangelical Magazine*, 1834, 265-269.
46. For Payne (1781-1848) see CYB, 1848, 234-6; DNCBP; E. Kaye, op.cit. For a memoir by J. Pyer and the reminiscences of Ralph Wardlaw, see Payne's *Lectures on Christian Theology*, 2 vols., 1850.
47. For Alliott (1804-1863) see CYB, 1865, 217-218; DNB; DNCBP; *Evangelical Magazine*, 1864, 129-135; A.R. Henderson, *Castle Gate*

Congregational Church, Nottingham 1655-1905, London: James Clarke, 1905; E. Kaye, op.cit.
48. C. Clemence, *Funeral Services for the Rev. R. Alliott.... Address delivered at the General Cemetery, Nottingham, December 28, 1863, by the Rev. C. Clemence.... Sermon delivered... January 3, 1864, with a Sketch by the Rev. G.B. Johnson,* London: Hamilton, Adams, [1864], 37.
49. R. Alliott, *Psychology and Theology: or, Psychology applied to the investigation of Questions relating to Religion, Natural Theology, and Revelation,* London: Jackson and Walford, 1855, vi.
50. Ibid., 56.
51. Ibid., 81.
52. Ibid., 85.
53. Ibid., 143.
54. Ibid., 278.
55. Ibid., 285.
56. See R. Alliott, 'Opening address,' CYB, 1859, 5-18. It would take us too far into theology to pursue the argument of this address in detail, but it may be said in passing that few papers of this vintage are, in their remarks on the doctrine of the atonement (to which Alliott refers in illustration of his argument), as pertinent to our present homiletic situation as this.
57. For Gaskell (1805-1884) see DNB; H. McLachlan, *The Unitarian Home Missionary College, passim.*
58. W. Gaskell, *The Investigation of Religious Truth. A Sermon ... preached at Cross Street Chapel, Manchester, on 18th March 1833* [on Proverbs 23: 23], in *Modern Sermons,* Manchester: Johnson & Rawson, n.d., 40.
59. Ibid., 45.
60. R. Alliott, 'Opening address,' 9.
61. G. Payne, *On the instrumentality of divine truth in the sanctification of the souls of men: a discourse* [on John 17: 17], Glasgow: James Curll, 1823, 26.
62. Quoted by G.B. Johnson, 'Sketch,' 36.
63. Ibid., 39.
64. Quoted in *Henry Robert Reynolds D.D. His Life and Letters. Edited by his Sisters, with Portraits,* London: Hodder and Stoughton, 1898, 171. Lest the inference be drawn that Reynolds was one of the 'pause for profile' school of princes of the pulpit, it should be noted that his health was indifferent; that he took the Cheshunt appointment because the strain of pastoral ministry was greater than he could bear; and that in the college chapel he occasionally read an address to the students whilst seated. See Stephen Orchard, *Cheshunt College,* [1968] published by the College, 12-13.
65. For John Moon Charlton (1817-1875) see CYB, 1877, 350-353; for Chapman (1828-1922) see CYB, 1923, 102-103.
66. Thomas Stenner Macey (d. 1926) has no obituary in CYB. He was trained at Western College, and ministered at Wiveliscombe (1881-1886). He served as tutor at Western College from 1886 until his death.
67. For Williams (1750-1813) see DNB; DNCBP; *London Christian Instructor,* IV, 1821, passim; J. Gilbert, *Memoir of the Life and Writings of the late*

Edward Williams, D.D., London, 1825; W.T. Owen, *Edward Williams DD 1750-1813,* Cardiff: University of Wales Press, 1963.
68. J. Gilbert, *Memoir,* 535.
69. For Falding (1818-92) see CYB 1894, 191-3; K.W. Wadsworth, *Yorkshire United Independent College,* London: Independent Press, 1954; E. Kaye, *For the Work of Ministry;*
70. See H.J.S. Guntrip, *Smith and Wrigley of Leeds,* London: Independent Press, 1944, 41. Smith and Wrigley arrived in college on the same day, shared the one pastorate for thirty-seven years, and were joint chairmen of the Congregational Union of England and Wales in 1928. For Smith (1864-1943 see CYB, 1944, 435-6; for Wrigley (1868-1945) see CYB, 1946, 457.
71. *Rotherham College. The Annual Report of the Committee,* Sheffield: Leader, 1883, 11.
72. For Rotherham College, and also for Airedale, see K.W. Wadsworth, *Yorkshire United Independent College;* Elaine Kaye, *For the Work of Ministry.*
73. E. Armitage, 'Who makes our theology?' *Hibbert Journal,* IV no. 2, January 1906, 359. For Armitage see CYB, 1930, 222-3; DNCBP; K.W. Wadsworth, op.cit.; E. Kaye, op.cit.
74. E. Armitage, *The Riddle of Life; or, the Testimony of the Soul,* London: Independent Press, 1930, 33.
75. Ibid., 87.
76. Ibid., 118.
77. Ibid., 249.
78. CYB, 1930, 223.
79. Thereby prompting local rivalry. See, for example, J. Horsfall Turner, *Nonconformity in Idle, with the History of Airedale College,* Bradford: T. Brear, [1876], 122.
80. For Vint (1768-1834) see DNB; J. Horsfall Turner, op.cit., 52-85; K.W. Wadsworth, op.cit.; E. Kaye, op.cit.
81. For Scott (1779-1858) see CYB, 1859, 218-221. His son, Caleb, was President of Lancashire Independent College, 1869-1902.
82. For Creak (1821-1864) see CYB, 1865, 230-232.
83. For Shearer (1832?-1907) see CYB, 1908, 197.
84. *Minutes of the Proceedings of a Conference of Delegates,* 21.
85. D. Fraser, 'The minimum of education which our colleges ought to furnish, and which all college-educated ministers should be expected to possess,' in *Minutes of the Proceedings of a Conference of Delegates from the Committees of the Theological Colleges and Institutions connected with the Congregational Churches of England,* London: Jackson, Walford and Hodder, [1865], 15, 16.
86. For Fairbairn (1838-1912) see DNB; DNCBP; W.B. Selbie, *The Life of Andrew Martin Fairbairn,* London: Hodder and Stoughton, 1914; DTLC, ch. 19; E.J. Price, 'Dr. Fairbairn and Airedale College: the hour and the man,' CHST, XIII no. 3, April 1939, 131-139; K.W. Wadsworth, op.cit.; Elaine Kaye, *Mansfield College Oxford. Its Origin, History and Significance,* Oxford: OUP, 1996; idem, *For the Work of Ministry.*

87. Though in 1885 eight students were at Glasgow, five at Edinburgh and one at Cambridge. So E. Kaye, *For the Work of Ministry*, 116. Albert Peel, the noted historian, and Arnold Mee, a gifted Hebraist and poet, were among Yorkshire United students who were graduates of Leeds, not of Edinburgh. For Peel (1887-1949) see CYB, 1950, 523-524. For Mee (1901-1966) see CYB, 1966-67, 460-461; Joan W. Moody [his daughter], *Arnold Francis Mee, 1901-1966*, privately printed.
88. For Simon (1830-1909) see CYB, 1910, 189-191; F.J. Powicke, *David Worthington Simon*, London: Hodder and Stoughton, 1912.
89. For Sortain (1809-1860) see CYB, 1861, 239-240; DNCBP; Bridget Margaret Sortain (his wife), *Memorials of Joseph Sortain*, 1861; Richard Alliott, *The Funeral Sermon for the late Rev. Joseph Sortain, A.B., Preached on Sunday morning, July 29, 1860, in North Street Chapel, Brighton*, Brighton: John Smith, 1860. Sortain combined his pastoral ministry with his teaching at Cheshunt.
90. Of Sortain it was said that his reading of Micaijah Towgood's *Letters on Dissent* 'quenched the desire to enter Cambridge University, and, subsequently, the English Church.' CYB, 1861, 239. That Towgood's letters of the 1740s should have made such an impact exemplifies their long-continuing influence in Nonconformist circles. See further DTLC, ch. 7, 663-665.
91. *The Calendar of the Congregational Colleges*, 1879, 51.
92. For Griffiths (1812-1891) see DWB; Geraint Dyfnallt Owen, *Ysgolion a Cholegau yr Annibynwyr*, Swansea: Union of Welsh Independents, [1939], ch. 9.
93. See *The Calendar of the Congregational Colleges*, 93. For Morris (1813-1896) see DWB.
94. For Rees (1869-1926) see CYB, 1927, 152; DWB. For Edwards (1873-1941) see CYB, 1942, 418-419.
95. For brief descriptions of Edwards's philosophical books see Alan P.F. Sell, *The Philosophy of Religion 1875-1980*, (1988), Bristol: Thoemmes Press, 1996, 30-31, 96-97.
96. *Evangelical Magazine*, 1830, 138. For Roby (1766-1830) see DNB; W. Gordon Robinson, *William Roby and the Revival of Independency in the North*, London: Independent Press, 1954; E. Kaye, *For the Work of Ministry*.
97. See Charles E. Surman, 'Roby's academy, Manchester, 1803-1808,' CHST, XIII no. 1, September 1937, 41-53; idem, 'Leaf Square academy, Pendleton, 1811-1813,' ibid., XIII no. 2, September 1938, 107-117 and 77.
98. For this academy see further R. Slate, *A Brief History of the Rise and Progress of the Lancashire Congregational Union; and of the Blackburn Independent Academy*, London: Hamilton, Adams, 1840.
99. For Fletcher (1784-1843) see DNB; Joseph Fletcher, Jr, *The Select Works and Memoirs of the Late Rev. Joseph Fletcher, D.D.*, London: John Snow, 1846; E. Kaye, *For the Work of Ministry*. Fletcher was a noted contributor of articles on theological topics to the *Eclectic Review*.
100. For Wardlaw (1798-1873) see CYB, 1874, 559-561; DNCBP. For his educational ideas see *Education for the Christian Ministry; an Address, delivered at the Annual meeting of the Committee and Friends of Blackburn*

Theological Academy, held June 24th, 1830, Manchester: John Clarke, 1830.
101. See Joseph Thompson, *Lancashire Independent College, 1843-1893*, Manchester: J.E. Cornish, 1893; Elaine Kaye, *For the Work of Ministry.*
102. 'Dr. Robert Vaughan,' *The Congregationalist*, VI, March 1877, 135-136. For Vaughan (1795-1868) see also DNB; DNCBP; J. Thompson, *Lancashire Independent College 1843-1893*, Manchester: J.E. Cornish, 1893; E. Kaye, *For the Work of Ministry.*
103. Quoted by F.J. Powicke, *David Worthington Simon*, 17. For Halley (1827-1885) – not to be confused with his father of the same name (for whom see DNB), see CYB, 1886, 175-177; for Bruce see CYB, 1909, 162-165.
104. *Report of the Senatus Academicus and Calendar of the Associated Theological Colleges of England and Wales*, 1885, 114-115. For Hodgson (1842-1923) see CYB, 1924, 97.
105. For Mackintosh (1858-1933) see CYB, 1934, 269; DNCBP; New DNB; George Phillips, 'Dr. Mackintosh,'*The Congregational Monthly*, March 1933, xi; Alan P.F. Sell, *Robert Mackintosh: Theologian of Integrity*, Bern: Peter Lang, 1977; idem, *Philosophical Idealism and Christian Belief*, Cardiff: University of Wales Press and New York: St. Martin's Press, 1995.
106. R. Mackintosh, 'Theism,' *Encyclopedia Britannica,* 11th edn., 1910-1911, vol. 26, 753.
107. Idem, *From Comte to Benjamin Kidd*, London: Macmillan, 1899, 21.
108. Ibid., 85.
109. Idem, 'Theism,' 747.
110. Ibid., 749.
111. Idem, *Hegel and Hegelianism,* Edinburgh: T. & T. Clark, 1903, 287.
112. Idem, 'The authority of the Cross,' *Congregational Quarterly*, XXI, 1943, 215. This is a paper of 1906, with annotations by P.T. Forsyth.
113. 'Recent philosophy and Christian doctrine,' *Proceedings of the Third International Congregational Council*, London: Congregational Union of England and Wales, 1908, 83.
114. Idem, *Hegel and Hegelianism*, 290-291.
115. Idem, *Values. A Bird's Eye Survey*, London: Independent Press, [1928], 51.
116. Idem, 'Theism,' 755. See further for Mackintosh's philosophy, Alan P.F. Sell, *Robert Mackintosh*, ch. 4.
117. Idem, *Essays Towards a New Theology*, Glasgow: Maclehose, 1889, 366.
118. Idem, *Albrecht Ritschl and His School*, London: Chapman and Hall, 1915.
119. Idem, *Essays Towards a New Theology*, 389.
120. See T.W. Manson, 'The first fifty years: a sketch,' in *Theological Essays in commemoration of the Jubilee*, Manchester: John Rylands Library and Manchester University Press, 1954, 7-18; Ronald H. Preston, 'The Faculty of Theology in the University of Manchester: the first seventy-five years,' in D.A. Pailin, ed., *University of Manchester Faculty of Theology Seventy-fifth Anniversary Papers 1979*, published by the Faculty, 1980, 1-24.
121. For Bubier (1823-1869) see CYB, 1870, 279-281.
122. *The Calendar of the Congregational Colleges*, 81-82. For apologetics at Spring Hill see Dale A. Johnson, 'The end of the "evidences": a study in

Nonconformist theological transition, JURCHS, II no. 3, April 1979, 62-72.
123. For a full account see Elaine Kaye, *Mansfield College Oxford.*
124. For Selbie (1862-1944) see CYB, 1945, 441; DNB; E. Kaye, *Mansfield College.*
125. See H.G. Tibbutt, 'The Cotton End Congregational Academy, 1840-74,' CHST, VIII no. 3, August 1958, 100-105. The Congregational Home Missionary Committee Minutes record that William Booth applied for entry to Cotton End, but withdrew his application, 'disapproving of the manner in which the Committee had conducted his examination on the disputed doctrines of Arminianism.' H.G. Tibbutt, art. cit., 104, quoting the Minutes of 5 October 1852.
126. See R.R. Turner, 'Cavendish Theological College (1860-1863). Joseph Parker's experiment in ministerial training,' CHST, XXI no. 4, October 1972, 94-101; R.R. Turner and Ian H. Wallace, *Serve Through Love. A History of Paton Congregational College, Nottingham*, privately printed, [1984]; E. Kaye, *For the Work of Ministry.* For Parker (1830-1902) see DNB; for John Brown Paton (1830-1911) see DNB; CYB, 1912, 161. Paton College merged with Northern College, Manchester, in 1968.
127. See *The Calendar of the Congregational Colleges,* 1879, 103.
128. Ibid., 94. See further R. Tudur Jones, *Diwinyddiaeth ym Mangor. Theology in Bangor 1922-1972*, Cardiff: University of Wales Press, 1972, chs. 1, 2. For the pugilistic Joneses (1787-1853) and (1822-1898) respectively, see DWB; G.D. Owen, *Ysgolion a Cholegau yr Annibynwyr.*
129. 'Academical theology,' *The Congregational Magazine*, N.S. VIII, 1844, 264.
130. *Minutes of the Proceedings of a Conference of Delegates,* 42.
131. Ibid., 44-49; cf. *Henry Roberts Reynolds, D.D. His Life and Letters,* edited by his Sisters, London: Hodder and Stoughton, 1898, 313-315.
132. A.M. Fairbairn in the *Nonconformist and Independent*, 26 May 1881, 505-505.
133. Idem, 'Dr. Fairbairn's reply to presidents Hyde and Slocum,' *Proceedings of the Second International Congregaitonal Council*, 1899, 275.
134. Charles Rignal, *Manchester Baptist College 1866-1916*, Bradford: Wm. Byles, 149.
135. A.J. Grieve, 'A hundred years of ministerial training,' CHST, XI no. 6, September 1932, 262.
136. See Kenneth D. Brown, *A Social History of the Nonconformist Ministry in England and Wales 1800-1930,* Oxford: Clarendon Press, 1988, 83.
137. J. Ernest Rattenbury, 'Didsbury – fifty years ago,' in W. Bardsley Brash and Charles J. Wright, eds., *Didsbury College Centenary 1842-1942*, London: Epworth Press 1942, 101. K.D. Brown (see previous note) quotes the last five words here, and says that Rattenbury 'reckoned that *as a denomination* the Wesleyans positively "discouraged pursuit of university degrees"' (84; my italics). This is a larger claim than Rattenbury made.
138. The full list of external examiners in all subject is printed in the *Report of the Senatus Academicus of Associated Theological Colleges, British and Colonial,* for 1901, printed for the Senatus, 1902, 8-12. For Caird and

other idealists see Alan P.F. Sell, *Philosophical Idealism and Christian Belief*; for these and other apologists see idem, *Defending and Declaring the Faith. Some Scottish Examples 1860-1920*, Exeter: Paternoster Press, 1987; *Confessing and Commending the Faith. Historic Witness and Apologetic Method*, Cardiff: University of Wales Press, 2002.

139. *Report of the Senatus Academicus and Calendar of the Associated Theological Colleges of England and Wales*, 1885, iv, xxv, xxvii, xxviii.
140. S.W. Green, 'Sketch of the history of the Faculty,' in *London Theological Studies by members of the Faculty of Theology of the University of London*, London: University of London Press, 1911, x.
141. Ibid., xi.
142. See ibid., x-xiii for further details. Divinity degrees were opened to Nonconformist students at Cambridge in 1913 and at Oxford in 1919. In 1920 the New Testament professor at Westminster [Presbyterian] College, Cambridge, C.A. Anderson Scott, became the first Nonconformist DD of Cambridge; the Old Testament scholar William Henry Bennett, of New and Lancashire colleges, had become the first Nonconformist DLitt of that university in 1902. For the former see R.S. Robson, *Our Professors. Brief notes of men who after occupying English Presbyterian pulpits have been appointed to chairs*, London: Presbyterian Historical Society, 1956, 12-13. For the latter see Alan P.F. Sell, Oxford DNB, forthcoming.
143. For Ryland (1753-1825) see DNB; *Baptist Magazine*, 1826, 1-9; Norman S. Moon, *Education for Ministry: Bristol Baptist College 1679-1979*, Bristol: Bristol Baptist College, 1979, 119 and passim.
144. For Thomas Steffe Crisp (1788-1868) see N.S. Moon, op.cit., 42-52, 121.
145. For Baynes (1823-1887) see DNB; DNCBP.
146. T.S. Baynes, 'Sir William Hamilton,' in *Edinburgh Essays by Members of the University*, Edinburgh: A. & C. Black, 1857, 297.
147. For Leechman see George Yuille, ed., *History of the Baptists in Scotland from Pre-Reformation Times*, Glasgow: Baptist Union Publications Committee, [1926], passim.
148. J.T. Gray, *Exercises in Logic*, London: Taylor and Walton, 1845, vi. For Gray (1809-1854) see DNCBP; Frederic Boase, *Modern English Biography*, Truro: Netherton and Worth, 1892; Stephen A. Swaine, *Faithful Men; or, Memorials of Bristol Baptist College, and some of its most Distinguished Alumni*, London, 1884, 315-317.
149. Ibid., 145, 146.
150. For Frederick William Gotch (1808-1890) see BH, 1891, 140-142; BDEB; N.S. Moon, op.cit., 121-122 and passim.
151. For James C. Culross (1824-1899) see BH, 1900, 209; N.S. Moon, op.cit., 124.
152. For Henderson (1843-1929) see N.S. Moon, op.cit., 125.
153. For Evans (1767-1827) see DNB. Moon, op.cit. 49, says that Evans served until 1818; DWB gives 1821, and DNB 1825.
154. See further A.C. Carter, *A Popular Sketch, Historical and Biographical, of the Midland Baptist College,* London: Kingsgate Press, 1925.
155. For Steadman see Thomas Steadman, *Memoir of William Steadman, D.D., Pastor of the First Baptist Church, Bradford*, London, 1838; Sharon James,

'Revival and revewal in Baptist life. The contribution of William Steadman (1764-1837),' *The Baptist Quarterly*, XXXVII no. 6, April 1998, 263-282.
156. For this Ryland (1798-1866) see DNB. Of a retiring disposition, he devoted most of his life to writing and translation.
157. For Godwin (1785-1871) see BH, 1872, 220-222; BDEB; DNCBP.
158. Reproduced by John O. Barrett, *Rawdon College (Northern Baptist Education Society) 1804-1954. A Short History*, London: Carey Kingsgate, 1954, 11. Barrett, p. 12, quotes Steadman thus: 'In studying the Classics . . . I allow them to avail themselves of translations as they greatly expedite the business.' For the Yorkshire Baptist colleges see also C.E. Shipley, *The Baptists of Yorkshire*, Bradford: Wm. Byles, 1912, 282-284. For a good summary account of Baptist ministerial training in the nineteenth century see J.H.Y. Briggs, *The English Baptists of the 19th Century*, Didcot: The Baptist Historical Society, 1994, 74-86.
159. For Acworth (1798-1883) see BH, 1884, 279-281; BDEB.
160. For Samuel Gosnell Green (1822-1905) see DNB.
161. For Medley (1837-1908) see BH, 1909, 477-479; DNCBP.
162. BH, 1909, 477, 479.
163. W. Medley, *Christ the Truth. An Essay towards the Organization of Christian Thinking*, London: Macmillan, 1900, 12. See also John O. Barrett, *Rawdon College*, 1954, 27.
164. Ibid., 18.
165. Ibid., 24.
166. Ibid., 184.
167. Ibid.
168. Ibid., 231.
169. For Tymms (1842-1921) see BH, 1922, 274; DNCBP.
170. *Report of the Senatus Academicus*, 1885, 106-107.
171. D. Mervyn Himbury, *The South Wales Baptist College (1807-1957)*, published by the College, 1957, 15-36. This includes a full account of Micah Thomas (1778-1853), for whom see also DWB.
172. For Thomas (1805-1881) see Himbury, op.cit., *The Dictionary of Welsh Biography*.
173. See D.M. Himbury,op.cit., 45.
174. For Lewis (1840-1880) see DWB. He was elected principal in 1877, but died three years later. His other subjects were English, French, German, Greek, Latin, Hebrew, English and Roman history, mathematics and natural philosophy.
175. For Edwards (1848-1929) see DWB; T.W. Chance, *The Life of Principal Edwards,* Cardiff: Priory Press, 1934.
176. See D.M. Himbury, op.cit., 60-61.
177. See T.M. Bassett, *The Welsh Baptists*, Swansea: Ilston House, 1977, 345-349; R. Tudur Jones, *Diwinyddiaeth ym Mangor. Theology in Bangor*, chs. 1, 2. Llangollen students had been attending courses in Bangor since 1885.
178. Quoted by E.A. Payne, 'The development of Nonconformist theological education in the nineteenth century, with special reference to Regent's Park College,' in E.A. Payne, ed., *Studies in History and Religion presented to Dr. H. Wheeler Robinson, M.A., on his seventieth birthday,* London:

Lutterworth, 1942, 234. The source given is S. Tomkins, Memoir prefixed to *Twelve Sermons on Various Subjects by the Rev. Solomon Young*, London, 1832, 29. Young's dates are 1783-1827.
179. See E.A. Payne, ibid., 235-236. For William Harris Murch (1784-1859) see BH, 1861, 100; BDEB; R.E. Cooper, *From Stepney to St. Giles*, London, 1960. For Tomkins see R.E. Cooper, op.cit.
180. For Dowson (1812-1884) see BH, 1886, 113-114.
181. C. Rignall, *Manchester Baptist College*, 48.
182. *Report of the Senatus Academicus*, 135. For Marshall (1850-1923) see BH, 1924, 298.
183. For Spurgeon (1834-1892) see DNB, his autobiography in four volumes, 1897-1900, and numerous biographies. For the college see Mike Nicholls, *Lights to the World. A History of Spurgeon's College 1856-1992*, Harpenden: Nuprint, 1994. This book extends the story told in the same author's two-part article, 'Charles Haddon Spurgeon: educationalist,' BQ, XXXI no. 8, October 1986, 384-401, and XXXII no. 2, April 1987, 73-94.
184. C.H. Spurgeon, *The Sword and the Trowel*, 1887, 509.
185. M. Nicholls, op.cit., 19.
186. Ibid., 114.
187. Quoted by V. D. Davis, *A History of Manchester College from its Foundation in Manchester to its Establishment in Oxford*, London: Allen & Unwin, 1932, 69. For Walker (1734?-1807) and Barnes (1747-1810) see DNB. For the early period see Ruth Watts, 'Manchester College and education 1786-1853,' in Barbara Smith, ed., *Truth, Liberty and Religion. Essays celebrating Two Hundred Years of Manchester College*, Oxford: Manchester College, 1986, 79-110.
188. John Kenrick, *Biographical Memoir of the Rev. Charles Wellbeloved*, London: Edward T. Whitfield, 1860, 89-90; cf. V. D. Davis, op.cit., 77. For Wellbeloved (1769-1858) see also DNB; Bibliography (b) at Schulman, F. Manchester College has always been open to lay students.
189. For Turner (1788-1853) see DNB.
190. For Hincks (1818-1899) see DNB.
191. See V. D. Davis, op.cit., 107. For Martineau (1805-1900) see DNB; DNCBP, and a vast literature. Recent studies include Ralph Waller, 'James Martineau: the development of his thought,' in Barbara Smith, ed., op.cit, 225-264; Alan P.F. Sell, *Commemorations. Studies in Christian Thought and History*, (1993), Eugene, OR: Wipf & Stock, 1998, chs. 1, 10.
192. J. Martineau, 'Scope of mental and moral philosophy,' 11.
193. See vols. I and IV of Martineau's *Essays, Reviews and Addresses*, London: Longmans, Green, 1890, 1891.
194. See C.B. Upton, *Dr. Martineau's Philosophy: A Survey*, London: Nisbet, 1905, 103, 219, 225. Cf. Alan P.F. Sell, *Commemorations*, 242-243.
195. For John James Tayler (1797-1869) see DNB; for Drummond (1835-1918) see DNB and V. D. Davis, *A History of Manchester College*, 179-180. For Charles Barnes Upton (1831-1920) see *The Inquirer*, 27 November 1920, 596 and 30 June 1923, 419-420; V. D. Davis, *op.cit.*, 180-181. For L.P. Jacks (1860-1955) see DNB.
196. For Beard (1800-1876) see DNB; DNCBP.

197. For Poynting (1813-1878) see *The Inquirer*, 2 March 1878, 133; 9 March 1878, 155-157; for John Edmonson Manning (1848-1910) see DNB.
198. For Mellone see DNCBP; *The Inquirer*, 28 July 1956, 249.
199. See H. McLachlan, *The Unitarian Home Missionary College*, 131-133.
200. S.H. Mellone, *Studies in Philosophical Criticism and Construction*, Edinburgh: W. Blackwood, 1897, 419.
201. S.H. Mellone, *The Dawn of Modern Thought. Descartes, Spinoza, Leibniz*, London: OUP, 1930, 117-118.
202. For Jones (1628-1697) see DNB. For the college see H.P. Roberts, 'The History of the Presbyterian academy Brynllywarch-Carmarthen 1662-1982,' UHST, IV no. 4, 1930, 333-364, V, 1931, 24-42; D. Elwyn Davies, 'Education and radical Dissent in Wales in the eighteenth and nineteenth centuries,' ibid., XIX, 1988, 92-101.
203. See the *Report of the Committee of the Memorial College, Aberystwyth, 1979-80*, Swansea: John Penry Press, 1980, 7. I am grateful to my colleague, Principal Eifion Powell, for supplying this information.
204. H.P. Roberts, art.cit., 360.
205. Ibid., 30. It would be interesting to know how far the Carmarthen tutors played a part in the 1840s debate over the question whether the knowledge of God is acquired through sensation, or is innate (and hence Locke was wrong). See D. Elwyn Davies, *They Thought for Themselves,* Llandysul: Gomer Press, 1982, 169.
206. For Morgan (1818-1884) see *The Dictionary of Welsh Biography*.
207. For Evans (1860-1941) see CYB, 1942, 435; and his autobiography, *My Spiritual Pilgrimage*, London: James Clarke, 1961.
208. Not the nineteenth century, as D. Elwyn Davies, by a slip, has it; art.cit., 100.
209. For Harris see DNB; *The Dictionary of Welsh Biography*; Geoffrey F. Nuttall, *Howel Harris 1714-1773. The Last Enthusiast*, Cardiff: University of Wales Press, 1965.
210. For Charles (1812-1878) see DNB; DWB. For Howells (1818-1888) see DWB. For Davies (1826-1891) see DNB; DWB. For Prys (1857-1934) see DWB.
211. For the syllabus see *The Story of Our Colleges*, 41. For Hannah (1792-1867) see DMBI; DNB. Jones began his ministry in 1835, and died in 1875 as a minister of the United Methodist Free Churches.
212. J. Ernest Rattenbury, *Didsbury College Centenary*, 97-98. The latter comment could have been applied to the fare provided during the same decade by Robert Mackintosh at Lancashire College.
213. For Moss (1850-1935) see *Minutes* of the Methodist Conference, 1936, 188; DMBI. For Simon (1843-1933) see *Minutes* of the Methodist Conference, 1933, 262-263; DMBI.
214. For Pope (1822-1903) see DMBI; DNB; DTLC, ch. 19. For Randles (1826-1904) see DMBI; DNB. For Platt (1859-1955) see *Minutes* of the Methodist Conference, 1955, 132; DMBI. For Bedale (1879-1919) see *Minutes* of the Wesleyan Conference, 1919.
215. For Findlay (1849-1919) see *Minutes* of the Wesleyan Conference, 1920, 116-117; DMBI.
216. E.S. Waterhouse, *Richmond College 1843-1943*, London: Epworth Press, 1944.

217. For Barrett (1808-1876) see BDEB; DMBI.
218. For Davison (1846-1935) see DMBI; DNCBP.
219. For Davison (1846-1935) see *Minutes* of the Methodist Conference, 1936, 187-188; DMBI.
220. W. Bardsley Brash, *The Story of Our Colleges*, 85. For Banks see *Minutes* of the Wesleyan Methodist Conference, 1917, 167-168; DMBI.
221. Some wished to site the college in Manchester, but Thomas Firth of Sheffield left £4500.00 for the college provided its location were Sheffield. For Allin (1784-1866) and Cooke (1806-1884) see BDEB; DMBI. For Stacey see *Minutes* of the United Methodist Free Churches Conference, 1891, 9; DMBI.
222. See Henry Smith, *Sketches of Eminent MNC Ministers*, [c. 1893], 78, quoted by E. Alan Rose, *Preachers All. Essays to celebrate the Silver Jubilee of the Yorkshire Branch of the Wesley Historical Society,* published by the Branch, 1987, 13.
223. See G. Packer, ed., *The Centenary of the Methodist New Connexion 1797-1897*, London: Geo. Burroughs, [1897], 161. For Hulme and Crothers see UMFC Conference *Minutes*, 1901, 7; 1903, 9 respectively; and DMBI.
224. R. Pyke, *Men and Memories*, London: Epworth Press, 1948, 36. Pyke had read widely before candidating for the ministry. He suspected that he owed his success before the candidates board to his knowledge of Henry Rogers's *The Superhuman Origin of the Bible* – a work of which one of the examiners was greatly enamoured. Ibid., 34. For Pyke (1873-1965) see DMBI.
225. See further, *The Story of Our Colleges,* ch. 12; Henry Smith, John E. Swallow, and William Treffry, eds., *The Story of the United Methodist Church*, London: Henry Hooks, [1932], 141-143.
226. For Petty (1807-1868) see *Minutes* of the Primitive Methodist Conference, 1868, 12-13; BDEB; DMBI.
227. G.E. Milburn, *A School for the Prophets,* 19.
228. For Antliff (1813-1884) see *Minutes* of the Primitive Methodist Conference, 1885, 11-13; BDEB; DMBI. For Greenfield see *Minutes* of the Primitive Methodist Conference, 1894, 15-16; DMBI.
229. For the college see W.A.L. Elmslie, *Westminster College Cambridge 1899-1949*, London: Presbyterian Church of England, n.d.; R. Buick Knox, *Westminster College Cambridge: Its Background and History*, Cambridge: the University Library and Westminster College and London: The United Reformed Church History Society, n.d.; David Cornick: '"Our school of the prophets". The Presbyterian Church in England and its College 1844-1876,' *The Journal of the United Reformed Church History Society*, V no. 5, November 1994, 283-298.
230. *Report of the Senatus Academicus*, 1885, 130.
231. For Lorimer see DNCBP; Chalmers (1812-1894) see *Messenger of the Presbyterian Church of England,* December 1894, 269; for William Gray Elmslie (1848-1889) see W. Robertson Nicoll and A.N. MacNicoll, *W.G. Elmslie, D.D.: Memoir and Sermons,* London: Hodder and Stoughton 1890; for Dykes (1835-1912) see *Who Was Who, 1897-1916;* for Oman (1860-1939) see DNB; *Biographical Dictionary of Twentieth-Century Philosophers*, London: Routledge, 1996. For brief sketches of all of the

Presbyterian professors see R. S. Robson, *Our Professors. Being brief notes of men who after occupying English Presbyterian pulpits have been appointed to chairs*, London: Historical Society of the Presbyterian Church of England, 1956. I am grateful to Principal David Cornick of Westminster College, Cambridge, for drawing my attention to this last source.
232. It is not implied that recourse is not had to these ploys to this day.

Notes to Chapter 5
Nonconformist Contribution to Ethics and Apologetics: 1800-1920
pages 149-205

1. *The Works of the Rev. Edward Williams, D.D.*, ed. Evan Davies, London: James Nisbet, 1862, IV,3.
2. Ibid., 4.
3. Ibid., 5.
4. Ibid., 78.
5. Ibid., 79.
6. Ibid., 101.
7. For Parry (1754-1819) see DNB. In later life he had to refute the charge that he had become a Unitarian. See *Evangelical Magazine*, 1818, 172.
8. W. Parry, *Strictures on the Origin of Moral Evil; in which the Hypothesis of the Rev. Dr. Williams is Investigated*, London: S. Couchman, 1808, 50.
9. E. Williams, *Works* IV, 216
10. For a comparison of Payne's ethical stance with those of Robert Mackintosh and Sydney Cave, see Alan P.F. Sell, 'A renewed plea for "impractical divinity"', *Studies in Christian Ethics*, VIII no. 2, 1995, especially, 74-79.
11. G. Payne, *Elements of Mental and Moral Science*, London: John Gladding, 2nd enlarged edn., 1842, 6.
12. Ibid., 254.
13. Ibid., 284.
14. Ibid., 356.
15. Ibid., 360.
16. This surprising claim is open to question. See, for example, J. Butler, *Butler's Fifteen Sermons & a Dissertation on the nature of Virtue*, ed., W.R. Matthews, (1914), London: G. Bell, 1953, 14-16, 38-40, 245-257.
17. G. Payne, *Elements of Mental and Moral Science*, 363.
18. Ibid., 375.
19. Ibid., 396, 397.
20. Ibid., 399.
21. Ibid., 412-413.
22. Idem, 'Conscience – its nature and claims,' in his *Lectures on Christian Theology*, London: John Snow, 1850, II, 336.
23. Ibid., 337.
24. Ibid., 341. For Grove (1684-1738) see chs. 2 and 3 above
25. Ibid., 346.
26. Ibid., 350.
27. Ibid., 355. I do not altogether understand how this squares with Payne's insistence that conscience's work is done *retrospectively* in relation to our

actions.
28. For Cox (1783-1853) see BDEB; DNB; John H.Y. Briggs, '"Active, busy, zealous" : The Reverend Dr. Cox of Hackney,' in William H. Brackney, *et al.*, eds., *Pilgrim Pathways. Essays in Baptist History in honour of B. R. White*, Macon, GA: Mercer University Press, 223-241; idem, 'F.A. Cox of Hackney: nineteenth-century Baptist theologian, historian, controversialist, and apologist,' BQ, XXXVIII no. 8, October 2000, 392-411.
29. See F.A. Cox, *The Nature and Design of Moral Government*, 9, 11-12.
30. For Wardlaw see BDEB; CYB, 1855, 240-43; DNB; DNCBP; DSCHT; W.L. Alexander, *Elisha's Cry after Elijah*, in *Discourss and Sermons on occasion of the Death of the late Ralph Wardlaw, D.D.*, London, 1854; idem, *Memoirs of the Life and Writings of Ralph Wardlaw, D.D.*, Edinburgh: 1856.
31. For Lawson (1749-1820) see BDEB; DNB; DSCHT; J. MacFarlane, *The Life and Times of George Lawson*, Edinburgh, 1862.
32. For Alexander (1808-1884) see CYB, 1886, 146-9; DNB; DNCBP; W.D. McNaughton, op.cit; J. Ross, *W. Lindsay Alexander, DD, LLD. His Life and Work, with Illustrations of his Teaching*, London, 1887.
33. W.L. Alexander, *Elisha's Cry after Elijah*, 66-7.
34. R. Wardlaw, *Christian Ethics; or, Moral Philosophy on the Principles of Divine Revelation*, London: Jackson and Walford, 2nd edn. 1834, vi.
35. Ibid., 26.
36. Ibid., 127.
37. Ibid., 139.
38. Ibid., 201.
39. Ibid., 298.
40. Ibid., 368.
41. See *Edinburgh Review*, LXI, 59.
42. W.L. Alexander, *Memoirs*, 330.
43. Ibid., 332.
44. Ibid., 332-333.
45. From Jackson's obituary in the Wesleyan *Minutes of Conference* (1873, 19-20), quoted by Gordon Rupp, *Thomas Jackson, Methodist Patriarch*, London: Epworth Press, 1954, 51-52. For Jackson (1783-1873) see further BDEB; DMBI; DNB; DNCBP; B. Frankland, ed., *Recollections of my own Life and Times, by Thomas Jackson*, 1878.
46. T. Jackson, *The Duties of Christianity Theoretically and Practically Considered*, 22nd edn., London, 1867, 2.
47. Ibid., 3.
48. We need not suppose that all moral philosophers at the beginning of Christianity's third millennium will endorse this analysis!
49. Ibid., 27.
50. Ibid., 36.
51. For Hinton (1791-1873) see BH, 1875, 277-280; BDEB; DNB; DNCBP; Ian Sellers,' John Howard Hinton, theologian,' BQ, XXXIII no. 3, July 1989, 119-132.
52. J.H. Hinton, *A Treatise on Man's Responsibility*, in *The Theological Works of the Rev. John Howard Hinton, M.A. In Six Volumes*, London: Houlston

& Wright, I, 1864, 474.
53. Ibid., 454.
54. Idem, *Elements of Moral Philosophy*, in *Works*, IV, 1865, 10.
55. Ibid., 11.
56. Ibid., 17.
57. Ibid., 19.
58. G.L. Turner, *Wish and Will: An Introduction to the Psychology of Desire and Volition*, London: Longmans, 1880, 265.
59. J.H. Godwin, *Active Principles; or, Elements of Moral Science*, London: James Clarke, 1885, viii.
60. Ibid., 3.
61. Ibid.
62. Ibid., 92.
63. Ibid., 121.
64. Ibid., 186.
65. Ibid., 187.
66. Ibid., 194.
67. Ibid., 254.
68. Ibid., 256, 259.
69. Ibid., 267.
70. Ibid., 279.
71. Ibid., 290, 291.
72. Ibid., 296.
73. Ibid., 296.
74. Ibid., 301.
75. Ibid., 303.
76. For Belsham (1750-1829) see chs. 2 and 3 above.
77. In 1866 he was an unsuccessful candidate for the Chair of Philosophy of Mind and Logic at University College, London. George Grote opposed his appointment on the ground that the College's stance on religious neutrality would be vitiated if one known to hold a strong religious position were appointed. Crabb Robinson and Augustus de Morgan, on the contrary, interpreted the College's principle as meaning that none should be excluded on religious grounds. The successful candidate was George Croom Robertson, the founding editor of *Mind*. See further Ralph Waller, 'James Martineau: the development of his religious thought,' in Barbara Smith, ed., *Truth, Liberty, Religion,* 225-264.
78. J. Martineau, *Biographical Memoranda* at Harris-Manchester College, Oxford, 19. See further, Alan P.F. Sell, *Commemorations*, ch. 10.
79. Ibid.
80. Idem, *Types of Ethical Theory*, 3rd edn. Revised, 1891, I, xii.
81. J. Martineau, *The Relation between Ethics and Religion: An Address at the Opening of the Session 1881-2 of Manchester New College, London,* London: Williams and Norgate, 1881, 3-4. The reference to the first series of Congregational Lectures cannot pass without comment. The author was, as we have seen, Ralph Wardlaw. It is true that Wardlaw argues that 'On every point that relates to religion and virtue, the mental powers of man are injuriously affected by his moral estrangement from God, the eternal

prototype of all excellence' (*Christian Ethics; or, Moral Philosophy on the Principles of Divine Revelation*, p. 30) – a fact which he faults moral philosophers for overlooking. He further regards as futile the philosophers' attempts to discover the principles of rectitude from an analysis of fallen nature. But if he over-emphasized the noetic effects of sin (and this would need to be argued, not simply asserted), it is arguable that Martineau, whom some felt was 'too easily good' underestimates them. See further, Alan P.F. Sell, *Commemorations*, pp. 24-26. For Wardlaw (1779-1853) see William D. McNaughton, *The Scottish Congregational Ministry 1794-1993*, Glasgow: The Congregational Union of Scotland, 1993, 166.

82. Ibid., 5.
83. Ibid., 17.
84. Ibid., 22.
85. Idem, *The Seat of Authority in Religion*, London: Longmans, Green, 1890, vi.
86. W.T. Davison, *The Christian Conscience. A Contribution to Christian Ethics*, London: T. Woolmer, 1888, 12
87. Ibid., 15.
88. Ibid., 48.
89. Ibid., 76.
90. Ibid., 86.
91. Ibid., 99.
92. Ibid., 100.
93. Ibid., 105.
94. Ibid., 137.
95. Ibid., 161.
96. Ibid., 173.
97. This work caused a fluttering in the Methodist dovecotes because of Findlay's openness to the milder forms of biblical criticism.
98. G.G. Findlay, *Christian Doctrine and Morals Viewed in their Connexion*, London: Charles H. Kelly, 1894. He quotes the fourth edition of Wace's Boyle Lectures for 1874-1875, *Christianity and Morality, or the Correspondence of the Gospel with the Moral Nature of Man*, 5.
99. For a good example of the genre see Robert Mackintosh, *Christian Ethics*, London: T.C. and E.C. Jack, 1909.
100. See, for example, J.W. Grant, *Free Churchmanship in England 1870-1940*, London: Independent Press, n.d.; Willis B. Glover, *Evangelical Nonconformists and Higher Criticism in the Nineteenth Century*, London: Independent Press, 1954; Dale A. Johnson, *The Changing Shape of English Nonconformity 1825-1925*, New York: OUP, 1999; DTLC, chs. 17, 19. For contemporary developments in Scotland see my *Defending and Declaring the Faith. Some Scottish Examples 1860-1920*.
101. A.M. Fairbairn, *The City of God. A Series of Discussions in Religion*, London: Hodder and Stoughton, (1883), 8th edn., 1903, 7-8.
102. For Aspland (1782-1845) see DNB; DNCBP; R. Brook Aspland [son], *Memoir of the Life, Works and Correspondence of the Rev. Robert Aspland*, London: E.T. Whitfield, 1850. His son (for whom see DNB), evidently no hagiographer, writes, 'Although in after life no one could surpass him in

the power, *when an emergency arose,* of bracing up his faculties and devoting his whole mind and will to a purpose . . . yet in his ordinary literary pursuits, when there was no pressure from without, unity of purpose and persevering application were too often wanting.' Op.cit., 52.

103. R. Aspland, *The Power of Truth. A Sermon preached before the Unitarian Society for Promoting Christian Knowledge, at Essex Street Chapel, on Thursday, April 13, 1818,* London: R. Hunter, 1815, 2.
104. Ibid., 6.
105. Ibid., 11.
106. Ibid., 27.
107. For Redford (1785-1860) see CYB, 1861, 230-233; DNB; DNCBP.
108. G. Redford, *The True Age of Reason,* London: B.J. Holdsworth, 1821, v.
109. Ibid., vi.
110. Ibid., 43.
111. Idem, *Body and Soul; or life, mind and matter, considered as to their peculiar nature and combined condition in living beings,* London: John Churchill, 1847, v.
112. For Bennett (1774-1862) see CYB, 1863, 206-8; DNB; DNCBP.
113. J. Bennett, *An Antidote to Infidelity. Lectures on the External Evidences of Divine Revelation* [including the] *Second Antidote to Infidelity,* London: Hamilton, Adams, n.d. (but second part delivered in February and March 1831), 18.
114. For Godwin (1785-1871) see BDEB; BH, 1870, 220-222; DNCBP.
115. See A. Gordon, 'Higginson, Edward, 1807-1880,' DNB. His father, an alumnus of Manchester College, was James Martineau's father-in-law.
116. E. Higginson, *The Christian Miracles, and the Place they hold in the Gospel Evidence; considered in reference to the Antisupernaturalist Theology,* London, 1842, 3.
117. Ibid., 8.
118. Ibid., 15.
119. Ibid., 19.
120. Ibid., 31.
121. Ibid., 38.
122. R. Alliott, *On the Evidences of Christianity. A Discourse, delivered on Sunday evening. November 17, 1844,* London, n.d., 169.
123. Ibid., 177.
124. Ibid., 179.
125. Idem, *Lecture on the Moral Evidence of Christainity,* London: Hamilton, Adams, n.d., 3.
126. Ibid., 24.
127. G. Wardlaw, *The Leading Christian Evidences, and the Principles on which to Estimate them,* Edinburgh: T. & T. Clark, 1870, vi.
128. See the remarks of R.W. Dale in his Memoir of Rogers, prefixed to the 8th edn. of the latter's *The Superhuman Origin of the Bible,* 1893, xii. Dale himself was influenced, as Rogers was not, by Thomas Erskine of Linlathen, John McLeod Campbell and F.W. Robertson. See A.W.W. Dale, *The Life of R.W. Dale of Birmingham,* London: Hodder and Stoughton, 1899, 704.
129. H. Rogers, *The Eclipse of Faith; or. A Visit to a Religious Sceptic,* London:

Longman, Brown, Green, and Longmans, 1852, 242.
130. Ibid., 348.
131. Ibid., 349. I confess to repeating these illustrations from my DTLC, 502-504; they do, however, epitomise Rogers's style, and they afford some light relief from apologetics of the more stolid kind.
132. Idem, *Defence of the Eclipse of Faith*, 30, 204.
133. To pursue further the tangled web of issues surrounding the rise and reception of modern biblical criticism would take us too far from matters philosophical. But see Willis B. Glover, *Evangelical Nonconformists and the Higher Criticism in the Nineteenth Century*, London: Independent Press, 1954; Alan P.F. Sell, *Theology in Turmoil. The Roots, Course and Significance of the Conservative-Liberal Debate in Modern Theology*, (1986), Eugene, OR: Wipf & Stock, 1998, ch. 2. Similarly, the inner-Christian polemics over Anglo-Catholicism and Ritualism, which are frequently more entertaining than edifying – and with equal frequency crushingly boring, cannot here detain us.
134. For Miall (1809-1881) see NB; DNCBP; Arthur Miall, *The Life of Edward Miall*, London: Macmillan, 1884.
135. Edward Miall, *Bases of Belief: An Examination of Christianity as a Divine Revelation by the Light of Recognised Facts and Principles*, London: Arthur Hall, Virtue, 1853, 155-156.
136. Ibid., 228.
137. Ibid., 238.
138. Ibid., 238-239.
139. Ibid., 240.
140. Ibid., 424.
141. Ibid., 425.
142. R. Vaughan, *The Credulities of Scepticism. A Lecture*, London: James Nisbet, 1885/6, 30.
143. J. Acworth, *The Internal Witness to Christianity. A Discourse delivered before the Ministers and Delegates of the Yorkshire Associated Baptist Churches, met in Trinity Road Chapel, Halifax, May 13, 14, and 15, 1856*, Leeds: J. Heaton, 1856, 3.
144. Ibid., 5-6.
145. Ibid., 9.
146. Ibid., 30.
147. Ibid., 31. This rhetorical question surely calls out for the insertion of the term 'ultimately', since, *pro tem*, the wicked frequently seem to flourish.
148. J.R. Beard, *Letters on the Ground and Objects of Religious Knowledge; addressed to a Young Man in a State of indecision*, 2 vols. London: Whitfield and Manchester: Johnson and Rawson, 1856, I, iii.
149. Ibid., II, 188.
150. H. Batchelor, *The Logic of Atheism. Three Lectures delivered in the Large Temperance Hall, Sheffield,* London: Judd and Glass, 1858, 23. For Batchelor (1823-1903) see CYB, 1904, 158. He ministered at Clemens Street, Leamington (1848?-1851), where R.W. Dale was in his congregation; Fetter Lane, London (1851-1853), Nether, Sheffield (1853-1859), Elgin Place, Glasgow (1859-1875), Blackheath, Kent (1875-1880,

St. James's, Newcastle-upon-Tyne (1881-1887) and Weston-super-Mare (1887-1903).
151. Ibid., 28.
152. Ibid., 207.
153. Ibid., 212.
154. *The Eclectic Review*, January-June 1859, 558.
155. Idem, *Rationalism: the Immediate Peril of the Free Churches. The Address by Rev. Henry Batchelor, Chairman of the Union.* [the Congregational Union of Gloucestershire and Herefordshire] *delivered at the Annual Sittings, March, 1891*, London: John F. Shaw, [1891], 2.
156. Ibid., 7.
157. For this complicated story see DTLC, ch. 5.
158. S. McAll, *The Sceptic's Credulity; or, the Logic of Atheism*, London: The Book Society, 2nd edn., [1868], iii.
159. Ibid., 5.
160. Ibid., 7.
161. Ibid., 14.
162. Ibid., 17.
163. Ibid., 23.
164. Ibid., 27.
165. Ibid.
166. Ibid., 33.
167. Ibid., 35.
168. Ibid., 40.
169. Ibid., 41.
170. Ibid., 42.
171. Ibid., 46.
172. Ibid., 51.
173. Ibid., 52.
174. Ibid., 52-53.
175. J. Stoughton, *The Nature and Value of the Miraculous Testimony to Christianity*, London: Hodder and Stoughton, 1871, 7. Stoughton's son, T. Wilberforce Stoughton was Hodder's partner in this well-known publishing house.
176. Ibid.
177. Ibid., 15.
178. Ibid., 16.
179. Ibid., 20.
180. Ibid., 23.
181. For Allon (1818-1892) see BDEB; CYB, 1893, 202; DNB; DNCBP; Alan Argent, 'Henry Allon of Union Chapel, Islington,' *Congregational History Circle Magazine*, III no. 1, Spring 1993, 12-31.
182. H. Allon, *The Argument for the Supernatural Character of Christianity, from its Existence and Achievements*, London: Hodder and Stoughton, 1872, 5.
183. Ibid., 8.
184. Ibid., 9-10.
185. Ibid., 45.

186. J.R. Thomson, *Modern Pessimism*, London: The Religious Tract Society, n.d., 45.
187. Ibid., 64.
188. Idem, *The Witness of Man's Moral Nature to Christianity*, London: The Religious Tract Society, n.d., 55.
189. Idem, *Utilitarianism: an Illogical and Irreligious Theory of Morals*, London: The Religious Tract Society, [1885], 59.
190. R. Waddy Moss, *Is Man a Machine?* London: Charles H. Kelly, n.d., 4.
191. For Scott Lidgett (1854-1953) see DMBI; DNB; DNCBP.
192. J. Scott Lidgett, *Spiritual Discernment, its Place in Christian Evidences*, London: Charles H. Kelly, 279.
193. Ibid., 279.
194. Ibid., 283.
195. Ibid., 293.
196. Ibid., 297.
197. J.S. Lidgett, *The Christian Religion, its meaning and Proof*, London: Robert Culley, [1907], 4.
198. Ibid.
199. Ibid., 11.
200. Idem, 'How to meet the un-Christian and anti-Christian teaching of the day,' CYB, 1878, 131.
201. Ibid.
202. Ibid.
203. Ibid., 132.
204. Ibid., 134.
205. Ibid., 134. See his 'Experience in theology: a chapter of autobiography,' *Contemporary Review*, XCI, January-June 1907, 554-573, for the way in which his sojourn in Germany prompted Fairbairn away from scholastic Calvinism towards what he called (p. 569) 'a larger and nobler Christianity' which emphasises the Fatherhood of God.
206. Ibid., 184.
207. Idem, *Catholicism, Roman and Anglican,* London: Hodder and Stoughton, 2nd edn., 1899, 388.
208. Idem, *Studies in Religion and Theology*, New York: Macmillan, 1910, 92.
209. Idem, 'Mr. Herbert Spencer's philosophy and the philosophy of religion,' *Contemporary Review*, XL, July-December 1881; cf. 'Herbert Spencer,' ibid, LXXXV, January-June, 1904.
210. Idem, *The Philosophy of the Christian Religion*, London: Hodder and Stoughton, (1902), 5th edn., 1907, x.
211. For a fuller account of Fairbairn see Alan P.F. Sell, *Dissenting Thought*, ch. 19. For a swingeing critique of his *The Philosophy of the Christian Religion* on the grounds of its terminological inexactitude and philosophical ineptness see Hakluyt Egerton [pseud. Arthur Boutwood], *A New Way in Apologetics*, London: A.R. Mowbray, [1907], appendix. More deferential is the verdict of one of Fairbairn's Baptist students, H. Wheeler Robinson. Fairbairn, he writes, 'has not written anything "epoch-making" in the true sense of a much abused word, not even in his greatest work *The Place of Christ in Modern Theology*. But he has won the fine and noble reward of

the teacher, in that the high qualities of character and of intellect, which found their realisation in him, have become the inspiring ideals of his many pupils throughout the world.' Quoted by E.A. Payne, *Henry Wheeler Robinson, Scholar, Teacher, Principal*, London: Nisbet, 1946, 33.
212. A.M. Fairbairn, *The Philosophy of the Christian Religion*, x.
213. P. Lorimer, 'Disbelief in miracles proved to be unscientific,' in J. Oswald Dykes, ed., *Some Present Difficulties in Theology. Being Lectures to Young Men delivered at the English Presbyterian College, London*, London: Hodder and Stoughton, 1873, 70-71.
214. Ibid., 78.
215. Ibid., 105.
216. Ibid., 107, 108.
217. Ibid., 120.
218. Idem, in *Credentials of Christianity*, London: Hodder and Stoughton, 1876, 184.
219. J. Martineau, *Religion as affected by Modern Materialism: An Address delivered in Manchester New College, London, at the opening of its 89th Session, on Tuesday, Oct. 6th, 1874*, London: Williams and Norgate, 5th edn., 1876, 14-15.
220. Ibid., 32.
221. Ibid., 35.
222. For Conder (1820-1892) see CYB, 1893, 214-217; DNCBP.
223. For John and Josiah Conder see DNB; BDEB.
224. E.R. Conder, *The Basis of Faith*, London: Hodder and Stoughton, 1877, xv.
225. Ibid., 60.
226. Ibid.
227. Ibid., 244.
228. Ibid., 257.
229. Ibid., 282.
230. For a range of responses to these see Alan P.F. Sell, *Mill and Religion. Contemporary Responses to Three Essays on Religion*, Bristol: Thoemmes Press, 1997.
231. E.R. Conder, *The Basis of Faith*, 282.
232. Ibid., 291.
233. Ibid., 292.
234. Ibid., 321.
235. Ibid., 324.
236. Ibid., 369.
237. Ibid., 404.
238. Ibid., 433.
239. W. Medley, *Our Attitude in relation to Religious Opinion and Belief*, London: Yates and Alexander, 1879, 9.
240. Ibid., 19.
241. Ibid., 21.
242. See BH, 1884, 44-52.
243. T.V. Tymms, *The Mystery of God. A Consideration of some Intellectual Hindrances to Faith*, London: Elliot Stock, 4th edn., 1890, ix.
244. Ibid.

245. Ibid., xi.
246. Ibid., 34.
247. Ibid., 35.
248. Ibid., 54.
249. Ibid., 65.
250. Ibid., 66.
251. Ibid., 91.
252. Ibid., 96.
253. Ibid., 180.
254. Ibid., 320.
255. Ibid., 330.
256. Ibid., 331.
257. Ibid., 342.
258. Ibid., 350.
259. Ibid., 353.
260. Ibid., 357.
261. Ibid., 358.
262. For Parker see CYB, 1903, 298 (b-e); DNB. He published his autobiography (1899), and there are biographies by Albert Dawson (1901) and William Adamson (1902).
263. See J. Parker, *Job's Comforters: Scientific Sympathy*, London: Hodder and Stoughton, 1874; abridged in *Mill and Religion*, 19-23.
264. For Solly see *The Inquirer*, 4 April 1925, 213.
265. For Solly's review see ibid., 28 November 1874, 774-775; reprinted in *Mill and Religion*, 43-49.
266. For Upton's review see *Theological Review*, XII, 1875, 127-145, 249-272; reprinted (slightly abridged) in *Mill and Religion*, 124-163.
267. I do not overlook Upton's younger contemporary, the Unitarian George Dawes Hicks. An alumnus of Owens College and Manchester Unitarian College, Hicks became professor of philosophy at University College, London. His main works, *The Philosophical Bases of Theism*, London: Allen and Unwin, 1937, and *Critical Realism. Studies in the Philosphy of Mind and Nature*, London: Macmillan, 1938, fall outside the period with which we are here concerned. See, however, Alan P.F. Sell, *The Philosophy of Religion 1875-1980*, (1988), Bristol: Thoemmes Press, 1996, 66, 107-108 for a brief account of his thought. For Anthony Quinton's judgment that Hicks 'had one good idea which he never succeeded in bringing to serious attention,' see Stuart Brown, *et al.*, eds., *Biographical Dictionary of Twentieth-Century Philosophers*, London: Routledge, 1996. See also DNB.
268. J.P. Kingsland, 'Lancashire College sixty-five years ago,' CHST, XIV no. 3, April 1943, 175.
269. J.M. Hodgson, *Philosophy and Faith: A Plea for Agnostic Belief*, Manchester: Brook and Chrystal, 1885, 6.
270. Ibid., 7.
271. Ibid.
272. Ibid., 8.
273. Ibid., 9, quoting *Evidences and Authority of the Christian Revelation*,

Edinburgh: Blackwood, 1814, 243.
274. Ibid., 10.
275. This is perhaps the point at which I should mention that a number of Nonconformist divines (and others) offered criticisms of the increasingly fashionable attempt to cash Christian thought in terms of philosophical idealism. Among criticisms most frequently offered were that idealism could not really accommodate an hisorical revelation, and that it could not provide an adequate account of evil (and therefore of the atonement), regarding it as but a stage on the way to a greater good. Among the Nonconformist critics were Robert Mackintosh and A.E. Garvie, both of whom had studied under Edward Caird in Glasgow. For a full treatment of this matter see Alan P.F. Sell, *Philosophical Idealism and Christian Belief.*
276. Ibid., 14.
277. Ibid., 26.
278. Idem, *Theologia Pectoris*, Edinburgh: T. & T. Clark, 1898, 9.
279. Idem, *Religion – The Quest of the Ideal*, London: James Clarke, 1911, 5.
280. Ibid., 7.
281. Ibid., 6-7.
282. A.E. Garvie, *A Handbook of Christian Apologetics*, London: Duckworth, 1913, vii. I had already decided to entitle the concluding volume of my own apologetics trilogy *Commending and Confessing the Faith* (2002) when I returned after some years to Garvie's book to find his use of the word 'commendation'.
283. The apologetic interest is never far from Garvie's mind in his many works, the most important of which were published after 1920.
284. For Forsyth see DNB. Recent works on his include Trevor Hart, ed., *Justice the True and Only Mercy. Essays on the Life and Theology of Peter Taylor Forsyth*, Edinburgh: T. & T. Clark, 1995; Leslie McCurdy, *Attributes and Atonement*, Carlisle: Paternoster Publishing, 1999; Alan P.F. Sell, ed., *P.T. Forsyth: Theologian for a New Millennium*, London: United Reformed Church, 2000.
285. See his *Monism*, London Society for the Study of Religion, printed for the Society, 1909; 'Some Christian aspects of evolution,' *London Quarterly Review*, October 1905, 209-239, reprinted as *Christian Aspects f Evolution*, London: Epworth Press, 1950; and 'The evidential value of miracles,' *London Quarterly Review*, July 1909, 1-7.
286. P.T. Forsyth, *The Person and Place of Jesus Christ*, (1909), London: Independent Press, 1961, 84. See further, Alan P.F. Sell, 'P.T. Forsyth as unsystematic systematician,' in T. Hart, op.cit., especially 126-134.
287. P.T. Forsyth, *The Justification of God*, (1917), London: Independent Press, 1948, 220-221.
288. W.T. Davison, *The Christian Conscience*, 99.
289. For a few brush strokes see Alan P.F. Sell, *The Great Debate. Calvinism, Arminianism and Salvation*, ch. 6. I hope in due course to attempt a fuller study of the dilution of Calvinism in nineteenth-century Congregationalism.
290. See further Alan P.F. Sell, *Philosophical Idealism and Christian Belief*, chs. 1-3; idem, *Theology in Turmoil*, chs. 1, 3. From the vast secondary literature on Darwinism and religion we may select John Dillenberger,

Protestant Thought and Natural Science, Garden City, NY: Doubleday, 1960; David C. Lindberg and Ronald L. Numbers, eds., *God and Nature*, Berkeley: University of California Press, 1966; James R. Moore, *The Post-Darwinian Controversies: A Study of the Protestant Struggle to Come to Terms with Darwin in Great Britain and America, 1820-1900*, Cambridge: CUP, 1979; and for the relation between the religion and science debate and biblical criticism see Willis B. Glover, *Evangelical Nonconformists and Higher Criticism in the Nineteenth Century*, London: Independent Press, 1954.

291. T. Rhondda Williams, *The Working Faith of a Liberal Theologian*, Lodon: Williams and Norgate, 1914, 205. Those theologians who too easily equated the onward march of progress with the coming of the Kingdom of God ignited – and to some degree deserved – the obloquy later heaped upon them by Barth and Niebuhr. Of course, hindsight often makes things easier.

292. A.E. Garvie, *The Christian Doctrine of the Godhead*, London: Hodder and Stoughton, 1925.

Note to Chapter 6
Epilogue
page 206

1. CYB, 1865, 217.

BIBLIOGRAPHY
of primary and secondary sources mentioned in the text and notes

(a) Primary Sources, including histories of academies and theological colleges

Acworth, James, *The Internal Witness to Christianity. A Discourse delivered before the Ministers and Delegates of the Yorkshire Associated Baptist Churches, met in Trinity Road Chapel, Halifax, May 13, 14 and 15, 1856*, Leeds: J. Heaton, 1856.

Alliott, Richard, *Lecture on the Moral Evidence of Christianity*, London: Hamilton, Adams, n.d.

On the Evidences of Christianity. A Discourse, delivered on Sunday evening, November 17, 1844, London, n.d.

Psychology and Theology: or, Psychology applied to the investigation of Questions relating to Religion, Natural Theology, and Revelation, London: Jackson and Walford, 1855.

'Opening address,' CYB, 1859, 5-18.

The Funeral Sermon for the late Rev. Joseph Sortain, A.B., Preached on Sunday morning, July 19, 1860, in North Street Chapel, Brighton, Brighton: John Smith, 1860.

Allon, Henry, *The Argument for the Supernatural Character of Christianity, from its Existence and Achievements*, London: Hodder and Stoughton, 1872.

Amory, Thomas, *Christ the Light of the World; or, the Principal Improvements made in Religion by Christianity. Represented in A Sermon preached at the Young Men's Lecture at Exon, Thursday, September 11, 1735*, London: R. Hett, 1735.

Ministers not Lords over the Faith of Christians, but Helpers of their Joy. A Sermon preached at Lewins-Mead, Bristol, at the Ordination of the Reverend Mr. William Richards, May the 22d. 1751, London: J. Waugh [1751].

Memoir of Henry Grove, *The Protestant Dissenter's Magazine*, III, March 1796, 81-84, abridged from his 'Account' of his uncle prefixed to *Sermons and Tracts; being the posthumous Works of Henry Grove*, 1740-1741.

Twenty-Two Sermons, London: T. Becket and P.A. de Hondt, 1766.

Annet, Peter (or Morgan, Thomas?), *Deism Fairly Stated and Fully Vindicated from the Gross Imputations and Groundless Calumnies of Modern Believers*, 1746.

Anon, 'An account of the Dissenting academies from the restoration of Charles the Second,' DWL, MS 24.59.25.

'Edward Williams,' *The London Christian Instructor, or Congregational Magazine*, IV, 1821, 169-75; 225-34; 281-88; and cf. 294-5.

'Academical education,' *The Congregational Magazine*, N.S. VIII, 1844.

Review of H. Batchelor, *The Logic of Atheism*, in *The Eclectic Review*, January-June, 1859, 558.

'Robert Vaughan', *The Congregationalist*, VI, March 1877, 129-148.

Credentials of Christianity, London: Hodder and Stoughton, 1876.

Annual *Report(s) of the Senatus Academicus and Calendar of the Associated Theological Colleges of England and Wales*.

Rotherham College. *The Annual Report of the Committee*, Sheffield: Leader, 1883.

Bristol Baptist College. 250 Years, 1679-1929, published by the College, [1929].

Report of the Committee of the Memorial College, Aberystwyth, 1979-80, Swansea: John Penry Press, 1980.

Armitage, Elkanah, 'Who makes our theology?' *Hibbert Journal*, IV no. 2, January 1906, 346-361.

The Riddle of Life: or, the Testimony of the Soul (ed. E.J. Price), London: Independent Press, 1930.

Aspland, Robert, *Bigotry and Intolerance Defeated*, 2nd edn., Harlow, 1811.

The Power of Truth. A Sermon preached before the Unitarian Society for Promoting Christian Knowledge, at Essex Street Chapel, on Thursday, April 13, 1818, London: R. Hunter, 1815.

Aspland, Robert Brook, *Memoir of the Life, Works and Correspondence of the Rev. Robert Aspland*, London: E.T. Whitfield, 1850.

Balguy, John, *Divine Rectitude, or a Brief Enquiry concerning the Moral Perfections of the Deity*, London, 1730.

Ball, John, *Some Remarks on a new Way of Preaching*, London, 1736.

Barnes, Thomas, *A Discourse delivered at the Commencement of the Manchester Academy, September fourteenth, one thousand seven hundred and eighty six*, Warrington: W. Eyres, [1786].

Barrett, Alfred, *Discourse on the Modern Mental Philosophy, viewed in its aspects on* Christianity: with Strictures on that Exposition of it prsented by Mr. J.D. Morell, *in his Philosophy of Religion . .* , 1850.

Barrett, John O., *Rawdon College (Northern Baptist Education Society) 1804-1954. A Short History*, London: Carey Kingsgate, 1954.

Batchelor, Henry, *The Logic of Atheism. Three Lectures delivered in the Large Temperance Hall, Sheffield*, London: Judd and Glass, 1858.

Rationalism: the Immediate Peril of the Free Churches. The Address by Rev. Henry Batchelor, Chairman of the Union [the Congregational Union of Gloucestershire and Herefordshire] *delivered at the Annual Sittings, March, 1891*, London: John F. Shaw, [1891].

Baxter, Richard, *The Saint's Everlasting Rest*, London, 1651.

Bayes, Thomas, *Divine Benevolence, or An Attempt tp prove that the Principal End of the Divine Providence and Government is the Happiness of His Creatures*, London: John Noon, 1731.

Baynes, Thomas Spencer, *An Essay of the new Analytic of Logical Forms*, 1850.

'Sir William Hamilton,' in *Edinburgh Essays by Members of the*

University, Edinburgh: A. & C. Black, 1857.
Beard, J.R., *Letters on the Ground and Objects of Religious Knowledge; addressed to a Young Man in a State of Indecision*, 2 vols., London: Whitfield, 1856
  A Manual of Christian Evidence, London: Simpkin, Marshall, 1868.
Belsham, Thomas, *Knowledge the Foundation of Virtue. A Sermon addressed to the Young Persons who attend at Gravel Pit Meeting, Hackney*, London: J. Johnson, 1795.
  Freedom of Enquiry, and Zeal in the Diffusion of Christian Truth, Asserted and Recommended in a Discourse delivered at Bristol, July 8, 1800, before the Society of Unitarian Christians, established in the West of England, for Promoting Christian Knowledge and the Practice of Virtue, by the Distribution of Books, London: G. Woodfall, 1800.
  Elements of the Philosophy of Mind, and of Moral Philosophy, to which is prefixed a Compendium of Logic, London: J. Johnson, 1801.
  Letters upon Arianism, and other Topics in Metaphysics and Theology, in reply to the Lectures of the Rev. Benjamin Carpenter, London: J. Johnson, 1803.
  A Summary View of the Evidence and practical Importance of the Christian Revelation, London: R. Taylor, 1807.
  The Rights of Conscience asserted and defined, in reference to the modern interpretation of the Toleration Act, London: J. Johnson, 1812.
  Discourses, Doctrinal and Practical; delivered in Essex Street Chapel, London: R. Hunter, 2 vols., 1826-1827.
Bennett, James, *An Antidote to Infidelity. Lectures on the Extrernal Evidences of Divine Revelation* [including the] *Second Antidote to Infidelity*, London: Hamilton, Adams, [1831].
Benson, George, *The Reasonableness of the Christian Religion as Delivered in the Scriptures*, London: John Noon,1743.
Bird, Benwell, 'The changes passing over religious thought, and the spirit in wich we should meet them,' BH, 1884, 44-52.
Bourn, Samuel, II, *The True Christian Way of striving for the Faith of the Gospel. A Sermon preached to a Congregation of Protestant Dissenters, Ministers, and Private Christians, at their Yearly Meeting at Dudley in Worcestershire. On May 23rd 1738, being Whitsun-Tuesday*, London: J. Robinson, 1738.
  A Charge delivered at the Ordination of the Reverend Mr. Job Orton; at Shrewsbury, September 18, 1745, Birmingham: T. Warren, 1745.
  A Vindication of the Principles and Practice of the Protestant Dissenters, London: J. Robinson, 1748.
Bourn, Samuel, III, *A Series of Discourses on the Principles and Evidences of Natural Religion and the Christian Revelation. And on some Practical Subjects*, London: R. Griffiths, 2 vols. 1760. N.B. The second volume has a different title page:
  Discourses on Various Subjects of Natural Religion and the Christian Revelation
  Fifty Sermons on various Subjects, Critical, Philosophical, and Moral, Norwich: R. Beatniffe, 1777.
Brash, W. Bardsley, *The Story of Our Colleges 1835-1935*, London: Epworth

Press, 1935.
Brash, W. Bardsley and Wright, Charles J, eds., *Didsbury College Centenary 1842-1942*, London: Epworth Press, 1942.
Brine, John, *A Vindication of some Truths of Natural and Revealed Religion*, 1746.
Bull, Josiah, *Memorials of the Rev. William Bull*, London: J. Nisbet, 1864.
Butler, Joseph, *Butler's Fifteen Sermons & a Dissertation on the nature of Virtue*, ed. W.R. Matthews, London: G. Bell, 1953.
Carpenter, R.L., *Memoirs of the Life of the Rev. Lant Carpenter, LL.D*, Bristol: Philp and Evans, 1842.
Carter, A.C., *A popular Sketch, Historical and Biographical, of the Midland Baptist College*, London: Kingsgate Press, 1925.
Chalmers, Thomas, *The Evidence and Authority of the Christian Revelation*, Edinburgh: Blackwod, 1814.
Chandler, Samuel, *Vindication of the Christian Religion*, London, 1725, 1728. *Plain Reasons for being a Christian*, London, 1730.
Clegg, James, *Extracts from the Diary and Autobiography of the Rev. James Clegg*, ed. Henry Kirke, Buxton: C.F. Wardley, 1899.
Clarke, Samuel, *The Scripture Doctrine of the Trinity*, London: James Knapton, 1712.
Clemence, C., *Funderal Services for the Rev. R. Alliott . . . Address delivered at the General Cemetery, Nottingham, December 28, 1863, by the Rev C. Clemence . . . Sermon delivered . . . January 3, 1864, with a Sketch by the Rev. G.B. Johnson*, London: Hamilton Adams, [1864].
Collier, Arthur, *Clavis Universalis: or, A New Inquiry after Truth, being a Demonstration of the Non-Existence or Impossibility of an External World*, London: Robert Gosling, 1713.
Collins, Anthony, *A Philosophical Inquiry concerning Human Liberty*, London, 1715 (reprinted and corrected, 1717).
Conder, Eustace R., *The Basis of Faith. A Critical Survey of the Grounds of Christian Theism*, London: Hodder and Stoughton, 1877.
Cooper, R.E., *From Stepney to St. Giles*, London, 1960.
Cornick, David, 'Our school of the prophets;. The Presbyterian Church in England and its College 1844-1876,' *The Journal of the United Reformed Church History Society*, V no. 5, November 1994, 283-298.
Cox, F.A., *The Nature and Design of Moral Government*, 1839.
[Crippen, T.G.], 'Richard Frankland and his academy,' *Congregational Historical Society Transactions*, II, 1905-1906, 242-249.
Crisp, Tobias, *Christ Alone Exalted, being the Compleat Works of Tobias Crisp, D.D.*, with a Preface by John Gill, London: J. Murgatroyd, 1791.
Daggett, David, *Sunbeams may be extracted from cucumbers, but the process is tedious. An Oration pronounced on the fourth of July 1799* . . . New Haven, Conn., 1799. See Boston University Library, Bartman YE 289 D99.
Dale, R.W., Memoir of Henry Rogers prefixed to the latter's *The Superhuman Originof the Bible*, 8th edn., q.v.
Darwin, Charles, *The Origin of Species by Natural Selection, or the Preservation of Favoured Raced in the Struggle for Life*, London: John Murray, 1859.
Davies, Gareth, 'Trevecka (1806-1964),' *Brycheiniog*, XIV, 1971.

Davis, V. D., *A History of Manchester College from its Foundation in Manchester to its Establishment in Oxford*, London: Allen and Unwin, 1932.

Davies, William, *The Tewkesbury Academy*, Tewkesbury, [c.1905].

Davison, W.T., *The Christian Conscience. A Contribution to Christian Ethics*, London: T. Woolmer, 1888.

Doddridge, Philip, *A Course of Lectures on the Principal Subjects of Pneumatology, Ethics, and Divinity: with reference to the most considerable Authors on each Subject*, London, 1763.

    The Works of the Reverend Philip Doddridge, ed. E. Williams and E. Parsons, with a Memoir by Job Orton, 10 vols., Leeds, 1802-1805.

Dodwell, Henry, the Younger, *Christianity not Founded on Argument*, London: T. Cooper, 1741.

Drummond, James and Upton, C.B., *Life and Letters of James Martineau*, London: Nisbet, 2 vols., 1902.

Edwards, Jonathan, *The Works of Jonathan Edwards, with a Memoir by Sereno E. Dwight; revised and corrected by Edward Hickman*, (1834), Edinburgh: The Banner of Truth Trust, 2 vols., 1974.

Egerton, Hakluyt [pseud. Arthur Boutwood], *A New Way in Apologetics*, London: A.R. Mowbray, [1907].

Elmslie, W.A.L., *Westminster College Cambridge 1899-1949*, London: Presbyterian Church of England, n.d.

Enfield, William, *A Funeral Sermon occasioned by the Death of the late Rev. John Aikin, D.D. Professor of Divinity at the Academy in Warrington*, Warrington: W. Eyres, 1781.

Eustachius de Saint-Paul, *Ethics*, Cambridge, 1654.

Evans, Caleb, *Elijah's Exclamation*, Bristol: W. Pine, 1781.

    and others, *A Charge and Sermon, together with an Introductory Discourse, and Confession of Faith, delivered at the ordination of the Rev. Mr. Caleb Evans,*

August 18, 1767, in Broad-Mead, Bristol, Bristol: S. Farley, 1767.

Fairbairn, A.M., 'The Miracles of Christ,' in *What is Christiaity?* London: Charles H. Kelly, n.d.

    'How to meet the un-Christian and anti-Christian teaching of the day,' CYB, 1878.

    'Mr. Herbert Spencer's philosophy and the philosophy of religion,' *Contemporary Review*, XL, July-December 1881.

    The City of God. A Series of Discussions in Religion, London: Hodder and Stoughton, 1883.

    Catholicism, Roman and Anglican, London: Hodder and Stoughton, 2nd edn., 1899.

    'Herbert Spencer,' *Contemporary Review*, LXXXV, January-June 1904.

    The Philosophy of the Christian Religion, London: Hodder and Stoughton, 1907.

    'Experience in theology: a chapter of autobiography,' *Contemporary Review*, XCI, January-June 1907.

    Studies in Religion and Theology, New York: Macmillan, 1910.

Findlay, G.G., *Christian Doctrine and Morals Viewed in their Connexion,*

London: Charles H. Kelly, 1894.
Flexman, Roger, *A Crown of life, the gratuitious Reward of the faithful Christian: A* Sermon preached at the Old Jewry, July 10. 1774. On the occasion of the Death of *the Rev. Thomas Amory, D.D. who died June 24, in his seventy-fourth year*, London: J. Buckland, 1774.
Ford, William, *A Sermon Preached at the Ordination of the Reverend Mr. John* Notcutt at the Meeting-House in Green-Street, Cambridge, on july 22, 1735, by William Ford. With the Charge then given him by the Revd. Mr. Tobias Wildboar; *and Mr. Notcutt's Confession of his FAITH*, 1735.
Forsyth, P.T., *The Justification of God*, (1916), London: Independent Press, 1948.
Foskett, Benjamin, *Pneumatology*, MS z.e.16 and 39 at Bristol Baptist College.
Foster, James, *The Usefulness, Truth and Excellency of the Christian Revelation defended against the Objections contain'd in a late Book, intituled, Christianity as old as the Creation, &c.*, London: J. Noon, 1731.
Discourses on all the Principal Branches of Natural Religion and Social Virtue, London: J. Noon, 1749, 1752.
Frankland, B., ed., *Recollections of my own Life and Times, by Thomas Jackson*, 1878.
Fraser, Daniel, 'The minimum of education which our colleges ought to furnish, and which all college-educated ministers should be expected to possess,' in *Minutes of the Proceedings of a Conference of Delegates from the Committees of the Theological Colleges and Institutes connected with the Congregational Churches of England*, London: Jackson, Walford and Hodder, [1865].
Fraser, Lucy A., ed., *Memoirs of Daniel Fraser . . . Half-a-Century of Educational Work*, London: Percy Lund, 1905.
Froman, Andreas, *De anima in genere*, Jena, 1620.
Fuller, Andrew, *The Complete Works of the Rev. Andrew Fuller*, London: Holdsworth and Ball, 1831-1832.
Garvie, A.E., *A Handbook of Christian Apologetics*, Lodon: Duckworth, 1913.
The Christian Doctrine of the Godhead, London: Hodder and Stoughton, 1925.
Gaskell, William, *The Investigation of Religious Truth. A Sermon . . . preached at Cross-Street Chapel, Manchester, on 18th March 1833* [on Proverbs 23: 23], in *Modern Sermons*, Manchester: Johnson & Rawson, n.d.
Gibbons, Thomas, *Memoirs of the Rev. Dr. Isaac Watts, D.D.*, London, 1780.
Gilbert, Joseph, *Memoir of the Life and Writings of the late Edward Williams, D.D.*, London, 1825.
Gill, John, *Complete Body of Doctrinal and Practical Divinity*, (1769-1770), Grand Rapids: Baker Book House, 1978.
Glover, Philips, *An Enquiry concerning Virtue and Happiness*, 1751.
Godwin, Benjamin, *Lectures on the Atheistic Controversy*, London, [1834].
The Philosophy of Atheism Examined and compared with Christianity, London, 1853.
Godwin, J.H., *Intellectual Principles; or, Elements of Mental Science*, London: James Clarke, 1884.
Active Principles; or, Elements of Moral Science, London: James Clarke,

1885.
Goveanus, Thomas, *Logica Elenctica*, Dublin, 1683.
Gray, Joshua T., *Immortality, its Real and Alleges Evidences*, 1843.
    Exercises in Logic, London: Taylor & Walton, 1845.
Grove, Henry, *Sermons and Tracts; being the posthumous Works of Henry Grove*, ed. T. Amory, 6 vols., 1740-1741.
    The Works of Henry Grove, containing all the Sermons, Discourses and Tracts published in his Life Time, ed. T. Amory, 4 vols., 1747.
    A System of Moral Philosophy by the late Reverend and Learned Mr. Henry Grove, of Taunton. Published from the Author's Manuscript, with his latest Improvements and Corrections by Thomas Amory, London: J. Waugh, 1749. [This work, together with the one immediately preceding has been reprinted with an Introduction by Alan P.F. Sell, Bristol: Thoemmes Press, 2000].
Guyse, John, et al., *A Sermon preached at the Ordination of Mr. Thomas Gibbons, October 27, 1743. At Haberdasher's Hall, London. By John Guyse, D.D. Together with an Introductory Discourse by Richard Rawlin. Mr. Gibbons's Confession of Faith. And an exhortation to him by Thomas Hall*, London, 1743.
Hagenbach, *German Rationalism, in its Rise, Progress, and Decline, in relation to Theologians, Scholars, Poets, Philosophers, and the People . . .*, ed. And trans. W.L. Gage and J.H.W. Stuckenberg, Edinburgh, 1865.
Hallett, Joseph, *A Defence of a Discourse*, 1731.
Harris, John, *The Importance of an Educated Ministry: A Discourse preached preparatory to the Opening of the Lancashire Independent College*, London, [1843].
Hebden, Samuel, *Baptismal Regeneration Disproved; The Scripture Account of the Nature of Regeneration explained; and the absolute Necessity of such a Change argued from the Native Corruption of Man since the Fall; In a Discourse on John 3: 5, 6. With remarks on some Passages in a late Book against Original Sin; and an Appendix Relating to Three different false Descriptions of Regeneration delivered in some Modern Books*, 1741.
Hester, Giles, *Attercliffe as a Seat of Learning and Ministerial Education*, London: Elliot Stock, 1893.
Hicks, G. Dawes, *The Philosophical Bases of Theism*, London: Allen and Unwin, 1937.
    Critical Realism. Studies in the Philosophy of Mind and Nature, London: Macmillan, 1938.
Higginson, Edward, *The Christian Miracles, and the Place they hold in the Gospel Evidence; considered in reference to the Antisupernaturalist Theology*, London, 1842.
Himbury, D. Mervyn, *The South Wales Baptist College (1807-1957)*, Cardiff: published by the College, 1957.
Hinton, J.H., *The Theological Works of the Rev. John Howard Hinton, M.A. In Six Volumes*, London: Houlston & Wright, 1864.
Hobbes, Thomas, *The English Works of Thomas Hobbes*, ed. William Molesworth, London: John Bohn, 1839.
Hodgson, J.M., *Philosophy and Faith: A Plea for Agnostic Belief*, Manchester: Brook and Chrystal, 1885.

Theologia Pectoris: Outlines of Religious Faith and Doctrine, Founded on Intuition and Experience, Edinburgh: T. & T. Clark, 1898.

Religion - The Quest of the Ideal, London: James Clarke, 1911.

Horsey, John, 'Institutes of Moral Philosophy,' DWL MS 69.5. [These were possibly used by Horsey].

'Lectures Introductory to the Study of the New Testament,' DWL MS 69.16, and 'Thoughts concerning the Inspiration of Scripture,' DWL MS 69.2. [He may have written these].

'Five Lectures on Government and thirteen on the British Constitution', DWL MS 69.3.

Lectures to Young Persons on the Intellectual and Moral Powers of man; the Existence, Character and Government of God; and the Evidences of Christianity, London: Samuel Leigh, 1828.

Houlbrooke, Theophilus, *A Sermon occasioned by the Death of William Tayleur, Esq.*, delivered at a Meeting of Unitarian Dissenters, in Shjrewsbury upon the *fifteenth day of May, 1796*, Liverpool: J. M'Creery, 1796.

Hume, David, *Essays, Moral and Political*, 2 vols. 1741-1742.

An Enquiry concerning the Principles of Morals, 1751.

Humphreys, J.D., *Correspondence and Diary of Philip Doddridge*, 5 vols., London, 1829-1831.

Hutcheson, Francis, *An Inquiry into the Original of our Ideas of Beauty and Virtue; in Two Treatises*, (1725), 4th corrected edn., London: D. Midwinter, 1738.

An Essay on the Nature and Conduct of the Passions and Affections. With Illustrations on the Moral Sense, London, 1728.

Jackson, Thomas, *The Duties of Christianity Theoretically and Practically Considered*, 1857.

Johnstone, J.C., 'The story of Western College,' *Congregational Historical Society Transactions*, VII, 1916-1918, 98-109.

Jones, J.A., *Bunhill memorials. Sacred Reminiscences of Three Hundred Ministers and other Persons of Note, who are Buried in Bunhill Fields, of every Denomination*, London: James Paul, 1849.

Jones, William, *Memoirs of the Life, Studies, and Writings of George Horne, late Bishop of Norwich*, London, 1809.

Jones, W.P. *Coleg Trefeca 1842-1942*, Llandysul: Gomer Press, n.d.

Kant, Immanuel, *Critique of Pure Reason*, (1781), trans. Norman Kemp Smith, 2nd impression, London: Macmillan, 1980.

- *Fundamental Principles of the Metaphysics of Ethics*, (1785), trans. T.K. Abbott, London: Longmans, Green, 10th edn., 1926.

- *Critique of Practical Reason*, (1788), see T.K. Abbott, trans., *Kant's Theory of Ethics*, 4th edn., London: Longmans, Green, 1889.

Kaye, Elaine, *Mansfield College Oxford. Its Origin, History and Significance*, Oxford: OUP, 1996.

For the Work of Ministry. A History of Northern College and its Predecessors, Edinburgh: T. & T. Clark, 1999.

Kenrick, John, *Biographical Memoir of the Rev Charles Wellbeloved*, London: Edward T. Whitfield, 1860.

Killingworth, Grantham, *A Forerunner to a Farther Answer, if need be, to the*

Rev. Dr. J. Taylor of Norwich, his Covenant of Grace, and Baptism the Token of it, London, 1758.
Kingsland, J.P., 'Lancashire College sixty-five years ago,' *Congregational Historical Society Transactions*, XIV no. 3, April 1943, 173-80.
Kippis, Andrew, *An Address delivered at the Interment of the late Rev. Dr. Richard Price on the twenty-sixth of April, 1791*, London, 1791.
Knox, R. Buick, *Westminster College Cambridge. Its Background and History*, Cambridge: the University Library and Westminster College, and London: The United Reformed Church History Society, n.d.
Leechman, John, *Logic: Designed as an Introduction to the Study of Reasoning*, 4th edn., Glasgow, 1845.
Lewis, O., 'The teaching of science in English Dissenting academies 1662-1800,' unpublished MPhil dissertation, The Open University, 1989.
Lidgett, J. Scott, 'Spiritual Discernment, its Place in Christian Evidences,' in *What is Christianity?* London: Charles H. Kelly, n.d.
   The Christian Religion, its meaning and Proof, London: Robert Culley, 1907.
Linkens, Derek, 'Timothy Jollie and the Attercliffe Academy,' *The Banner of Truth*, 173, February 1978, 22-28.
Locke, John, *An Essay concerning Human Understanding*, (1690), ed. Peter H. Nidditch, Oxford: Clarendon Press, 1975.
   Essays on the Law of Nature, ed. W. von Leyden, Oxford: Clarendon Press, 1954.
   The Reasonableness of Christianity, (1695), ed. John C. Higgins-Biddle, Oxford: Clarendon Press, 2000.
   Works, ed. Bohn, 1854.
Lorimer, Peter, 'Disbelief in miracles proved to be unscientific,' in J. Oswald Dykes, ed., *Some Present Difficulties in Theology. Being Lectures to Young Men delivered at the English Presbyterian College, London*, London: Hodder and Stoughton, 1873. See his lecture in Anon, *Credentials of Christianity*, above.
McAll, Samuel, *The Sceptic's Credulity; or, the Logic of Atheism*, London: The Book Society, 2nd edn., [1868].
McCosh, James, *Christianity and Positivism*, New York, 1871.
Mackintosh, Robert, *Essays Towards a New Theology*, Glasgow: Maclehose, 1889.
   From Comte to Benjamin Kidd, London: Macmillan, 1899.
   Hegel and Hegelianism, Edinburgh: T. & T. Clark, 1903.
   Christian Ethics, London: T. C. and E. C. Jack, 1909.
   'Theism,' *Encyclopedia Britannica*, 11th edn., 1910-1911, XXVI.
   Albrecht Ritschl and his School, London: Chapman and Hall, 1915.
   Values. A Bird's Eye Survey, London: Independent Press, 1928.
   'The authority of the Cross,' *The Copngregational Quarterly*, XXI, 1943, 209-218.
McLachlan, H., *The Unitarian Home Missionary College 1854-1914*, London: Sherratt and Hughes, 1915.
   'The old Hackney College, 1786-1896,' *Transactions of the Unitarian Historical Society*, III no. 3, October 1925.

English Education under the Test Acts, Manchester: Manchester University Press, 1931.
    Warrington Academy, its History and Influence, Manchester: The Chetham Society, N.S. CVII, 1943.
Martineau, James, *Biographical Memoranda*, at Harris-Manchester College, Oxford.
    Religion as affected by Modern Materialism: An Address delivered in Manchester New College, London, at the opening of its 89th Session, on Tuesday, Oct. 6th, 1874, London: Williams and Norgate, 5th edn., 1876.
    The Relation between Ethics and Religion: An Address at the Opening of the Session 1881-2 of Manchester New College, London, London: Williams and Norgate, 1881.
    A Study of Spinoza, 1882.
    A Study of Religion, Oxford: Clarendon Press, 2 vols., 1887.
    The Seat of Authority in Religion, London: Longmans, Green, 1890.
    Essays, Reviews and Addresses, 4 vols., London: Longmans, Green, 1890-1891.
    Types of Ethical Theory, 3rd edn., revised, 2 vols., 1891.
Medley, William, *Our Attitude in relation to Religious Opinion and Belief*, London: Yates and Alexander, 1879.
- *Christ the Truth. An Essay towards the Organization of Christian Thinking*, London: Macmillan, 1890.
Medway, John, *Memoirs of the Life and Writings of John Pye Smith, DD, LLD*, 1853.
Mellone, S.H., *Studies in Philosophical Criticism and Construction*, Edinburgh: W. Blackwood, 1897.
    Introductory Text Book on Logic, 1903.
    The Dawn of Modern Thought. Descartes, Spinoza, Leibniz, London: OUP, 1930.
    Elements of Modern Logic, 1934.
Miall, Edward, *Bases of Belief: An Examination of Christianity as a Divine Revelation by the Light of Recognised Facts and Principles*, London: Arthur Hall, Virtue, 1853.
Miall, James G., *Congregationalism in Yorkshire. A Chapter in Modern Church History*, London: John Snow, 1868.
Milburn, G.E. *A School for the prophets. The Origins of Ministerial Education in the Primitive Methodist Church*, privately published, [1981].
Mill, John Stuart, *Three Essays on Religion*, (1874), London: Longmans, 1885.
Moon, Norman, *Education for Ministry: Bristol Baptist College 1679-1979*, Bristol: Baptist College, 1979.
Morell, J.D., *An Historical and Critical Review of the Speculative Philosophy of Europe in the Nineteenth Century*, 2 vols., London, 1846.
    Handbook of Logic, 2nd edn., London, 1855.
    Modern German Philosophy: its Characteristics, Tendencies and Results, London, 1856.
Morris, Arthur D., *Hoxton Square and the Hoxton Academies*, privately printed, 1957.
Moss, R. Waddy, 'Is Man a Machine?' in *What is Christianity?* London: Charles

H. Kelly, n.d.
A Manual of the History of Philosophy, 1884.
Newth, S., ed., *The Calendar of the Congregational Colleges of England and Wales. Including the Countess of Huntingdon's College at Cheshunt*, printed for the editor, 1879.
Newman, Francis, *Phases of Faith; or, Passages from the History of my Creed*, London, 1850.
Newton, John, *The Works of the Rev. John Newton*, 6 vols., London, 1808.
Nicholls, Mike, *Lights to the World. A History of Spurgeon's College 1856-1992*, Harpenden: Nuprint, 1994.
Notebook, New College MS L185 at DWL.
Nuttall, Geoffrey F., *New College, London and its Library*, London, 1977.
  'Welsh students at Bristol Baptist College,' *Transactions of the Hnourable Society of Cymmrodorion*, 1978.
  The Significance of Trevecca College 1768-91, London: Dr. Williams's Trust,1969.
O'Brien, Padraig, *Warrington Academy 1757-86, its Predecessors & Successors*, Wigan: Owl Books, 1989.
Oldfield, Joshua, *An Essay towards the Improvement of Reason in the Pursuit of Learning and Conduct of Life*, London, 1707.
Orchard, Stephen, *Cheshunt College*, published by the College, [1968].
Orton, Job, *Memoirs of the late Reverend Dr. Philip Doddridge*, Shrewsbury: J. Cotton and J. Eddowes, 1766.
Overton, Richard, *Mans Mortallitie*, Amsterdam or London,1643.
  An Arrow against all Tyrants or Tyranny, London, 1646.
Owen, Geraint Dyfnallt, *Ysgolion a Cholegau yr Annibynwyr*, Swansea: Union of Welsh Independents, [1939].
Owen, John, *The Works of John Owen*, ed. William Goold, (1850-1853), London: The Banner of Truth Trust, 1968.
Paley, Wiliam, *Horae Paulinae, or the Truth of the Scripture History of St. Paul* Evinced, by a comparison of the Epistles which bear his Name, with the Acts of the *Apostles, and with one another*, 1790.
  A View of the Evidences of Christianity, 1794.
Palmer, Samuel, *A Defence of the Dissenters Education in their Private Academies*, London, 1703.
Parker, Irene, *Dissenting Academies in England*, Cambridge: CUP, 1914.
Parker, Joseph, *Job's Comforters: Scientific Sympathy*, London: Hodder and Stoughton, 1874.
  A Preacher's Life: An Autobiography and an Album, London: Hodder and Stoughton, 1899.
Parry, William, *A Vindication of Public and Social Worship, containing an Examination of the Evidence concerning it in the new Testament, and of Mr. Wakefield's Enquiry into its propriety and Expediency*, London, 1792.
  Strictures on the Origin of Moral Evil; in which the Hypothesis of the Rev. Dr. Williams is Investigated, London: S. Couchman, 1808.
Payne, E.A., 'The development of Nonconformist theoogical education in the nineteenth century, with special reference to Regent's Park College,' in idem, *Studies* in History and Religion presented to Dr. H. Wheeler

Robinson, M.A., on his *seventieth birthday*, London: Lutterworth, 1942.
Payne, George, *On the instrumentality of divine truth in the sanctification of the souls of men: a discourse* [on John 17: 17], Glasgow: James Curll, 1823.
    Elements of Mental and Moral Science, 2nd enlarged edn., London, 1842.
    Lectures on Christian Theology, 2 vols., London, 1850.
Powicke, F.J., *David Worthington Simon*, London: Hodder and Stoughton, 1912.
Price, E.J., 'Dr. Fairbairn and Airedale College: the hour and the man,' *Congregational Historical Society Transactions*, XIII no. 3, 1939, 131-139.
Price, Richard, *A Review of the Principal Questions and Difficulties in Morals*, London, 1758.
    The Nature and Dignity of the Human Soul. A Sermon preached at St. Thomas's, January the First, 1766. For the Benefit of the Charity-School in Gravel-Lane, *Southwark*, London: A. Millar, 1766.
    The Vanity, Misery, and Infamy, of Knowledge without suitable Practice; represented in a Sermon preached at Hackney, November the 4th, 1770, London: J. Buckland, 1770.
    The Evidence for a future period of Improvement in the State of Mankind, with the means and Duty of promoting it, represented in a Discourse, delivered on Wednesday the 25th of April, 1787, at the Meeting-House in the Old Jewry, London, in Support of a new Academical Institution among Protestant Dissenters, London: H. Goldney, 1787.
    Four Dissertations, London: A. Millar and T. Cadell, 1767.
    and see Price's *Observations on the Nature of Civil Liberty* (1776), *Observations on the Importance of the American Revolution* (1785), and *A Discourse on the Love of our Country* (1789), in D.O. Thomas, *Richard Price, Political Writings*, see below.
    and Priestley, Joseph, *A Free Discussion of the Doctrines of Materialism, and Philosophical Necessity*, London: J. Johnson, 1778.
Priestley, Joseph, *Memoir of Dr. Priestley*, 1805.
    The Theological and Miscellaneous Works of Joseph Priestley, ed. J.T. Rutt, 25 vols., 1817-1831; reprinted Bristol: Thoemmes Press, 1999.
    and Price, Richard, *A Free Discussion,* see above.
Ramus, P., *The Logike of the moste Excellent Philosopher P. Ramus Martyr*, London, 1574.
Redford, George, *The True Age of Reason; or A Fair Challenge to Deists. A candid* Examination of the Claims of Modern Deism, containing a Demonstration of the *Insufficiency of Unassisted Reason to lead Mankind to Virtue*, London: B.J. Holdsworth, 1821.
    Body and Soul; or life, mind and matter, considered as to their peculiar nature and combined condition in living beings, London: John Churchill, 1847.
Rees, Thomas, *Address delivered at the Old Jewry Chapel in Jewin Street, on* Saturday, the 19th day of June, 1825, over the body of the late Rev. Abraham Rees, *D.D., F.R.S., &c,&c, previously to his Interment in Bunhill Fields*, London: Longman, 1825.
Reid, Thomas, *Works*, ed. William Hamilton, Edinburgh, 1846.

Bibliography

Ridgley, Thomas, *A Body of Divinity wherein the Doctrines of the Christian Religion are expounded and defended. Being the substance of several lectures on the Assembly's Larger Catechism*, London: D. Midwinter and A. Ward, 1731.
Rignal, Charles, *Manchester Baptist College 1866-1916*, Bradford: Wm. Byles, n.d.
Rippon, John, *A Brief Essay towards an History of the Baptist Academy at Bristol*, in *The Baptist Annual Register*, II, 1795.
Roberts, H.P., 'Nonconformist academies in Wales,' *Transactions of the Honourable Society of Cymmrodorion*, 1930.
 'The history of the Presbyterian academy Brynllywarch-Carmarthen,' *Transactions of the Unitarian Historical Society*, IV no. 4, October 1930.
Robinson, Robert, *Arcana: or the Principles of the late Petitioners to parliament for Relief in the Matter of Subscription*, Cambridge: Fletcher & Hodson, 1774.
Rogers, Henry, *Essays selected from the Edinburgh Review*, 3 vols. London, 1850-1855.
 The Eclipse of Faith; or, a Visit to a Religious Sceptic, London: Longman, Brown, Green, and Longmans, 1852.
 Defence of the Eclipse of Faith, London, 1854.
 The Superhuman Origin of the Bible, 8th edn., London: Hodder and Stoughton, 1893.
Rose, E. Alan, 'Ranmoor College 1864-1919,' in *Preachers All. Essays to celebrate the Silver Jubilee of the Yorkshire Branch of the Wesley Historical Society*, published by the Branch, 1987, 11-17.
Rowe, Mortimer, *Unitarian College, Manchester. A Centenary Address*, privately printed, 1954.
[Seymour, A.C.H.], *The Life and Times of Selina, Countess of Huntingdon*, London: William Edward Painter, 2 vols. 1840.
Sherlock, Thomas, *Vindication of the Doctrines of the Trinity and of the Incarnation*, 1690.
Simms, T.H., *Homerton College 1695-1978*, Cambridge: Trustees of Homerton College, 1979.
Slate, R., *A Brief History of the Rise and Progress of the Lancashire Congregational Union; and of the Blackburn Independent Academy*, London: Hamilton, Adams, 1840.
Smiglecki, Martinus, *Logica*, 1618.
Smith, Barbara, ed., *Truth, Liberty, Religion. Essays Celebrating Two Hundred Years of Manchester College*, Oxford: Manchester College, 1986.
Smith, Henry, Swallow, John E., and Treffry, William, eds., *The Story of the United Methodist Church*, London: Henry Hooks, 1932.
Smith, J.W. Ashley, *The Birth of Modern Eduaction: The Contribution of the Dissenting Academies 1660-1800*, London: Independent Press, 1954.
Sortain, Bridget Margaret, *Memorials of Joseph Sortain*, 1861.
Sortain, Joseph, *A Lecture Introductory to the Study of Philosophy*, 1839.
 The Life of Francis, Lord Bacon, [1851].
Steadman, Thomas, *Memoir of William Steadman, D.D., Pastor of the First Baptist Church, Bradford*, London, 1838.

Stennett, Samuel, *The Mortality of Ministers contrasted with the Unchangeableness of* Christ: *in a Sermon, occasioned by the Decease of The Rev. Caleb Evans, D.D., Who departed this Life Aug. 9, 1791, in the 54th Year of his Age . . . To which is added the Address delivered at his Interment, by the Rev. John Tommas*, London: Rivington and Marshall, 1791.

Stewart, Alexander, *Autobiography* (extract), ed. Albert Peel, *Congregational Historical Society Transactions*, XV no. 2, April 1946, 75-84.

Stoughton, John, *The Nature and Value of the Miraculous Testimony to Christianity*, London: Hodder and Stoughton, 1871.

[Strickland, Gough], *Enquiry into the Causes of the Decay of the Dissenting Interest*, London, 1730.

Summers, W.H., Gibbons, 'Dr. Thomas Gibbons' diary,' *Congregational Historical Society Transactions*, I, 1901-1904, 313-329, 380-397, II, 22-38.

Surman, Charles E., 'Roby's Academy, Manchester, 1803-08,' *Congregational Historical Society Transactions*, XIII no. 1, September 1937, 41-53.

'Leaf Square Academy, Pendleton, 1811-1813,' *Congregational Historical Society Transactions*, XIII no. 2, September 1938, 107-117 and 77.

Swaine, Stephen A., *Faithful Men; or, Memorials of Bristol Baptist College, and some of its most Distinguished Alumni*, London: Alexander, 1884.

Taylor, Abraham, *An Introduction to Logick, with a few Lectures, on Perception, the first part of that Science*, 1739; DWL MS 69.24.

Taylor, John, *A Narrative of Mr. Joseph Rawson's Case: or, an Account of several Occurrences relating to the Affair of his being excluded from Communion with the Congregational Church in Nottingham. With a Preface in Defence of the Common Rights of Christians*, [1737], 2nd edn., 1742. (The anonymous *Narrative* is by Rawson, the Preface by Taylor).

A Defence of the Common Rights of Christians; and of the Sufficiency and Perfection of Scripture, without the aid of Human Schemes, Creeds, Confessions, &c., [1737], London: The British and Foreign Unitarian Association, 1839.

A Further Defence of the Common Rights of Christians, 1738.

The Scripture-Doctrine of Original Sin proposed to Free and Candid Examination, London, 1740.

A Supplement to the Scripture-Doctrine of Original Sin, &c., containing some Remarks upon two Books, viz. The Vindication of the Scripture-Doctrine of Original Sin, and The Ruin and Recovery of Mankind, 1741.

Remarks on such Additions to the Second Edition of the Ruin and Recovery of Mankind As *relate to the Arguments Advanced in the Supplement to the Scripture-Doctrine of Original Sin*, 1743.

The Scripture-Doctrine of Atonement Examined, 1751.

The Hebrew Concordance adapted to the English Bible, 2 vols. 1754-1757.

The Covenant of Grac, and Baptism the Token of it, Explained upon Scripture Principles, 1757.

An Examination of the Scheme of Morality advanced by Dr. Hutcheson, late Professor of Morality, in the University of Glasgow, London: J. Waugh, 1759.

A Sketch of Moral Philosophy; or, an Essay to demonstrate the Principles of Virtue and Religion upon a New, Natural, and Easy Plan, London: J. Waugh, 1760.

A Scheme of Scripture Divinity, 1762.

Thompson, Joseph, *Lancashire Independent College, 1843-1893*, Manchester: J.E. Cornish, 1893.

Thomson, J,. Radford, *Auguste Comte and 'The Religion of Humanity'*, London: The Religious Tract Society, n.d.

Modern Pessimism, London: The Religious Tract Society, n.d.

The Witness to Man's Moral Nature to Christianity, London: The Religious Tract Society, n.d.

Utilitarianism: an Illogical and Irreligious Theory of Morals, London: The Religious Tract Society, [1885].

Tibbutt, H.G., 'The Cotton End Congregational Academy, 1840-74,' *Congregational Historical Society Transactions*, VIII no. 3, August 1958, 100-105.

Tomkins, S., Memoir prefixed to *Twelve Sermons on Various Subjects by the Rev. Solomon Young*, London, 1832.

Tommas, John, see under Stennett, Samuel, above.

Toothill, Jonathan, *The Foundation of the Dying Christian's Triumph, in the Prospect of Nature's Dissolution. A Sermon, preached, Feb. 2, 1783, at heckmondwike in Yorkshire; on occasion of the Death of the Rev. Mr. James Scott, late Pastor of the Church, and Tutor to an Academy at that Place*, Huddersfield: J. Brook, 1783.

Toulmin, Joshua, *Memoirs of the Revd. Samuel Bourn, for many years one of the* Pastors of the United Congregations of the new Meeting in Birmingham and of the *Meeting in Coseley*, Birmingham: Belcher, 1808.

An Historical View of the State of the Protestant Dissenters in England, Bath, 1814.

Towgood, Micaijah, *The Dissenting Gentleman's Answer to the Reverend Mr. White's three letters; in which a separation from the Establishment is fully justified; the Charge of Schism is refuted and retorted; and the Church of England and the Church of Jesus Christ, are impartially compared, and set in Contrast, and found to be Constitutions of a quite Different Nature*, 1746.

Turner, George Lyon, *Wish and Will: an Introduction to the Psychology of Desire and Volition*, London: Longmans, 1880.

Original Records of Early Nonconformity under Persecution and Indulgence, 3 vols., London: T. Fisher Unwin, 1911-1914.

Turner, J. Horsfall, *Nonconformity in Idle, with the History of Airedale College*, Bradford: T. Brear, [1876].

Turner, R.R., 'Cavendish Theological College (1860-1863). Joseph Parker's experiment in ministerial training,' *Congregational Historical Society Transactions*, XXI no. 4, October 1972, 94-101.

Turner, R.R. and Wallace, Ian H., *Serve Through Love. A History of Paton*

Congregational College, Nottingham, privately printed, [1984].
Turner, William, *The Warrington Academy*, articles reprinted from *The Monthly Repository*, VIII, IX, X, 1813-1815, Warrington: Library and Museum Committee, 1957.
Lives of Eminent Unitarians, 2 vols., London,1840-1843.
Tymms, T.V., *The Mystery of God. A Consideration of some Intelelctual Hindrances to Faith*, London: Elliot Stock, 4th edn., 1890.
Upton, C.B., see Drummond, James, above.
Lectures on the Bases of Religious Belief, Lodon: Wiliams and Norgate, 1894.
Dr. Martineau's Philosophy: A Survey, London: Nisbet, 1905.
Vaughan, Robert, *Congregationalism: or the Polity of Independent Churches, viewed in relation to the State and Tendencies of Modern Society*, 2nd edn. Revised and enlarged, 1842.
The Credulities of Scepticism. A Lecture, London: James Nisbet, 1885/6.
Wace, Henry, *Christianity and Morality, or the Correspondence of the Gospel with the Moral Nature of Man*, 1876.
Waddington, John, *Congregational History 1700-1800*, London: Longmans, Green, 1876.
Wadsworth, Kenneth W., *Yorkshire United Independent College*, London: Independent Press, 1954.
Wakefield, Gilbert, *Memoirs of the Life of Gilbert Wakefield*, by himself, London, 1792.
Walker, George, *On the Right of Individual Judgment in Religion. A Sermon preached at Chewbent [sic], Lancashire, on the 25th June, 18—, at the Annual provincial Meeting of the Ministers of the Presbyterian Persuasion*, Manchester: J. Johnson, [1800].
Wardlaw, Gilbert, *Education for the Christian Ministry; an Address, delivered at the Annual Meeting of the Committee and Friends of Blackburn Theological Academy, held June 24th, 1830*, Manchester: John Clarke, 1830.
Experimental Evidence a Ground for Assurance that Christianity is Divine, Glasgow,1849.
The Leading Christian Evidences, and the Principles on which to Estimate them, Edinburgh: T. & T. Clark, 1870.
Wardlaw, Ralph, *Christian Ethics; or Moral Philosophy on the Principles of Divine Revelation*, London: Jackson and Walford, 1852.
Waterhouse, E.S., *Modern Theories of Religion*, London: Charles H. Kelly, 1910.
Richmond College 1843-1943, London: Epworth Press, 1944.
Watts, Isaac, *The Works of the Rev. Isaac Watts, D.D.*, 7 vols., Leeds: Edward Baines, 1800.
Wayland, Francis, *The Elements of Moral Science*, Boston, Mass., 1844.
Wesley, John, *Free Grace*, London, 1740.
Wesley, Samuel, *A Letter from a Country Divine to his friend in London, concerning the Education of Dissenters in their private Academies*, London: R. Clavel, 1703.
White, John, *To a Gentleman Dissenting from the Church of England*, Three

letters: 1743, 1745, 1745.
Whitefield, George, *Journals*, London: The Banner of Truth Trust, 1960.
Williams, John, *Memoirs of the late Rev. Thomas Belsham*, 1833.
Williams, T. Rhondda, *The Working Faith of a Liberal Theologian*, London: Williams and Norgate, 1914.
Wilson, Walter, *History and Antiquities of Dissenting Churches and Meeting-houses in London, Westminster and Southwark*, London: W. Button, 1808-1812.
Wollaston, William, *The Religion of Nature Delineated*, London: Sam Palmer, 1724.
Yates, John, *A Funeral Discourse, occasioned by the death of the Dr. Barnes, preached at Cross-Street Meeting-House in Manchester on Sunday, 15th July 1810*, Liverpool, 1810.

(b) Secondary Sources

Adamson, William, *The Life of the Rev. Joseph Parker*, Glasgow: Inglis, Ker, 1902.
Alexander, W.L., *Elisha's Cry after Elijah*, in *Discourses and Sermons on occasion of the Death of the late Rev. Ralph Wardlaw, D.D.*, London, 1854.
— *Memoirs of the Life and Writings of Ralph Wardlaw, D.D.*, Edinburgh, 1856.
Argent, Alan, 'Henry Allon of Union Chapel, Islington,' *Congregational History Circle Magazine*, III no. 1, Spring 1993, 12-31.
Azad, Yusef, 'The limits of university: the study of language in some British universities and academies 1750-1800,' *History of Universities*, VIII, 1988, 117-147.
Barth, Karl, *Church Dogmatics*, III.i, Edinburgh: T. & T. Clark, 1958.
Bassett, T.M., *The Welsh Baptists*, Swansea: Ilston House, 1977.
Beaty, Michael, Carlton Fisher and Mark Nelson, eds., *Christian Theism and Moral Philosophy*, Macon, GA: Mercer University Press, 1998.
Beckerlegge, Oliver A., *The United Methodist Free Churches*, London: Epworth Press, 1957.
Bellot, H. Hale, *University College, London 1826-1926*, London: University of London Press, 1929.
Berg, J. van den, and Nuttall, Geoffrey F., *Philip Doddridge (1702-1751) and The Netherlands*, Leiden: Brill, 1987.
Bill, E.G.W. *Education at Christ Church, Oxford 1660-1800*, Oxford, 1988.
Boase, Frederic, *Modern English Biography*, Truro: Netherton and Worth, 1892.
Bolam, C.G., et al., *The English Presbyterians*, London: Allen and Unwin, 1968.
Briggs, J.H.Y., *The English Baptists of the Nineteenth Century*, Didcot: The Baptist Historical Society, 1994.
— '"Active, busy, zealous": The Reverend Dr. Cox of Hackney,' in William H. Brackney and Paul S. Fiddes, with John H.Y. Briggs, *Pilgrim Pathways. Essays in Baptist History in Honour of B.R. White*, Macon, GA: Mercer University Press, 1999, 223-241.
— 'F.A. Cox of Hackney: nineteenth-century Baptist theologican, historian, controversialist, and apologist,' *The Baptist Quarterly*, XXXVIII no. 8,

October 2000, 392-411.

Broglie, G. de, 'Le vraie notion thomiste des "praeambula fidei"' *Gregorianum*, XXIV, 1953, 341-389.

Brown, Kenneth D., 'Nineteenth-century Methodist theological college principals: a survey,' *Proceedings of the Wesley Historical Society*, XLIV pt. 4, May 1984, 93-102.

A Social History of the Nonconformist Ministry in England and Wales 1800-1930, Oxford: Clarendon Press, 1988.

Burns, Robert M., *The Great Debate on Miracles from Joseph Glanvill to David Hume*, Lewisburg, PA: Bucknell University Press, 1981.

Byrne, Peter, *Natural Religion and the Nature of Religion*, London: Routledge, 1989.

Cambridge History of English Literature, IX: From Steele and Addison to Pope and Swift, Cambridge, 1912.

Chance, T.W., *The Life of Principal Edwards*, Cardiff: Priory Press, 1934.

Clark, Gordon H., *Biblical Predestination*, Nutley, NJ: Presbyterian and Reformed Publishing Company, 1966.

Dale, A.W.W., *The Life of R.W. Dale of Birmingham*, London: Hodder and Stoughton, 1899.

Davies, D. Elwyn, *They Thought for Themselves*, Llandysul: Gomer Press, 1982.
'Education and Radical Dissent in Wales in the eighteenth and nineteenth centuries,' *Transactions of the Unitarian Historical Society*, XIX no. 2, 1988, 92-101.

Davis, Arthur Paul, *Isaac Watts, his Life and Works*, London: Independent Press, 1948.

Dawson, Albert, *Joseph Parker, D.D. His Life and Ministry*, London: S.W. Partridge, 1901.

Deacon, Malcolm, *Philip Doddridge of Northampton 1702-1751*, Northampton: Northamptonshire Libraries, 1980.

Dillenberger, John, *Protestant Thought and Natural Science*, Garden City, NY: Doubleday, 1960.

Earwarker, J.P., ed., *Lancashire and Cheshire Wills and Inventories at Chester*, Manchester: The Chetham Society, N.S. III, 1884.

Eddy, G.T., *Dr Taylor of Norwich: Wesley's Arch-heretic*, Peterborough, Epworth Press, 2003.

Ella, George M., *John Gill and the Cause of God and Truth*, Eggleston, Co. Durham: Go Publications, 1995.

Eusden, J.D., 'William Ames,' in *Dictionary of Seventeenth-Century British Philosophers*, Bristol: Thoemmes Press, 2000.

Evans, Evan Keri, *My Spiritual Pilgrimage*, London: James Clarke, 1961.

Evans, George Eyre, *Midland Churches. A History of the Congregations on the Roll of the Midland Christian Union*, Dudley: *Herald* Printing Works, 1899.

Fitzpatrick, Martin, 'Varieties of candour: Scottish and English style,' *Enlightenment and Dissent*, VII, 1988, 35-56.

Fletcher, Joseph, Jr., ed., *The Select Works and Memoirs of the Late Rev. Joseph Fletcher, D.D.*, 3 vols. London: John Snow, 1846.

Flint, Robert, *Anti-Theistic Theories*, (1879), 6th edn., Edinburgh: Blackwood, 1899.

Gascoigne, John, *Cambridge in the Age of the Enlightenment. Science, Religion and Politics from the Restoration to the French Revolution*, Cambridge: CUP, 1989.
Gee, Henry and Hardy, William John, *Documents Illustrative of English Church History*, London: Macmillan, 1896.
George, Timothy and Dockery, David S., eds., *Baptist Theologians*, Nashville: Broadman Press, 1990.
Glover, Willis B., *Evangelical Nonconformists and the Higher Criticism in the Nineteenth Century*, London: Independent Press, 1954.
Gordon, Alexander, *Freedom after Ejection*, Manchester: Manchester University Press, 1917.
    Addresses Biographical and Historical, London: The Lindsey Press, 1922.
Grant, J.W., *Free Churchmanship in England 1870-1940*, London: Independent Press, n.d.
Green, S.W., 'Sketch of the history of the Faculty,' in *London Theological Studies by members of the Faulty of Theology of the University of London*, London: University of London Press, 1911.
Grieve, A.J., 'A hundred years of ministerial training,' *Congregational Historical Society Transactions*, XI no. 6, September 1932, 258-264.
Griffiths, Olive M., *Religion and Liberty*, Cambridge: CUP, 1935.
Haakonssen, Knud, *Natural Law and Moral Philosophy*, Cambridge: CUP, 1995.
Hall, G. Stanley, 'On the history of American college text-books and teaching in logic, ethics, psychology and allied subjects,' *Proceedings of the American Antiquarian Society*, N.S. IX, 1894.
Hans, Nicolas A., *New Trends in Education in the Eighteenth Century*, London: Routledge & Kegan Paul, 1951.
Harding, Diana, 'Mathematics and science education in eighteenth-century Northamptonshire,' *History of Education*, I no. 2, 1972, 139-159.
Hayden, Roger, 'The contribution of Bernard Foskett,' in William H. Brackney and Paul S. Fiddes, eds., *Pilgrim Pathways. Essays in Baptist History in Honour of B.R. White*, Macon, GA: Mercer University Press, 1999, 189-206.
Haykin, Michael G., ed., *The Life and Thought of John Gill (1697-1771). A Tercentennial Celebration*, Leiden: Brill, 1997.
Henderson, A.R., *Castle Gate Congregational Church, Nottingham 1655-1905*, London: James Clarke, 1905.
Henderson, Henry F., *The Religious Controversies of Scotland*, Edinburgh: T. & T. Clark, 1905.
James, Sharon, 'Revival and renewal in Baptist life. The contribution of William Steadman (1764-1837),' *The Baptist Quarterly*, XXXVII no. 6, April 1998, 263- 282.
Jay, William, *Memoirs of the Life and Character of the Late Rev. Cornelius Winter*, London: Williams and Smith, 1809.
Jeremy, Walter D., *The Presbyterian Fund and Dr. Daniel Williams's Trust*, London: Williams and Norgate, 1885.
Johnson, Dale A., 'The end of the "evidences": a study in Nonconformist theological transition,' *Journal of the United Reformed Church History*

Society, II no. 3, April 1979, 62-72.
   The Changing Shape of English Nonconformity 1825-1925, New York: OUP, 1999.
Jones, R. Tudur, *Diwinyddiaeth ym Mangor. Theology in Bangor 1922-1972*, Cardiff: University of Wales Press, 1972.
Laboucheix, Henri, *Richard Price as Moral Philosopher and Political Theorist*, Oxford: The Voltaire Foundation at the Taylor Institution, 1982.Lindberg, David C. and Numbers, Ronald L., eds., *God and Nature*, Berkeley: University of California Press, 1966.
MacFarlane, John, *The Life and Times of George Lawson,* Edinburgh, 1862.
MacIntyre, Alasdair, *A Short History of Ethics*, London: Routledge & Kegan Paul, 1967.
McKim, Donald K., *Ramism in William Perkins' Theology*, New York: Peter Lang, 1987.
McLachlan, H., *Essays and Addresses*, Manchester: Manchester University Press, 1950.
McNaughton, William D., *The Scottish Congregational Ministry 1794-1993*, Glasgow: Congregational Union of Scotland, 1993.
Manson, T.W., 'The first fifty years: a sketch,' in *Theological Essays in commemoration of the Jubilee* [of the Faculty of Divinity], Manchester: John
 Rylands Library and Manchester University Press, 1954.
Maudlin, Frank Louis, 'Truth, heritage, and the eighteenth-century Baptists,' *The Baptist Quarterly*, XXXV no. 5, January 1994, 211-28.
Moore, James R., *The Post-Darwinian Controversies: A Study of the Protestant Struggle to Come to Terms with Darwin in Great Britain and America, 1820-1900*, Cambridge: CUP, 1979.
Muller, Richard, 'John Gill and the Reformed tradition,' in Michael A.G. Haykin, ed., op.cit.
Nicholl, W. Robertson, and MacNicoll, A.N., *W.G. Elmslie, D.D.: Memoir and Sermons*, London: Hodder and Stoughton, 1890.
Nicholls, Mike, 'Charles Haddon Spurgeon: educationalist,' *The Baptist Quarterly*, XXXI no. 8, October 1986, 384-401, and XXXII no. 2, April 1987, 73-94.
Nuttall, Geoffrey F., *The Puritan Spirit*, London: Epworth Press, 1967.
   'Philip Doddridge's library,' *Congregational Historical Society Transactions*, XVII no. 1, January 1952, 29-31.
   Howel Harris 1714-1773. The Last Enthusiast, Cardiff: University of Wales Press, 1965.
   Philip Doddridge 1702-1751, His Contribution to English Religion, London: Independent Press, 1951.
   ed., *Calendar of the Correspondence of Philip Doddridge, DD (1702-1751)*, London: HMSO, 1979.
Owen, H.P., *The Moral Argument for Christian Theism*, London: Allen and Unwin, 1965.
Owen, W.T. *Edward Williams DD 1750-1813: His Life, Thought and Influence*, Cardiff: University of Wales Press, 1963.
Packer, G., ed., *The Centenary of the Methodist New Connexion 1797-1897*,

London: Geo. Burrough, [1897].
Payne, Ernest A., *Henry Wheeler Robinson, Scholar, Teacher, Principal*, London: Nisbet, 1946.
Peach, W. Bernard, see under Thomas, D.O., below.
Pfizenmaier, T.C., *The Trinitarian Theoogy of Dr. Samuel Clarke*, Leiden: Brill, 1997.
Phillips, George, 'Dr. Mackintosh,' *Congregational Monthly*, March 1933, xi.
Preston, Ronald H., 'The Faculty of Theology in the University of Manchester: the first seventy-five years,' in D.A. Pailin, ed., *University of Manchester Faculty of Theology Seventy-fifth Anniversary Papers 1979*, published by the Faculty, 1980.
Pyke, Richard, *Men and Menories*, London: Epworth, 1948.
Pyle, Andrew, 'Introduction' to *Selected Works of Isaac Watts*, 7 vols., Bristol: Thoemmes Press, 1999.
Redford, George and James, John Angell, eds., *The Autobiography of William Jay*, (1854), Edinburgh: The Banner of Truth Trust, 1974.
Reid, H.M.B., *The Divinity Professors in the University of Glasgow*, Glasgow, 1923.
Reynolds sisters, *Henry Robert Reynolds D.D. His Life and letters. Edited by his Sisters, with Portraits*, London: Hodder and Stoughton, 1898.
Rivers, Isabel, *Reason, Grace, and Sentiment. A Study of the Language of Religion and Ethics in England 1660-1780*, Cambridge: CUP, II, 2000.
Robinson, W. Gordon, *William Roby and the Revival of Independency in the North*, London: Independent Press, 1954.
Robson, R.S., *Our Professors. Being brief notes of men who after occupying English Presbyterian pulpits have been appointed to chairs*, London: Historical Society of the Presbyterian Church of England, 1956.
Rogers, J. Guinness, *An Autobiography*, London: James Clarke, 1903.
Ross, J., *W. Lindsay Alexander, DD, LLD. His Life and Work, with Illustrations of his Teaching*, London, 1887.
Rupp, E. Gordon, *Thomas Jackson, Methodist Patriarch*, London: Epworth Press, 1954.
Schulman, Frank, *A Fine Victorian Gentleman: The Life and Times of Charles Wellbeloved*, Oxford, Harris Manchester College, 1999.
Searby, Peter, *A History of the University of Cambridge*, III, Cambridge: CUP, 1997.
Selbie, W.B., *The Life of Andrew Martin Fairbairn*, London: Hodder and Stoughton, 1914.
Sell, Alan P.F., *Robert Mackintosh: Theologian of Integrity*, Bern: Peter Lang, 1977.
The Great Debate. Calvinism, Arminianism and Salvation, (1983) Eugene, OR: Wipf & Stock, 1998. Korean edn., Seoul: Word of Life Press, 1989.
Church Planting. A Study of Westmorland Nonconformity, Worthing: H.E. Walter, (1986), Eugene, OR: Wipf & Stock, 1998.
Theology in Turmoil. The Roots, Course and Significance of the Conservative- Liberal Debate in Modern Theology, (1986), Eugene, OR:

Wipf & Stock, 1998.
Defending and Declaring the Faith. Some Scottish Examples 1860-1920, Exeter: Paternoster Press and Colorado Springs: Helmers & Howard, 1987.
The Philosophy of Religion 1875-1980, (1988), Bristol: Thoemmes Press, 1996.
Dissenting Thought and the Life of the Churches. Studies in and English Tradition, Lewiston, NY: Edwin Mellen Press, 1990.
Commemorations. Studies in Christian Thought and History, Calgary: University of Calgary Press and Cardiff: University of Wales Press (1993), Eugene, OR: Wipf & Stock, 1998.
Philosophical Idealism and Christian Belief, Cardiff: University of Wales Press and New York: St. Martin's Press, 1995.
'A renewed plea for "impractical divinity",' *Studies in Christian Ethics*, VIII no. 2, 1995, 68-91.
John Locke and the Eighteenth-Century Divines, Cardiff: University of Wales Press, 1997.
ed., *Mill and Religion. Contemporary Responses to Three Essays on Religion*, Bristol: Thoemmes Press, 1997.
Review of Pfizenmaier, q.v., in *Enlightenment and Dissent*, XIII, 1999, 270-275.
'Introduction' to *Henry Grove: Ethical and Theological Writings*, Bristol: Thoemmes Press, 6 vols., 2000, I, v-xxxix.
'*The Gospel its own Witness* : deism, Thomas Paine and Andrew Fuller,' forthcoming, *festschrift* for A.A. Trites, Macon, GA: Mercer University Press.
Confessing and Commending the Faith. Historic Witness and Apologetic Method, Cardiff: University of Wales Press, 2002.
The Dissenting Witness: Yesterday and Today, forthcoming.
Sellers, Ian, 'The old General Baptists 1811-1915,' *The Baptist Quarterly*, XXIV, 1971, 30-41, 74-88.
'John Howard Hinton, theologian,' *The Baptist Quarterly*, XXXIII no. 3, July 1989, 119-132.
Shipley, C.E., *The Baptists of Yorkshire*, Bradford: Wm. Byles, 1912.
Sidgwick, Henry, *Outlines of the History of Ethics for English Readers*, (1886), London: Macmillan, 1949.
Smith, Henry, *Sketches of Eminent MNC Ministers*, [c.1893].
Stephen, Leslie, *History of English Thought in the Eighteenth Century*, (1876), New York: Harcourt, Brace & World, 2 vols., 1962.
Stephens, John, 'The epistemological strategy of Price's *Review of Morals*,' *Enlightenment and Dissent*, V, 1986, 39-50.
Stoughton, John, *Reminiscences of Congregationalism Fifty Years Ago*, London: Hodder and Stoughton, 1881.
John Stoughton. A Short Record of a Long Life, by his Daughter [Georgina King Lewis], London: Hodder and Stoughton, 1898.
Streiff, Patrick, *Reluctant Saint? A Theological Biography of Fletcher of Madeley*, Peterborough: Epworth Press, 2001.
Sutherland, L.S. and Mitchell, L.G., *The History of the University of Oxford. V. The Eighteenth Century*, Oxford: Clarendon Press, 1986.

Thomas, D.O., *The Honest Mind. The Thought and Work of Richard price*, Oxford: Clarendon Press, 1977.
    ed., *Richard Price, Political Writings*, Cambridge: CUP, 1991.
    and W. Bernard Peach, *The Correspondence of Richard Price*, Durham, NC: Duke University Press and Cardiff: University of Wales Press, 3 vols., 1983, 1991, 1994.
Thomas, D.O., Stephens, John and Jones, P.A.L., *A Bibliography of the Works of Richard Price*, Aldershot: Scolar Press, 1993.
Veitch, John, 'Philosophy in the Scottish universities,' *Mind*, II, 1877, 74-91, 207-234.
Vos, Arvin, *Aquinas, Calvin and Contemporary Protestant Thought*, Washington: Christian University Press, 1985.
Ward, W.R., *Religion and Society in England, 1790-1850*, London: Batsford, 1972.
    ed., *The Early Correspondence of Jabez Bunting*, Camden 4th series, 11, London: Royal Historical Society, 1972.
    Early Victorian Methodism, Oxford: OUP, 1976.
Weddle, David, 'Jonathan Edwards on men and trees, and the problem of solidarity,' *Harvard Theological Review*, LXVII, 1974, 155-175.
Wills, Gregory A., 'The spirituality of John Gill,' in M.A.G. Haykin, ed., see above.
Wogaman, J. Philip, *Christian Ethics: A Historical Introduction*, London, SPCK, 1993.
Wykes, David L., 'The contribution of the Dissenting academy to the emergence of rational religion,' in Knud Haakonssen, ed., *Enlightenment and Religion. Rational Dissent in Eighteenth-Century Britain*, Cambridge: CUP, 1996.
Yuille, George, ed., *History of the Baptists in Scotland from Pre-Reformation Times*, Glasgow: Baptist Union Publications Committee, [1926].

In addition to articles consulted in the sources listed under 'Abbreviations' above, pieces, in many cases unsigned, from the following have been drawn upon, and are referred to in the text:

Baptist Magazine
Biographical Dictionary of Twentieth-Century Philosophers, 1996
The Eclectic Review
Evangelical Magazine
The Inquirer
The Messenger of the Presbyterian Church of England
Minutes of the Primitive, United and Wesleyan Methodist Conferences
The Monthly Repository
The Nonconformist and Independent
The Sword and the Trowel

Indices

In this Index the following abbreviations are used, though we should recall the ecclesiastical fluidity of the period 1662-1700, denominations as we have come to know them having their institutional origins in the nineteenth century:

[B] Baptist; [BC] Bible Christian; [C] Congregational; [CH] Countess of Huntingdon's Connexion; [G] a general, not exclusively a theological, education provided; [M] Methodist; [MNC] Methodist New Connexion; [P] Presbyterian; [PCE] Presbyterian Church of England; [PM] Primitive Methodist; [U] Unitarian; [UNC} United Methodist Church; [UMFC] United Methodist Free Churches; [URC] United Reformed Church; [W] Wesleyan

Index of Academies, Colleges and Universities

Aberdeen University, 26, 29, 34, 121, 132, 167, 231
Abergavenny Academy (1757, migratory) [C] 36, 45-6, 48, 149
Abergavenny Baptist College (1807-36), 135
Airedale Independent College (1800-88) 106, 119-121, 167, 186, 235
Associate Secession Church Theological Hall, 155
Attercliffe Academy (1690-1720) [G] [C], 25, 28, 49, 212
Axminster Academy (1795-1829) [C], 28, 115

Bala-Bangor Independent College (1892-1988), 122-3, 238
Bala College (1841-92) [C], 128
Bedworth Academy (1710?-50) [C], 25
Bethnal Green Academy (1680?-1708?) [G] [P], 24
Blackburn Independent Academy (1816-43), 46, 123,-4, 173, 236
Bonn University, 110
Bridgwater Academy (1688-1747) [P], 17, 49
Bridport Academy (1765-80) [C], 28, 115
Bristol Baptist College (1679 -), 37, 42-3, 45, 103, 105, 118, 132-4, 154, 158, 177, 213, 216, 231
Bristol Theological Institute (1863-1891) [C], 128
Bristol University, 118, 134
Brynllywarch Academy (1689-97) [C], 140, 215, 242
Bury Baptist College (1844-73), 136-7

Cambridge University, 10, 24-5, 102, 128, 130, 208-9, 211, 230, 235-6
Cardiff University College, 122, 130
Carmarthen Academy (1668 -) [G, originally] [C/P/U], 36-7, 45,

140-1, 171, 242
Cavendish Theological College
  (1860-3) [C], 128, 184, 238
Chancefield Academy (1736?-
  1741?) [C], 36
Cheshunt College (1792-1965) [CH/
  C], 106, 115, 118, 122, 127, 129,
  160, 183, 234, 236
Christ Church, Oxford, 9
Christ's College, Cambridge, 25
Clerkenwell-Deptford Academy, see
  Homerton
Congregational College, Melbourne,
  Australia, 130
Cotton End College (1840-74) [C],
  128, 238
Coventry Academy (1663-1700) [P],
  25
Coward College (1833-50) [C], 110,
  114

Daventry Academy (1752-89) [G]
  [C]. 28-9, 47, 52-3, 77, 86, 213
Didsbury College (1843-1967) [W],
  130, 142, 185, 199, 238, 242

Edinburgh University, 26, 29, 111-
  12, 121, 130, 132, 140, 145, 149,
  154, 158, 184, 186, 197, 200,
  235
Elmfield College, York (1865-8)
  [PM], 145
English Presbyterian College (1845-
  99), 145, 188; see also
  Westminster College
Evangelical Union Hall, 186
Exeter Academy (1690?-1722) [G]
  [P], 31-2
Exeter Academy (1829-1845) [C],
  46, 115, 123
Exeter College, Oxford, 164

Findern Academy (1710?-54) [G]
  [P], 27-8, 30, 67
Firth College, 119
Free Church Divinity Hall, Glasgow,
  130
Free/United Free Church College,
  Aberdeen, 130

Geneva University, 134
Glasgow Theological Academy [C],
  155
Glasgow University, 26-7, 30, 46,
  67, 71, 110-11, 115, 117, 119,
  130, 132-3, 151, 155, 168, 173,
  177, 197, 200, 212, 235
Gloucester Academy, see
  Tewkesbury
Gosport Academy (1780?-) [C], 47-
  8, 169
Göttingen University, 134

Hackney College (1786-96) [G] [U],
  12, 35-6, 53, 78, 215, 227
Hackney Congregational College
  (1803-1924), 114-15, 160, 179,
  184, 200
Hackney Unitarian Academy (1812-
  19), 167-8
Halle University, 26
Handsworth College, Birmingham
  (1881-1970) [W/M], 143, 164
Harris Manchester College, see
  Manchester College, Oxford
Hartley Primitive Methodist College
  (1881-1934), 144
Hartley Victoria College (1934-),
  [M]145
Haverfordwest Baptist College
  (1839-94), 136
Headingley College, Leeds (1868-
  1967) [W/M], 143, 166
Heckmondwike Academy (1756-83)
  [C], 46, 118, 120
Highbury College, see Hoxton
  Independent College
Hinckley Academy, see Kibworth
Homerton Academy (1730-1850)
  [C], 11, 28, 43-4, 53, 109-10,
  115, 150, 232
Horton College, Bradford (1804-
  1849) [B], 134, 170, 177
Hoxton Academy (1701-85) [C], 21,
  29, 33, 36, 41, 44, 48, 51, 217
Hoxton/Highbury Independent
  College (1778-1850), 46, 111-12,
  114, 142, 151, 168, 182, 232

Indices

Hoxton/Islington General Baptist College (1795-1818), 134
Hoxton Square Academy (1699-1729?) [G] [P], 25, 217

Idle Independent Academy (1800-26), 121
Islington Academy (1672-1707?) [G] [P], 211

Kibworth Academy (1715-23) [G] [C], 34, 49, 212, 218
Killyleagh Academy (1690s-1724), 26

Lancashire Independent College, 106-7, 110-11, 120, 123-7, 130, 160, 176, 197, 214, 223, 235-6, 242, 253
Leaf Square Academy, Pendleton (1811-13) [C], 123, 236
Leeds University, 121, 135, 235
Leiden University, 23, 26, 48-9
Llangollen Baptist College (1862-92), 136, 240
London University, 105, 110, 114, 121-3, 127, 131, 134, 136, 144, 176, 182-3, 185, 196, 246

Manchester Academy (1699-1713) [G] [P], 29, 87, 248
Manchester Academy (1786-1803) [G] [P/U], 11, 93, 137, 207-8
Manchester Baptist College (1873-1963), 130, 137, 238, 241
Manchester College, Oxford (1889-), 137, 213, 219, 241, 246
Manchester College, York (1803-40) [U], 110, 117, 137-8, 163, 171
Manchester New College, London (1853-89) [U], 117, 137-9, 163, 252
Manchester New College, Manchester (1840-53) [U], 137-8, 163, 196
Manchester Unitarian Home Missionary Board/Unitarian College, Manchester (1854-), 107, 117, 139, 178, 241, 253
Manchester University, 124, 127, 130, 137, 144-5, 237

Mansfield College, Oxford (1886-) [C], 121, 123, 127, 128-9, 186, 200, 237
Marlborough Academy (1785?-88) [C], 106
Memorial College, Aberystwyth (1980-) [C], 141, 242
Memorial College, Brecon (1837-1959) [C], 122, 140
Memorial College, Swansea (1959-1980), 141
Midland Baptist College (1789-1914?), 134, 239
Mile End Academy, see Homerton
Moorfields Academy, see Hoxton Academy (1701-85)

New College, London (1850-1977) [C], 112, 114, 122, 129, 183-4, 200, 233
Newington Green Academy (1666?-1706) [G] [C], 28, 37, 211
Newington Green Academy (1675?-1706?) [G] [C]. 27
Newport Pagnell Academy (1782-1820) [C], 12, 18, 29, 37, 47, 178
Northampton Academy (1729-51) [G] [C], 17-18, 26-7, 47, 50-51, 103, 213, 223
Northern College, Manchester (1958-) 18, 209, 238
Northowram Independent Academy (1783-95), 118, 120-21
North Wales Baptist College, Bangor (1892), 136, 240
North Wales University College, Bangor, 136, 141
Nottingham Congregational Institute/Paton College (1863-1968), 128, 238

Ottery-St-Mary Academy (1752-65), 18, 28, 115
Owens College, 117, 120, 124, 253
Oxford University, 10, 24-5, 27, 102, 128, 130, 208-9
Pastor's/Spurgeon's College (1856-) [B], 137, 241

Paton Congregational College, see Nottingham Congregational Institute
Pen-Twyn Academy [C], 36
Pontypool Baptist College (1836-99), 135-6

Ranmoor College, Sheffield (1863-1919) [MNC], 144, 243
Rathmell Academy (1670-98) [G] [P], 10, 24
Rawdon Baptist College (1849-1963), 130, 134-5, 177, 192-3, 239-40
Regent's Park Baptist College (1856-), 136, 193, 240
Richmond College (1843-1972) [W/M], 142-3, 157, 164-5, 200, 242
Roby's Academy (1803-8) [C], 123, 236
Rotherham Independent Academy (1795-1888), 46-7, 109, 118-122, 169, 232, 235

St. Andrews University, 121, 132
St. John's College, Oxford, 25
Scottish Congregational Theological Hall, 122, 124, 197
Serampore College, 133
Shebbear College (1842-) [BC], 144
Sheffield University, 119, 121
Sheriffhales Academy (1663-97) [G] [P], 24, 101, 106
Shrewsbury Academy (1680?-1715?) [G?] [P], 24, 30, 48
South Wales Baptist College (1899-), 136, 240
Spring Hill College, Birmingham (1838-1886) [C], 111, 115, 122, 127-8, 190, 237
Stepney Baptist College (1810-56), 132-3, 136, 240
Sulby Academy (1680-88) [G?] [C?]
Sunderland Theological Institute (1868-81) [PM], 145, 243

Taunton Academy (1670?-1758) [G] [P], 17, 25, 28, 30-33, 153, 206
Taunton Academy (1780-95) [C], 28, 115
Tewkesbuty Academy (1708?-24) [G] [P], 28, 49, 215, 220
Theological Institution, Hoxton (1835-42) [W], 107, 142
Trefeca Welsh Presbyterian College (1842-1906), 141, 146
Trevecca Academy (1768-92) [CH], 17, 46, 106, 122, 217
Trinity College, Dublin, 119

United Free Church College, Glasgow, 130
United Presbyterian College, Edinburgh, 130
United Theological College, Aberystwyth (1906-2003), 141

Victoria Park College, Manchester (1871-1932) [UMFC/UMC], 144

Warrington Academy (1757-83) [G] [P], 12, 17-18, 28, 30, 34-5, 37, 67, 71, 102, 106, 137, 208, 214
Western College, Bristol (1901-70) [C], 115, 118, 133, 234
Western College, Plymouth (1845-1901) [C], 105, 115, 118, 122, 128, 234
Westminster College, Cambridge (1899-) [PCE/URC], 145-6, 243-4
Whitehaven Academy (1708-29) [G] [P], 29, 67, 213
Wickhambrook Academy (1678?-96) [G] [P], 27
Wymondley Academy (1799-1833) [C], 54, 105, 110, 150, 175, 208, 219

Yale University, 32
Yorkshire United Independent College (1888-1958), 119, 121-2, 235

Index of Persons

Abbott, T.K., 229
Acworth, James, 134, 177, 240, 249
Adamson, Peter, 130, 141
Adamson, William, 253
Aikin, Anna Laetitia (see Barbauld, Mrs.)
Aikin, John, 17, 26, 34, 56, 102, 208
Alexander, Samuel, 109
Alexander, W.L., 155, 157, 245
Allin, Thomas, 143, 243
Alliott, Richard, Sr., 115
Alliott, Richard, 115-18, 122, 127, 147, 171-2, 179, 205-6, 233-34, 236, 248
Allon, Henry, 183, 250
Ames, William, 23-4, 55, 211
Amory, Thomas, 14, 33-4, 61, 64-6, 89, 94-5, 99, 212, 214, 220-22, 226, 228
Anne, Queen, 17
Annet, Peter, 30, 214
Anselm, 122
Antliff, William, 145, 243
Argent, Alan, 250
Aristotle, 23-4, 122, 143
Arius, 18
Arminius, Jacobus, 210
Armitage, Elkanah, 119-20, 147, 235
Arnold, Matthew, 195
Ashworth, Caleb, 28-9, 47, 52, 77, 86, 213, 223
Aspland, Robert, 19, 105, 167-8, 209, 247
Aspland, Robert Brook, 105, 209, 231, 247
Athanasius, 18
Avery, Benjamin, 18
Azad, Yusef, 230

Bacon, Francis, 24, 111, 122, 149, 188
Bain, Alexander, 160
Balguy, John, 31
Ball, John, 32, 214
Banks, John Shaw, 143
Barbauld, Mrs., 208
Barnes, Thomas, 11-12, 137, 207-8, 230, 241

Barrett, Alfred, 142-3, 242
Barrett, John O., 239-40
Barth, Karl, 199, 255
Bassett, T.M., 240
Batchelor, Henry, 178-9, 249-50
Baur, F.C., 188
Baxter, Richard, 20, 50, 102, 218, 231
Bayes, Thomas, 31
Baynes, Thomas Spencer, 132, 239
Beard, John Relly, 107, 139, 178, 241, 249
Beattie, James, 52, 86
Beckerlegge, Oliver A., 232
Bedale, Charles L., 142, 242
Bellot, H.H., 207
Belsham, Thomas, 52-3, 77-80, 86, 91, 96, 98, 101-02, 138, 163, 218-19, 223, 224-5, 227, 229, 246
Benion, Samuel, 26, 212
Bennett, James, 47, 169-70, 248
Bennett, W.H., 203, 239
Benson, George, 30, 51, 213
Bentham, Jeremy, 184, 201
Berg, J. Van den, 212
Berkeley, George, 119, 143
Bill, E.G.W., 211-12, 230
Bird, Benwell, 193
Boase, Frederic, 239
Bogue, David, 47
Bolam, C.G., 209
Bonnet, T., 52
Bosanquet, Bernard, 140
Bourn, Samuel (1648-1719), 71, 222
Bourn, Samuel (1689-1754), 71, 87-8, 91, 222, 226-8
Bourn, Samuel, III, 71-2, 90, 95, 98, 222
Boyle, Robert, 43
Brackney, William H., 216, 244
Bradbury, Thomas, 17
Bradley, F.H., 126, 140
Brick, E., 107
Brash, W. Bardsley, 232, 238, 243
Briggs, J.H.Y., 240, 244
Brine, John, 20, 33, 210, 214
Broadbent, William, 36

Broglie, G. De, 22, 211
Brown, Kenneth D., 231, 238
Brown, Stuart, 253
Brown, Thomas, 151-3
Browne, Peter, 79
Bruce, A.B., 130
Bruce, Robert, 124, 237
Bubier, George, 127, 237
Buckland, A.R., 232
Bull, William, 12, 29, 47-8, 213, 217
Bunting, Jabez, 107, 232
Bunyan, John, 174, 201
Burder, Henry Foster, 110-11, 155, 232
Burgersdyck, Franco, 23-5, 50
Burns, Robert M., 217
Butler, Joseph, 28, 52, 73, 75, 79, 102, 111-12, 114, 126, 137, 142, 144, 152, 156, 166, 173, 187, 201, 203, 220, 244
Byrne, Peter, 210

Caird, Edward, 14, 109, 125, 130, 200, 206, 238, 254
Caird, John, 198
Calamy, Edmund, 28
Calvin, John, 85, 142
Campbell, John, 196
Campbell, John McLeod, 248
Carey, William, 133
Carmichael, Gershom, 26, 30, 212
Carpenter, Benjamin, 86, 225
Carpenter, Lant, 53
Carpenter, R.L., 219
Carter, A.C., 239
Case, John, 24
Cave, Sydney, 244
Chalmers, Thomas, 198
Chalmers, William, 146, 243
Chance, T.W., 240
Chandler, Samuel, 49, 217
Chapman, Charles, 118, 234
Charles, David, 141, 242
Charlton, John, 118, 234
Chauncy, Isaac, 41
Chillingworth, William, 29
Chorlton, John, 29, 87, 213
Cicero, 46-7, 56, 63
Clark, Gordon H., 229
Clark, Samuel, 29, 50, 213, 218

Clarke, Adam, 107, 232
Clarke, Samuel, 18, 30-1, 36, 52, 57-8, 71, 73, 77, 79, 98, 155, 164
Clegg, James, 24
Clemence, C., 233
Cocker, William, 144
Colbert, J.B., 24
Coleridge S.T., 109, 163
Collier, Arthur, 31, 214
Collins, Anthony, 49, 85
Comte, Auguste, 109, 125, 138, 164, 184, 189
Conder, Eustace Rogers, 190-2, 202, 252
Conder, John, 28, 190, 213, 252
Conder, Josiah, 190, 252
Conder, Thomas, 190
Condillac, E.B. de, 38, 111
Condorcet, Marquis de, 111
Coningham, John, 29, 87, 213
Cooke, William, 144, 213
Cooper, Anthony Ashley, 56-7, 80, 96, 164
Cooper, R.E., 240
Cornick, David, 243
Cornish, William, 66
Coward, William, 53, 110
Cox, Francis Augustus, 154, 201, 244-5
Cradock, Samuel, 27, 213
Creak, Henry Brown, 121, 235
Crippen, T.G., 207
Crisp, T.S., 132, 239
Crisp, Tobias, 20
Crosbie, W., 119
Crothers, T.D., 144, 243
Cudworth, Ralph, 25, 43, 46, 58, 67, 71, 73, 77, 98, 155, 164
Culross, James, 133, 239
Cumberland, 25, 57, 64, 79

Dale, A.W.W., 248
Dale, R.W., 233, 248-9
Dalton, John, 102
Darwin, Charles, 166, 186
Davies, Benjamin, 46, 217
Davies, D. Charles, 141, 242
Davies, D. Elwyn, 217, 242
Davies, Evan (Carmarthen), 37, 215
Davies, Evan (missionary/editor), 244

Davies, Gareth, 217
Davies, William, 217
Davis, A.P., 215
Davis, V.D., 241
Davison, John, 41
Davison, William Theophilus, 143, 164-6, 201-02, 242, 247, 254
Dawson, Albert, 253
Deacon, Malcolm, 212
Derham, William, 44
Derodon, David, 25
Descartes, René, 22, 24, 37, 39, 49, 57, 64, 111, 143, 164
Dillenberger, John, 255
Dixon, Thomas, 29, 67, 213, 221
Dockery, David S., 219
Doddridge, Philip, 17-18, 26-7, 34, 43, 47, 50-3, 82-3, 101-03, 110, 212-13, 218, 220, 223
Dodwell, Henry, 30, 51, 213
Doolittle, Thomas, 211
Downame, George, 24
Dowson, Henry, 136, 241
Drummond, James, 139, 196, 219, 241
Duncan, William, 36
Dunscombe, Thomas, 43
Dwight, Timothy, 156
Dykes, J. Oswald, 146, 243, 252

Eames, John, 33, 36, 41, 44, 48, 214
Earwarker, J.P., 211
Eddy, G.T., 221
Edwards, David Miall, 122-23, 236
Edwards, Jonathan, 20, 43, 84-6, 151-2, 156, 159-61, 225, 227
Edwards, William, 136, 240
Egerton, Hakluyt (pseud. Arthur Boutwood), 251
Ella, George M., 219
Elmslie, W.A.L., 243
Elmslie, W.G., 146, 243
Emlyn, Thomas, 25, 27, 210
Empedocles, 131
Enfield, William, 34-5, 215, 219
Entwisle, Joseph, 107
Erskine, Thomas (of Linlathen), 248
Euclid, 68
Eusden, J.D., 22, 211
Eustache (Eustachius de Saint-Paul), 24-5, 211
Evans, Caleb, 45, 92-3, 103, 220
Evans, Evan Keri, 141, 242
Evans, George Eyre, 213, 225
Evans, Hugh, 43, 45, 216
Evans, John, 28, 36
Evans, John (General Baptist), 143, 239
Ewald, H.G.A., 134

Fairbairn, A.M., 14, 121, 123-4, 128, 146, 167, 186-8, 199-200, 203, 235, 238, 247, 251-2
Falding, F.J., 119, 122, 234
Ferguson, Adam, 36
Fichte, J.G., 110
Fiddes, Paul S., 216
Findlay, George G., 142-3, 166, 242, 246
Firth, Thomas, 243
Fisher, G.P., 136
Fitzpatrick, Martin, 212
Flavel, John, 36-7
Fleming, Caleb, 210
Fleming, Henry, 24
Fletcher, JohnWilliam, 45-6, 217
Fletcher, Joseph, 111, 123, 154-5, 236
Fletcher, Joseph, Jr., 236
Flexman, Roger, 90, 226
Flint, Robert, 130, 210
Forsyth, P.T., 200-01, 237, 254
Foskett, Bernard, 42-3, 82, 102, 216
Foster, James, 32-3, 214
Frankland, Richard, 10, 24-5, 211, 245
Fraser, A. Campbell, 189
Fraser, Daniel, 106, 121, 231, 235
Fraser, Lucy A., 231
Freeman, Stephen, 134
Fromenius (Andreas Froman), 24, 30, 211
Fuller, Andrew, 19, 98, 155, 210, 225, 229

Gale, John, 32-3
Gale, Theophilus, 46
Garvie, A.E., 14, 200, 203, 254-5
Gascoigne, John, 230
Gaskell, William, 117, 234
Gassendi, Pierre, 111
Gay, John, 78
Gee, Henry, 207

George II, 17
George III, 19
George, Timothy, 219
Gibbons, Thomas, 44-5, 216-17
Gilbert, J., 234
Gill, John, 20, 43-4, 55-6, 96-7, 101, 135, 206, 210, 291-20, 229
Gisborne, Thomas, 60
Gisburne, Jophn, 19
Glover, Philips, 67, 221
Glover, Willis B., 247, 249, 255
Godwin, Benjamin, 134, 170, 202, 239, 248
Godwin, John Hensley, 112-14, 147, 160-2, 201, 206, 233, 246
Godwin, William, 80
Goodwin, John, 210
Goodwin, Timothy, 27
Goodwin, Thomas, 110
Gordon, Alexander, 33, 42, 86, 171, 212-14, 216, 223-5, 248
Gotch, F.W., 133, 239
Gough, Strickland, 102, 230
Govean (Thomas Goveanus), 24, 211
Grant, J.W., 247
Gray, J.T., 133, 136, 146, 239
Greaves, R., 209
Green, S.G., 134, 240
Green, S.W., 131, 239
Green, T.H., 109, 140
Greenfield, Thomas, 145, 243
Grieve, A.J., 130, 238
Griffith, Roger, 48, 217
Griffiths, Henry, 122, 236
Griffiths, Vavasor, 36, 215
Grosvenor, Benjamin, 212
Grote, George, 246
Grotius, Hugo, 50, 55-6, 216
Grove, Henry, 14, 17, 28, 30-4, 39-40, 43, 56, 61-7, 71, 81-2, 87, 91, 97, 101-2, 153, 206, 209, 212, 214, 220-1, 224, 226, 228, 244
Guntrip, H.J.S., 235

Haakonssen, Knud, 207, 219
Hagenbach, K.R., 114
Haldane, James, 155
Haldane, Robert, 155

Hall, G. Stanley, 214, 229
Hall, Robert, 151, 225
Hallett, Joseph, Jr., 31-2, 34, 214
Halley, Robert, 124, 237
Halyburton, Thomas, 181
Hamilton, William (1669-1723), 26
Hamilton, William (1788-1856), 111, 131-2, 138, 189, 215
Hannah, John, 142, 242
Hans, Nicolas, 230
Harding, Diana, 230
Hardy, W.J. 207
Harris, Howel, 141, 242
Harris, John, 106, 231
Hart, Trevor, 254
Hartley, David, 24, 35, 53, 78, 80, 163, 215
Hartley, William, 145
Hartmann, K.R.E. von, 184
Hayden, Roger, 216
Haykin, Michael A.G., 219, 229
Hebden, Samuel, 83, 225
Heerebroord, Adrian, 23-4, 49
Hegel, G.W.F., 112, 119, 127, 194
Helm, Paul, 209
Henderson, A.R., 233
Henderson, Henry F., 212
Henderson, William J., 133, 239
Henry VIII, 9
Henry, Matthew, 36-7
Herbert, Lord, of Cherbury, 181
Hester, Giles, 212-13
Hick, John H., 209
Hicks, G. Dawes, 253
Higginson, Edward, 171, 248
Hill, Noah, 52, 218
Hill, Thomas (Findern), 30, 67, 214, 221
Hill, Thomas (Homerton), 110, 232
Himbury, D. Mervyn, 240
Hincks, William, 138, 241
Hinton, John Howard, 158-9, 201, 245
Hobbes, Thomas, 56-7, 62-5, 96, 100-101, 160, 181, 219, 221
Hodder, M.H., 250
Hodgson, James Muscutt, 124, 197-9, 205, 237, 253
Holyoake, J.G., 178-9
Hoppus, John, 136

Horne, George, 35, 215
Horsey, John, 53-4, 105, 219
Horsley, Samuel, 35, 215
Hort, Josiah, 28
Houlbrooke, Theophilus, 91, 227
Howe, John, 31, 180
Howells, William, 141, 242
Hudson, W. Donald, 209
Hulme, Samuel, 144, 243
Hume, David, 14, 48, 53, 73, 77, 80, 111-12, 116, 130, 143, 155, 169-71, 173, 175-6, 183, 186, 189, 192, 202, 224
Humphreys, J.D., 218
Huntingdon, Selina, Countess of, 122
Hutcheson, Francis, 26-7, 34, 36, 57-8, 61, 69-71, 73-4, 77, 79, 98, 153, 155, 164, 201, 212, 222
Huxley, T.H., 186, 193, 196

Iverach, James, 130

Jacks, Lawrence Pearsall, 139, 241
Jackson, Thomas, 157-8, 201, 245
James, John Angell, 231
James, Sharon, 239
James, T. Courtenay, 13
James, William, 140
Jardine, David, 37, 215
Jay, William, 106, 231
Jennings, David, 48, 217
Jennings, John, 49-50, 218
Jeremy, Walter D., 212-13
Jevons, W. Stanley, 136, 145
Johnson, Dale A., 237, 247
Johnson, G.B., 115, 234
Johnstone, J.C., 233
Jollie, Timothy, 25, 28, 49, 212
Jones, J.A., 232
Jones, Michael, 128, 238
Jones, Michael Daniel, 128, 238
Jones, Noah, 36-7, 52, 215
Jones, P.A.L., 215
Jones, R. Tudur, 238, 240
Jones, S., 215
Jones, Samuel (Brynllywarch), 140, 242
Jones, Samuel (Pen-twyn), 36, 215
Jones, Samuel (Tewkesbury), 26, 48-9, 213, 217, 220

Jones, Samuel (Methodist), 142, 242
Jones, W.P., 231
Jones, William, 35, 215

Kant, Immanuel, 14, 98-100, 125-27, 160, 165, 173, 202-02, 206, 229
Kaye, Elaine, 209, 217, 234-8
Keill, John, 36
Kello, John, 110, 232
Kelly, Charles H., 184, 186
Kenrick, John, 241
Kenrick, Timothy, 52, 218
Ker, John, 24, 211
Killingworth, Grantham, 19, 209
Kingsland, J.P., 253
Kippis, Andrew, 29, 77, 213, 223
Knox, R. Buick, 243

Laboucheix, Henri, 93
Lardner, Nathaniel, 18, 209
Latham, Ebenezer, 27-8, 30, 213
Lavington, John, 28, 213
Lawson, George, 155, 245
Le Clerc, Jean, 24-5, 30, 38, 49, 211
Lee, Atkinson, 145
Leechman, John, 133, 146, 239
Leechman, 26, 212
Leibniz, G.W., 43, 52, 111, 119, 140
Lessing, G.E., 138
Lewis, Georgina King, 232
Lewis, O., 230
Lewis, W. Mortimer, 135, 174
Leyden, W. Von, 220
Lidgett, John Scott, 185-6, 199, 251
Limborch, Philipp von, 24, 29, 211
Lindberg, David C., 254
Linkens, Derek, 212
Locke, John, 20-1, 23-6, 29-30, 35-7, 39-44, 49-52, 57, 62, 65, 73, 78, 81-2, 85, 94, 96, 111, 119, 125, 140-41, 143, 151, 160, 211, 213, 218-19, 221, 228, 242
Lorimer, Peter, 145, 188-9, 243, 252
Luther, Martin, 163

McAll, Samuel, 114, 179-82, 202, 233, 250
M'Alpin, James, 26
McCosh, James, 114, 160

McCurdy, Leslie, 254
Macey, Thomas, 118, 234
MacFarlane, J., 245
MacKenzie, J.S., 130
McKim, Donald K., 211
Mackintosh, Robert, 14, 124-7, 147, 199, 205-6, 237, 242, 244, 247, 254
MacIntyre, Alasdair, 220
McLachlan, Herbert, 36, 208, 212-13, 215-16, 218, 222, 234, 241
McLean, Archibald, 155
McNaughton, W.D., 245, 247
MacNicoll, A.N., 243
Macovius, Johannes, 55
McTaggart, J.M.E., 126
Mahomet (sic) 30
Malebranche, Nicolas, 50, 143, 164
Manning, J.E., 139, 241
Manning, William, 210
Manson, T.W., 237
Manton, Thomas, 36-7
Marckius (Johannes Marck), 26, 44
Marshall, J.T., 137, 241
Martineau, James, 132, 138-40, 147, 163-5, 189-90, 196-7, 202, 206, 241, 246, 248, 252
Mather, Cotton, 32
Matthews, W.R., 244
Maudlin, F.L., 229
Maurice, F.D., 163
Medley, William, 134-5, 147, 192-3, 206, 240, 252
Medway, John, 207, 232
Mee, Arnold F., 235
Mellone, S.H., 139-40, 146-7, 205, 241-2
Merle d'Aubigné, J.H., 134
Miall, Arthur, 249
Miall, Edward, 175-6, 249
Miall, James G., 228
Milburn, G.E., 231, 243
Mill, James, 136, 197
Mill, John Stuart, 124, 138, 160, 184, 188-9, 191, 194-7, 202
Milton, John, 24
Mitchell, L.G., 209
Moffat, Robert, 123
Molesworth, William, 219

Moody, Joan W., 235
Moon, Norman S., 216, 239
Moore, James R., 254
More, Henry, 24-5, 57
Morell, John Daniel, 110, 116, 136, 143, 232
Morgan, Augustus de, 122, 246
Morgan, Thomas, 30, 214
Morgan, William, 141, 242
Morgan-Wynne, J.E., 216
Morison, James, 121
Morris, Arthur D., 217
Morris, John, 122, 236
Morton, Charles, 27, 211, 213
Moss, R. Waddy, 142, 185, 242, 251
Muller, Richard, 55, 219
Murch, W.H., 136, 240
Murray, A. Victor, 218
Muschenbroeck, Peter van, 36
Mylne, James, 123

Neal, Daniel, 30
Newman, Francis, 173-4, 188
Newman, John Henry, 174
Newth, Samuel, 231
Newton, Isaac, 24-5, 37
Newton, John, 12, 47, 217
Nicholls, Mike, 241
Nicoll, W. Robertson, 232
Nidditch, Peter H., 219-20
Niebuhr, Reinhold, 255
Notcutt, John, 22, 211
Numbers, Ronald L., 254
Nuttall, Geoffrey F., 209, 212-13, 217-18, 242

O'Brien, P., 208
Oldfield, Joshua, 25-6, 212
Oman, John Wood, 146, 243
Orchard, Stephen, 234
Orr, James, 130
Orton, Job, 51-2, 218, 226
Overton, Richard, 220
Owen, G.D., 215, 236, 238
Owen, James, 24, 30, 48, 211
Owen, John, 9, 94, 228
Owen, Robert, 154, 170
Owen, W.T., 234

Packer, G., 243
Pailin, David A., 209, 237
Paine, Thomas, 53, 170, 210
Paley, William, 53, 80, 111-12, 114, 147, 156, 166, 173, 175, 180
Palmer, Samuel, 211
Parker, Edward, 130
Parker, Irene, 24, 102, 207, 211, 230
Parker, Joanna, 219
Parker, Joseph, 109, 128, 196, 238, 253
Parker, Theodore, 188
Parry, William, 105, 150, 208, 219, 244
Pascal, Blaise, 111
Paton, J.B., 128, 238
Payne, Ernest A., 240, 251
Payne, George, 14, 36, 46-7, 111, 115, 117, 123, 151-4, 165, 205-6, 233-4, 244
Peach, W. Bernard, 227
Peake, A.S., 203
Peel, Albert, 235
Peirce, James, 51
Perkins, William, 23-4, 55, 211
Petty, John, 145, 243
Pfizenmaier, T.C., 209
Phillips, George, 214, 237
Pictet, Benedict, 36
Plato, 119, 143, 164, 169
Platt, Frederic, 142, 242
Pope, William Burt, 142, 242
Powell, Baden, 188-9
Powell, Eifion, 242
Powicke, F.J., 236-7
Poynting, T. Elford, 139, 241
Preston, Ronald H., 237
Price, E.J., 120, 230, 235
Price, Richard, 14, 18, 35-6, 53, 67, 71, 73-7, 79, 84-5, 90, 95-6, 98-102, 151-52, 155, 164, 201, 206, 209, 215, 220-21, 223, 225, 227-29
Priestley, Joseph, 17-18, 20, 28-9, 35, 48, 52-3, 77-8, 84-6, 90, 98-9, 101-02, 138, 163, 208-10, 213, 215, 220, 223, 225, 227, 229
Pringle-Pattison, A.S., 140
Pryce, Robert Vaughan, 114, 122, 233
Prys, Owen, 141, 242
Pufendorf, Samuel, 36, 42, 50, 55-6, 216

Pyer, John, 233
Pyke, Richard, 144, 243
Pyle, Andrew, 215

Quinton, Anthony, 253

Ramus, Peter, 23-4
Randles, Marshall, 142, 242
Raphael, D.D., 223
Rashdall, Hastings, 200
Rattenbury, J. Ernest, 130, 238, 242
Reader, Thomas, 28, 213
Redford, George, 168-9, 202, 223, 231, 233, 248
Redford, Robert A., 114
Reed, Stella, 216
Rees, Abraham, 29, 48, 213, 217
Rees, Thomas, 217
Rees, Thomas (Brecon/Bala-Bangor) 122, 236
Reid, H.M.B., 212
Reid, Thomas, 35, 52, 73, 79, 123, 125, 149-51, 201, 206, 215
Renan, J.E., 178, 194
Reynolds, H.R., 118, 129, 234
Richards, William, 33
Ridgley, Thomas, 21-2, 41-2, 92, 210, 216, 220, 227
Rignal, Charles, 238, 241
Rippon, John, 45, 102, 216, 230
Rivers, Isabel, 220
Roberts, H.P., 213, 215, 242
Robertson, F.W., 248
Robertson, George Croom, 246
Robinson, Crabb, 246
Robinson, H. Wheeler, 251
Robinson, Robert, 93, 98, 228
Robinson, W. Gordon, 236
Robson, R.S., 239, 243
Roby, William, 123, 236
Rogers, Henry, 105, 110-12, 120, 124, 127, 147, 166, 173-5, 190, 200, 202, 206, 233, 243, 248-9
Rogers, J. Guinness, 106, 231
Rooker, James, 28, 213
Rose, E. Alan, 243
Ross, J., 245
Rotheram, Caleb, 26, 212-13
Rowe, Mortimer, 232

Rowe, Thomas, 28, 30, 37
Royce, Josiah, 126
Rupp, Gordon, 245
Rutherforth, Thomas, 79
Rutt, J.T., 208
Ryland, John, 132, 225, 239
Ryland, John Collett, 42, 216
Ryland, J.E., 134, 239

Sacheverell, Henry, 17
Sallust (Sallustius Crispus), 45
Saunders, Julius, 25 212
Saunders, Thomas, 50
Savage, Samuel Morton, 29, 51-2, 213, 218
Saville, David, 53
Schleiermacher, F.D.E., 116, 128, 143, 147, 200
Schopenhauer, Arthur, 184
Schulman, F., 241
Scott, A.J., 117
Scott, Caleb, 235
Scott, C. Anderson, 239
Scott, James, 36, 215
Scott, James (Heckmondwike), 46, 93, 217, 228
Scott, Walter, 121, 235
Searby, Peter, 207
Secker, Thomas, 28, 49, 217
Seddon, John, 71, 222
Seeley, J.R., 194
Selbie, W.B., 128, 235, 237
Sell, Alan P.F., 207-10, 212-14, 218-19, 221, 224-6, 228-9, 232, 236-9, 241, 244, 246-7, 249, 251-4
Sellers, Ian, 209, 245
Seymour, A.C.H., 217
Shaftesbury (see Cooper, Anthony Ashley)
Shearer, William Campsall, 121, 235
Sherlock, William, 210
Shipley, C.E., 240
Shuttlewood, John, 25, 27, 212
Sidgwick, Henry, 56-7, 136, 140, 184, 219-20
Simms, T.H., 232
Simon, David Worthington, 122, 127-8, 236
Simon, John Smith, 142, 199, 242

Simpson, Robert, 46, 217
Simson, John, 26, 212
Skinner, John, 146
Slate, Richard, 236
Small, James, 28, 115, 213, 233
Smiglecius (Martinus Smiglecki), 24, 211
Smith, Adam, 79, 155
Smith, Barbara, 208, 241, 246
Smith, Bertram, 119, 235
Smith, Henry, 243
Smith, John Pye, 11, 109-10
Smith, J.W. Ashley, 47, 207, 217-8, 230
Smith, Norman Kemp, 229
Socrates, 169
Solly, Henry Shaen, 196, 253
Sortain, Bridget Margaret, 236
Sortain, Joseph, 122, 236
South, Robert, 210
Spear, Robert, 123
Spencer, Herbert, 125, 184, 188, 193
Spinoza, Baruch de, 63, 138, 140, 164, 188, 194
Spurgeon, C.H., 137, 241
Stacey, James, 144
Steadman, Thomas, 239
Steadman, William, 134, 177, 239-40
Stennett, Samuel, 92, 227-8
Stephen, Leslie, 102, 231
Stephens, John, 215, 218, 222
Stewart, Alexander, 111, 233
Stewart, Dugald, 111, 123, 127, 151
Stillingfleet, Edward, 20
Stoughton, John, 111, 114, 182-3, 232-3, 250
Stoughton, T. Wilberforce, 250
Strauss, D.F., 112, 174, 178, 188-9, 194
Streiff, Patrick, 217
Surman, Charles E., 236
Sutcliff, John, 225
Sutherland, L.S., 209
Swaine, Stephen A., 216, 239
Swallow, John E., 243

Tallents, Francis, 24, 211
Tatham, Edward, 24
Tayler, J.J., 139, 241
Tayleur, William, 91
Taylor, Abraham, 43-4, 48, 216

Indices

Taylor, A.E., 126
Taylor, Isaac, 189
Taylor, John, 17-20, 26, 28-30, 34, 67-71, 82-5, 88-89, 91, 98, 100, 156, 209, 213, 220-22, 224, 226-7, 229
Tetlaw, Renald, 24
Thomas Aquinas, 22, 185, 211
Thomas, D.O., 215, 227-8
Thomas, George, 135, 172
Thomas, John Heywood, 209
Thomas, Micah, 135, 240
Thomas, Samuel, 36-7, 215
Thomas, Thomas, 135
Thomas, Urijah R., 118
Thompson, Joseph, 236
Thompson, William, 124
Thomson, J. Radford, 114-15, 183-4, 233, 250
Tibbutt, H.G., 237-8
Tindal, Matthew, 32
Tomkins, Samuel, 136, 240
Tommas, John, 92, 228
Toothill, Jonathan, 93, 228
Toulmin, Joshua, 101, 211-12, 222, 229
Towgood, Micaijah, 18-19, 209, 236
Treffry, William, 243
Trigg, Roger, 209
Trites, Allison A., 210
Turner, George Lyon, 114, 124, 160, 201, 233, 246
Turner, J. Horsfall, 235
Turner, R.R., 238
Turner, William, 138, 163, 241
Turner, William, II, 208, 222
Turner, William, III, 210, 212
Tymms, T. Vincent, 129-30, 135, 146, 193-6, 206, 240, 252
Tyndall, John, 189-90, 193, 196

Upton, Charles Barnes, 139-40, 196-7, 219, 241, 253

Vaughan, Robert, 105, 107, 110, 114, 123-4, 175-7, 223, 232, 236, 249
Veitch, John, 212, 230
Vint, William, 121, 235
Virgil, 46
Voltaire (Françoise Marie Arouet), 111, 199-200
Vos, Arvin, 22, 211

Wace, Henry, 166, 247
Waddington, John, 216, 218
Wadsworth, K.W., 212, 217, 228, 231, 234-5
Wakefield, Gilbert, 12
Walker, George, 93, 137, 228, 241
Wallace, Ian H., 238
Waller, Ralph, 219, 241, 246
Ward, James, 140
Ward, W.R., 231-2
Wardlaw, Gilbert, 123-4, 173, 201-2, 236, 248
Wardlaw, Ralph, 154-7, 201-2, 233, 245-7
Warner, Ferdinando, 28
Warren, Matthew, 25, 30, 212
Waterhouse, Eric S., 142, 200, 242
Watson, Thomas, 55
Watts, Isaac, 14, 28, 36-43, 46-7, 49, 52-3, 56, 58-61, 80-81, 83, 94, 97, 99, 102, 123, 206, 209, 213, 215-16, 220, 224, 228-9
Watts, Ruth, 241
Wayland, Francis, 136, 145
Weddle, David, 225, 227
Wellbeloved, Charles, 138, 241
Wesley, John, 20, 84, 135, 200, 210, 213
Wesley, Samuel, 211
Whately, Richard, 124, 127, 136, 145
Whewell, William, 138
Whichcote, Benjamin, 56
White, John, 19
Whitefield, George, 20, 210
Wiche, John, 28
William of Orange, 10
Williams, Daniel, 20
Williams, Edward, 46-7, 109, 118-19, 149-51, 155, 201, 234
Williams, John, 218, 223
Williams, T. Rhondda, 203, 255
Wills, Gregory A., 229
Wilson, Joshua, 215
Wilson, Walter, 214
Wilton, Samuel, 52
Winter, Henry, 29, 213
Winter, Cornelius, 106
Wiseman, Nicholas Patrick Stephen, 174

Witsius, Hermann, 55
Wogaman, J. Philip, 220
Wolff, Christian, 38
Wollaston, William, 31, 36, 46-7, 50, 67, 79, 221
Woodhouse, John, 24, 211
Wordsworth, William, 163

Wright, Charles J., 238
Wrigley, Francis, 119, 235
Wykes, David L., 207

Yates, John, 34, 214
Yolton, John, 209
Young, Solomon, 136, 240

Select Index of Subjects

academies; see also, curriculum, teaching method
   more evangelical, 41-8
   more liberal, 29-37
   more theologically diverse, 48-54
agnosticism, 101, 120, 160, 166, 173, 186, 191, 198, 202
antinomianism, 20, 56
apologetics, 13, 109, 114, 121, 124, 130, 135, 137, 142, 144-7, 166-203, 205-6, 249, 254
Arianism/Arians, 18, 32, 37, 41, 48, 67, 86, 92, 97, 101, 141, 167, 179, 210, 226, 231
Arminianism/Arminians, 19-21, 28, 41, 44, 50, 56, 106, 134-5, 141, 209-10, 225, 238
Associate Secession Church, 155
associationism, 78-9, 113
atheism, 37, 60, 96, 99, 101, 125, 154, 166, 168, 170, 173, 178-82, 191, 202

baptism, 19
Baptists, 10, 19, 27, 33, 41-2, 45, 92-3, 98, 105, 107, 130, 132-7, 146, 151, 154, 158, 167, 170, 177, 192, 225, 251
   General Baptists, 18, 28, 32
   New Connexion General Baptists, 134
Baxterianism, 50, 218

Calvinism/Calvinists, 19-21, 28, 32-3, 42, 44-7, 50-1, 53, 55, 85-6, 91-3, 97-9, 106, 109, 119, 134-5, 137, 155-6, 167, 202, 210, 217, 225, 229, 231, 251
Cambridge Platonists, 25, 56-7
Christian Evidence Society, 182-3, 189, 199
Church of England, 9-10, 19, 95, 109, 205, 210, 220
Civil War, 9
common sense, 34-5, 67, 86, 150
Congregationalism, -ists, 12, 17, 20-1, 27-8, 36-7, 43, 45-7, 105-7, 109-128, 133, 141, 146, 149, 155, 157, 160, 168-9, 173, 175, 178, 183, 186, 190, 197, 200, 203, 208, 210-11, 213, 235, 238, 246-7
conscience, 29, 53, 58-60, 62-3, 69, 72, 75, 87-94, 97, 114, 152-3, 157, 160, 162, 164-5, 184, 189-90, 244
cosmological argument, 21-2, 41, 72, 190, 194
curriculum, 11-13, 30-32, 34-7, 42-7, 49-51, 71, 102, 109-11, 114-15, 118-19, 121, 132, 134-40, 142, 144-5, 205-6, 230-31

deism, 20-21, 31-3, 37-8, 49, 56, 60, 65, 168, 170, 176, 187, 202

English language, 27
Enlightenment, 84
establishment question, 13, 19, 94-6, 109, 155, 175, 178, 205, 236
ethics, see moral philosophy
Evangelical Revival, 17, 21, 45, 89, 94, 106, 200
evolution, 108, 165, 186-8, 190-1, 193, 202-3

freedom, 58, 68, 75, 77, 79, 141, 149, 159, 183, 185, 194, 210
   and necessity, 14, 42, 52, 80-7, 98-100, 150, 160, 225
   of belief, 57
   of conscience, 65, 87-94, 98, 100
   of worship, 10, 57, 94-6, 99, 100

happiness, 38, 62, 65-6, 69-70, 76, 78-80, 97-8, 159
humanism, 101, 166, 189

Independents, see Congregationalists
individualism, 84, 100
idealism, 108, 120, 125-7, 140, 147, 183, 198, 203, 206, 254
innate ideas, 39, 151, 242

liberty, see freedom

logic, 23-5, 30, 37-9, 42-5, 47, 49-50, 52-3, 109, 111, 114, 117-19, 123-4, 128, 133-44, 146, 161, 193, 205-6

materialism, 30-1, 48, 57, 85, 96, 125, 160, 166, 169, 173, 180-1
Methodism, -ists, 13-14,106-8, 130, 141-6, 184, 247
    Bible Christians, 144
    New Connexion, 143-4
    Primitive Methodists, 106-7, 144-5, 203, 231-2
    United Methodist Free Churches, 144
    United Methodists, 144
    Wesleyans, 107, 130, 142-3, 157, 164, 185, 199-200, 238
    Wesleyan Association, 107
moral philosophy, 13, 24, 26, 30, 32, 36, 42, 45, 47, 51-4, ch. 3, 109, 114-15, 119, 122-3, 127-8, 135-41, 143-4, 147, 149-66, 201-2, 205-6, 245
moral sense, 57, 59, 69-71, 73, 78-9, 98, 152, 159, 222

naturalism, 166, 186-7, 202
natural law, 51, 56-60, 63-4, 96, 99-100, 152
natural theology, 21-2, 33-5, 45-7, 89, 98, 101, 116, 147, 152, 156, 173, 180, 186, 190, 202
neonomianism, see Baxterianism

original sin, 82-5

pantheism, 191, 193-4
personal identity, 40, 51
pessimism, 184, 202
positivism, 173, 183-4, 198, 200, 202
pragmatism, 126
Presbyterians, 18-20, 27-8, 30-2, 67, 71, 86-8, 101, 141, 161, 171, 179, 206, 210, 220
    Presbyterian Church of England, 107, 130, 145-6, 188, 239
    Welsh, 106, 141, 146
psychology, 108, 112-13, 115-16, 128, 130, 139-40, 147, 151, 160-2, 173, 197-8, 201, 206
Puritans, 55, 96-7

rationalism, 179, 202, 229
reason, 21-2, 29-35, 38, 40, 42-3, 51, 57-61, 66-8, 70-71, 73-7, 80-81, 88, 97-8, 102-3, 113, 116, 153, 157-8, 160, 167-9, 179, 187, 193, 198, 200, 216
Religious Tract Society, 183
revelation, 21, 29, 32-4, 37-8, 42-3, 52, 56, 60-61, 65, 68-9, 71, 88, 91, 97-100, 117, 127, 152, 158, 165, 168-70, 174-5, 183-5, 188, 191-2, 194, 198-200, 202-3
Roman Catholic Church, 9, 44, 88, 90, 96, 99, 163
Romanticism, 108, 173, 203

Salters' Hall Conference, 18
Sandemanians, 28
Schism Bill, 17
secularism, 166
Senatus Academicus, see Theological Senatus
Separatists, 9
Socinianism, 20, 29, 41, 43, 53, 86, 93, 110, 155, 210, 219

teaching method, 27, 50, 101-2, 117-18, 207, 218, 229-30, 240
Theological Senatus, 108, 128-32, 136, 146
toleration, 29, 94-6, 210
Toleration Act, 10, 17, 94
Trinity, 12, 18, 41-3, 210
truth, 35, 51, 60-1, 68-9, 73, 76, 79, 88-9, 98, 112, 117, 120, 134-5, 140, 152, 156, 161, 168, 195

Unitarianism/Unitarians, 18-9, 28, 53, 77, 91, 93, 101, 107, 110, 132, 137-41, 146, 167, 178-9, 189, 196, 201, 244, 253
utilitarianism, 162, 164, 184, 201-2

Westminster Assembly, 21, 89

Printed in the United Kingdom
by Lightning Source UK Ltd.
R131000001B/R1310PG00000X00001B/51